Mount Radford Re

A HISTORY OF THE
BRETHREN MOVEMENT

This is the first comprehensive history of
The Brethren Movement, which began over
140 years ago and has spread throughout
the world. It is the only such history that
gives an account of the Independent or Open
element that was the original genesis and
became by far the largest part of the Movement.

After tracing the rapid growth of the Movement in the British Isles and its worldwide
expansion overseas, the author considers
some of the outstanding characters thrown
up by the Movement, and also its significant contribution to the hymnody of the
Church. He concludes with an objective
assessment of the Movement in relation to
the situation today of the Church world-
wide.

Titles in this Series

A HISTORY OF THE BRETHREN MOVEMENT

Its Origins, its Worldwide Development and its Significance for the Present Day

by

F. ROY COAD, F.C.A.

EXETER:

THE PATERNOSTER PRESS LTD.

ISBN: 0 85364 164 1

AUSTRALIA:
Emu Book Agencies Pty., Ltd.,
63 Berry Street, Granville 2142, N.S.W.

SOUTH AFRICA:
Oxford University Press,
P.O. Box 1141, Oxford House, 11 Buitencingle St., Cape Town

Made and printed in Great Britain for
The Paternoster Press, Paternoster House,
3 Mount Radford Crescent, Exeter, Devon,
by Butler & Tanner Limited,
Frome and London

TO
MY PARENTS

BY WHOM I BECAME THE FOURTH GENERATION
OF MY FAMILY WITHIN THE MOVEMENT OF
WHICH THIS BOOK SPEAKS, AND WITHIN
WHICH I HAVE LEARNED WHAT
I HAVE KNOWN
OF THE GRACE
OF GOD

AUTHOR'S PREFACE

ALL HISTORICAL STUDIES MUST CONTAIN AN ELEMENT OF interpretation. This book is essentially an interpretation of a movement by one who owes to it one of the greatest debts which a man can acknowledge: that of a deeply-rooted faith.

The word "movement" has been used deliberately, for the characteristics of the main stream of Brethren have been those of a movement rather than those of a formal denomination. Brethren are still shadowy figures to many even of their fellow-Christians. This fact arises partly from their quixotic (though well-intentioned) practice of anonymity. Their meeting-places are common enough in Britain, and the halls of the extreme "exclusives" are distinguished by a stark standard announcement which is distinctive enough, but the buildings of the main body of Brethren are rarely indicated by a name or by activities which mark them out from other mission halls and chapels. The most significant identification, to the knowledgeable, is the regular weekly celebration of the Lord's Supper on a Sunday morning, and the absence of the name of any pastor or minister. Another reason for their shadowiness arises from a vague reputation for narrow sympathies which attaches (and often with scant desert) to them. The sources of that reputation this book will itself make clear.

Past histories of Brethren, even from the main stream, have suffered from a morbid pre-occupation with the quarrels which have marked the aberrations of exclusivism. If this book helps to correct that perspective, and to bring into prominence something of the extraordinarily rich and positive history of the independent Brethren during the second half of the nineteenth century, I shall be satisfied. I have given much space to the first great convulsion, which took place when exclusivism broke away from the independents, because an understanding of the processes which lay beneath that convulsion are today still of vital importance to the understanding of the movement. May I nevertheless express the hope that the time may not be far distant when a history of the movement will be able to pass over in a few pages even that deep trauma? The record of the *independent* Brethren in regard to division in fact compares favourably with that of the first century of almost any other section of the Church.

An interpretative approach to the history has made necessary a detailed

7

examination of the personal histories and characteristics of the first leaders of the movement. My readers will be as conscious as I am myself that as a result I have passed far too sketchily over the still untrodden ground of the half-century which marked the main expansion of independent Brethren. There is rich material there, waiting for a chronicler with more ability and time for original research than I possess. I would, however, express an especial debt in this aspect of the history to D. J. Beattie's study, *Brethren, the Story of a Great Recovery*. Beattie's book is not documented and is badly arranged, and is inclined to the hagiographic, but it seems to preserve much oral information which would otherwise have been lost, and covers ground which no other work touches.

I am indebted to Dr. H. H. Rowdon for bringing to light the work of Robert Gribble, and for his study of the developments in Darby's thought in Switzerland. The chapters in this book which cover the same ground as Dr. Rowdon's own work were largely prepared before I saw his thesis, but I believe that the two accounts will be found to complement each other. To Mr. T. C. F. Stunt I owe the discovery of the importance of seceders from the Society of Friends in the early movement. I have not read the thesis of the late Dr. Peter Embley, but have reason to believe that it contains original matter of considerable importance. It is to be hoped that its author's untimely and tragic death will not prevent his work from becoming more generally available.

Numerous friends have helped me by providing books and advice. I would in particular thank Mr. D. C. Cameron, Mr. C. E. Fry and Mr. G. C. D. Howley, who have all provided me with access to rare and essential material relating to the very early period of the movement. I cannot speak too gratefully of the interest and practical suggestions which I have received from my publisher, Mr. B. Howard Mudditt, during the preparation of this book (and, indeed, of his gentle persistence, without which the book would have been neither conceived nor written), nor of the encouragement of Professor F. F. Bruce, and for his help in reading the manuscript and in making numerous valuable suggestions. Dr. J. S. Andrews and Mr. W. Grunbaum have also helped me with suggestions from their own fields. The book itself is, of course, my own responsibility alone. Finally may I thank my wife and family for their patient forbearance through the disruptions of home life which inevitably resulted from the addition of the writing of a book such as this to the normal cares of a busy professional life.

I would repeat the warning which the book itself contains concerning statistics which appear in it. To present a meaningful picture of the movement it has been necessary to attempt to present some figures, and I have tried to take those I have quoted from sources which are likely to be reliable. Nevertheless, official Brethren statistics do not exist, and such information as is available is often subjective and approximate.

The nature of this study has necessitated the use of quotations, which in some cases have extended well beyond the usual tolerance. I have therefore to acknowledge with gratitude the permission given for the use of quotations as set out below:

To the Rev. Paul G. Guinness for the use of quotations from his mother's book *Peculiar People*.

To Messrs. William Heinemann Ltd. for the use of quotations from *Father and Son* by Sir Edmund Gosse.

To Messrs. Hodder and Stoughton Ltd. for the use of quotations from *A History of the Plymouth Brethren* by W. Blair Neatby.

To Messrs. John Murray for the use of two verses of the poem "Undenonominational" from the *Collected Poems* of Mr. John Betjeman, in the heading to chapter eleven.

To Messrs. Routledge & Kegan Paul for the use of quotations from *The Life of Philip Henry Gosse* by Sir Edmund Gosse.

If I have unwittingly infringed other copyrights, I express my apologies and hope for the forbearance of those concerned. The sources of all quotations are fully acknowledged in the book.

AUTHOR'S PREFACE TO THE SECOND EDITION

IT HAS BEEN A SOURCE OF VERY CONSIDERABLE PLEASURE TO me to see how much interest in the history of the Brethren movement has grown in the few years since the first edition of this book was published; and not the least part of that pleasure has been the opportunity to have contacts with young and enthusiastic students and researchers in different parts of the world. One can look forward with pleasure to the fruit of those studies – and in due course to the publication of a *History* which will be free from the limitations and deficiencies of which I am only too aware in this work.

In the meantime, I must thank those many reviewers and correspondents whose questions and suggestions have led to a number of distinct improvements in this second edition.

Two further remarks remain. The first is to remove once and for all the impression which some who remain intensely loyal to the memory of J. N. Darby seem to have taken away from the first edition: that I was in some way suggesting that that considerable theologian taught the docetic heresy as such. I thought that I had chosen my words advisedly, and with the careful discussion of this subject by Professor F. F. Bruce in his essay on "The Humanity of Jesus Christ" in *CBRF Journal 24* (September 1973) before us, I do not feel that any of my comments on the docetic tendencies inherent in Darbyism (or indeed in aspects of the modern charismatic movement where ideas in that movement brush against similar thinking) need amendment. But that Darby himself was consciously docetic is, I judge, an absurd idea.

The second is a more constructive comment. As I write this foreword, reports are coming in of the great International Congress on World Evangelization in Lausanne: and if those reports are to be believed then the future ecclesiology of international and interconfessional evangelicalism is going to draw much more deeply than has been generally acknowledged from currents of thinking that are exemplified in this book. Alas! – even as classical pentecostals are beginning to lament that the Spirit of God is possibly passing them by in developments which they pioneered, so it must be acknowledged that much of Brethrenism also has withdrawn into a hard self-satisfaction that fails to see when the hand of God is giving to others gifts it thought were its own prerogative. If some are awakened to understand the contribution they can make to a revived and vigorous worldwide evangelical churchmanship: and if some from those wider circles can learn from this history some of the rocks and shoals that lie in their path, I shall feel my labours justified.

19th August 1974

CONTENTS

CONTENTS

FOREWORD

by Prof. F. F. Bruce

MR. COAD'S ACCOUNT OF A PHASE OF EVANGELICAL Christianity which has lasted for over 140 years is the fruit not only of original research, involving personal experience and the study of unpublished as well as published documents, but also of keen and sympathetic insight into the state of the church today and the service which can be rendered to the advance of Christ's kingdom by such independent congregations as are described in these pages.

I am glad, among other things, that he has emphasized the profound influence of the mid-nineteenth century revival on the life and thought of the movement with which he deals. In my own part of the British Isles (North-East Scotland) many of these independent churches, including that in which I was brought up, came into existence as the result of the 1859 revival and its aftermath, without any prior knowledge of the independent churches formed earlier in Dublin, Plymouth and Bristol. Against this different background the record of these English and Irish churches is read with keen interest but with considerable detachment too. The Christians with whom I first enjoyed local church fellowship, when hearing or reading about movements between 1825 and 1848, did not feel that this was where *they* came in, and appeals to them to conform their ways to those of "the early brethren" would meet with the response, "Why should we?" But, be the background that of North-East Scotland or of South-West England, many of us who belong to independent churches of this general pattern find membership in them specially congenial because of the exhilarating atmosphere of spiritual freedom which we breathe in them: long may it be so!

Nearly twenty years ago a symposium on *The Church*, produced by some members of these churches, received the following notice in *The Times Literary Supplement:* "Little societies which accept some such view of the Church as is expressed in this book are to be found all over the world, providing one of the problems of divided Christendom. The essays in this book are patently sincere and might profitably be considered by those who tend to be over-optimistic about the prospects of Reunion." The ecumenical movement has advanced far since then, but these independent brethren and others like them still present a challenge to the patience and tolerance of its leaders. No truer word is spoken in the following pages than that at the foot of p. 284: "The society which acknowledges, in reality and not in pretence, the free liberty of the independent, without suppression by physical or psychological pressures, alone can retain its integrity." If the ecumenical vision can embrace such independents in Christian charity, without asking them to give up any of their independence, this will effectively refute the suggestion of totalitarian overtones which Professor Ian Henderson discerns in the slogan "one church." From within the independent camp Mr. Coad shows himself able to appreciate the ecumenical point of view, and able therefore to interpret the one side to the other.

CHAPTER I

THE CONCERN OF AN INDIVIDUAL

I REMEMBERED a saying of the noble-hearted Groves: 'Talk of loving me while I agree with them! Give me men that will love me when I differ from them and contradict them: those will be the men to build up a true Church.'

F. W. Newman, *Phases of Faith*

IT IS ODD THAT A CAVIL OF CONSCIENCE SHOULD HAVE BROUGHT matters to a head. Anthony Norris Groves was giving up his profession and studying for the ministry of the Church of England, and his chief ambition was to go to the East as a missionary. Then a friend had approached him for advice. This friend had a job in a shady business house, who required him to sell under false descriptions. His conscience was troubled: what should he do? Groves gave the obvious advice, and the friend resigned his position.

Groves was not counting on his friend producing a "do thou likewise": but, shortly after, it came. Did not Groves hold strong pacifist views? How then, asked his friend, could he subscribe the last sentence of Article thirty-seven: "It is lawful for Christian men, at the commandment of the Magistrate, to wear weapons, and to serve in the wars"?

The question was hardly unanswerable. But Groves was a man of that transparent simplicity that cannot bear subterfuge. Just how and why that cavil of conscience had the decisive effect it did, is a longer story.

Anthony Norris Groves was born on 1st February 1795, and he was thirty-two when he faced his crisis of conscience. He had been born near Lymington in Hampshire, where his father, who had formerly been a prosperous business man, had lost most of his wealth through a penchant for engaging in ill-starred business ventures (a trait which years later, in India, was to appear also in his son). Norris Groves himself had trained as a dentist. After studying chemistry with the firm of Savory and Moore in London, he had served an apprenticeship with his uncle, a well-to-do dentist with a practice off Hanover Square, while he also "walked the hospitals" and gained there such practical experience as was available. It was the common inadequate training of the day. He was able to start his own practice in Plymouth on his nineteenth birthday, and as he was successful, he married his cousin, Mary Bethia Thompson, the daughter of his dentist uncle, some two and a half years later. After marriage, he moved his practice to Exeter.

In Plymouth Groves had moved in a circle of cultured and devout men, with whom he remained in touch after his move to Exeter. In Exeter he provided a refuge for several of his relatives and friends who were in need. A deaf mason's boy had been educated by a group of these Plymouth friends, and was taken into Groves's household. Later this young man became the well-known Biblical scholar Dr. Kitto. He paid a striking tribute to Groves's loyalty through some of the setbacks of his earlier life:

> Mr. Groves is the only representative of that which, before I had gone out into the world, I thought all men to be . . . And when I have fallen, he did not say to me, as others have done, "Lie in the bed of your own making": but, although the most aggrieved, has come forth repeatedly to my help.[1]

Another interesting man whom Groves helped at this time was Michael Solomon Alexander, who in 1841 became first Anglican Bishop of Jerusalem. Having been formerly the Jewish Rabbi in Plymouth, he suffered considerable opposition after he received Christian baptism in 1825, and it was in Groves's house in Exeter that he found refreshment and relief at this time of trial.

While Groves was in Plymouth he had come under deep spiritual influence through two clergymen friends. This influence revived in him a half-forgotten boyhood whim, which thereafter became the central ambition of his life: this was a conviction of a call to missionary service. While in Plymouth he had gone so far as to offer himself to the Church Missionary Society, but after his marriage he had found that his wife was resolutely opposed to his plans, and for a time he abandoned them. Yet, despite increasing success in his profession, his heart was fixed. There is something intensely pathetic in the picture which Groves later drew of himself at this time, as, happily married and outwardly contented, he ate his heart out for a vision:

> Often did I, with every earthly thing that man could desire, feel most miserable. I had a wife who loved me, dear little children, and a most lucrative profession, yet I had not the Lord's presence as in days past, and therefore I was miserable.[2]

This state of affairs lasted for six years, while the Groves family in their Exeter home withdrew into their personal family life. It was in such a frame of mind that Groves, in about the year 1822, began to read his Bible passionately (and for a time virtually to the exclusion of other books).

To devote oneself to the Bible with the single-minded purposiveness which Groves brought to his studies is liable to produce startling results. It has been said that what we find in the Bible is a good indication of the sort of people we are. It was characteristic that Groves should find in it things to challenge his own way of life – and that in the material prosperity and comfort which was its chief consolation.

Groves's practice was bringing him in a thousand pounds a year (a substantial enough sum in those days) and was increasing annually. He was a man of sympathetic nature and self-conscious over his good fortune. His reading of the Bible therefore centred naturally upon the right use of his wealth. The first sign of developing convictions came when Groves and his wife together decided to distribute one tenth of their income regularly among the needy in the district, his wife taking responsibility for the necessary visitation and distribution. It was the crisis point for Mary Groves, as she met grinding poverty, and real faith alive in the midst of it.

With a mind in turmoil, and worried by the secret fear that her opposition to her husband's missionary plans was keeping him from responding to a genuine divine call, Mary Groves at first showed signs of retreating into ill-health. She soon overcame this morbid reaction, however, and fell in more enthusiastically with her husband's convictions. In the face of the need of which they now had personal experience, she agreed that they should give away not a tenth but a quarter of their income. They had three children, and in her words, they were to allow their giving "to stand as one, and be a fourth."[3] It was not long before this decision also was revised, and the Groveses began to give all their income, beyond modest immediate needs, to the service of God.

These matured convictions Groves embodied in a booklet, of which the first edition was published in 1825. *Christian Devotedness* was a remarkable publication. The standard evangelical literature of the time, represented at its best in the popular tracts of Hannah More and her contemporaries, was content to accept the social divisions of the day with what seems to us an intolerable smugness. It used religion to alleviate the symptoms of social injustice even while bolstering the very structure which caused injustice. Groves, on the other hand, was blissfully regardless of social distinction or barriers. His response was personal and practical. Possessions, to him, were simply a means of Christian service; wealth a positive danger to its possessors and to their dependants. Taking the words of Christ in their simple literal sense, Groves regarded the deliberate accumulation of wealth as a plain hindrance to personal piety: indeed, he considered that there existed a clear duty to spend all one's goods in the service of God. The consequences of this "rashness," both for self and dependants, were to be left to the fatherly providence of God, and to the Christian responsibility of others. He summed up his theme: "The Christian motto should be – labour hard, consume little, give much, and all to Christ." Groves was far from being a radical or a revolutionary, but it is hardly surprising that some who saw the social implications of his principles (of which he scarcely seemed aware) opposed his pamphlet fiercely.

Some of Groves's deductions from the Scriptures may seem extreme, and his economics naïve, but it is difficult not to be captivated by the strong simplicity of his faith, or indeed by the logic of his position. The root of his ideas was in his personal piety: the entire devotion of possessions and talents which he advocated springing not from political or economic theory, but solely from a deep personal devotion to Christ. As he wrote of the early Church, so he wished to see Christian love in practice in his own time:

> This manifestation of love he believes to have been made by the entire and real (not figurative) devotion of themselves, their property, time and talents to Christ, their Lord and King.[4]

It was not common for Groves to express himself with asperity concerning others – yet may we not detect a certain impatience with some of the platitudes of his day, in one of the footnotes to his pamphlet?:

> ... the guinea dedications and speeches from the rich, would pass out altogether as no longer needed; for one *action* of real dedication would contain more argument than a thousand *speeches* about it, from those who are living in all the luxuries of life, and yield more help than a thousand guineas.[5]

To criticize Groves's ideas is easy, but one feature lends a hollow ring to all criticism. Groves did not only talk about his principles – he put them into practice.

At about this time, a visit to the Groves household by Bishop Chase of Ohio, a man of similar convictions and sacrifices to themselves, led again to the raising of missionary ambitions (Ohio was at that time a frontier state). This time Mary Groves, after a first reaction of dismay, changed her direction completely, and began to support her husband's plans with enthusiasm. The Church Missionary Society was approached, and a visit from Edward Bickersteth, secretary of that Society, in July 1825, led to the Groveses being accepted as missionary candidates for Bagdad, a place for which the Society had been seeking a missionary for years. Groves's ambition was at last on the point of realization. He could hardly have foreseen that achieving it was to lead to the breaking up of the whole of his church position.*

In preparation for his missionary service, Groves started studies at Trinity College, Dublin, intending to take a theological degree before ordination. He continued to live in Exeter, and travelled to Dublin for quarterly examinations, while his dental practice in Exeter was cared for by a young relative, to whom he later gave it outright. Groves also cast

---

* Groves was at that time far from regarding service with a regular Missionary Society as being other than on authentic lines of faith – there were in his mind none of the facile distinctions which were drawn later by advocates of "Faith Missions". "I know no state where such close communion with God is necessarily kept up, as where you are almost placed, like the ravens, to be fed day by day from your Father's hands," he remarks, when writing of his missionary plans to a friend on 22nd June 1825. (*Memoir* p. 12.) Later, however, when he had seen at first hand the bad results inherent in the power structure of every organized society, he reacted violently against them. (*Christian Witness*, April 1840, Vol. VII, pp. 127–41.)

about for a suitable home tutor for his own studies, and for those of his two young sons. After some time he secured the services of a young Scot, a son of the manse, Henry Craik. Craik, ten years his junior, had just graduated from St. Andrews, where he had studied with some distinction under Hunter and latterly under Chalmers. He arrived at the Groves household on 21st August 1826, recording nine days later an almost lyrically enthusiastic impression of his employer (though faintly leavened with his native Scottish caution):

> He is a most interesting, a most noble character. The chief features of his mind are generosity, heavenly-mindedness, great talent, persuasive eloquence, gentleness, humility, learning. I know not what faults I may yet discover, but as yet I have reason to believe there scarcely does exist a more noble character.[6]

Groves had need of such qualities! Craik records:

> I arrived in Exeter on 21st August 1826, and immediately commenced my classical readings with Mr. Groves. During the first period of our studies (from the above date to 9th October), we read together eight books of Homer, the Epistles of Horace, together with portions of Lucian, Juvenal, etc. Among the works with which I privately employed myself were: Heber's *Life of Jeremy Taylor*, Cecil's *Life of Newton*, Brown's *History of Missions*, since finished; James's *Semi-sceptic*, Irving's *Orations*, *Adams on Religion*, afterwards finished; with other works, the *perusal* of which I did not accomplish.[7]

Meanwhile, Groves's frequent visits to Dublin (it was a Dublin visit which brought the first session under Craik's tuition to an end on 9th October 1826) were bringing him into contact with a new circle of friends in that city: a circle of immense importance to our own story.

Groves was now past thirty, with convictions and ideals that had matured through many years of discouragement. Of these convictions, two were to characterize deeply the remainder of his days. One was that personal devotedness to Christ, which, nourished by his open-hearted reading of the Bible, had led him and his family into their course of self-denying service. The other was related to it. His was a naturally sympathetic and generous temperament, and he was instinctively alive to the convictions of others. So there was growing in his mind a sense of the depth of true Christian unity.

Although a strict churchman on his own acknowledgement, Groves and his wife had for many years enjoyed a close friendship with two Nonconformist ladies in Exeter, the Misses Paget, and their influence was affecting him deeply as to the tragedy of Christian divisions. Now, finding himself in Dublin in a situation very different from that in Exeter, Groves realized that his friendship with these Nonconformist ladies had prepared his mind for a decisive shift of perspective. In Dublin, members of the Protestant Anglo-Irish minority found themselves thrown upon each other's company, with a consequent loosening of denominational distinctions. The habit of meeting for discussion and Bible study in private houses, which was cultivated among them, itself tended to break down artificial barriers: and it brought Groves face to face with the problems which denominational barriers raised between equally sincere Christians. Groves's mind had been deeply influenced during the period of his earnest study of the Bible by the uninhibited freedom and fellowship of the apostolic church. He must have felt the similarity between the little groups in the hostile city, and the situation of the New Testament Christians.

In Dublin Groves enjoyed a particularly close friendship with an Irish barrister of his own age, John Gifford Bellett, a classical prizeman of Trinity College. Bellett had spent some of his boyhood in Exeter, and the common ties which this circumstance must have forged between the two men were strengthened by a marked compatibility of temperament. Groves stayed in Bellett's home on his visits to Dublin, and there he was introduced to one of the most gifted of the circle of Christians who were accustomed to meet for private prayer and discussion: a young curate from Wicklow, John Nelson Darby.

That Groves's mind was rapidly developing under the stimulus of these varied influences is plain. In the spring of 1827 he took Miss Bessie Paget with him to Dublin, and it is to her that we owe the story of an incident which shows just how radically his views were changing from the strict churchmanship of a year or two before:

> Miss Paget remembers the occasion on which one of the party, Mr. Bellett, a dear friend of Mr. Groves, said to her, "Groves has just been telling me, that it appeared to him from Scripture, that believers, meeting together as disciples of Christ, were free to break bread together, as their Lord had admonished them; and that, in as far as the practice of the apostles could be a guide, every Lord's day should be set apart for thus remembering the Lord's death, and obeying his parting command."[8]*

Groves himself, some years later, recorded in his diary (under date 14th December 1833):

> I was almost forgetting, till a letter from Mr. Bellett of Dublin reminded me, that I was the first to propose that simple principle of union, the love of Jesus, instead of *oneness* of judgement in minor things, things that may consist with a true love to Jesus.[9]

Miss Paget was quick to capitalize upon his changing views. She suggested, when they returned to Exeter, that Groves should take charge on Sundays of a little Nonconformist congregation at the village of Polti-

* Groves's widow (his second wife), who edited the *Memoir* after his death, adds after this: "This suggestion of Mr. Groves was immediately carried out by himself and his friends in Dublin." She does not state whether this information came from Miss Paget or was her own deduction: Bellett in his account seems to know nothing of this. (But see the account of Parnell's group, page 30.)

more for which she had made herself responsible. Groves, who was after all still a candidate for Anglican ordination, was still not free of all his scruples. He wrote:

> I cannot, perhaps, convey to you the repugnance that I had; first, because I really disapproved in principle; and, secondly, because I saw that it would stand in the way of my procuring ordination; yet it worked on my mind till I could not but go; and I went. . . . Yet I only allowed this going to Poltimore as a particular exception, in consequence of the notorious inadequacy of the clergyman there. I had never yet gone near a dissenting place of worship.[10]

Events now moved rapidly. The next visit to Dublin was due in the summer of that same year, 1827, after which Groves would need to make no more journeys there until he attended to take his degree at Easter 1828. Shortly before this summer visit was due a strange series of incidents occurred.

A missionary from Calcutta, visiting Exeter, met Groves, and they turned to discussing his plans for Persia. This missionary asked Groves why he was "wasting his time" going through College, when he intended going to the East. To this Groves made the reasonable reply that it would qualify him the better for ministry at home, if his health were to cause him to return. Moreover, he was about to make his final journey to Dublin, and his degree was only nine months away – to change his plans now would neither improve his reputation for consistency, nor particularly hasten his departure for Persia.

His wife, however, pressed the question. For the moment they agreed to differ, but two nights before his departure for Dublin their home was burgled, and the money set aside for the Irish visit was stolen. They appear to have regarded this incident as closing the question:

> As I was returning up stairs, I met dearest Mary in the hall, and said, "Well, my love, the thieves have been here, and taken all the money." "And now," she said, "you won't go to Dublin." "No," I replied, "that I won't" – and we spent one of the happiest Sundays I ever recollect, in thinking on the Lord's goodness, in so caring for us as to stop our way up, when He does not wish us to go. Some thought it right; others thought it foolish; it mattered not to us, we had not a doubt it was of the Lord.[11]

The bonds were being rapidly loosened. First, there had been that almost naïve simplicity of heart in response to the reading of the Bible. That simple-hearted devotion to Christ had led to a growing realization of the implications of true Christian unity; and as a direct result to the loosening one after the other of the restrictions of denominational discipline. To Groves, excited as he must have been by the rapid development of his own thinking, and with an increasing sense of a divine over-ruling of his circumstances, no incident could have seemed too trivial to be the carrier of a divine command.

It was at this point that he found himself facing the question posed to him by his friend. Groves described the circumstances himself:

> During this time, dear Hake came and consulted me about certain difficulties, which involved his leaving his wife and children penniless, so far as he knew, or following a course that his conscience disapproved. I gave my opinion clearly; and he with that holy simplicity which has ever characterized him, acted out what his conscience dictated. Shortly after this, he called on me, and asked me if I did not hold war to be unlawful. I replied, "Yes.'· He then further asked, how I could subscribe that article which declares, "It is lawful for Christian men to take up arms at the command of the civil magistrate." It had, till that moment, never occurred to me. I read it; and replied, "I never would sign it"; and thus ended my connection with the Church of England, as one about to be ordained in her communion.[12]

So Groves took what, in retrospect, must appear the crucial step in his churchly path. Yet he still continued with his missionary plans, so sure was he of the calling which he had received. For the moment, he made up his mind to go out with the Church Missionary Society as planned, but as a lay worker. On 1st January 1828 he handed over his dental practice to the young relative who had been caring for it in his absence. Then the discipline of the Church put its last stumbling block in his way. The Church Missionary Society informed him that, as a layman, he would not be able to celebrate the communion with any converts of his mission, in the absence of an ordained clergyman.

Groves was faced with a denial of the very convictions which he had outlined to Bellett barely a year before. Yet, for a time, a still greater point of conscience remained: "I saw not yet my liberty of ministry to be from Christ alone, and felt some ordination to be necessary, but hated the thought of being made a sectarian."[13]

With our knowledge of the development of his thinking, we can readily guess the solution to his dilemma. Like many another in a similar situation, he turned back to the simple and uninhibited joy of the early church. "One day the thought was brought to my mind, that ordination of any kind to preach the gospel is no requirement of Scripture. To me it was the removal of a mountain."[14] He adds – and of this we shall hear more later – "in my last visit to Dublin, I mentioned my views to dear Mr. Bellett and others."[15]

Groves and his wife continued their plans to go to Bagdad: but it would be at their own charges, and as freemen of Christ. Financially, they had little problem, for they had received a substantial inheritance on the death of Mrs. Groves's father a year before. This, like their other goods, was now to be applied to the service of Christ. A group of friends in Dublin was keenly interested in their plans, and several had thoughts of joining them at a later date. So, on 12th June 1829 they sailed from Gravesend for St. Petersburg, from which city they were to travel overland, through

Russia, into Persia and on to Bagdad. Sailing with them was Kitto, Groves's protégé of earlier days, and they were accompanied as far as St. Petersburg by another interesting companion, one of the Dublin group, who had arranged the charter of a friend's yacht for this first part of the journey. This was John Vesey Parnell, son of Sir Henry Brooke Parnell, a leading Irish Member of Parliament who was later to be created Baron Congleton.

It says much for the tolerant goodwill of the Church Missionary Society – and indeed for Groves himself – that their parting appears to have been on friendly terms: in a letter written during his journey he describes how the Society would forward letters and small packets to him, adding "I take this most kindly at their hands."[16]

The break with the Church of England had not been accomplished without some pain: particularly as Groves's study of the Bible had convinced him of the necessity for believer's baptism, and he had accepted the ordinance before his departure. A friend (later to become his second wife after the death of Mary Groves in Bagdad) had met him shortly after the ceremony and had said: "Of course, you must be a Baptist now you are baptized." Groves's reply was typical:

"No! I desire to follow all in those things in which they follow Christ; but I would not, by joining one party, cut myself off from others." Then taking up the ring on which his keys hung, he said, "If these keys were to hold by one another, all would go if one fell; but as each of them is attached to this strong ring, so should we each take hold of Christ, not of any of the systems of men, and then we shall be safe and united: we should keep together, not because of any human system, but because Jesus is *one*."[17]

One of the Groveses' closest friends was the Anglican curate of Claybrook, Mr. Caldecott, in whose ordination in 1826 Groves had taken a considerable personal interest and delight. Not unexpectedly, the developments in Groves's views alarmed Caldecott (although later he was to follow in a similar course), and although he offered to share in the expenses of the Persian journey his letter had been reproachful. Groves replied:

You say I quitted *your* communion; if you mean by that, that I do not now break bread with the Church of England, this is not true; but if you mean that I do not *exclusively* join you, it is quite true, feeling this spirit of exclusiveness to be of the very essence of schism, which the apostle so strongly reproves in the Corinthians. I therefore know no distinction, but am ready to break the bread and drink the cup of holy joy with all who love the Lord and will not lightly speak evil of His name. I feel every saint to be a holy person, because Christ dwells in him, and manifests Himself where he worships; and though his faults be as many as the hairs of his head, my duty still is, with my Lord, to join him as a member of the mystical body, and to hold communion and fellowship with him in any work of the Lord in which he may be engaged.

You ask again, am I exercising the ministry on my own nomination? I trust not, for if I am, the work will come to nought; I trust I exercise it on the nomination of my Lord by His Spirit; if you can point out any other nomination as necessary, or that there are persons excluded until they are appointed by man, I hope I am willing to weigh the evidence you bring. I wish you, however, distinctly to understand, I do not object to ordination by men, if it be exercised on principles consistent with Scripture, but if they think they confer any thing more than their permission to preach in their little part of the fold of Christ, I should decline it until they show how they came by that authority from the word of God, and what are the scriptural rules and limitations of this authority. . . . As bodies, I know none of the sects and parties that wound and disfigure the body of Christ; as individuals, I desire to love all that love Him. Oh! when will the day come, when the love of Christ will have more power to unite than our foolish regulations have to divide the family of God (16th December 1828).[18]

Five-and-a-half years later, Groves was to write in his diary:

I am so sure of the truth of those blessed principles the Lord has taught me, that I glory in their propagation. Simple obedience to Christ alone; recognition of Christ alone in my brother, as the Alpha and Omega of terms of communion; lastly, unreserved devotion to Christ alone (25th June 1834).[19]

Quotation References – Chapter 1

1. *Memoir of Anthony Norris Groves containing extracts from his letters and journals* (2nd edn. 1857), compiled by his widow, p. 6.
2. Ibid., p. 27.
3. Ibid., p. 29.
4. *Christian Devotedness* (1825) (2nd ed., 1829), reproduced in G. H. Lang *Anthony Norris Groves* (2nd edn., 1949) – quotation on p. 72.
5. Ibid., p. 96 n.
6. *Passages from the Diary and Letters of Henry Craik of Bristol*, W. Elfe Tayler (1866), p. 81.
7. Ibid., p. 80.
8. *Memoir*, pp. 38–39.
9. Ibid., p. 259.
10. Ibid., p. 40.
11. Ibid., p. 42.
12. Ibid., pp. 40–41.
13. Ibid., p. 42.
14. Ibid., p. 42.
15. Ibid., p. 43.
16. Ibid., p. 53.
17. Ibid., p. 36.
18. Ibid., pp. 48–49.
19. Ibid., p. 321.

CHAPTER 2

BREAD UPON THE WATERS

As any system is in its provision narrower or wider than the truth, I either stop short, or go beyond its provisions, but I would INFINITELY RATHER BEAR *with all their evils*, than SEPARATE from THEIR GOOD. These were the *then* principles of our separation and inter-communion; we had resolved never to try to *get men to act* in UNIFORMITY *farther than they* FELT IN UNIFORMITY; neither by frowns, or smiles; and this for one simple reason, that we saw no authority given us from God thus to act.

A. N. Groves – *Letter to J. N. Darby* (10th March 1836).

DURING 1827 THERE CAME TO DUBLIN A YOUNG MAN WHO bore a name that was to become famous. This was Francis William Newman, younger brother of the great John Henry. But, while the older brother was to pass from his evangelical upbringing into leadership of the Tractarian movement, and thence to the red hat of a Roman cardinal, Francis was to pass through changes no less conspicuous, through the early Brethren movement, then into unitarianism, and free thought. He had obtained first-class honours in classics and mathematics at Worcester College, Oxford, in the previous year, and had also become a Fellow of Balliol. Now he had been engaged as a private tutor in the household of a leading Irish lawyer, Serjeant Pennefather, later to become Lord Chief Justice of Ireland.*

In the household of Pennefather he met an unusual man.

This was a young relative of his – a most remarkable man – who rapidly gained an immense sway over me. I shall henceforth call him "the Irish clergyman." His "bodily presence" was indeed "weak"! A fallen cheek, a bloodshot eye, crippled limbs resting on crutches, a seldom-shaven beard, a shabby suit of clothes and a generally neglected person, drew at first pity, with wonder to see such a figure in a drawing-room. It was currently reported that a person in Limerick offered him a halfpenny, mistaking him for a beggar; and if not true, the story was yet well invented. This young man had taken high honours in Dublin University and had studied for the Bar, where under the auspices of his eminent kinsman he had excellent prospects; but his conscience would not allow him to take a brief, lest he should be selling his talents to defeat justice. With keen logical powers, he had warm sympathies, solid judgement of character, thoughtful tenderness and total self-abandonment. He before long took Holy Orders,

* Professor Basil Willey, in his essay on Newman in *More Nineteenth Century Studies – A Group of Honest Doubters*, says (wrongly) that it was in the household of Lord Congleton (p. 18).

25

and became an indefatigable curate in the mountains of Wicklow. Every evening he sallied forth to teach in the cabins, and roving far and wide over mountain and amid bogs, was seldom home before midnight. By such exertions his strength was undermined, and he so suffered in his limbs that not lameness only, but yet more serious results were feared. He did not fast on purpose, but his long walks through wild country and indigent people inflicted on him much severe deprivation: moreover, as he ate whatever food offered itself – food unpalatable and often indigestible to him – his whole frame might have vied in emaciation with a monk of La Trappe.

Such a phenomenon intensely excited the poor Romanists, who looked on him as a genuine "saint" of the ancient breed. The stamp of heaven seemed to them clear in a frame so wasted by austerity, so superior to worldly pomp, and so partaking in all their indigence. That a dozen such men would have done more to convert all Ireland to Protestantism, than the whole apparatus of the Church Establishment, was ere long my conviction; though I was at first offended by his apparent affectation of a careless exterior. But I soon understood, that in no other way could he gain equal access to the lower and lowest orders, and that he was moved not by asceticism, nor by ostentation, but by a self-abandonment fruitful of consequences. He had practically given up all reading except that of the Bible; and no small part of his movement towards me soon took the form of dissuasion from all other voluntary study.

. . . In spite of the strong revulsion which I felt against some of the peculiarities of this remarkable man, I for the first time in my life found myself under the dominion of a superior. When I remember, how even those bowed down before him, who had been to him in the place of parents – accomplished and experienced minds – I cease to wonder in the retrospect, that he riveted me in such a bondage... he *only* wanted men "to submit their understandings *to God*," that is, to the Bible, that is, to his interpretation ! . . . Such was Ignatius Loyola in his day.[1]

The "Irish clergyman" was none other than Bellett's friend, John Nelson Darby, and how he came to be at this time in the household of his brother-in-law in this crippled and yet compelling state of person, is the next part of our own story.

Darby was born on 18th November, 1800, the son of a well-to-do Irish landowner and merchant, and had received his second Christian name* in tribute to the great Lord Nelson himself (his uncle, Admiral Sir Henry Darby, commanded the *Bellerophon* at the Nile). The family home was at Leap Castle, Offaly (then known as King's County). Educated at Westminster School, Darby had entered Trinity College, Dublin, at the age of fifteen, and in 1819 had graduated there as Classical Gold Medallist. After being called to the Irish Bar, as Newman recounts, he had abandoned his career for the Church, being ordained deacon in 1825 and priest in 1826, His first charge was as curate of Calary in County Wicklow.

At this time the question of Catholic emancipation was a burning one,

* The often reported statement that Nelson was godfather to Darby needs to be substantiated.

but it would also appear that Protestantism was beginning to make some unexpected headway among the Irish people. For some reason – perhaps because of the resultant political risks – Archbishop Magee of Dublin in 1827 delivered a charge to his clergy, who published a declaration to Parliament claiming State protection against the Roman Catholic Church. Magee seems to have considered that the time required a more open demonstration of the claims of the Protestant clergy to be loyal upholders of the English domination, and he therefore added to the offence of the petition yet another – the requirement that all converts from Roman Catholicism should take the oaths of allegiance and supremacy.

There can scarcely have been a more maladroit act. Its effect upon the Irish was precisely what might have been expected, and Darby many years later described it (in an account possibly somewhat exaggerated):

> I ought to have somewhere a copy of my letter to the Archbishop. I forget it. But his course was ruinous – really stopped the deliverance from Popery of masses, perhaps of all Ireland; they were leaving from seven to eight hundred a week. He required the oath of supremacy and abjuration: it stopped as by a shot.[2]

The effect upon Darby himself was little less decisive. His first act – a sufficiently bold one for a curate of barely two years in orders – was to draw up and circulate among his fellow-clergy a strong protest against the miserable view of the Church's calling which could so reduce it to subservience to the State (this may have been the "letter to the Archbishop" to which he refers). The pamphlet was followed in the next year by the first of Darby's voluminous public writings – a booklet entitled *On the Nature and Unity of the Church of Christ*, of which we shall have more to say later.

The shock to Darby's mind was permanent: and a further event in that same year of 1827 was to deepen the movement of his thought. After he had been for two-and-a-quarter years in his curacy, he was thrown by his horse against a doorpost, and forced to remain in convalescence for some time – it was undoubtedly this accident that had brought him to the home of his brother-in-law at the time of F. W. Newman's arrival, and which accounted for the crutches of which Newman spoke (the eye-trouble was more deep-rooted, and there are recurring references to it in Darby's correspondence). Darby later wrote:

> During my solitude, conflicting thoughts increased; but much exercise of soul had the effect of causing the Scriptures to gain complete ascendancy over me. I had always owned them to be the word of God.[3]

With Darby himself passing through this period of tension, there is little wonder that Newman found the impact of his ideas to be frightening!

Darby's understanding of the Church was being changed radically as a result of these events. At one time, on his own showing, he had been an extreme sacramentalist in his church views, but he now turned to very different thoughts:

> It then became clear to me that the church of God, as He considers it, was composed only of those who were so united to Christ, whereas Christendom, as seen externally, was really the world, and could not be considered as "the church," save as regards the responsibility attaching to the position which it professed to occupy – a very important thing in its place. At the same time, I saw that the Christian, having his place in Christ in heaven, has nothing to wait for save the coming of the Saviour, in order to be set, in fact, in the glory which is already his portion in Christ.
>
> The careful reading of the Acts afforded me a practical picture of the early church, which made me feel deeply the contrast with its actual present state, though still as ever, beloved by God.[4]

This later recollection possibly over-simplifies the movement of his mind at this time, but the general trend of his thinking is plain enough. His writings show that he was already gone beyond the traditional dissenting concept of the Church (if, in fact, he ever shared or understood it) and was reaching for characteristic mystical insights. For the moment, like Groves, he found his inspiration in the picture of the early church found in the New Testament.

Darby's friend J. G. Bellett had fallen under the influence of Groves. Groves's visit in the spring of 1827 had (as we have seen) faced Bellett with some of the implications of the newly-developing ideas. Then, late in 1828, Groves paid a farewell visit to his friends in Dublin. By now, Groves had reached his final position on matters of church order, and he seems to have been eager to discuss it with his friends. As to those friends themselves, the eventful eighteen months since Groves had last been in Dublin had prepared the ground for fresh advances. Bellett describes the effect upon him of his conversation with Groves:

> . . . by the entrance of these thoughts the whole question was raised in his mind, so that he (Groves) not only abandoned his connection with College, but viewed as he never before had done, the whole matter of the Established Church and the claims of Dissenting bodies. In the close of 1828 he visited Dublin, though he had seceded from the College. He preached in Poolbeg Street at the request of dear Dr. Egan, then in connection with the little company formed there, of whom Richard Pope, well-known in Ireland at the time, was one. Walking one day with him, as we were passing down Lower Pembroke Street, he said to me, "This, I doubt not, is the mind of God concerning us, that we should come together in all simplicity as disciples, not waiting on any pulpit or minister, but trusting that the Lord would edify us together, by ministering as He pleased and saw good from the midst of ourselves."
>
> At the moment he spoke these words I was assured my soul had got the right idea, and that moment – I remember it as if it was yesterday, and could point

you out the place – it was the birth place of my mind, dear James, may I so speak as a brother.[5]*

Yet Darby and Bellett had still not wholly broken with the Established Church. Darby had returned to his curacy, then, resigning it, began to travel widely, but still as a clergyman.

Small groups of Christians had been meeting in different parts of the city, unable to find a home for conscience within the existing churches. One such group had formed shortly before the events we have described around a Dr. Edward Cronin, a convert from Roman Catholicism, from Cork. On arriving in Dublin, Cronin had at first been welcomed as visitor by various Nonconformist Churches, but later they stipulated that, as a resident, he could not partake of communion without stated membership of one church. Reasonable as this requirement might seem,* it offended Cronin's sense of the unity of all Christians to find himself obliged to join one specific section to the exclusion of others. His doubts, instead of attracting sympathy, led to a public denunciation of Cronin from one of the Nonconformist pulpits.

This untoward act caused the resignation of a handful of members from the church concerned, in sympathy with Cronin. Among them was one of the deacons, Edward Wilson, who was also the assistant secretary of the Dublin branch of the Bible Society. These few began to meet for prayer and the Lord's Supper in a room of Wilson's home, and continued there for a time until Wilson left for England.

Wilson's association with the group led to its becoming known, and in due course a friendship formed between Cronin and one of the circle to which Darby and Bellett belonged. This was Francis Hutchinson, son of the Archdeacon of Killala, Sir Samuel Synge (the archdeacon had assumed the additional surname of Hutchinson on succeeding his uncle to the title).[6] Bellett, Darby and Hutchinson were away from Dublin for the summer of 1829, but by their return in November 1829 Hutchinson "was quite prepared for communion in the name of the Lord with all, whomseoever they might be, who loved Him in sincerity."[7] Hutchinson offered the use of a room in his house in Fitzwilliam Square, and five persons met

---

* Professor Basil Willey, op. cit., pp. 19, 20, states that "At this very time Congleton and Groves received a joint communication, of a mystical character, concerning the mind of God towards them: 'that we should come together not waiting on any pulpit or minister, but trusting that the Lord would edify us together by ministering as He pleased.' This revelation ... was the basis of Plymouth Brethrenism"! (Professor Willey quotes from Miss Sieveking's life of F. W. Newman.) Amusing though it is to find Groves's sober proposal that they should dispense with the services of the clergy and manage among themselves, thus transmuted Ariel-like into something rich and strange, the misunderstanding is not without pertinence, in the light of later developments in some sections of Brethren towards an "impulsive" participation in public ministry of the Word. Groves was to fight this development fiercely.

* There are places where precisely this requirement would be imposed by present-day Brethren churches.

there to discuss the position – Bellett, Brooke, Cronin, Darby and Hutchinson. Hutchinson was careful to lay down a simple order of service and to fix a time which permitted members of the group to attend church services elsewhere. On the following Sunday four of them met to celebrate Communion – Brooke was absent, having (according to a tart note of Darby's) been "frightened away by Hutchinson."[8]

There was another small group, which had for some years been meeting to "break bread" in similar fashion, which was soon drawn to join forces with the newly-formed fellowship. Once again, the reason for their secession from the existing churches had been their inability to find a church fellowship which would welcome them all, from their differing backgrounds, and not exclude one or other of them. William Stokes and Groves's friend Parnell had been two of their number. When they learned of the establishment of the fellowship in Hutchinson's house, the two groups joined forces. Parnell (who had recently returned from his journey to St. Petersburg with Groves) soon became concerned over the privacy of the little group's proceedings, and in May 1830, proposed that they should move their meeting-place to a more public room which he hired in Aungier Street. (Miss A. M. Stoney, who became associated with the Brethren in Dublin some years after this, has left on record the suggestion that the move was also made in order that poorer folk might attend with less embarrassment than they would have felt – in those days of great class distinction – in entering the home of a wealthy man.)[9] Hutchinson and Bellett were at first shy of the open challenge which was presented to the discipline of other churches by the formation of such a public fellowship, but after some hesitation they joined with the new venture. Darby was probably in England at the time.

The early days of the little church were fresh and delightful, but it soon lost some of the most gifted of its members. In September 1830,[10] a party had left to join Groves in Bagdad, among them Parnell, Cronin and his sister, and F. W. Newman (who had come from Oxford to join them). The story of that tragic episode does not belong to this part of our account. Of the remaining leaders at Dublin, Darby was only occasionally present, while Hutchinson died in April 1833. The happy early spirit continued, and numbers increased: but the congregation also had its troubles, traces of which appear in the reminiscences of Bellett and of Cronin, and also in Darby's contemporary letters. The settled order of worship which had characterized the early days in Fitzwilliam Square was gradually replaced by a completely free character of proceedings, even a recognized eldership being renounced – a development in which Darby's own altering views are apparent. The story of the little church now becomes linked with that of other events near to Dublin, which must be described in a later chapter of this book.

Darby was still not wholly committed to a total breach with the Established Church. Indeed, Bellett writes of him as, even as late as 1834, "*all but* detached from the Church of England":[11] and another clash with his Archbishop (now Whately) in 1832 and an outright breach with many members of the Church of Ireland at Powerscourt in 1833 had intervened between these two dates. The clash with Whately took the form of an open letter by Darby in relation to the Irish Education Measure. Whately was identified with proposals to restrict severely the teaching of the Scriptures in Irish schools, in deference to that same Roman Catholic problem over which his predecessor had fallen foul of the erstwhile curate of Calary. In his letter of 1832, Darby did not content himself with a bitter attack on an "unholy marriage between Infidelity and Popery, the devil's apostate counterpart of the union between the bride, the Lamb's wife, and the great Head of the Church," but went on to a strong personal attack on Whately himself in relation to his alleged Sabellianism.[12]

Before we leave Dublin to consider developments elsewhere, it is important to give more attention to the first of Darby's many public writings: the pamphlet to which we have already referred, entitled *On the Nature and Unity of the Church of Christ*. The pamphlet would be important, if for no other reason than that it provides us with contemporary evidence of the development of Darby's thinking – and by implication of that of many of the circle around him* – at an interesting and critical point of their early history. But the pamphlet has an especial fascination from the fact that two quite different editions are extant: for the development between their respective dates is of intense interest to any who would try to understand later events.

The earlier edition appears in modern reprints under the dateline "Dublin, 1828."[13] It thus followed quickly upon the controversy over Archbishop Magee's actions in relation to the Roman Catholic converts. Its style was tortuous and difficult (a characteristic of Darby's writings), and it justified (as the later edition did not) the description which was given to it by Neatby – "strikingly lacking in definiteness of suggestion, and . . . plainly either the writing of a man who does not yet see his own way clearly; or of one who deliberately prefers to keep his own counsel."[14]

Nevertheless, it was produced by a man feeling deeply the pain of division among earnest Christians, and distressed by the worldly ambitions he sees within the Church. His analysis of the causes of these divisions traced them back to the Church's historic subservience to the secular power – an analysis obviously inspired by his recent experiences.

Darby faintly commended certain contemporary efforts at co-operation among Christians, in the Bible Society and in missionary work, but

* Neatby points out (*History of the Plymouth Brethren* 2nd edn, p. 33), that Groves makes an apparent rough quotation from it in the letter of 16th December 1828, from which we have quoted on p. 24.

condemned recent attempts to solve the problem of disunity by secession as "defective, in not practically waiting upon His will." He went on: "it has failed for the reason mentioned, as in act it ran before the general progress of the divine counsels."

He then expressed the ideal of unity. It is grounded in "the purpose of God in Christ to gather in one all things in heaven and on earth, reconciled unto Himself in Him," and leads on to the truth that Christian believers are "*so* to be all one, as that the *world* might know that Jesus was sent of God; in this we must all confess our sad failure."

The summary reads familiarly enough to those who are conversant with modern literature on the subject of Christian unity, and it is at first difficult to remember that we are dealing with a writing of as early a date as 1828, until we reach the sequel. For it was at this point that Darby's dilemma asserted itself. He had stressed the urgent need for unity. Mutual co-operation was insufficient: though good, it was but a step in the right direction, having "partially inherent in it, though not recognized in its power, the germ of true unity". On the other hand, he had deplored an attempt to secede and form yet another communion in which unity might try to find expression. There might seem to be one obvious alternative: the union of existing bodies. Yet Darby renounced it: "In the first place, it is not a formal union of the outward professing bodies that is desirable; indeed, it is surprising that reflecting Protestants should desire it; far from doing good, I conceive it would be impossible that such a body could be at all recognized as the Church of God. It would be the counterpart to Romish unity; we should have the life of the Church and the power of the Word lost, and the unity of spiritual life utterly excluded."

Darby's dilemma was complete. He insisted: "No meeting, which is not framed to embrace all the children of God in the full basis of the kingdom of the Son, can find the fulness of blessing, because it does not contemplate it – because its faith does not embrace it." Any more restricted bond of communion, he went on, "puts me in mind indeed (as all doubtless have some separate portion of the form of the Church) of those who parted the Saviour's garments among them." How, then did he propose to demonstrate this ideal?

Darby first went back to Scriptural principles. Unity is centred in Christ – "In *Him* alone can we find this unity" . . . Then, referring first to John 11: 51, 52, he goes on to John 12: 32, 33 – "our Lord in the vision of the fruit of the travail of His soul declares 'I, if I be lifted up from the earth, will draw all men unto me. This he said signifying what death he should die.' It is then Christ who will draw – will draw to *Himself* . . . and draw to Himself by being lifted up from the earth. In a word, His death is the centre of communion till His coming again, and in this rests the whole power of truth. Accordingly, the outward symbol and instrument of unity is the partaking of the Lord's Supper – 'for we being many are one body, for we are all partakers of that one bread.'"

We are now at the profound heart of the argument, and look for its practical application – but we find none. "The essence and substance of unity," Darby continued, "which will appear in glory at His coming, is conformity to His death, by which that glory was all wrought." He had given a theological and mystical answer to a matter of practical Church action – with no plain indication as to how that devotional answer is to be translated into deed. Oddly enough, there is a hint of Pelagianism in the answer: unity is not seen as the result of God's work in the death of Christ, so much as the result of the Christian's conforming to that death. It is an idea which coloured all Darby's later teachings.

A profound mystical insight, then, led to spiritual exaltation; only to leave its readers with little clear practical direction – and therefore with the risk of dangerous misunderstanding. Darby pointed out that the early Church enjoyed unity "when none said anything was his own," but that it lost it first in quarrels over possessions. Thus, in the only practical hint he had to give, conformity to the death of Christ was equated by implication with asceticism, with an outlook that rejected the material for the spiritual. His development of this thought was ominous. Other viewpoints were soon referred to as "the spirit of the world," "the spirit which gradually opened the door to the dominion of apostasy." Unity "can only be in the things of the Spirit, and therefore can only be perfected in spiritual persons."

But was this true? Is not unity – like salvation – the result of God's sovereign act of redemption? Who was to define "the world" and the "spiritual persons"? More pointedly, who was to classify himself as between these categories? Without clear definition, was there not all the material here for a merely ascetic definition of Christianity, and for a still more frightening recurrence of that very spirit of "he followeth not with us" which Darby himself had condemned? It is only just, of course, to read his comments in the light of his revulsion from sheer worldly ambitions within the churches. It was understandable that Darby should have deplored churches which seek an alliance with the world for secular advantage: but it was emphatically unjust for him to reject sincere attempts towards unity as "not the unity of the Church, but confederacy and denial of the nature and hope of the Church."

When at last Darby posed to himself the question "If you see these things, what are you doing yourself?" he had no answer. All that he could say in this first edition of the pamphlet was: "I can only deeply acknowledge the strange and infinite shortcomings, and sorrow and mourn over them: I acknowledge the weakness of my faith, but I earnestly seek for direction." Unity "cannot possibly be found till the common object of those who are members of it is the glory of the Lord, who is the Author and Finisher of its faith: a glory which is to be made known in its brightness at His appearing, when the fashion of this world shall pass away, and therefore acted up to and entered upon in spirit when we are planted together in the likeness of His death."

In raising the question which he had failed to answer, what other tendencies had Darby set in train? That the question received no coherent, practical answer, until secession had hardened spirits and thoughts, was the tragedy of Darbyism.

For, as we have already stated, the pamphlet appeared in a second edition. We have referred to the troubled pathway which Darby trod between the dates of the two editions. But, in Plymouth, he had found a group of men who shared much of his outlook, among them another seceding Anglican clergyman, Henry Borlase, formerly curate of St. Keyne in Cornwall. In January 1834 there appeared a new periodical, issued from Plymouth, under the editorship of Borlase. In that first number of *The Christian Witness*[15] was printed the revision of Darby's pamphlet *On the Nature and Unity of the Church of Christ*. But the ending of the earlier edition was replaced by a longer and altogether more bitter ending. The first edition, for all its deploring of the pathway of other churches, still recalled their virtues with warmth: "I earnestly care for them; for the Dissenters, for their integrity of conscience, and often deep apprehensions of the mind of Christ; and for the Church, if it were but for the memory of those men, who, however they may have been outwardly entangled with what was not of their own spirit and failed in freeing themselves from it, seem to have inwardly drunk more deeply of the Spirit of Him who called them, than any since the days of the apostles; men in whose communion I thankfully delight myself, whom I delight to honour."

But, in the new edition, he saw himself "in the closing scene of revolution, moral as well as political." "The Dissenters have sought – have joined the world; and if the Establishment has been amalgamated with it, the eagerness of actual pursuit has marked the steps of the Dissenters. . . . They have sought the world, and the world they will have, but the world in its infidel state."

It is significant that many of the sentiments in the close of this new edition are identical with those expressed elsewhere by Borlase himself. Christians have a direct title to meet together to break bread – and if this is dubbed schism, then it ceases to be schism when it is schism from that which is worldly. It is the duty of Christians to separate quietly from the present evil, not "pretending to set up churches," but simply as the two or three gathered together. "If schism be charged, schism from the world is always right, and is now above all, a duty to Christ, and the dishonour of His Church is the chief dishonour to Him."

The direct right of Christians to break bread together in simplicity. They were as the words of Groves – but the spirit in which that right was to be exercised was the spirit of something very different from anything which Groves had foreseen or desired.

Quotation references – Chapter 2.

1. *Phases of Faith,* F. W. Newman (1850), pp. 27, 28, 33, 34.
2. *Letters of J. N. D.,** Vol. I, p. 397 (the letter is dated Toronto, 1865). Groves appears to make a reference to the Irish revival in a letter of 2nd April 1827 – "What a wonderful state of things appears to be arising in Ireland." (*Memoir,* p. 20.)
3. *Letters of J. N. D.,* Vol. III, p. 298 (Letter to Professor Tholuck of 185–).
4. Ibid., p. 298 (same letter).
5. *Interesting Reminiscences of the Early History of "Brethren"* (reprint undated), containing various letters. That quoted is an undated letter of J. G. Bellett to James McAllister. The printed copy differs in minor particulars from the manuscript copy quoted by Neatby in his *History of the Plymouth Brethren.* Quotation from pp. 4, 5.
6. This is taken from the biographical details given in *Chief Men Among the Brethren* (1931 edn), p. 57. The Archdeacon of Killala, Sir Samuel Synge, assumed the name Hutchinson when he succeeded his uncle, Sir Francis Hutchinson (T. C. F. Stunt in *The Harvester,* May 1968, p. 78).
7. *Interesting Reminiscences, etc.* From the letter of Bellett already cited, p. 5.
8. Ibid. Footnote by J. N. Darby, p. 14.
9. From a MS copy of notes of Miss Stoney in the possession of Mr. O. W. Ware of Capetown. Miss Stoney's recollection is not wholly reliable, and she dates the events in 1827.
10. Bellett, op. cit., p. 7, says 1831, but F. W. Newman, op. cit., p. 45, has 1830, and references in Groves's diary, reproduced in the *Memoir,* show Newman to be correct.
11. Op. cit., p. 8 (italics not Bellett's).
12. The letter is extensively reprinted in *John Nelson Darby,* W. G. Turner (1944), pp. 26–31.
13. Quotations are from a reprint of a number of early tracts of J. N. Darby, undated, and collectively entitled *The Faith once delivered to the Saints.*
14. *History of the Plymouth Brethren* (2nd edn, 1902), p. 18.
15. Quotations are taken from the original (bound) volumes.

* All references to Darby's *letters* in this book are to the Stow Hill edition.

CHAPTER 3

AN UNEXPECTED PARTNERSHIP

The Church is her true self only when she exists for humanity. As a fresh start she should give away all her endowments to the poor and needy. The clergy should live solely on the free-will offerings of their congregations, or possibly engage in some secular calling.
>> Dietrich Bonhoeffer, *Letters and Papers from Prison.*

WHEN GROVES DECIDED TO SAIL FOR BAGDAD, HENRY CRAIK was out of a job.* The anonymous well-wisher who spoke for him to John Synge of Buckridge House, Teignmouth, could not have foreseen that he was to be the indirect cause of as fruitful a partnership in practical Christianity as any the world has known.

That well-wisher may have been Groves himself (and it would have been characteristic of him to take concern for the young tutor he was leaving without employment). For Synge was only temporarily in Teignmouth – he was a Dublin man who in 1831 inherited the estate of Glanmore Castle, near Dublin, and he was one of the circle with which Groves had been in contact in that city, being a cousin of Francis Hutchinson. Craik had left Groves's employment early in 1828, and had returned to Scotland in March, after several unsuccessful attempts to find a post, in order to assist his ailing father at the village school.

Then, after a short interval, came the unexpected invitation to Teignmouth, to act as tutor to Synge's two sons. Synge was to prove a good friend during the next three years, encouraging Craik in his linguistic studies, and financing the publication of his *Principia Hebraica* in 1831. Synge was also to further the links between Craik and the Dublin group. But the most fruitful result of Craik's move to Teignmouth came from another friendship which he formed there.

Craik arrived back in Exeter in June 1828, and after a short period in that city, during which he occupied himself with linguistic and theological studies, took up his appointment at Teignmouth. His personal intellectual régime was a strenuous one, and his ideas of mental relaxation his own – on one occasion, having spent five-and-a-quarter hours on close work on the Greek roots in the Septuagint, he found himself forced by a headache to look for lighter reading. This he found in a work which he describes as "truly admirable" – Bishop Jewel's *Apologia Ecclesiae*

---

* He had received a strong invitation to accompany the party to Bagdad, but had declined because of his own family circumstances.

Anglicanae! His admiration for Jewel's *Apology* did not, however, prevent Craik from rejecting the doctrine of infant baptism while at Buckridge, and he began to preach regularly in the Baptist Chapel at Shaldon. In December 1829 he met Mr. Carey* in Exeter, to discuss the prospect of joining the latter in India with the Baptist Missionary Society, but the proposals came to nothing.

In July 1829 a visitor came to Teignmouth from a very different background than any we have yet met. George Müller was a young German, born (like Craik) in 1805. He had been trained for the Lutheran ministry, but, despite his proposed career, he had led a dissolute and profligate life. Then, in November 1825, while at Halle University, he had been quietly and suddenly converted during the course of a prayer meeting in a private house. Against the initial opposition of his father (his mother had died when he was fourteen) he had decided to devote himself to missionary service. Early in 1829 he came to London on an introduction from Professor Tholuck of Halle for training with the London Society for Promoting Christianity among the Jews (later to become the Church Mission to the Jews). Two months after his arrival, his health broke down, and he came to Teignmouth on convalescence.

Müller and Craik struck up an immediate friendship. They must have seemed oddly matched, the erstwhile profligate German and the ultra-earnest, introspective Scot. Yet the friendship was to remain close and unbroken until Craik's death in 1866. After Craik's death, Müller recorded their mutual attraction in his somewhat ponderous prose:

> That which drew me to him was not that we both were then nearly twenty-four years of age; nor was it that we both had had a university education; nor was it that we both, with great love and earnestness, at that time, pursued the study of the Hebrew language; nor was it even, that both of us had been about the same time brought to the knowledge of the Lord Jesus, whilst at the university; but it will be seen in what follows, what it was that drew me to him. . . . While at Teignmouth, I became acquainted with Mr. Craik, and *his warmth of heart towards the Lord* drew me to him. It was this which was the attraction to me.[1]

Müller remained in Devon for a few weeks, and found himself spiritually attracted by friends he met there. His friendship with Craik had brought him into contact with the teaching of Groves, of whom he had already heard while in London. In January 1830, after developing views similar to those of Groves on ordination and establishment, and with Groves's example before his mind, he broke in friendly manner with the Jews' Society. He had returned to Exmouth in December to visit friends there, and now resolved to remain in Devon. An invitation to minister to a small congregation at Ebenezer Chapel, Teignmouth, soon followed, and

* I am indebted to the Revd. Ernest A. Payne, in his review of the first edition of this book in *The Baptist Times*, for pointing out that this could not have been William Carey, but was probably Eustace.

his contact with Craik was resumed. "On the Monday evening," he wrote, "I preached for brother Craik, at Shaldon, in the presence of three ministers, none of whom liked the sermon."[2] Then, on 7th October 1830, he married Groves's sister Mary.

Through this period Müller's views had been developing rapidly. Study of the New Testament had changed his previous views on baptism, and he had himself accepted believers' baptism – a step which cost him half his salary. He had also started to celebrate the Lord's Supper weekly, and had adopted the principle of freedom to speak, both at this and at other meetings of the church.

Most interesting of all, in the light of Müller's later development, was the decision which he and his wife made just after their marriage, to renounce a regular salary entirely and to rely upon the voluntary giving of their congregation for their support. This decision was largely based upon dislike of the system of pew rents: Müller disliked the social distinctions to which it gave rise (the better seats were more expensive!), and the element of compulsion about it. He felt also that the system might hinder him in the free expression of his views to a greater extent than the anonymous support of free-will offerings. Yet the influence of Groves's ideas is also apparent in their decision, for at the same time Müller and his wife decided to renounce all private property, and also to refrain from making any requests for personal support. A box was placed in the chapel for the receipt of contributions to their support; a practice which continued in Bristol also until 1841, when even this was removed as giving a false impression of their relationship to their congregation. This, however, is to anticipate later developments in the views of Müller and Craik.

By these decisions the Müllers set the pattern of the remainder of their lives. There was no supernatural ease about the experiences which followed. Only a month later, the Müllers found themselves penniless: an experience which was to become commonplace to them. Yet they firmly kept to their decision to give no hint of their need, and within hours the need was met. The experience was repeated time and again (not least because the church treasurer was not as punctual as he might have been in opening the box intended to receive gifts for their maintenance!). They also adopted a highly necessary corollary to this manner of living – they refused to incur debt for any reason (basing their refusal on Romans 13: 8), and provided for any accruing liabilities well before they fell due. Their eccentric manner of living (as it was accounted locally) brought much gossip, some of which was malicious, but this gossip itself served only to increase the interest of sympathizers. Entries in Müller's diary, dated 12th June 1831 and 14th January 1832, are typical:

> June 12th. Lord's day. On Thursday last I went with brother Craik to Torquay, to preach there. I had only about 3s. with me, and left my wife with about 6s. at home. The Lord provided beds for us through the hospitality of a brother.

I asked the Lord repeatedly for money; but when I came home my wife had only about 3s. left, having received nothing. We waited still upon the Lord. Yesterday passed away and no money came. We had 9d. left. This morning we were still waiting upon the Lord, and looking for deliverance. We had only a little butter left for breakfast, sufficient for brother E. and a relative living with us, to whom we did not mention our circumstances, that they might not be made uncomfortable. After the morning meeting, brother Y. most unexpectedly opened the box, and, in giving me quite as unexpectedly the money at such a time, he told me that *he and his wife could not sleep last night on account of thinking that we might want money.* The most striking point is, that after I had repeatedly asked the Lord, but received nothing, *I then prayed yesterday that the Lord would be pleased to impress it on brother Y. that we wanted money, so that he might open the box.*[3]

January 14th. This morning we had nothing but dry bread with our tea; only the second time since we have been living by simple faith upon Jesus for temporal supplies. We have more than £40 ready money in the house for two bills, which will not be payable for several weeks, but we do not consider this money to be our own, and would rather suffer great privation, God helping us, than take of it. . . . We were looking to our Father, and He has not suffered us to be disappointed. For when we now had but 3d. left, and only a small piece of bread, we received 2s. and 5s., the particulars concerning which would take up too much space to relate.[4]

The support which was given to them was thus erratic, but not ungenerous. Müller records at the end of 1831 that in fact they had received in total substantially more than his previous salary.

In the meantime Craik had fulfilled his service to the Synge family, and in April 1831 had taken charge of the Baptist Chapel at Shaldon, a nearby village. In the summer of that year he had married, and his diary at the beginning of August shows the happiness of those days:

On the very eve of my twenty-sixth birthday, I desire to record, with unfeigned gratitude, the mercies of my dear Lord:

1. A good hope, through grace, that I am interested in the blood of my dear and precious Christ.

2. Some love to Him, His people, and His ways.

3. A loving, praying wife – dear, gentle, frugal, diligent.

4. An affectionate people and kind friends.

5. A sufficiency of temporal provision.

"O Lord, what shall I render unto Thee for all Thy benefits toward me?"[5]

In addition to his pastoral duties, he set himself an exacting and meticulous programme of Bible study, and recorded his plans in a curiously detached style:

. . . Let me inquire what it may be, for the glory of the Lord, that I should attempt to accomplish.

1. . . . . the daily reading of the Psalms, and other parts of experimental truths . . .

2. The regular reading of the English Old Testament, and attempting to impress upon the memory the detail of its Historical facts.

3. The Historical portion of the New Testament in the same way – the Gospels and Acts of the Apostles.

4. The study of the Didactic parts of Scripture – Job, and the writings of Solomon.

5. The inquiry into prophecy.

6. Experimental reading of the Epistles, with a view of determining what are the suitable experiences of a true believer.

7. The study of the New Testament, with a view to determine the external character of believers.

8. The character of our blessed Lord.

9. Preparation for pulpit exposition.

10. Exact knowledge and improvement in the Hebrew Bible and Greek Testament. . . . [6]

This quiet happiness was not to last for long. In September, only weeks after their marriage, his wife began to show signs of the onset of consumption, and on 1st February 1832 she was dead. Craik was heartbroken, and sensed the spiritual crisis which had come upon him: "This is the most important month in my life," he had written as he and his friend Müller wrestled in unavailing prayer for his dying wife.[7] Again, the two men stand in odd contrast. Less than three weeks later Müller suffered a haemorrhage of the stomach and, receiving an assurance of recovery in prayer, insisted on carrying out his pastoral engagements against urgent medical advice, without ill effect. Müller was already building up his characteristic way of life.

> About this time, I repeatedly prayed with sick believers till they were restored . . . In some instances, however, the prayer was not answered . . . The way in which I now account for these facts is as follows: It pleased the Lord, I think, to give me in such cases something like the gift (not grace) of faith, so that unconditionally I could ask and look for an answer. The difference between the *gift* and *grace* of faith seems to me this. According to the *gift of faith* I am able to do a thing, or believe that a thing will come to pass, the not doing of which, or the not believing of which *would not be sin*; according to the *grace of faith* I am able to do a thing, or believe that a thing will come to pass, respecting which I have the Word of God as the ground to rest upon, and, therefore, the not doing of it, or the not believing it, *would be sin*. For instance, *the gift of faith* would be needed, to believe that a sick person would be restored again, though there is no human probability: for *there is no promise to that effect*; *the grace of faith* is needed to believe that the Lord will give me the necessaries of life, if I first seek the kingdom of God and His righteousness: for *there is a promise to that effect* (Matt. vi. 33).[8]

During the previous three years Craik had been receiving urgent requests that he should settle in Bristol. They came from an Anglican layman, a Mr. Chapman, who had been converted many years before in London under the ministry of the evangelical William Romaine. He had heard Craik preach in 1829 during a holiday in Teignmouth, and had been impressed by him. Craik had paid a short visit to Bristol at Chapman's invitation, and had preached in various chapels there. Then, in March 1832, a request more urgent than the earlier ones arrived. To understand its importance we must go back a few years.

In the early years of the nineteenth century, a group of members of one of the five Independent (or Congregational) Chapels in Bristol, Penn Street Tabernacle, had seceded from that congregation, apparently under the influence of the teachings of the celebrated Anglican Calvinist Robert Hawker of Plymouth. They built for themselves a chapel in Newfoundland Street which they named "Gideon Chapel," and, looking around for a pastor, made the unfortunate choice of the eccentric William Hunt (or Huntington) of Providence Chapel, London, the leader of an antinomian movement, and a self-taught preacher of some current vogue. Huntington arrived in Bristol, apparently in 1810, the same year as his chapel in London was burned down. A larger building was, however, built for him in Gray's Inn Lane, London, and he seems to have stayed in Bristol only for a very short time.

The congregation which he left was soon heavily in debt, and after a few years of struggle they gave up the chapel. It was then taken by another group, of more interest to our own story. This was a group of persons who were leaving the Anglican Church in order to form a new congregation on lines which the historian of Gideon Chapel describes as those "which are now known as those of the Plymouth Brethren,"[9] under the leadership of a seceding clergyman, Mr. Cowan.* This group was already building its own larger chapel, Bethesda, elsewhere in the city and their use of Gideon was only temporary. They continued to use it for occasional services for a time, but in 1820 it was closed with a heavy debt still outstanding upon it.

The chapel did not remain in this sorry state for long. In 1821, Thomas Wilson, the builder of Highbury College, visited Bristol and was the means of reviving the work as a regular Independent or Congregational Church. The first minister, John Wooldridge, was called in 1822. The church flourished under his pastorate, and was soon enlarged to accommodate the increased congregation; at the same time its missionary interests

---

* L. P. Nott describes him as "Mr. Cowan" (*Gideon 1810–1910*, p. 23), and the information that the builder of Bethesda Chapel was "an ex-clergyman of the Church of England" is given by E. T. Davies (*Bethesda Church Bristol*, p. 8) and by E. K. Groves (*Bethesda Family Matters*, p. 14). A Rev. T. C. Cowan is linked by H. H. Rowdon ("Secession from the Established Church in the Early Nineteenth Century," *Vox Evangelica No. 3* (1964), p. 79) with the "Western Schism" of the years 1815 and after, when a number of Anglican clergymen in the west of England seceded: a leading figure among them was James Harington Evans, later minister of John Street Chapel, Grays Inn, who will appear later in our story. This group also was accused (unjustly) of antinomianism (ibid).

grew. Wooldridge himself volunteered his services in 1831 to the London Missionary Society, and left as a missionary for Jamaica.

Here, then, was a flourishing leaderless work in a chapel with a turbulent background. The building, moreover, was held upon the original trusts of 1808, and thus had an in-built eccentricity in its constitution. There was every reason for its sympathizers to wish to see it under a wise and stable leadership. Craik agreed to visit the church for a month, and arrived on 30th March 1832.

His coming caused much interest, and he found himself preaching to increasing congregations, until on the third Sunday a considerable number were unable to find a place in the building. Craik had already decided that he would not accept a call to Bristol unless he could be accompanied by Müller, a decision which was in part made because of their developing views on the non-exclusive nature of the ministry. Müller joined Craik at the latter's invitation for the last week of his stay in Bristol.

Müller himself had been growing unsettled in his Teignmouth pastorate. When he accepted it, he had stated that he felt a call to an itinerant ministry, and he had in fact been preaching throughout Devon, even as far as Barnstaple. He had even preached twice in different places on the journey to Bristol. Both men were therefore strongly attracted by requests that they should remain in Bristol, but they decided that they should return to Teignmouth in order to reach a decision away from the excitement of their successful visit to the city.

Within a month of their return, the invitations from Bristol were urgently renewed. Müller felt that they should go, but Craik, back among his friends in Devon, and in a spot with so many memories, not least of the young wife he had so soon lost, was torn. After considerable prayer and discussion they sent a reply to Bristol with a number of stipulations:

> ... for the present to consider us only as ministering among them, but not in any fixed pastoral relationship, so that we may preach as we consider it to be according to the mind of God, *without reference to any rules among them*: *that the pew-rents should be done away with*; *and that we should go on, respecting the supply of our temporal wants, as in Devonshire.*[10]

There was another attraction drawing them to Bristol. Cowan's congregation at Bethesda Chapel had broken up as a result of erroneous teaching, and an offer had been made to take this empty building also for them. Here then was an opportunity to build up a work entirely on the lines which they had come to feel to be scriptural, from a fresh start, and in a building whose trusts and origins would be wholly favourable to their desires.

The reply to their stipulations, from the congregation at Gideon, was a prompt acceptance. Without waiting for a final arrangement concerning Bethesda, therefore, they decided to move to Bristol. It was a decision full of significance.

The Müllers left for Exeter on 24th May 1832, and waited there for Craik in the house which Groves had formerly occupied: now the home of Groves's friend, William Hake. With them was Mrs. Müller's father, Groves senior. Craik followed the next day, and on Friday 25th May the party arrived in the city which was to be the setting for their remarkable partnership.

From the moment of their arrival in Bristol the two friends found themselves engulfed in a whirlwind of pastoral activity. First, they found that it was necessary to repeat to the congregation of Gideon Chapel the conditions which they had attached to their taking up their work. No hindrance appearing, they launched into energetic pastoral activities. Craik himself was battling against ill-health, but this did not affect the extent or energy of their joint teaching or pastoral visitation. They also launched a full round of church activities, of prayer, teaching and inquiry meetings.

They preached alternately – one Lord's-day Mr. Craik preached in the morning, and Mr. Müller in the evening; the next Lord's-day the order was reversed. From the first they attracted great attention; the chapel, especially at night, was crowded to excess.[11]

Less than two months after their arrival in Bristol, tragedy struck the city. On 13th July the first reports reached them of a cholera outbreak, and within days it was taking an appalling toll. Men and women, alive and well in the morning, were dead by evening. Reports of sudden illness and death reached them from every side. The two young men threw themselves into this new need, answering frequent calls for visitation from the sick and dying, with striking self-abandonment. Early morning meetings for prayer were arranged at Gideon Chapel. On 24th August Craik wrote in his diary:

Rose about 5. Prayer meeting as usual. Readings of St. Luke on to 5th chapter. Last evening we were called to a person in Wade Street, dying of cholera. He said nothing, but by holding up his hand, made a sign of understanding us. Our neighbour, Mrs. Williams, a few yards from us, was attacked about 3 this morning, and died about 3 in the afternoon. Her husband was also attacked, and is not expected to recover. *The bell is incessantly tolling; it is an awful time.*[12]

Müller wrote on the same day:

This morning a sister in the Lord, within fifty yards of our lodgings, was taken ill with cholera, and died this afternoon. Her husband, also a believer, has been attacked, and may be near death. The ravages of this disease are becoming daily more and more fearful. We have reason to believe that great numbers die daily in this city. Who may be the next, God alone knows. I have never realized so much the nearness of death. Except the Lord keep us this night, we shall be no more in the land of the living tomorrow. Just now, ten in the evening, the funeral bell is ringing, and has been ringing the greater part of this evening. It rings almost all the day.[13]

The outbreak continued until October, when it gradually died away.

Even while the cholera epidemic was raging, Müller and Craik had engaged in an important new venture. At last the arrangements concerning the empty Bethesda Chapel had been completed, and a well-wisher had provided the first year's rent. They now had the opportunity for which they wished, to start a new work from the beginning on the lines which had become a matter of conviction to them. On 6th July they started preaching at Bethesda as well as at Gideon. Then, on 13th August 1832, Müller recorded in his diary:

> This evening one brother and four sisters united with brother Craik and me in church fellowship at Bethesda, *without any rules, desiring only to act as the Lord shall be pleased to give us light through His Word.*[14]

With two growing congregations and a considerably wider pastoral ministry, the two men – both only 27 – had found their calling. No longer did Müller hanker after an itinerant ministry. Then, after a few months, an invitation arrived to put them into perplexity.

> 1833. January 4th. This morning we received letters from Bagdad. The missionary brethren there invite brother Craik and me to go and join them in their labours. The invitation was accompanied by drafts to the amount of £200, for our travelling expenses.[15]

Müller then listed the points which would support the invitation, and added, "these are the points which must appear of no sufficient weight in comparison with the importance of our work *here*, before I can determine *not* to go."

The mission in Bagdad was in crisis. An outbreak of plague in 1831 – only a year before the cholera in Bristol – had devastated Bagdad, and had taken with it Groves's dearly loved wife and infant daughter. The relieving party had at length reached him, but they too had lost the two women of their party, one of whom, Cronin's sister, had married Parnell only a short time before. Things were not going well with the workers themselves, and Groves was in poor health. The two friends in Bristol were in a quandary.

> January 5th. I considered with brother Craik about going to Bagdad. We see nothing clearly. If the Lord will have me to go, here I am. January 9th. I again asked the Lord concerning Bagdad, but see nothing clearly respecting it. I told the Lord I should stay at my post unless He Himself should most evidently take me away, and I did not feel afterwards my remaining here to be against His will. January 14th. I feel more and more satisfied that it is not of the Lord that I should go to Bagdad. January 19th. For some days past I have been reading brother Groves's Journal of his residence at Bagdad, both for the sake of information respecting his position there, and . . . to show me clearly whether I should go or stay. Blessed be His name that I have no desire of my own in this matter![16]

The decision to stay in Bristol was barely taken, when there appeared in Müller's diary a casual entry:

February 9th. I read a part of Franke's life. The Lord graciously help me to follow him, as far as he followed Christ.[17]

Müller had taken up the book which was to give him his life's work.

On 29th May 1833, Müller looked back over their first year in Bristol:

Review of the last twelve months, since we have been in Bristol, as regards the fruits of our labours. (1) It has pleased the Lord to gather a church, through our instrumentality, at Bethesda, which increased to 60 in number, and there have been added to Gideon church, 49: therefore the total number of those added to us within the year has been 109. (2) There have been converted, through our instrumentality, *so far as we have heard and can judge respecting the individuals*, 65. (3) Many backsliders have been reclaimed, and many of the children of God have been encouraged and strengthened in the way of truth. What clear proofs that we were not suffered to be mistaken as regards our coming to Bristol![18]

Six months later a further forty-four had been added to their fellowship, and by the end of 1834 the additions were well over 200. They had also paid a brief visit to Teignmouth and Shaldon in May 1833, renewing their happy friendships there. In September 1833 they visited Ireland at the invitation of Craik's former patron, John Synge, meeting other early Brethren leaders there and attending the Powerscourt conference on prophecy, and in the following year Craik, whose health was still poor, visited his relatives in Scotland.

Their family lives were also developing. The Müllers' only child to survive infancy, their daughter Lydia, was born on 17th September 1832, in the later stages of the cholera epidemic. Craik had remarried on 20th October 1832, and on 18th January 1834 his son Henry was born.

The two friends had settled into a fruitful field of work. Neither was wealthy nor had prospects of wealth, but their ambitions were satisfied in the task which had been given to them. Their links with more distant places and friends were being strengthened, and visitors to Bristol from elsewhere were becoming more frequent. One important visitor had, however, noticed something still lacking. J. N. Darby wrote to a friend on 15th October 1832:

The Lord sent us a blessing, and disposed the hearts of the saints much towards us at Bristol, and many also to hear. We preached in both chapels. The Lord is doing a very marked work there, in which I hope our dear brothers M. and C. may be abundantly blessed, but I should wish a little more principle of largeness of communion. I dread narrowness of heart more than anything for the church of Christ, *especially now*.[19]

It was an observation which was to have a strange sequel.

With all his growing responsibilities, Müller continued to look around

him with a young man's restless energy. Bristol teemed with social problems. He had written in his diary in 1833:

> May 28th. This morning, whilst sitting in my room, the distress of several
> brethren and sisters was brought to my mind, and I said to myself, "Oh that it
> might please the Lord to give me means to help them!" About an hour afterwards
> I received £60 from a brother, whom I had never seen, and who then lived, as
> he does still, at a distance of several thousand miles. . . .

> June 12th. I felt, this morning, that we might do something for the souls of those
> poor boys and girls, and grown-up or aged people, to whom we have daily
> given bread for some time past, in establishing a school for them, reading the
> Scriptures to them, and speaking to them about the Lord.[20]

A frugal meal was provided early in the morning, and this was followed
by an hour's tuition in reading and in the Scriptures. Penniless themselves,
living from day to day on the free-will gifts of their congregations and of
interested friends, they could apparently do little more for the hungry
people and particularly the children around them. They were concerned
too for their educational needs – but further extension of the work might
well have seemed beyond them.

Yet Müller combined with his spiritual vision an unexpectedly practical and matter-of-fact business mind. He recorded his plans methodically
and objectively. First, he would deal with some of the educational needs:

> February 25th (1834). . . . I was led again this day to pray about the forming of a
> new Missionary Institution, and felt still more confirmed that we should do so.
> The Institution will be called "The Scriptural Knowledge Institution for
> Home and Abroad."[21]

The Institution was to be a Bible Society in miniature. He recorded its
objects:

> 1. To assist and establish new day-schools, Sunday schools and adult schools
> "in which instruction is given upon *scriptural principles*." For this latter qualifica-
> tion Müller insisted that all the teachers must be believing Christians, and the
> instruction must not be opposed to the principles of the Gospel.
> 2. To circulate Bibles and Testaments.
> 3. To aid missionary efforts, adding as a rider "we desire to assist those mis-
> sionaries whose proceedings appear to be most according to the Scriptures."

He also recorded seven principles:

> 1. He believed Christians bound to help the cause of Christ, and felt confident
> in expecting God to forward a "work of faith and labour of love."
> 2. He would not seek "the patronage of the world" (by which he meant the
> patronage of unconverted persons of rank or wealth).
> 3. He would not ask money of unconverted persons, although he would not
> refuse unsolicited gifts.
> 4. He would use only believing Christians as helpers.

5. He would never contract debts, but would act only according to the means which God would give.

6. Success would be reckoned by God's blessing, not by numerical standards.

7. They would avoid "needless singularity," but would "go on simply according to Scripture, without compromising the truth."

It is characteristic of their whole vision that such plans should have been laid down in the face of daunting financial obstacles. Only a few days later Müller wrote in his diary:

"March 7th. Today we have only one shilling left."[22]

In January 1835 Groves arrived back from India, to which country he had moved from Bagdad, on a visit to Europe. He wished to find recruits for his mission, and at the end of February Müller left with him as his interpreter when he made a six weeks' visit to Germany to help in this purpose (Groves was in touch with German missionaries in India). Just before they left, Müller recorded that the fifth day-school had come under the auspices of the Scriptural Knowledge Institution.

A few days before Müller and Groves returned from the Continent, Craik fell ill. He had been in poor health for some time, and now found himself obliged to retire into the country for a complete rest – which he took as a heaven-sent opportunity for further theological and linguistic researches! The illness persisted, however, until he seriously considered resigning his place at Bristol. His father had died some years before, and he had thoughts of moving to Scotland to his mother's home, and devoting himself to a project close to his heart – a personal revision of both Old and New Testaments of the Authorized Version of the Bible. The strong reaction of both churches to the suggestion, however, convinced him of his place in Bristol. It was during this first illness that Craik published his *Pastoral Letters* to the two congregations.

Craik's health was never robust again, and he was increasingly to spend the time which he could spare from his pastoral responsibilities thereafter in the quieter field of Biblical studies. For these, he received in January 1849 an offer from Professor Alexander, of St. Andrews University, of nomination for a doctorate, but he declined the honour – as he did a second time a few years later. His family life was overshadowed by bereavement. Although the oldest boy survived, the Craiks lost three further children in infancy during the ten years after 1834, and it was not until 1847 and 1849 that two further children survived. Yet, despite these shadows, and a certain melancholy which is marked in his diary, he left a reputation for great personal cheerfulness and humble kindliness. His diary shows him to have been in correspondence with many of the great Biblical scholars of his day: yet he was said to have been accessible to the simplest. In many ways, Craik is one of the most attractive and level-headed of all the men who were brought together in the early days of the Brethren movement.

He lived until 22nd January 1866, and his partnership with Müller lasted to that day, in Müller's words, "without one jar" – even when their views differed.[23]

Müller was still intensely active during Craik's illness of 1835, while Craik's place was filled temporarily by Groves's old friend Caldecott. On 3rd June 1835 Müller recorded:

> Today we had a public meeting on account of the Scriptural Knowledge Institution for Home and Abroad. It is now fifteen months, since, in dependence upon the Lord for the supply of means, we have been enabled to provide poor children with schooling, circulate the Holy Scriptures, and aid missionary labours. During this time, though the field of labour has been continually enlarged, and though we have now and then been brought low in funds, the Lord has never allowed us to be obliged to stop the work. We have been enabled during this time to establish three day-schools, and to connect with the Institution two other charity day-schools, which, humanly speaking, otherwise would have been closed for want of means. The number of children that have been thus provided with schooling amounts to 439.[24]

Later that same month the Müllers suffered two severe personal losses. Mrs. Müller's father, Groves senior, died on the 22nd June after several weeks' illness, and four days later they lost their fifteen-months-old son from a chest inflammation.

Most men would justifiably have felt that their energies were occupied enough: yet it was at this time that a further reading of Francke's life revived earlier ideas. As a young student, he had known well the great orphan houses in Halle which August Francke, a German pietist, had established in 1696, and which had at one time been the largest of their kind in the world. For a short time Müller himself had lodged there as a poor student. On the 20th November 1835 he wrote:

> I have frequently for a long time, thought of labouring in a similar way, though it might be on a much smaller scale; not to imitate Franke (sic), but in reliance upon the Lord.[25]

The next day he recorded his determination to establish an orphan house himself, and a few days later wrote:

> December 5th. This evening I was struck in reading the Scriptures, with these words: "Open thy mouth wide, and I will fill it" (Ps. 81: 10). Up to this day I had not prayed at all concerning the means or individuals needed for the Orphan-House. I was now led to apply this Scripture to the Orphan-House, I fell on my knees, and asked the Lord for premises, for £1,000, and for suitable individuals to take care of the children.[26]

A public meeting was held on 9th December, at which Müller announced his plans, and, methodical as ever, he examined himself and recorded his motives in his diary. His own experience of simple reliance on God for his daily needs had been such that he felt that "the Lord had not given me this simple reliance on Him merely for myself, but also for others. Often, when I saw poor neglected children running about the streets at Teignmouth, I said to myself: 'May it not be the will of God, that I should establish schools for these children, asking Him to give me the means?'" So he had founded the Scriptural Knowledge Institution, and now repeatedly he had had the urge to found an Orphan House.[27] Later, he extended his analysis. "I had constantly cases brought before me, which proved that one of the special things which the children of God needed in our day, was, *to have their faith strengthened*. I longed to have something to point to as a visible proof, that our God and Father is the same faithful God as ever He was . . ."[28]

Gifts, in money and kind, and offers to assist in the work, began to come in. Such gifts Müller strictly reserved for the Orphan Homes, although he and his family were often in considerable personal need during the months that followed. Groves left for India with his wife (he had remarried during his visit) and the party of helpers he had collected, on 1st March 1836. On 11th April, Müller took in the first of his children at a house which he had rented in Wilson Street, a street abutting the back of Gideon Chapel. A month later he had admitted twenty-six children between seven and twelve years of age, and the number was growing daily. It is of interest that Müller engaged the helpers both in the schools and in the orphan homes on the basis of a regular salary – he did not expect them to share completely his own way of living, although they knew well that their salaries were contingent on funds being provided for the work.

> July 28th (1836). For some weeks past we have not been able to pay the salary of the masters and governesses a *month in advance*, but have been obliged to pay it *weekly* . . . we were now brought so low, that we should not have been able to pay even this *weekly* salary of the teachers had not the Lord most remarkably helped us again today . . .[29]

The need around was great, and the pressure on Müller's venture was great with it. In October 1836 a second orphan home, for infants, was opened. From that time, the orphan work grew to be the preponderant part of the work of the Scriptural Knowledge Institution. Despite illness and church cares, and against disappointments resulting from the opposition of neighbours, a third orphan home was opened in October 1837. The years which followed were years of living, financially, from hand to mouth.

> Sept. 5th (1838). Our hour of trial continues still. The Lord mercifully has given enough to supply our daily necessities: but He gives *by the day* now, and almost *by the hour*, as we need it. Nothing came in yesterday. I have besought the Lord again and again, both yesterday and today. It is as if the Lord said: "*Mine hour is not yet come.*" But I have faith in God. I believe that He will surely send

help, though I know not whence it is to come. Many pounds are needed within a few days, and there is not a penny in hand.[30]

Yet, time and again, the necessary funds or provisions arrived at the moment of need. At first, Müller would not share the emergencies with any of the workers, beyond Craik and one other colleague: but later he took them all into confidence, and many of them sank savings and personal possessions in the homes. Through it all, Müller kept firmly to his financial principles. He would not incur debt, and therefore when financial need was extreme he stopped even the weekly tradesmen's accounts, settling all purchases for cash. He would not divert money from one purpose, if it had been given for that purpose, to another – however urgent the need, or however sure he might be of the donor's agreement. Provision was made in advance for accruing expenses. The story is as remarkable for the methodical business-like record of its hazards, as it is for their constant satisfaction. Despite all the stringency, the orphans never went without food and shelter. "I further state," wrote Müller in December 1838, "that the Orphans have never lacked anything. Had I thousands of pounds in hand, they would have fared no better than they have; for they have always had good nourishing food, the necessary articles of clothing, etc."[31]

Never would Müller give any indication of his financial needs to any person outside the homes, even in response to a direct request. Each year, however, he published a detailed annual account of his stewardship, regarding such an account as a public duty to be punctiliously observed: its publication was only delayed on rare occasions, when needs were particularly acute, and its appearance might be regarded as an appeal for funds.

The period of extreme stringency lasted for several years. It may be a matter of debate whether this would have been remedied if open appeals had been made for money. It is probable that the need would always have outrun the funds with which it could have been supplied, for Müller was pioneering in appalling social conditions. But Müller felt that if his own principle of faith was to be plainly and publicly demonstrated, then, if he was doing what God desired, God would supply the means to do it. Any temptation to depart from a course which showed plainly that transparent trust in God, must be firmly resisted.

November 19th (1840). Since September 18th 1838, this has been, perhaps, of all the days the most trying. The poverty has been exceedingly great for the last six days. There had come in no money since yesterday. On this account no bread could be taken in, as far as the natural prospect went. Nor was there any money at three in the afternoon to take in milk for tea, when brother B. came to me. However, we prayed together, and the Lord had mercy. For one of the labourers found that he was able, which he knew not before, to give of his own 10s., so that there were the means to take in the milk, by the time it is usually brought.

This evening about six there came in still further 10s. 3d. by the sale of Reports. Thus, by the good hand of our God upon us, we were able to take in bread as usual. How very kind of the Lord that He sent us an abundance of potatoes and two large sacks of oatmeal, before this season of deep poverty, as to pecuniary means, commenced!

November 20th. Nothing more had come in this morning. It was nearly three o'clock this afternoon, when brother B. called on me, to see whether anything had come in; but I had received nothing. I was obliged to go out with a brother from Devonshire, and therefore requested him to wait until I returned. About a quarter past three I came back, when, among several persons who were waiting at my house to converse with me, there was a sister whom I much desired to see about some church affair. I did so. When I had ended the conversation with her, about half-past three, she gave me £10 for the Orphans. More sweet, and more needed, were none of the previous deliverances. . . . In none of the houses was milk for tea, and in one even no bread, and there was no money to purchase either. It was only a few minutes before the milkman came, when brother B. arrived at the Orphan-houses with the money. Yet even now it was more than an hour before the usual tea-time. The Lord be praised for this deliverance! Such a week of deep poverty as we have had since November 13th, we never had before. Yet, thanks to the Lord! We have lacked nothing, and we have been kept from dishonouring Him by unbelief.[32]

To read the detailed account which Müller kept of those years is to wonder at the sheer adventure of faith in which he and his helpers engaged. The whole responsibility for the three orphans' homes, some hundred persons, not to speak of the day-schools and the other ventures associated with the Scriptural Knowledge Institution, was being met over a period of many years on a hand-to-mouth basis, waiting on God moment by moment for the very primary necessities of life. Time and again funds were exhausted, money arriving at the very time of need. Apparent accidents – the posting of a gift a little earlier than intended, a man intending to call in the evening but instead calling in the morning – meant the difference between a meal when due or hunger.

Though our trials of faith during these seventeen months (to May 1842) lasted longer, and were sharper than during any previous period, yet during all this time the Orphans had everything that was needful in the way of nourishing food, the necessary articles of clothing, etc. Indeed I would rather at once send the children back to their relatives than keep them without sufficient maintenance.[33]

The timely answers to prayer, the miraculous continued survival of the work, as it seems to any reader of the narrative, are the first immediate causes of wonder: but in a broader perspective the detailed occurrences seem less wonderful than the sheer daring of the conception which inspired Müller's faith and sustained it through that incredible first decade of the orphan homes. It is not the least striking event of those years that, in 1841, in the middle of this period of financial stringency, Müller and Craik removed from the chapel the boxes placed there for their personal support, because they conflicted with their developing views of their relationship to the church, and marked them off too obviously as "the ministers."

The importance of their example to the Brethren ideal – impractical and visionary as that ideal seemed – should not be underestimated. For all their sacrifices and devotion, men like Groves and Darby were men of private means: but here were men of no means at all applying the same ideals of faith. Others were not slow to recognize this. Müller records that R. C. Chapman, finding on a visit to the Continent that Christians were hesitant to put into practice the things he taught them, for fear of the consequences for themselves and their families, urged upon him the publication of his *Narrative* in German: advice which coincided with more direct invitations, and so led to Müller's visit to Germany in 1843 and 1844, and to the formation of a Brethren assembly in Stuttgart on the lines of Bethesda.

In 1843, Müller found himself receiving more applications for admission of children to the homes than he could meet. Then he received a gift of £500, coinciding with the offer of the occupation of another house adjoining the homes. Despite the poverty of the earlier years, he therefore opened the fourth house in July 1843. Funds, for a time, began to come in more steadily, including a gift towards work in Germany which allowed him to make the visit to Germany, with his wife, to which reference has been made. The Müllers were away from Bristol from 9th August 1843 until 6th March 1844, and during the whole of that time there was no difficulty as to means, although for a period later in the year there were further occasions of difficulty, when needs were barely supplied.

So matters continued until 30th October 1845, when they received a disturbing letter:

> I received from a gentleman, who lived in the street where the four Orphan-Houses were, a polite and friendly letter, in which he courteously stated to me that the inhabitants in the adjoining houses were in various ways inconvenienced by the Orphan-Houses being in Wilson Street. He left to myself the judgment of the case.[34]

Müller's reaction was in character. "On Monday morning, however, November 3rd, I set apart some hours for the prayerful consideration of the subject, and after I had besought the Lord to guide me to a right decision, I wrote down the reasons which appeared to me to make it desirable that the Orphans should be *removed* from Wilson Street, and also the reasons *against removing*."[35] His final decision was that they should cease to rent, but that he should build an orphan home to accommodate three hundred persons, against the one hundred and twenty of the existing homes. Reckoning the cost, he decided that he would need at least £10,000. "I was not discouraged by this," he added, "but trusted in the living God."[36] It might be remarked that funds were now coming in much more freely, but the total might have been ten times as large, for all the prospects that were apparent of raising such a sum!

Yet raise the sum he did, and that without any appeal beyond the announcement of his intention. Monies received for the building were set on one side, so that they might remain separate from the day-to-day needs of other branches of the work. In December 1845 an architect, a stranger, offered his services free of charge. In February 1846, Müller bought a plot of seven acres on Ashley Down, the sympathetic owner reducing the price from £200 to £120 per acre. Work started in July 1847, and the first of the great buildings on Ashley Down was ready for occupation in mid-1849. The cost, with the furnishings and equipment, had been just £15,000 and the whole sum had arrived before the building was completed – a final donation of £2,000 coming in just a month before the opening.

Müller's responsibilities had been multiplied nearly three times by the opening of the new home, but the increased facilities only opened his eyes to the scale of the need. Within two years he was planning another house, this time to house a further seven hundred children. He had reached that stage of expansion when the overall administrative burden was becoming too great for one man. He had no secretary, and yet dealt with three thousand letters a year himself. On top of all this, Müller also retained responsibilities at Bethesda Chapel. The answer to his problem was a further expansion: great enough to allow for a full administrative staff. Once again, he methodically listed the reasons for and against the new venture.

In November 1857 the second house was opened. By 1870 five great orphan houses stood on Ashley Down. When Müller died in 1898, over ten thousand orphans had passed through his hands in sixty-two years, and about a million pounds had been spent on them. In addition one hundred and fourteen thousand children had attended the day-schools and Sunday schools of the Scriptural Knowledge Institution. The total budget of this Institution, apart from that of the orphan homes, had amounted to four hundred and sixty thousand pounds since 1834, of which some hundred thousand pounds had been spent on the schools, and the remainder had been sent to missionaries, or used in the provision of Bibles and other literature. It is interesting to notice that the Scriptural Knowledge Institution was a mainstay of Hudson Taylor's China Inland Mission in its earliest days. When the man who had raised this money by the example of his faith died on 10th March 1898, he left behind a personal estate which was sworn in the sum of £160, of which £100 was the value of his personal furniture and books, and most of the rest was money in hand for distribution.

In his later years, Müller had passed the administration of his homes to his successors. With up to two thousand children under care at any one time, the homes inevitably became severely institutionalized. Müller's own Germanic method and discipline were developed according to current Victorian practice, and these methods persisted, as is the habit of a strong tradition. Eventually, however, the great social changes of the twentieth century changed the orphan homes as well, while the need for the day-schools has long since disappeared. Today the work of the Müller Homes for Children continues in Bristol and district, with some hundred and fifty children who are cared for, in modern fashion, in smaller family house-holds under the care of house-parents. The work retains its original spiritual impetus and ideals, and its needs are still supplied by private donation without appeals or publicity. The Scriptural Knowledge Institu-tion continues its own work, both through its bookshop in Bristol, and especially by the distribution of considerable funds to missionaries and to children's homes overseas. The great buildings on Ashley Down, no longer needed for their original purpose, have been renovated and mod-ernized, and now house the Bristol Technical College – as fitting a tribute as could be paid to the businesslike thoroughness both of Müller himself and of the architect and builders.

While the orphan homes were growing, Bethesda Chapel also flour-ished. Some of the development of its early years will be referred to in a later chapter, for it is of some importance in the account of the growth of the movement to see how Müller and Craik hammered out a coherent church order within the broad scope of their own principles. Gideon Chapel, however, was surrendered in 1840: the old traditions of the con-gregation had been longer in dying than either of the two leaders realized, and they were shocked to discover in that year that, despite the abolition of pew rents, certain of the congregation still regarded their pews as private property, as distinct from the ordinary benches that the chapel also contained. When they realized this, and found that the traditions were not capable of amendment, they decided to withdraw from Gideon, although most of the congregation moved over to Bethesda. Later, a replacement for Gideon was found in Salem Chapel.

By the date of Craik's death in 1866, the combined membership of Bethesda and its associated congregation at Salem Chapel totalled about one thousand: they had received into fellowship over the whole period some two thousand five hundred persons. When Müller died in 1898, the single congregation of Bethesda had become ten congregations, six being independent churches, and the remaining four numbering some twelve hundred persons. Bethesda Chapel itself was destroyed during the air raids of the Second World War, and its traditions are maintained at its daughter church, Bethesda, Alma Road.*

The influence of Bristol upon the open section of Brethren has been incalculable. From the complex of churches that developed around Bethesda have arisen some of the most constructive movements of thought and action among them: perhaps the most notable being the Missionary Study Class movement which led to a great expansion of their missions in the years before and immediately following the First World War. From Bristol or its influence has come a high proportion of those leaders among them who have contributed positively to the wider evangelical life of this country.

George Müller's faith, like John Wesley's Aldersgate experience, has become part of the stock in trade of evangelical tradition. Like Wesley's experience also, an undiscriminating piety has made of it one of those near-legends which can shift the balance of popular thinking, and in the process obscure their real significance. Müller's desire to prove by his trust the perpetual faithfulness of God arose from genuine pastoral concern, but popular legend has overlaid its real lesson by a mysticism which is quite foreign to the methodical practicality of his methods. The legend emphasizes one side of the coin: the intensity of Müller's trust. It has often forgotten the other side – that the funds to supply the need came from men and women who were partners in Müller's faith in God. If I am to exercise a simple childlike faith like Müller's, then I must be certain that the venture for which I am exercising it is one worthy of inspiring the faithful response of other men and women. Mere credulity belongs to the isolated individual, but faith of this nature is essentially a partnership. Müller was the inspirer and focus of a great movement of faith among earnest men and women, and the expression of that faith was in practical action to meet the

* In 1875, C. H. Mackintosh, a popular writer among Exclusive Brethren, wrote an open letter to a friend to explain the differences between Bethesda and the followers of J. N. Darby. He wrote: "As you are doubtless aware, there was a congregation of Baptists who met for worship at a chapel called 'Bethesda,' in Bristol. There was an associated body meeting at 'Salem' chapel; ... Well, then, some years previous to the time above referred to, this Baptist congregation was received into fellowship with Brethren – received as a body. The whole assembly, professedly and ostensibly, took the ground occupied by Brethren. ... It has been my conviction, for many years, that this reception of a congregation was a fatal mistake on the part of Brethren." (*Things New and Old*, Vol. 18, pp. 317-18). It is only necessary to quote this, because this account of events has become part of the folklore of Exclusive Brethren, and is still to be found in their writings. Its accuracy can be judged from this chapter. The account – by one who was well acquainted with all the principal participants on the Exclusive side of later events – is a melancholy example of how religious strife can cause the best of men to deceive themselves: its substance probably derived from some off-hand comments of J. N. Darby after his quarrel with Bethesda (*Letters*, Vol. I, p. 516: letter of 1868).

spiritual and material needs of their fellow-men. Müller's expression of faith was founded on a Scriptural principle: namely, the obedience of Christian people in devoting to God's use the material resources they had diligently earned by the gifts He had given them.

Müller's influence among Brethren has been powerfully felt, and not least in the financial aspects of their work. It has almost completely prevented them from engaging in those frantic appeals for money which are the least attractive aspect of so much fine Christian work: but it has also been seen in some of their more eccentric characteristics, and not least in their reluctance to make any regular provisions for the financial support of full-time ministers of the Word of God among them. It is significant therefore that Müller seems to have regarded his own example as relevant in the first place to men and women in normal secular occupations, and not primarily to the evangelist or Bible teacher. On one occasion at least he indicated specifically that he could favour very different arrangements for a full-time Christian worker, from those normally current among Brethren. After the death of Craik, some members of the Bethesda congregation suggested the name of a well-known speaker as a replacement.

> After prayer, Mr. Müller said, "Dear brethren, what you mean of course is, that we should give a call to Mr. Guinness to come and labour among us." They rather shrank back at that, and said, "we did not mean it quite in that way." Mr. Müller added, "If you were to invite Mr. Guinness to labour among us, you ought to back the invitation up with at least £500 a year."[37]

The entire reluctance of Brethren to make any form of regular provision for their teachers – severely reproved by Scripture – stems from other causes, although it is often popularly traced back to Müller. One cause is their fear of the creation of a ministerial caste among themselves, which would deny the basic principle of their doctrine of the ministry. The examples of Müller and Craik provided an obvious way of countering this fear: but there was an even more powerful and direct precedent. In 1839, at the height of his revulsion from the whole system of the Established Church, J. N. Darby had written: "I have a very strong objection – I am, in fact, entirely opposed – to sending anyone into the Lord's field with a salary of so much per annum."[38] Yet even Darby wrote with no necessity for any abiding structure in mind, or any proposals to establish enduring churches, for in the same letter he expresses his assurance that the Second Advent is near at hand;[39] a church living so near to its removal from the scene of its activities has no need to create the structure of an enduring teaching ministry.

Müller laid down in the famous passage we have quoted earlier his principle that to trust God for one's daily sustenance was not the "gift" of faith to be exercised by a few, but the "grace" of faith necessary to all believers. For this reason he went so far as to deprecate insurance, or any saving for old age. In this he wholly followed Groves. Without discussing at this point whether or not his deduction was sound, we can at least suggest that a practice which applies the principle more rigorously to the full-time Christian worker than to his secular brother is neither logical nor in Müller's own tradition.*

* William James, in *The Varieties of Religious Experience*, described Müller's experiences fairly and at length (Fontana edition, pp. 447–51). His parting reaction is, however, strongly reminiscent of that "children-in-the-market-place" attitude of which our Lord complained in the Jews of His day (Luke 7: 31–35). It is all very well to complain of the "extraordinary narrowness of the man's intellectual horizon," and to contrast Müller with Emerson and Phillips Brooks: but it is absolutely beside the point. The whole glory of Müller's achievement was precisely in his practical assurance and demonstration to the "tradesmen and others in Bristol," of whom James speaks so slightingly, that the God of the far ranges *was* a God intimately concerned with their own lives and with the appalling social conditions with which they were surrounded.

Quotation References – Chapter 3.

1. *Passages from the Diary and Letters of Henry Craik of Bristol*. W. Elfe Tayler (1866). Introdn., pp. xi, xii.
2. *Autobiography of George Muller* (compiled from Müller's own *Narrative of the Lord's Dealings with George Muller* by G. Fred. Bergin) (1905), p. 40.
3. Ibid., p. 50.
4. Ibid., p. 52.
5. *Craik's Diary*, pp. 129, 130.
6. Ibid., pp. 130–1.
7. Ibid., p. 141.
8. *Autobiography*, pp. 53–54.
9. *Gideon 1810–1910, the Vicissitudes of a City Chapel*, L. P. Nott (1909), p. 23.
10. *Autobiography*, pp. 57–58.
11. *Craik's Diary*, pp. 151–2.
12. Ibid., p. 158.
13. *Autobiography*. p. 60.
14. Ibid., p. 60.
15. Ibid., p. 61.
16. Ibid., pp. 61–62.
17. Ibid., p. 62.
18. Ibid., p. 62.
19. *Letters of J. N. D.* Vol. I, p. 8 (letter from Granard 15 October 1832).
20. *Autobiography*. p. 62.
21. Ibid., p. 64.
22. Ibid., p. 66.
23. *Craik's Diary*, pp. 302 and xvi.
24. *Autobiography*, p. 77.
25. Ibid., p. 80.
26. Ibid., p. 82.
27. Ibid., p. 83.
28. Ibid., p. 80.
29. Ibid., p. 91.
30. Ibid., p. 105.
31. Ibid., p. 118.

32. Ibid., pp. 143–4.
33. Ibid., p. 172.
34. Ibid., p. 246.
35. Ibid., p. 246.
36. Ibid., p. 249.
37. *Bethesda Church, Great George Street, Bristol* (1917). From the *Historical Review* by E. T. Davies, p. 17.
38. *Letters of J. N. D.* Vol. I, p. 32 (letter from Neuchâtel of 22nd November 1839).
39. See the discussion of this matter in Chapter 8 of this book (p. 119), and in particular the reference to Darby's dating of the Second Advent for 1842. The wording in the letter itself is: "For me, the near coming of the Saviour, the gathering together of His own, and the sanctification and joy of those who are manifested, are always the thoughts predominant in my soul. There is every appearance that the Lord is hastening the time; for the rest, our duty is certain."

CHAPTER 4

THE BRETHREN FROM PLYMOUTH

> Plymouth, I assure you, has altered the face of Christianity to me, from finding Brethren, and they acting together.
>
> J. N. Darby, Letter of 13th April 1832.

> . . . . that slough of love. . . . (attributed to Edward Irving, on the Plymouth congregation of Brethren) (*B. W. Newton's reminiscences*).

FRANCIS NEWMAN STAYED IN IRELAND FOR FIFTEEN MONTHS, before he returned to Oxford. He arrived back there in 1828, under the powerful influence of Darby's personality, and enthusiastic over Groves's missionary plans. At Oxford he had a close friend, Benjamin Wills Newton, a Fellow of Exeter College, who later in life recounted how Newman had accosted him with an excited account of his new acquaintance, the Irish clergyman. Some months later, Newman was able to persuade Darby to visit Oxford, where he arrived in the earlier part of 1830* as the guest of Dr. Hill, the Vice-Principal of St. Edmund Hall. Benjamin Newton's old age recollection of his meeting with Darby indicates his first impression of a man who was later to affect his own life in such stormy fashion:

A few months afterwards [Newman] came to me saying "Now Newton, that friend has come to Oxford and is to have tea with me: I insist on your coming to meet him". I replied that I was tired, and didn't at all want to come. But he urged and insisted. "You shall," he said; and (so to speak) dragged me. I sat at one end of the room and was rather distant in manner; but towards the end of the evening they asked him to expound, and he took a Psalm. I was so pleased in what he said in so doing, that I afterwards went up to him & asked if he was going to stay any time in Oxford, and would he come to my room.[1]

It is in character that Newton, seven years Darby's junior, seems to have gone to some lengths to cross-question the older man, when he

---

* Darby's correspondence gives varying dates for this visit, but other evidence fixes it as mid-1830. In one place Darby dates it after July 1830, but we know that Newton and Wigram, whom Darby met on the visit, were both absent from Oxford at the end of that month, as there is a letter extant written from Newton in Plymouth to Wigram in Scotland dated 31st July 1830. (This is in the Fry collection.) Neatby suggests that the visit must have been between July and Newman's departure for Bagdad in September – but the descriptions make it plain that it was not in vacation-time. We are thus left with the early summer months of 1830. (Since the first edition of this book appeared, Mr. T. C. F. Stunt has confirmed that Darby was in Oxford by May 1830 – *The Harvester*, May 1968, p. 78.)

took up the invitation, in order to satisfy himself on Darby's doctrinal orthodoxy. Equally interesting, in view of later developments, is the fact that they agreed on the interpretation of certain prophetic scriptures – a unity which was not destined to last for long.

B. W. Newton was not the only man to fall under Darby's spell. Francis Newman wrote:

> Most striking was it to see how instantaneously he assumed the place of universal father-confessor, as if he had been a known and long-trusted friend. His insight into character, and tenderness pervading his austerity, so opened young men's hearts, that day after day there was no end of secret closetings with him.[2]

Darby paid several visits to Oxford during the next two years. William Kelly, who joined Darby some years later, wrote that "the same visit of his acted more privately (not on Mr W. E. Gladstone, who saw and heard him then) but on G. V. Wigram, Sir L. C. L. Brenton, B. W. Newton and W. Jarrett, as well as others too halting in faith to make a decided stand and endure the consequences."[3]

One name among those mentioned by Kelly demands further attention at this point. George Vicesimus Wigram was a close friend of B. W. Newton at Oxford. He was born in 1805, the twentieth child (hence his curious second name), of Sir Robert Wigram, a wealthy London Irish merchant, another of whose sons was to become Bishop of Rochester. George Wigram had served in the Guards. Experiencing conversion, he had resigned his commission, and entered Queen's College with the purpose of taking orders. At this time, Wigram was an eccentric character, prodigal with his wealth in some respects, yet affecting a slovenliness in dress as a means (Newton alleged) of self-mortification. Newton (who later had reason to regard his erstwhile friend rather sourly) recounted how he would rub a new coat on the wall to make it shabby: adding tartly that the self-denial was on the part of those who were seen out with him! Wigram was said by Newton to have had a wide selection of friends – among them the celebrated Scottish lay theologian, Thomas Erskine (a friendship which Newton regarded as "very objectionable"[4]). It is interesting in this connexion to notice that Wigram was also briefly in touch with another Scottish theologian who was ill regarded by his orthodox Church of Scotland contemporaries: McLeod Campbell of Row* (now Rhu).

---

* It is not apparent whether Campbell's universalist views had any influence with Wigram, but it is not without interest that a later exponent of conditional immortality claimed that in the earliest days of the Brethren movement there was a tendency to question orthodox doctrine concerning human destiny (*The Bible Echo* for 1874, quoted by Le R. E. Froom, *The Conditionalist Faith of our Fathers*, Vol. II, pp. 399, 436.). Whatever might have been the early position, the later position of the movement was fiercely orthodox on this point, and counted deviation a matter for excommunication – not only within Darby's circle, but even within the much milder churches at Bristol, and at Barnstaple where R. C. Chapman was the chief influence. Darby was always aware of the Platonic origins of the doctrine of the immortality of the soul.

Whatever Wigram's connexions and friendships, they were all sunk in the loyalty he now gave to the new friend and leader he found in Darby: a loyalty so strong that it was later to lead to the complete sacrifice of older friendships, and even of courtesy and of fair judgment in controversy.

These storms were yet in the future. The association of these men led to a step which can be seen as one of the most formative and fateful in the growth of the new movement. Not long after their meeting Newton invited Darby to go with him to his home in Plymouth, where it seems that Wigram had already settled (there is a suggestion that he may have had a very brief curacy nearby). There they met others who had been taken up by the intense interest then attaching to study of the Bible prophecies, an interest of which more will be said in a later chapter. Newton and Wigram had both been influenced by these teachings through friends in Oxford, and they had been a major concern of Darby's in Dublin. At Plymouth they found an interesting man who was actively preaching these doctrines. This was Percy Francis Hall, whose father had been Regius Professor of Divinity, and Dean of Christ Church. Hall had attained the rank of naval Commander, but had resigned his commission and sold his possessions. Like Groves, he had put forward his views in a booklet entitled *Discipleship*, in which he adopted extreme pacifist grounds, which caused him to go so far as to insist that a Christian could not be a civil magistrate, and thus be obliged to pass sentence upon persons found guilty in his court:

> For what is "a christian magistrate" to do when a broken-hearted man pleads for his wife and starving family, acknowledges the sinfulness of his heart, tells him of the temptations of the world to all, but specially to the poor, and the power of Satan, and prays for pardon? Will he say, "no, you are guilty, and I am not the minister of mercy, but of law; you must go to the hulk, or the jail, or it may be to death?" Would Jesus have done so? will he do so now? is this grace? and is such a person a servant of the Lord Jesus Christ *in the act*?[5]

Hall was, however, in command of the coastguard station at Plymouth. Seeing the possibility of the establishment of a permanent work, Wigram acquired a chapel★ where regular preaching (particularly on prophetic subjects) was to be given. The addresses were widely attended by Christians, both clerical and lay. Wigram's early intention may not

---

★ Newton suggests that this was the chapel in Raleigh Street, and Tregelles (*Three Letters*, p. 7) quotes a letter addressed to Newton at Raleigh Street. W. H. Cole, who joined the Plymouth meeting a few years later, states in his reminiscences that it had started "in a small house in King Street" (quoted by G. H. Lang, *Anthony Norris Groves*, p. 326), and a letter of Darby's dated 15th October 1832 refers to the "poor souls in K. Street" (*Letters*, Vol. I, p. 8). Wigram registered a chapel, known as Providence Chapel, in St. Andrews parish, in December 1831. This appears to have been the Raleigh Street chapel.

have been to establish more than a useful preaching centre, although Newton suggests in his reminiscences that the Lord's Supper was taken privately at an early date, and that shortly thereafter it was taken formally in the chapel. Neither Darby nor Newton himself were fully in accord with this early step, for neither was yet completely detached from the Church of England. Indeed, Darby continued to preach in Anglican churches, as a clergyman, long after Newton himself had seceded: in this the situation is similar to that described by Bellett in Dublin, and the testimony of both Newton and Bellett as to Darby's position at this time is strikingly consistent.

Hall's preaching attracted numbers of hearers to the chapel. Other able men soon joined them, and there was before long a strong independent church, far exceeding in spiritual abilities both Dublin and Bristol. Only Newton of the original four remained in Plymouth, where his influence soon became páramount. Darby was essentially a traveller, and Wigram and Hall moved to establish new churches at London and Hereford respectively.

The history of the man who thus became the leading influence at the most important centre of the new movement calls for a short digression. Benjamin Wills Newton was at this time still in his twenties. He was born on 12th December 1807, his father having died eleven days before his birth, and he had grown up to be an austere and dominating man, of high personal honour. It is of interest that Darby too became an orphan at an early age – in his case he lost his mother, at the age of five – and we might speculate upon the effect of these circumstances upon the characters of these two dominating men whose later personal controversies were nearly to wreck the movement in which they both played so large a part.

Newton came of Quaker stock, although he himself was a member of the Church of England, and he was connected by marriage, through his mother, to Samuel Lloyd the banker, to the Fox family, and other prominent members of the Society of Friends. There is an amusing incident which has survived from his childhood, on an occasion when he was teased by a relative on his precocity. "My mamma has not as much money as you have, Aunt Fox," he had replied, "and therefore I must learn." Aunt Fox's observation to a friend was tart: "My child is a baby to him, but I do not desire such forward chicken."[6]

"Forward chicken" he proved to be. After education at grammar schools at Lostwithiel and Plymouth, and private tuition from a severe Calvinist clergyman, Newton matriculated and entered Exeter College, Oxford, in December 1824. He was just seventeen. With him at Oxford were the Newman brothers, Gladstone, and Hurrell Froude the early tractarian and older brother of J. A. Froude, the historian. He took a first-class degree in 1829, but had already been elected a Fellow of Exeter College before taking the degree.

At Oxford Newton received very considerable spiritual benefit through his friend Henry Bellenden Bulteel, curate of St. Ebbe's Church; and it was events concerning Bulteel which brought about the decisive change in his circumstances which took him from Oxford to Plymouth. On 6th February 1831, Bulteel preached a dramatic sermon in the University Church, denouncing the Establishment, and resigning his charge. In this step Newton supported him, and Darby (who was in Oxford at the time) sprang to Bulteel's defence in a spirited pamphlet. In the following August, Bulteel's curate's licence was withdrawn by his Bishop as a result of his preaching in Nonconformist churches. But then came disaster (in Newton's view). Within a few weeks Bulteel was taken up violently by the rising craze for the "gifts" of healings and tongues so soon to be identified with the Irvingite movement. Wigram and Darby, at Newton's suggestion, had already investigated these "gifts" in the course of visits paid to their first place of occurrence at Row in Scotland, and had rejected them.[7] Newton, repelled by these developments at Oxford, left the city and returned to Plymouth. There, on 15th March 1832, he married, thus vacating his Exeter College Fellowship. He was never to return to Oxford.

In this way, Newton became the first major accession to the new church. Darby and others had met with him in its early days to determine the order of its proceedings, for Hall's preaching was attracting considerable numbers, many of them being illiterate persons, and it was felt that ungifted or otherwise unsuitable persons might be tempted to hold the platform. A presiding elder was therefore appointed to maintain order at the meetings, and restrain any plainly unprofitable participants. B. W. Newton was the first to hold this duty, which he relinquished after three or four years in favour of another.[8]

It is plain, therefore, that Darby, even if only occasionally present, was a leading influence in the determination of the order and procedure of the new church, and that he had not yet developed his later extremely "spiritual" doctrine of the ministry. It is equally plain that he soon developed an almost paternal protectiveness concerning Plymouth, for his earliest letters show how deeply he identified himself with the church there, writing in a style which is almost apostolic in feeling.

There seems to have been considerable unrest among evangelical clergy in the then Exeter diocese: possibly not unconnected with the unpopular consecration of Henry Philpotts as Bishop of Exeter in 1830. Philpotts was an extreme sacramentalist, who later became the centre of national controversy as a result of the Gorham case, which would not endorse his refusal to induct an evangelical clergyman on the issue of baptismal regeneration. Having lost his case, Philpotts later excommunicated the Archbishop of Canterbury!

The Plymouth congregation was strengthened in the same year of

1831 by the accession, as one of its earliest members, of a seceding evangelical, the curate of Plymstock, James Lampen Harris.* Harris, born in 1793 and therefore not yet forty, was the oldest of the men whom we have met so far – a significant indication of the youthful nature of the movement. An old Etonian, of a wealthy Plymouth family, he had been a Fellow of Exeter College until his marriage in June 1829, and had met Newton in Oxford when, in 1829, he had come to Oxford to vote for Peel at the famous Catholic emancipation by-election.

Two other able men joined the church within the next year or two. Henry Borlase, curate of St. Keyne, Cornwall, resigned and threw in his lot with the new church, and later published an erudite and trenchant account of his reasons for leaving the Established Church. We have already referred to the mutual influence of Borlase and Darby upon each other: Borlase was to die in November 1835, following the rupture of a blood vessel in early 1834, and Newton later regretted his loss in words that have a poignant significance:

> He left the church in consequence of my secession and that of others with me in Plymouth, and became intimate with us, joined the Brethren. And if he had lived, Brethrenism would have taken a different turn to what it did. He saw exactly as I did, except about infant baptism.[9]

There is significance in this last remark, for Darby stood almost alone in the earliest days in not discarding the doctrine of infant baptism, and the support of a man such as Borlase must have been a strong encouragement to him in retaining this one, somewhat illogical, remnant of his earlier position – which was later taken up by most of those who followed him in his section of the movement.†

In his pamphlet *Reasons which have constrained me to withdraw from the Ministry of the Established Church*, Borlase described how an inquiry into the true and Scriptural purpose of Communion had led him to consider the character of fellowship of believers in his day, and more particularly in his own Church. The anti-Scriptural state of things which he saw there, he concluded, arose from the utter absence of any power of discipline: and this in turn derived from the establishment of the Church, its incor-

---

* One of Groves's early friends in Plymouth had been a Mr. Lampen (*Memoir* p. 3). Although Harris's second name is frequently quoted as "Lampden," the spelling "Lampen" appears in the official registration of Ebrington Street Chapel (see "Dissenters Meeting Houses in Plymouth to 1852" by Edwin Welch in *Transactions of Devon Association*, Vol. XCIV, 1962, [contributed by Mr. R. F. S. Thorne of Plymouth]).

† It ought to be remarked that the more moderate but (in Britain) minority sections of Exclusives have always retained a very open attitude to baptism, and include among their members upholders both of infant and of believers' baptism. William Kelly himself rejected infant baptism. This is an interesting feature in relation to current ecumenical trends.

poration with the State, and its subordination to the civil power. The burial service had been turned into a solemn mockery, by the requirement that hopes applicable to those who sleep in Jesus should be pronounced over persons of abandoned and profligate lives.★ In the ordinance of baptism, he wrote, "there is not the smallest room for the exercise of faith: the child may be presented by ungodly parents; the sponsors may be persons of irreligious lives; yet the minister is obliged to pronounce "regenerate", and ever after to consider as "a child of God by adoption and grace," one who, as is inevitably too often the case, has been presented without faith, who may be nurtured in ungodliness, and pass from the cradle to the grave without the slightest exhibition of the change which the Baptismal service affirms to have taken place within."[10] (This was of course written before the Gorham case had limited and defined the meaning of the language of the Book of Common Prayer.)

As for the service of Holy Communion, which should be "the outward symbol and instrument of Unity amongst His people"[11] – the whole purpose and character of the ordinance had been destroyed by indiscriminate admission, itself the result of the figment of baptismal regeneration – "the sign being uniformly put for the thing signified."[12] The result was an irremediable impurity of communion and a Church incapable of exercising discipline. "A Church," Borlase concluded, "consists not in rites and ceremonies, but 'where two or three are gathered together in His Name, there is He in the midst of them,' and such a refuge is open to the weakest of His people."[13]

Another paper, first appearing in *The Christian Witness* for July 1834, took the title "Separation from Apostacy not Schism." In it Borlase adopted the view, then common to Newton and Darby, but later to be developed by Darby in ways which dismayed Newton, that every dispensation of God's dealing with mankind had contained in it the seeds of apostasy. The Reformation had preserved in the churches the essence of this apostasy, by continuing their identification with the world. In fact, Borlase insisted, "The Church of England's own definition of the visible Church (often urged and as often disregarded), as a 'congregation of *faithful* men, in which the pure word of God is preached,' etc . . . utterly destroys her own title to be considered a Church."[14] Modern dissent, also, Borlase rejected: "with infinitely less of spirituality among individuals, it is more connected with the irreligion and ungodliness of popular feeling."[15] The only course was to separate from the evil: such separation from apostasy would not be schism, for it was no church in the proper sense which

★ An identical view had earlier been expressed in a sermon preached in the parish church at Stadhampton, Oxfordshire, on 11th December 1831, by another Anglican minister who later seceded under Darby's influence. This was the Rev. L. C. L. Brenton, later Sir L. C. L. Brenton, baronet, and the translator of the Septuagint (2 vols., 1844).

was being left. In the meantime, Borlase considered, there would be a gradual movement toward external union of the churches: "if a judgment may be formed from the aspect of the times, a period is rapidly approaching when every conceivable degree of iniquity will be tolerated to enforce an external union, and all godly turning away from it denounced as schism."[16]

The fourth notable acquisition came in early 1835, when Samuel Prideaux Tregelles, a member of a Quaker family, joined the congregation. He had been converted through his contacts with Newton, his cousin by marriage. Ostracized by his family as a result, he lived for a few months with Newton and his wife, until arrangements were made for his employment by Wigram on the early stages of the latter's *Englishman's Greek and Hebrew Concordances* – a work which launched Tregelles on the career which later placed him in the forefront of Biblical textual critics.

When Tregelles joined the church it numbered about eighty. Numbers continued to expand rapidly, and a few years later many hundreds were in fellowship. Henry William Soltau, a Cambridge man and a barrister, and his brother-in-law Richard Hill, another ex-clergyman, were two other notable additions. Darby, in a somewhat depreciatory comment in 1868, stated that "there were never more than seven hundred there."[17] Because of the increasing numbers, Raleigh Street Chapel was given up as the main meeting-place in 1840, although it was retained as a subsidiary chapel, and a new chapel was built in Ebrington Street, to a design which was favoured elsewhere by early Brethren.* The centre front of the chapel was occupied by the communion table, and it was the custom of speakers to address the congregation from that point. To this end, the seating was arranged in gradually ascending tiers. In the large building at Plymouth, these tiers were arranged in three blocks, each centring on the communion table in an approximate semicircle, thus giving an effect of a table in the centre of the congregation, while retaining the advantages of a point from which the whole congregation could be conveniently addressed.

The church at Plymouth was not totally preoccupied with its own expansion, but it also became the centre for an active evangelistic work, untiringly fostered by its leaders, throughout the surrounding countryside. The congregation at first lived a semi-communal life, visiting freely in each others' homes for meals and for spiritual fellowship. Newton, after isolation and controversy had soured him, spoke of those early customs:

> The Brethren lived a great deal in each other's houses and company. There was no such thing as domestic privacy among the very early Brethren. I always had seven or eight to dinner besides my own household, and in my ill-health [Newton refers to a serious illness he suffered], it was dreadful. I could not alter it and hardly knew how to endure it. When was this? Oh, in 1836.[18]

* It is said to have been adopted in London. The chapel at Stafford, which is still in use, has the same sloping floor.

The women of the congregation seem to have been far less inhibited in their participation in church activities than was later the practice, for Newton in his reminiscences speaks of Richard Hill's wife, whom he describes as "a gifted person in meetings," and whom he "urged to go on, and even rebuked her because she was neglecting her gift," when she began to devote herself more entirely to the care of her family. Newton went on:

> I was wrong, very wrong, for all her children grew up to be remarkably good Christians.[19]

The Plymouth leaders adopted a much more aggressive attitude towards other churches than had been the case at Dublin, and certainly than was the case at Bristol. The tenor of the teaching was strongly apocalyptic, calling out Christians from a world and from churches that were under imminent judgment, into a fellowship of simple devotion. Yet this emphasis was matched by an intense devotedness and sincerity, and attracted people in large numbers. A stable church of seven hundred persons is not built merely on excited prophesyings. Neither comfort nor health was permitted to stand in the way of the work to be done, and those who had means of their own gladly gave all their energies to the work. The well-to-do cultivated a deliberate simplicity of life, so that nothing might stand in the way of free intercourse with the poorer members: a habit which often led to quaint extremes of personal asceticism.

> I remember [Robert Chapman's] coming to me: I wasn't well off myself, but he was worse: he had been walking about all day having had no food but a loaf they had found on a common in answer to prayer. That sort of thing. Once I remember he went to a physician who had come to the meetings, whose wife was a Christian – he went to their house, inquired for the servant, had tea in the kitchen with the cook, and never asked for the lady. This as a sort of Christian testimony to lowlymindedness. Similarly, Lord Congleton on some occasion or other would have his coachman to dine and one of the servants who couldn't say two words on any subject.[20]

Lord Congleton, as his biographer, Henry Groves, tells us, though in possession of an independent income of £1,200 a year, took a house in Teignmouth of which the rent was £12, furnished it with wooden chairs and a plain deal table, steel forks and pewter tea-spoons, and wholly dispensed with carpets. The deal table, "by concession to the housemaid, was afterwards stained, because of the trouble it gave in constant scouring to keep it clean." Carpets seem to have been regarded with singular disfavour by the Brethren. The late Benjamin Wills Newton, I have been told, lived at one time in a large and handsome house in the same carpetless state. He also was a man of considerable means.

A symptom of the same general condition was a tendency to a kind of Pentecostal communism. It is related of one of the Brethren – Sir Alexander Campbell, if I mistake not – who had property in the West of England, that he insisted on his servants' sitting down with him at table. One day, coming in late for dinner, he found that his servants had already made some progress with the meal. They explained that, as he was so late, they thought they had better begin without him.[21]

The first periodical of the movement was issued from Plymouth in January 1834, under the title *The Christian Witness*, and appeared quarterly until its discontinuance with the January 1841 issue. Its first editor was Borlase, and after his death he was succeeded by J. L. Harris. It was also on sale in London, Limerick and Dublin. The establishment, not later than 1838,* of a Bible and Tract Depot, under Clulow and Soltau, two of the members of the church, indicates the church's growing influence and the number of pamphlets being issued from Plymouth. After Newton's serious illness in 1836, he was released from his pastoral work by Harris and Soltau, to enable him to concentrate on his writing and his spoken ministry.

Of the vigour and the remarkable character of the church at Plymouth there can be no doubt. For a period of fourteen years it enjoyed a success, and rejoiced in gifts, such as few single churches have experienced. Yet its documents make one conscious of a radical weakness from the beginning. Much of the teaching and testimony of the church was based upon prophetic interpretation, and upon the apocalyptic expectations of apostasy and judgment which that study generated. Its devotion and ardour were admirable and real, yet much derived from appeals for separation from corruption and apostasy in others. Some of these features, as we shall see in a later chapter, gave grave concern to Groves when he visited the church on his brief visit to this country, as early in its history as 1835. For the moment we merely note the fact. The outworking of the principles and events at Plymouth will call for a later discussion.

* The depot first appears on the title page of an issue of *The Christian Witness* in the 1838 volume. Soltau joined the church in 1837.

Quotation References – Chapter 4.

1. *Fry MS book*, p. 237. The Fry collection of Newtonian literature and MSS is held by Mr. C. E. Fry of Newport, Isle of Wight. For a detailed description and evaluation see H. H. Rowdon, *The Origins of the Brethren* (1967). Quotations are taken from a large MS book into which much of the material has been transcribed by one of Newton's disciples.
2. *Phases of Faith*, p. 45.
3. Quoted in W. G. Turner, *John Nelson Darby*, p. 70.
4. *Fry MS book*, pp. 262–3.
5. *Discipleship: or, Reasons for Resigning his Naval Rank and Pay*, P. F. Hall (London reprint, undated), p. 26.
6. *Fry MS book*, p. 45.
7. Wigram's visit is evidenced from a letter in the Fry collection (see *MS book* p. 264) written from Newton in Plymouth to Wigram in Scotland on 31st July 1830. Darby's visit is evidenced by Newton's reference (ibid., p. 237),

and by his own statement in *The Irrationalism of Infidelity*, p. 376, in reply to
F. W. Newman's description of his visit in *Phases of Faith*, p. 178.

8. *Three Letters*, S. P. Tregelles (1849 – reprinted 2nd edn. 1894), pp. 6–8.
9. *Fry MS book*, p. 289.
10. *Reasons*, etc., reprinted in *The Present State of the Church* (1892), pp. 8, 9.
11. Ibid., p. 12.
12. Ibid., p. 13.
13. Ibid., p. 33.
14. *The Christian Witness* (1834), p. 339.
15. Ibid., p. 354.
16. Ibid., p. 356.
17. *Letters*, Vol. I, p. 515 (letter dated 1868).
18. *Fry MS book*, p. 306.
19. Ibid., p. 315.
20. Ibid., p. 315.
21. *History of the Plymouth Brethren*, W. B. Neatby, pp. 41–42.

CHAPTER 5

WIDENING CIRCLES – ENGLAND

". . . majors, captains, even lords, retired merchants, men who, although independent, long for something to do."

W. Reid, *Plymouth Brethrenism Unveiled and Refuted.*

THE ANCIENT NORTH DEVON SEAPORT OF BARNSTAPLE FOUND an interesting subject for gossip in the summer of 1831. A fashionable young London solicitor – of all persons – was preaching – of all things – at the Pilton almshouses – of all places. Such events were no small sensation in those quiet days: and not least because this solicitor had been invited to Barnstaple by a local lawyer with a reputation for mild eccentricity, Thomas Pugsley. Pugsley had become particularly religious in recent years, and had been inviting various outlandish strangers to preach in local chapels – only in the previous year he had invited a young German from Teignmouth, George Müller.

When the local Strict Baptist congregation at Ebenezer Chapel wanted a pastor in the following year, having had no less than four ministers in nine years, they were not a little surprised to hear that this young solicitor had just given away his private fortune, and was willing to give up a successful London practice to become their pastor. His preaching had not been very striking, but his personality had been. Someone had in fact suggested to him that his preaching gift was hardly adequate to such a call, but he had replied: "There are many who preach Christ, but not so many who live Christ: my great aim will be to *live* Christ."[1]

So, in 1832, Robert Cleaver Chapman, the patriarch of Barnstaple, began his connexion with the town which was to be his home until his death, in his hundredth year, in 1902. Chapman, the son of a wealthy merchant family from Whitby, Yorks, had been born in Elsinore, Denmark, on 4th January 1803. After a private education he had served articles with the famous law firm of Freshfields, and had qualified as a solicitor in 1823, practising on his own account in Copthall Chambers, Throgmorton Street, and later in Cornhill.

In 1823 Chapman had been converted under the ministry of James Harington Evans at John Street Chapel, Gray's Inn. Evans, an Oxford man with a first-class academic record, had himself experienced an evangelical conversion after his ordination. His ardent evangelical preaching was the cause of a small revival around his curacy of Milford in Hampshire in the

70

years from 1810 to 1815, when opposition to his teachings led to his dismissal from his curacy.* He had already become concerned as to the Biblical teaching on baptism, and in 1816 received believer's baptism at Taunton. Evans was one of a number of Anglican clergymen who left the Church of England at this time, in a minor movement known as the "Western Schism." He himself moved to London, where Henry Drummond the banker, generous supporter of evangelical enterprise, built for him in 1818 the chapel in John Street, where he exercised a fruitful ministry for many years until his death in 1849.

Evans's influence on Chapman was profound. Despite his personal Baptist convictions, Evans was no strict Baptist, nor was Chapman. Moreover, Evans had encouraged him in views which were not dissimilar to those which Müller and Craik were later to develop in Bristol,* and had also impressed him with a sense of the true unity of all God's people.

This was the man, then, whom the Strict Baptists of Barnstaple invited to their church. Chapman would not come under false pretences, and he stipulated that if he was to come he could only do so on the condition that he should be free to teach all that he found in the Bible. Yet Chapman was no disrupter of churches, as a letter of 1893 shows:

> When, sixty years since, I came to this place, I waited for unity of heart and judgment among the company who called themselves Baptists, and when by the power of the Scriptures the greater part of them were minded to throw down their wall, we waited on in patience for fulness of unity of judgment. For this I was blamed by men of much grace, who at that time were endeavouring in the South of Devon to bring about a joint testimony of saints to the full truth of God. What we now enjoy here of mutual love and the Spirit's unity would never have been our portion had any other course been taken.[2]

Ebenezer Chapel lay in a poor and miserable part of the town, known as "Derby" from the lace factory which a Derbyshire man had built there some years before. Chapman was no stranger to squalor; since his conversion he had been spending his spare time in London in the poverty-stricken areas around Gray's Inn Road. First taking lodgings in a worker's cottage in Barnstaple, Chapman later took a tiny house in New Buildings in the middle of this district. With quiet patience and pastoral care he built up the congregation, spending his time in visitation and relief work, and

---

* It is interesting that these events took place in a parish hard by Groves's boyhood home at Lymington – although probably too late to have influenced Groves.

* W. H. Bennet, a leading Open Brother of his day, goes so far as to refer in his life of Chapman to "the assembly" (a term normally reserved for Brethren churches) of Christians in London to which Mr. Harington Evans ministered the Word (p. 28.) Evans himself in later years deplored the divisive influence, as he saw it, of Brethren teaching. (*Memoir and Remains of the Rev. James Harington Evans*, J. J. Evans (1852), p. 75.)

holding open house for all visitors. After a time, difficulties arose with some of the stricter members of the church, which Chapman later described—

> When I was invited to leave London and go to minister the Word of God in Ebenezer Chapel, then occupied by a community of Strict Baptists, I consented to do so, naming one condition only – that I should be quite free to teach all that I found written in the Scriptures. This I continued to do for some time with blessing from the Lord. A brother who visited me in those days urged me to set aside the strict rule that none but baptized believers should be allowed to break bread. I replied that I could not force the consciences of my brethren and sisters; and I continued my ministry, patiently instructing them from the Word. I well knew at that time that I could have carried the point with a large majority, but I judged it to be more pleasing to God to toil on to bring all to one mind. I was enabled to bear with their unduly pressing a *right* course; I could not have thus waited had they been pressing a *wrong* thing, such as infant baptism. In due time, through patiently waiting, and by the blessing of God upon us, we were brought to be all of one mind.
>
> A little time after that some Christians resident in Barnstaple, who held the strict views which we had abandoned, demanded that we should give up the use of the chapel. I carefully examined the Trust Deed, and found that in not one particular did we set aside its provisions. *Yet* we gave them the chapel, just as I should give my coat to a man who demanded it. You will not be surprised when I tell you that ere long the Lord gave us a much better chapel. He will be no man's debtor.[3]

A promising site nearby came to Chapman's notice, and he had contracted to buy it, when it came to his notice that the Anglican authorities had planned to use this site for a new church. Again, characteristically, Chapman surrendered his right to the site, and the congregation found temporary accommodation until, several years later, a chapel was built for their use in Grosvenor Street.[3a] The exact date of the building is not known, but it is interesting that George Müller spent some months in the district in 1842, and that in July 1843 his diary records a gift "to complete the payment of the expenses incurred by building a chapel for the meeting of the saints at Barnstaple."[4] The chapel, when built, contained no baptistry, as it was Chapman's custom to baptize in the river.

The work at Barnstaple grew to be a centre for considerable activity in the villages of North Devon. For twenty years since 1815 Robert Gribble, a Devonshire tradesman, had been evangelizing the villages throughout the north of the county. Many of the little churches he formed, although nominally under Independent or Baptist auspices, found the new principles from Barnstaple and Bristol to be ideally suited to their needs: indeed the denominational lines of demarcation were very indistinct in the villages of the whole area. Gribble himself adopted the new principles soon after Chapman's move to Barnstaple, and Pugsley too helped in the building of village chapels. In 1858 Gribble's *Recollections* were published by the Brethren publisher William Yapp in London.

The Barnstaple church also introduced its own new blood into the district and the movement at large. A convert of Chapman's, William Bowden, with George Beer, a convert of Gribble's, helped in the work, until, on Groves's return to this country, the two men joined the missionary party which Groves took back with him to India in March 1836. A circle of little churches sprang up in the villages around Barnstaple, some of them as the result of the work of another convert, a farmer named George Lovering. The most notable acquisition was Henry Heath, the young schoolmaster of Tawstock, who was studying for Holy Orders when he met Chapman in 1839. He worked with Chapman in the district until 1848, when he moved to Hackney in London to become a mainstay of the congregation there: later still he moved to Suffolk, where he was largely responsible for the establishment of a series of village congregations around Woolpit.

Chapman's long life and the simple holiness of his character made him the outstanding patriarch and counsellor of nineteenth century Open Brethren. It is difficult to study the life of any prominent man among them during any part of the century, who was not influenced in some way by this outstandingly godly and humble man. Barnstaple became a "Mecca" of Brethren. Miss Bessie Paget moved there after the death of her sister and took another cottage in New Buildings. It was there that Groves visited her for the last time in October 1852, during the last year of his life. With the addition of a woman's practicality and concern, the engagement of the church in the social needs surrounding it increased, Sunday schools, a soup kitchen, and other ventures being started. When Miss Paget died in 1863, Groves's other old friend William Hake, who had recently suffered a severe breakdown in mental health, which had caused havoc at the school he ran in Bideford, took over her cottage where he made a full recovery and continued in close partnership with Chapman until his death in 1890. Others who spent the later years of their life in Barnstaple included the Plymouth pioneer H. W. Soltau.

Chapman himself, who was an accomplished linguist, travelled extensively, often on foot. His name is particularly associated with Brethren work in Spain, as well as in Ireland. Barnstaple remained, however, his centre and chief love. Perhaps the aptest comment on his life and character is contained in the story – apocryphal or not – that the Post Office once delivered safely to him an envelope which was addressed simply to "R. C. Chapman, University of Love, England."[5]

The pattern of Barnstaple was repeated elsewhere. It is significant that lasting work was often the result of gifted men settling in a district and devoting themselves to building up churches in the surrounding area. This pattern of activity has in more recent years been largely lost among Brethren, in their recoil from any form of settled ministry, and has been replaced by a haphazard "system" of peripatetic preaching, which bids fair to weaken them more quickly than any other peculiarity.

Another of such early centres was at Hereford, where the ground had been prepared by the teaching of the vicar of St. Peter's, the Rev. Henry Gipps; whose daughter later married William Kelly, a prominent leader of Exclusive Brethren later in the century. Gipps died a young man in 1832, and was succeeded by the Rev. John Venn, who, although an evangelical of the Clapham Sect, failed to satisfy the congregation. After one of them had visited Plymouth and had there heard the fascinating preaching of Captain Percy Hall, Hall was invited to settle in Hereford, where he arrived in 1837.

It was not long before some hundreds were attending his preaching. Hall had absorbed Darby's general scheme of doctrine, and this gave to his preaching a coherence and devotion which the congregation found lacking elsewhere. Venn (who later in life was himself to be accused of "Plymouth Brethrenism") reacted naturally with outright opposition. The result was a general secession from the churches of the district, and the establishment of a large congregation which included a number of the more prominent local citizens; among them a Mr. Yapp, a well-to-do merchant who later, as a publisher, was to invent and give his name to the familiar "yapp-edged" Bibles, a surgeon, Dr. Griffiths, and Mr. Humphrys, a solicitor.

It is an interesting pointer to the general ecclesiastical climate of those days that news of the formation of this independent congregation of Christians travelled widely. In Scarborough, another medical man, Dr. Rowan, had been meeting independently with a group of Christians on somewhat similar lines. This town was associated also with R. M. Beverley, author of a trenchant anti-clerical pamphlet, drawing on historical and scriptural data, *An Inquiry into the Scriptural Doctrine of Christian Ministry*. Hearing of the establishment of the Hereford assembly, Dr. Rowan contacted them, and later moved to Hereford, and joined them. Still later he moved to London, where his family was associated with the group at Hackney, of which more will be said in a later chapter.

The Hereford assembly was gifted with financial resources which far outstripped those of Barnstaple or Bristol, but it was no less devoted. The leading members placed their homes and their wealth at the disposal of the church, both locally and more widely. The district for miles around was evangelized thoroughly, and churches established throughout the villages and towns of the surrounding counties. Help was sent generously to missionaries and churches in other places. Later teachers included Captain William Rhind, another ex-naval officer who had surrendered his commission and studied for the ministry under Simeon at Cambridge, before joining with Brethren as a result of the influence of John Synge and the Powerscourt Group. He had been in touch with Groves's old circles in

Plymouth. Rhind lived in Hereford from 1838 until he moved to Ross-on-Wye in 1843. Captain the Hon. William H. G. Wellesley, a nephew of the Iron Duke, also renounced his commission and joined the new assembly. Thomas Maunsell, previously of Limerick, lived at Hereford from 1858 until his death in 1880, and another notable member was William Seward, whose connexion lasted for seventy years until his death in 1908. Darby visited the congregation at Hereford on several occasions in its earliest days: a fact sufficiently explained by his friendship with Hall, although his mother's family had connexions in the Hereford district.

In south-west Devon the Brethren teachers from Plymouth travelled out into the surrounding countryside. Newton later recounted how he had written his *Thoughts on the Apocalypse* during intervals snatched at inns and other resting-places during the course of such journeyings. At the same time, from the north of the county, the work centred on Barnstaple spread into central Devon and towards Exeter, into the areas evangelized by Gribble. In the south-east of Devon, Groves's old friend Caldecott had resigned his curacy at Claybrook, and was working around Sidmouth. There were also churches in Exeter and in Müller's old church at Teignmouth. Parnell lived in the latter town from 1837 to 1842, after his return from the East. Nearby, a group of Christians in Torquay, formerly Anglicans, had begun meeting in 1834 on Brethren lines, under the leadership of one John Vivian. The movement soon spread into the neighbouring counties of Somerset and Dorset. Early in the 1830s, Bellett had found interest in Brethren in the Somerset home of his Irish friend, the hymn-writer Sir Edward Denny, who himself joined the movement. A congregation was early established in Bath (according to Tregelles, as early as 1835 – Tregelles also mentions one in Salcombe, South Devon, by that date). Later, Gribble was to move into the western end of Somerset, and still later the Somerset-Devon border country of the Blackdown Hills was to be the centre of the outstanding (and still continuing) work of the Brealey family. Another hymnwriter, J. G. Deck, an ex-Indian army officer studying for ordination, was brought into contact with the movement in Devon, and later moved to Wellington in Somerset and Weymouth in Dorset. In that last county there were spontaneously-formed churches which were soon brought into touch with the wider movement of Brethren. Several of the meetings in Somerset and Dorset were later consolidated by the ministry of two brothers, friends of Deck, who had been connected with the Plymouth assembly, William and (at a later date) Henry Dyer.

While the movement was thus spreading throughout the west of England, from Plymouth in Devon to as far north as Leominster in Herefordshire, London was not overlooked. The precise early growth of the movement in London is obscure, but it is known that a church was started in the early 1830s, largely on the initiative of G. V. Wigram. Darby later wrote that "it began in London about the same time (as Plymouth), through one I had met in Oxford,"[6] and B. W. Newton speaks of a meeting in a private room near Regent Square in 1833. This congregation was soon meeting in Rawstorne Street, Camden Town. Another congregation met in Orchard Street, St. Marylebone, later moving to Welbeck Street. It was in these two congregations that Parnell settled in 1842, when he left Teignmouth on succeeding to the title of Lord Congleton. W. H. Dorman, writing on leaving the Independents in 1838, mentions only one assembly known to him in London, in Little Portland Street, but a well-informed Exclusive Brother* indicates that the congregations had become numerous by that date:

> Wigram was active in the initiation of a like testimony in London, where by the year 1838 a considerable number of gatherings were formed on the model of that at Plymouth, and he began to feel that some kind of organization was needed whereby these neighbouring companies should act in concert; hence his letter to J. N. Darby, which will be found on page 60 of W. B. Neatby's *History*. The formation of a London Saturday-evening administrative "central meeting" dates from that year.[7]

This letter was written on 6th October 1838: the very considerable change in the structure of the movement which it advocated was to have devastating consequences in the Exclusive or Darbyite section of Brethren, but that is a story for a different chapter of this book.

It was in 1838 that two further events occurred in the London area which were to have a considerable influence within the movement. William Henry Dorman, the minister of Islington Independent Chapel, had been developing views characteristic of Brethren since the beginning of his ministry there three years before. "The priesthood of believers," he wrote to his congregation, "the unscriptural distinction of clergy and laity – liberty of ministry – the simple principle of the communion of saints – the unscripturalness of seat-rents – plurality of elders – are no new doctrines at Islington Chapel; and many of you can bear me witness what efforts I have made to model things among you after this order."[8] He and a few others had at one time projected a "Society of Reformed Pastors" to put these views into circulation, but the proposal had come to nothing. Increasingly he found himself out of sympathy with the creaking structure of the chapel's government, and even the furnishings of the chapel began to irritate and perplex him: "The organ, the graduated desks – from the clerk's upward to the pulpit – the brass trellis-work, to separate the poor from the rich; the gates, at the end of the aisles, effectually to shut out those who could not pay for a seat; and, above all, the fact that the floor of the chapel is made six inches lower in the compartment appro-

---

* The article is signed with the initials "E.E.W." – apparently E. E. Whitfield, who wrote the article on Plymouth Brethren in Herzog's *Religious Encyclopedia*.

priated to the poor (which has the effect, whether intended or not, of marking more effectually the distinction), and that at the greatest distance from the pulpit."[9]

The crisis for Dorman came after a visit to Bristol. In Bristol he had preached at the new Independent Brunswick Chapel, and had there declined use of the gown and pulpit, and had preached from the clerk's desk. In his preaching he had been carried away in his enthusiastic exposition of I Cor. 2: 14. The result was an alarmed letter from Bristol to Islington, whose deacons, in Dorman's caustic words, "like all other deacons among the Dissenters, imagined their office to be episcopal, and to have to do with the order of ministry."[10] Dorman eventually reached London, after first visiting Stafford, where a secession had also recently taken place. In London, he found that his own church and pulpit were virtually closed to him. At a general meeting of church members on 26th June 1838 he "resigned back into the hands of the members and seat-holders the power they had given me to minister in that chapel, but retaining the pastorship of souls, which the Lord Jesus had, in infinite mercy and condescension, committed to me."[11] He offered to preach temporarily as a supply, and to explain on other occasions the Scriptural evidences for his views, but both offers were refused. Dorman, forced into the Brethren movement in this way, was to prove a notable acquisition.

In Tottenham, a few miles farther to the north of London, a Brethren congregation gathered around two former members of the Society of Friends, who had been disturbed by the "Beaconite" controversy within the Society. These were Robert and John Eliot Howard, both members of the chemical manufacturing firm of Howard and Sons. The latter was to become well known for his scientific work, later becoming a Fellow of the Royal Society and of the Linnaean Society. They had left the Society of Friends and been baptized a year or two before, and a small meeting was started by them in a house in Stoneleigh South in 1838. There they were joined by their father, Luke Howard the meteorologist, who had been disowned by the Friends in that same year. In 1839 they opened a chapel (which is still in use) in Brook Street, off Tottenham High Road. By 1842 eighty-eight persons were in communion. Later in the century this congregation was to become influential within the movement. Among its members, for a short time before he left for China, was James Hudson Taylor.

Each of these two developments was connected with movements in other parts of the country which spread the influence of the Brethren into the Midlands and the North. Dorman had visited Stafford, a town with which he had family connexions, on his way back from Bristol. There, a short time before, a Presbyterian minister, Alexander Stewart, had resigned his ministry and associated himself with a meeting of Christians on Brethren lines. Stafford was to become another strong centre of the movement, and in its early days was a minor "ecumenical" gathering, with Christians from Anglican and Free Churches meeting in unity. Darby visited Stafford at least as early as January 1839, so the church there was plainly in touch with the wider movement from the start. Stewart may well have been the Presbyterian minister who had seceded after a large conference of brethren from the whole of England and Ireland in 1837 or 1838, to whom Darby refers in a letter written from Hereford about this time.

The other developments, in Tottenham, were linked with events which were to bring into the movement a number of its influential and able leaders. The Society of Friends had been seriously divided for over a decade by disputes between members who supported their traditional teachings, with an emphasis on the "Inner Light" that tended to unitarianism, and a strong evangelical party whose Christian doctrines were more orthodox, and who gave more emphasis to the authority of Scripture. In England the controversy flared to the point of open secession after 1835, when Isaac Crewdson of Kendal and Manchester published his *A Beacon to the Society of Friends*. Crewdson was of the evangelical party, and the resultant controversy led to many Friends joining Anglican and Baptist Churches.

In such a situation it was inevitable that a new movement so very similar in many of its practices to the Society of Friends, and which shared its emphasis upon the simple unity of all Christians, in contrast to the settled denominationalism of older bodies, should attract many of those leaving the Quakers. Moreover, B. W. Newton's blood relationship with that closely-knit web of inter-connected families which formed the background of the Society of Friends, provided a direct link to the Brethren.

Two separate lines led directly to the heart of the evangelical group among the Quakers, the influential Crewdsons themselves. B. W. Newton's family connexions with them were close, and he visited them at their home in Kendal during an early preaching tour, finding them moving rapidly towards the Brethren position. The second line was equally important. Through local Anglican friends, the Crewdsons had links with Darby's relatives, the Pennefathers of Dublin, and they very soon were in contact with Darby and (probably by both links) with Hall. By the later 1830s, the Crewdsons, with their banking partner Wakefield, were part of a strong Brethren church in Kendal: although the new ideas were strongly opposed by the evangelical Quaker matriarch there, Anna Braithwaite. Wakefield was later one of the first trustees of Müller's orphan buildings.

B. W. Newton contributed to the "Beaconite" controversy with a pamphlet *A Remonstrance to the Society of Friends*, and the Howards of Tottenham had also taken a prominent part in the controversy. These developments around Kendal gave Brethren a strong footing in the North, which extended to the Midlands in 1840, when Samuel Lloyd of Birmingham, the banker, and his son Sampson, who were connected by marriage both to Newton and to the Howards, left the Quakers to join a Brethren meeting there. Peter Greenhill Anderson, a Scottish schoolmaster, was also active in Birmingham.

Bethesda at Bristol also received accessions from the Society of Friends, perhaps the most important being that of James Ireland Wright, who was baptized there in 1837, and whose son James, after contributing largely to Brethren growth in Hackney, London, married Müller's daughter Lydia as his second wife in 1871. He later joined Müller as co-director of the Orphan Homes.

Other developments in the North contributed to the spread of the movement there. Controversy within the Methodist New Connexion in Yorkshire brought into the Brethren an able young minister from that county, William Trotter. About 1842 the mystical Andrew Jukes, an Anglican clergyman in Hull, formed a congregation which was soon linked with Brethren, and which Darby visited soon after its formation. Jukes, an Old Harrovian and friend since his schooldays of F. W. Faber, had while at Cambridge in 1840 won the Hulsean Prize with an essay on *The Principles of Prophetic Interpretation*. He married the daughter of Admiral Hole of Barnstaple in January 1842, and was ordained in June of that year, being licensed to the curacy of St. John's, Hull. He never took priest's orders. The Oxford Movement, which took Faber, had some slight influence with him, as he described later in his life in a typically witty comment:

> I shall never forget my first reading of Dr. Pusey's first tract, in the *Tracts for the Times*, on Fasting. In my poor way I had always tried to practise abstinence, but Pusey's tract gave me direction and encouragement; for the good Pharisees among whom I then was cast had improved upon the old Pharisee's prayer, and while they yet said, "God, I thank Thee that I am not as other men," they concluded by saying, "I do *not* fast at all; I do *not* give tithe of all that I possess." What a change has come over the Church since then! It has been like springtime after frost.[12]

But the Oxford Movement could not satisfy his personal difficulties over infant baptism and other aspects of the subscription to the Prayer Book then required of all the clergy. He was suspended from his curacy, and began preaching in the open air, was baptized, and met with those who joined him in simple fashion, akin to other Brethren – though at first they suffered much from the indiscipline of self-assertive men who joined with them and took advantage of their liberty. Jukes was always an individualist. He corresponded with F. D. Maurice, and studied deeply in the mystical writers. In 1866, after much heart-searching, he built a chapel in Hull, cruciform in shape, which he called the Church of St.

John the Evangelist, and where he used some of the Anglican forms of service – to the horror of many of his associates! Shortly after, he published a book *The Second Death and the Restitution of All Things* in which he denied the doctrine of eternal punishment and finally alienated himself from the Brethren, who were fiercely orthodox on this point following the earlier debates within their churches. During his time with the Brethren, Jukes's writings – notably *The Law of the Offerings* and *The Types of Genesis* – had had a great and lasting influence on Biblical interpretation among them, and (together with Soltau's works on the Tabernacle) were in no small degree responsible for the typology which later became second nature to them.

The earlier of Jukes's works were the bane of the infant Edmund Gosse:

> There was, for instance, a writer on prophecy called Jukes, of whose works each of my parents was inordinately fond, and I was early set to read Jukes aloud to them. I did it glibly, like a machine, but the sight of Jukes's volumes became an abomination to me, and I never formed the outline of a notion what they were about.[13]

Which was a pity, because, whatever he might have thought of the author of another work imposed on him by his parents at a tender age – a "book of incommunicable dreariness, called Newton's *Thoughts on the Apocalypse*,"[14] Edmund Gosse would surely have savoured the wit which the later Jukes showed in his personal correspondence.

Quotation References – Chapter 5.

1. *Robert Cleaver Chapman of Barnstaple*, W. H. Bennet (1902), p. 31.
2. *Letters*, R. C. Chapman (1903), pp. 64–5.
3. Quoted, W. H. Bennet, op. cit., pp. 32–3.
3a. Chapman's *Letters* show that the church met for many years in Bear Street.
4. *Muller's Autobiography*, p. 196.
5. *Brother Indeed*, Frank Holmes (1956), p. 92.
6. *Letters*, Vol. I, p. 515 (letter dated 1868).
7. *Chief Men Among the Brethren*, ed. Hy. Pickering (2nd edn. 1931), p. 41.
8. *Reasons for Retiring from the Independent or Congregational Body* (otherwise known as *Principles of Truth*), W. H. Dorman (1862 reprint), pp. 95–96.
9. Ibid., pp. 100–1.
10. Ibid., p. 105.
11. Ibid., p. 107.
12. *Letters of Andrew Jukes*, ed. H. H. Jeaffreson (1903), p. xxi.
13. *Father and Son*, Edmund Gosse (Four Square Book 1959), pp. 20–21.
14. Ibid., p. 39.

CHAPTER 6

WIDENING CIRCLES – IRELAND
AND THE CONTINENT

TWELVE years ago Dr. Alexander, the present Primate of Ireland, described the warfare of his own church in the following remarkable terms: "The hill up which our little host must march is steep, and the hail beats in our faces. We hear the steady tramp of the serried ranks of Rome round us; the shout of the marauders of Plymouth rises, as they, ever and anon, cut off a few stragglers. We draw close, and grip our muskets harder."

W. B. Neatby, *A History of the Plymouth Brethren.*

THROUGHOUT THE YEARS FROM 1830 TO 1845 THE GROWTH of the movement engaged the untiring energies of J. N. Darby. Apart from the work by Müller in Stuttgart, to which reference has been made on p. 52 of this book, the story of the expansion outside England during those years is largely a part of Darby's biography.

To trace the story we must go back to the beginning of the century, when two brothers, James and Robert Haldane, started itinerant preaching in Scotland. Both had been naval officers, and were of a wealthy and cultured Scottish family. Their preaching in this unorthodox manner therefore attracted considerable attention, and no little support. Opposition arose from the established churches, and they therefore formed congregations of their own and started a training school for young preachers. In this way, the influence of the Haldanes spread widely throughout Scotland and into Ireland, while Robert Haldane visited the Continent and deeply influenced a number of young men in Geneva.

The Haldanes had links with the Brethren movement which came a few years later. Groves was in touch with a daughter of James Haldane in India, and her brother Robert married as his second wife the daughter of one of James's friends, Richard Burdon-Sanderson, an Oxford man who joined the Brethren in 1837. Their son Richard Burdon Haldane, who was born in 1856, became the great statesman Viscount Haldane of Cloan. Richard Burdon Haldane did not grow up to share the faith of his parents, but his mother remained a dominating and tolerant influence upon him for the whole of her long life.

The work of the Haldanes was a prominent example of a tendency which was becoming increasingly marked. Small groups of Christians in many different places were becoming disillusioned with the regular churches, and were breaking off to form independent congregations of their own. Where local leadership was strong, these groups often grew large, and there may well have been considerable disorganized contact between them. Where strong-minded leaders arose, groups of such churches would tend to form around them, as around the hymnwriter Thomas Kelly in Ireland, with whom a number of churches were associated in the early decades of the nineteenth century: or the violently Calvinist groups known as Walkerites who followed the lead of Walker, a Fellow of Trinity College, Dublin, and chaplain of the Bethesda Chapel there, at about the same time.

In Camowen Green, near Omagh in Northern Ireland, one such group had been formed in 1807 by a local man, James Buchanan, who had been influenced by the Haldanes and who was also later in touch with Walker (although his views were far less violent, and he differed from Walker in adopting Baptist principles). James Buchanan became British Consul in New York in 1819, having emigrated there in 1816, and it is interesting that a printed collection of correspondence survives from the years 1818–1820, between a similar church in New York and twenty-two such congregations, mainly in Scotland and Northern Ireland, but including groups in England, and three others in North America. Buchanan's own church in Camowen Green was included, and his brother John was a signatory to the reply. Trace has now been lost of most of these congregations: many doubtless later joined with the Baptist and Congregational bodies, others died out, while yet others may well have been absorbed by the growing Brethren movement. We do know that both a Baptist Church and a present-day Brethren congregation can trace their origin back to Buchanan's group in Omagh.

That Darby was soon aware of the existence of such bodies is clear. "I hear the north (of Ireland) is dotted with little bodies, meeting as you do, though I do not know the places," he wrote in a letter of 30th April 1833.[1] But his own entrance on the Irish scene was stormy, and is connected with the extremely unsettled state of the Church of Ireland. The dispute over Archbishop Magee's Erastianism had been followed by Darby's visit to England. There he had fully associated with the suspect evangelicals of Oxford, and had then* supported Bulteel's secession, in a vigorous pamphlet on certain Anglican doctrines. He returned to Ireland under a deep cloud, so far as the Established Church was concerned. "There was great feeling against J.N.D. when I came out, because of the secessions at Oxford about that time," wrote J. B. Stoney, who first associated with Brethren when at Trinity College, Dublin, in 1833, "so much so, that it was notified to me that both Dr. Saddler and Dr. Singer had conferred on the propriety of taking my rooms from me, because I had asked Mr. Darby to lecture in them."[2]

* Although the pamphlet was published anonymously, it is plain from J. B. Stoney's remarks quoted that Darby's authorship soon became known.

Further drama was to follow. In 1832, after visiting Plymouth and Bristol in the summer, Darby returned to Dublin, where he clashed with Archbishop Whately over the Irish Education Measure, and added publicly to the offence by the assertion that Whately was heretical in doctrine. Then, in October 1832, he set out on a tour of Ireland to visit some of the little bodies of which he had heard: visiting, as he himself said, two or three places a day to investigate them or to preach there.[3] In this, he was following the example of many clergy in Ireland, but the habit was already under official disapproval. After a wide tour he reached Limerick, having found groups in several towns. There he stopped for a while, and the successive extracts from his letters indicate the progress of things. First: "we have set up weekly Scripture reading meetings";[4] then, "a little church has been formed, or rather body, like the one at Plymouth, for communion";[5] and, in the following April (and apparently after another visit to Plymouth) "the church at Limerick have so multiplied, that they must seek some place of meeting."[6] Darby was still not wholly easy in mind: "This is a cause of anxiety to me, whilst I wait on the Lord's will, for I feel the importance of the moral character of the step, for unless called for, it would have the same tendency" (i.e. to sectarianism).[7]

By August 1833, Darby was excited by great events in Ireland. On the one hand, he found expressions of a widespread craving for deeper devotion and Scripture knowledge:

> by Scripture-reading meetings, and by the clergy themselves in many instances making churches, not with communion, but admitting all Christians, and many little bodies springing up, things are assuming a new shape, though unformed, and there will be an entirely new state of things in a year or two.[8]

At Limerick in 1833 Darby heard of "Hardman, a dear brother in the Lord, a clergyman,"[9] who had recently paid them a visit there. This contact brought him into touch with another breakaway movement, this time at Westport, in the north-west, and to a clash with yet a third Archbishop – this time le-Poer Trench of Tuam. Hardman became an Irvingite, but two others of the clergy from the Westport district, Charles Hargrove and John Marsden Code, left the Church of Ireland in 1835 and 1836 respectively, and were to become honoured leaders in the Brethren.*

---

* ". . . a letter written to the Rev. Charles Hargrove, requesting him to lose no time in coming back amongst his old friends, to teach them how to do without a lawful minister, and how to construct themselves into an ecclesiastico-republican society, after the newest and most approved *separating* model, as invented by the Rev. John Darby, to whose system he had unfortunately given in his own adhesion . . . he despatched no less a person than Mr. Darby himself, to give them the advantage of his own subtle reasoning, which few, if any, amongst them were competent to understand; and to drill them, according to his own regimental tactics, into an irregular corps, pledged to hatred of the Church, and unceasing war against her."

(From J. D'Arcy Sirr, *Memoir of the Hon. and Most Rev. Power le-Poer Trench, last Archbishop of Tuam* (1845), pp. 343–4.)

This, Darby's third tilt at an archiepiscopal windmill, proved finally fatal to his links with the Establishment. Openly, he attacked the preaching and parochial arrangements of the Established Church: and to this period also may confidently be dated a celebrated pamphlet which he kept unpublished for several years. Its embittered title seems deliberately provocative: *The Notion of a Clergyman dispensationally the Sin against the Holy Ghost.* In it, Darby attacked the established order with a vehemence that would not have done discredit to the violence of writing of an unknown contemporary in Denmark, Søren Kierkegaard, twenty years later.[10]

Yet the work in Ireland at this time seems to have been far less enduring than elsewhere. It was founded so largely in controversy, and yet the stormy environment of its birth was not the whole reason for its eclipse. Perhaps a deeper explanation is to be found in the factors of which the actions of Archbishop Magee, which shut the door to the hearts of the Irish peasantry, were a symptom. Thereafter, not only Darby's work in his curacy of Calary was destroyed: perhaps the access way for Protestant evangelicalism into the sympathies of the native Irish was destroyed for good. The Brethren themselves made quick headway, but the headway was largely among the Anglo-Irish, and particularly in their upper classes. The names of so many of the leaders are evidence enough of this: Darby of Leap Castle, Offaly; Lady Powerscourt; Stoney of Emell Castle, Offaly; Lord Congleton; Sir Edward Denny of Tralee Castle, Co. Kerry; and, still later in the century, the Hon. Somerset Maxwell (later Lord Farnham), the Earl of Cavan, and the Earl of Carrick.

Moreover, many of these leaders had roots in England as well as in Ireland, and it was largely England that received their gifts – Congleton in Teignmouth and London, Maunsell in Hereford, Code in Bath, Hargrove too, and Sir Edward Denny. So Darby could lament in August 1843:

> In Ireland they have been neglected, but in Dublin they are much blessed, more than ever, and they walk in peace elsewhere, but there is no work.[11]

It is significant that when D. J. Beattie, in the 1930s, tried to trace back the origins of twentieth-century Open Brethrenism in Ireland, he could find little evidence of survivals from those early days. Even at Limerick he found no record of a link with the church which Darby knew: only at Bandon, Co. Cork, did he find a link back to 1843 – and that, oddly enough, was the parish where J. G. Bellett's brother George (who never seceded from the church) had been curate, his teaching leaving an impression upon the founders of the assembly. Beattie even suggested that the Dublin church itself went into eclipse – although, as we have seen, Darby found them flourishing in 1843, and Bellett lived in Dublin throughout his life, except for a brief period between 1846 and 1854 during which period the North London churches were in touch with Dublin. In April 1848 Robert Chapman found "between two and three hundred breaking bread at Brunswick St." in Dublin.[11a] The present influential Open Brethren assembly has its building at Merrion Hall which was opened in 1863.

It is not surprising that Darby should have left Ireland after the Westport troubles, to find a field to pioneer elsewhere. He did visit Westport again in 1837, and found refreshment with his friends there, although he wrote of the Irish congregations that "the enmity against them increases every day."[12] His main journeys were, however, to be elsewhere. In England, where he visited the vigorous works which soon grew up in Hereford, Stafford and London, and of course in his beloved Plymouth, he found the work in the hands of gifted and competent men. He attended the large meeting of a hundred or more brethren from most parts of England and from Ireland of which we have already spoken. The work, he wrote soon after this date, was spreading in the two most populous areas of England, in London and Lancashire, while in Hereford, Cumberland ("a great increase") and Edinburgh ("where thirty-six are gathered together") there were other congregations. He was weary with controversy, yet controversy would not leave him:

> It is a refreshment now to sit down and write a line simply as in the Lord, from settling controversy with heresy, and looking over papers for the *Witness* and the like, all of which I suppose needful, but in which one's spirit no way flows free and blessed in Christ as when in the sphere, and so unhinderedness in principle, of one's own joys – of Christ's joys (what a blessing to be made partakers of them – may we – and what holiness it requires!) of His sorrows too.[13]

Outside England, another field was beckoning to Darby. It is difficult to date precisely his first visit to Switzerland, but references in his letters and by the editor of his *Spiritual Songs* indicate a short visit to Geneva in or before 1837. The Plymouth group knew of a movement close to their own hearts, both in French-speaking Switzerland, and also in France around Lyons: and an account of these movements was published in *The Christian Witness* for January 1834. It is those movements which we now consider.

Moravian influence had persisted in Geneva since Zinzendorf lived there in the 1740s. Unitarian influence had become strong there by the nineteenth century, but there was a revival of evangelical interest among the Moravian groups about 1810, affecting a number of students in Geneva. This interest was developed by Robert Haldane and was encouraged by the visits first of a follower of Whitefield, Wilcox, and later by the banker, Henry Drummond.* The result was the founding in Geneva, in 1817, of the first church of *L'Ancienne Dissidence*, Drummond being dubbed by its

---

* The dates of the visits were: 1816 to January 1817 Wilcox, from January 1817 Haldane, about September 1817 Drummond.

opponents "the banker of the new doctrine." Bitter opposition soon arose, fomented by a sarcastic press, and mob violence was also directed against the new church.

In the canton of Vaud, north of Lake Geneva, with Lausanne as its centre, evangelical work had developed more slowly. There was some influence from Geneva, and an English lady, a Miss Greaves, had carried on a spiritual work from her home about 1815, until she was later expelled from Lausanne. Others from Geneva worked there, including Felix Neff, who had at first been a bitter opponent of the movement in Geneva, but became its ardent supporter. The State Church, led by the formidable evangelical Curtat, *le doyen Curtat*, and fearing the growth of dissent, reacted with foolish violence against the signs of spiritual revival. Protests by pastors and people, and attempts to remedy a sterile formalism by the alteration of established forms of service, by private meetings for prayer and edification, and by the establishment of the *Société Vaudoise des Missions*, were countered by the suspension or striking off the roll of several ministers, and even by banishment, while a decree of 15th January 1824 forbade private meetings – although it plainly became a dead letter almost immediately.

This panic opposition inevitably forced the disruption it was intended to avoid. The expulsion of Charles Rochat, the pastor of Vevey, in 1824, led to the formation by a number of his followers of a separate congregation there. Within a few years the movement had spread, and Marc Fivaz, one of the men who had been struck off the roll of ministers, listed *assemblées dissidentes* in 1828 in fourteen places besides Lausanne itself. The debate simmered within the State Church for years, even while the independent congregations were growing, and eventually it led to a further breakaway of 153 ministers in 1845, and in 1847 to the formation of the Free Vaudoise Church.

In Geneva and Vaud, therefore, there had sprung up in the later 1820s a movement very similar to the movement in the British Isles of a few years later. In Neuchâtel also several congregations had been formed, and there was also a remarkable evangelical movement in Lyons, associated with Adolphe Monod; this movement drew as much from Roman Catholics as from Protestants.

In the middle 1830s the movement was disturbed by external influences. Henry Drummond's espousal of Irvingism in England had its influence in the Swiss congregations, and there was also dispute over Wesleyan doctrines on perfectionism, championed by one of the Vaudois leaders, Henri Olivier.

Such was the situation when Darby arrived in Geneva. His first visit in 1837 was a short one, but he arrived back in Switzerland in the autumn of 1839, the beginning of a stay of four years on the Continent. His work was at first constructive. The congregations were restored to harmony, and the dissident teachings ceased – no small cause being Henri Olivier's embracing of Darby's teachings. Groups of young men, inspired by Darby's example, were taught privately by him, and went out not only into Switzerland, but well into France. Some of them suffered assault and violence, but the work spread remarkably quickly. As early as 1837, the October issue of *The Christian Witness* had carried a letter (attributed to Darby's brother W. H. Darby) describing contacts earlier that year with a Christian in Nice who had "occasionally broken bread with a few saints who were sojourning there" and had afterwards been imprisoned under shocking conditions for reading his Bible.[14]

In January 1843, John Darby wrote from Lausanne of a visit he had paid to France:

> In France there is progress, and I found the brethren well, and walking near the Lord in general. There is now a large field open in the Gard ... At St. Hippolyte, though others labour equally, several true men (finding that our brethren walked more with the Lord, and had His blessing) who had been exceedingly prejudiced, have drawn towards the brethren and avowed it. There will be opposition there, at least, on the westward, but there is testimony. In the Isère there is a commencement of blessing, and in the Drôme, at Montmeyran, where they are however weak; this place will bring probably excessive enmity on me. I saw brethren from this place when in France. I could not go there when in the Ardèche. At Annonay and Vernoux they came as much as eighteen leagues to read and confer; this shows the awakening to the state of things which exists. It is chiefly, though not exclusively, among simple brethren; they are devoted and zealous – this is a remarkable feature. One in Switzerland has been severely beaten, but is happy in his work; one who is much blessed, has left all recently (a lithographist), and felt led to go out at once, without reading with us at Lausanne. Five more are come to read, of whom three I trust will be valuable labourers in different ways. The brethren meet to break bread in France, in places of which I knew not the existence before I went there this last trip. Many of them receive next to nothing, being unmarried: their zeal has awakened the goodwill of those among whom they labour; they receive them, and even give them clothing as presents.[15]

We may take a brief glance at the later development of the remarkable movement which became permanently associated with Darby's name, so that the French and German churches became known as "Darbyists." By 1855 it had spread throughout French-speaking Switzerland, in which Darby reckoned some fifty congregations, the largest of which numbered two hundred persons. Most of these had been established within a few years of his first starting there. For a period, Darby wrote at that time, "there was no preaching without a conversion."[16] In France itself the progress was even more marked, and the assemblies of Darbyites spread across the whole southern part of the country to the Spanish border – "from Bâle to the Pyrenees, with a fairly large gap in the districts of which Toulouse forms the centre."[17] Readers of *Travels with a Donkey in the*

Cevennes will remember how R. L. Stevenson came across a Darbyite peasant in a remote French Department in 1878. There were many meetings also formed at that time in the Rhineland, with a strong movement in the northern part around the Ruhr (Darby was then, in 1855, in Elberfeld, now a part of the city of Wuppertal) and into Holland. In view of the common reputation of Darbyism, it ought to be emphasized that much of this expansion was by genuine evangelistic effort.

But there was another side to the work in Switzerland. In March 1840 Darby had been planning to return from Geneva to England, but he had travelled no farther than Lausanne, when, in his own words, he found himself suddenly arrested in his course.[18] Again, after an illness later in the same year, he attempted to leave, but again he was called back. To explain the sequel requires some understanding of Darby's own mood at this time.

Darby had arrived in Switzerland after a decade of continuous controversy with the established churches in England and Ireland. The controversies had developed in his mind distinctly idiosyncratic views, both concerning the Church, and concerning his own especial calling. He had developed, also, a mystical idea of the hidden workings of heresy. Some of these developments will be traced in more detail in a later chapter, but it is in point to add here that Darby seems to have had an almost physical revulsion from any form of teaching which he regarded as erroneous. To him error was something evil, directly involving the honour of the Godhead. This, combined with his conviction of an almost apostolic calling towards his fellow Christians, in what he then regarded emphatically as the last days of the dispensation*, betrayed him into an intensity of feeling and expression over any form of opposition to his own teachings, which is otherwise scarcely understandable in a man of such warm humanity and self-abandonment. Nothing else can explain, for example, the language which he used in Switzerland concerning the Wesleyan doctrine which he opposed, or, a little later, concerning the devoted François Olivier, the brother of his friend and disciple Henri.

In Switzerland, then, Darby came into contact with a movement, which, while not dissimilar from the movement he knew in England and Ireland, had become firmly established with its own convictions and traditions forged in the heat of persecution and repression. It was a movement, also, in that stage of development when the first enthusiasm is growing dim. Darby seems to have made no allowance for this new situation. To him, the Swiss dissenters, like those in Britain, were still part of the ruined Church – respect them as he might for their past sufferings and their principles. For their part, they welcomed with open arms this foreign teacher who seemed so whole-heartedly in accord with their aspirations.

Then came the pressing call in 1840 to stay in Lausanne to deal with

* For a justification of this, see p. 119.

difficulties there. To Darby, there seemed to be a reprehensible lack of concern on the part of responsible leaders in the city over the activities of a troublesome teacher, and he felt that the churches called out for pastoral care. So he settled in Lausanne, and the churches were grateful for his pacifying influence.

Once settled, Darby began regular teaching. He himself was at a critical stage of his development. Thoughts which had been developing for the past ten years, fed by the controversies with Anglicanism, and by the influence of Borlase and of Darby's other friends in Plymouth, now took definite shape as described later, in Chapter 8. For their part, the Swiss congregations awoke with a start to find teaching with revolutionary implications suddenly presented to them: teaching the more startling because it reached them in its developed state, without the long preparatory struggles which the English churches had known. A series of lectures in Geneva in 1840 was followed by a long and wordy dispute, in the course of which Darby developed his views in a series of pamphlets (some published for the first time, and some translations of earlier pamphlets) that are foundational to Darbyism. Both Established Church and Dissenters opposed his teachings: the Established Church by Professor J. J. Herzog of the Lausanne theological college, and the Dissenters by two veterans of the troubles of fifteen years before, Auguste Rochat of Rolle, the brother of Charles Rochat of Vevey, and François Olivier. Firmly, they contradicted Darby's views on the ruin of the Church. To Rochat Darby was respectful, to Olivier scarcely courteous. In September 1842 a meeting of ministering brethren from among the Dissenters met Darby and repudiated his teaching. Darby's behaviour at the meeting alienated many of his friends, while he for his part was indignant and ready to impute unworthy motives:

> In comparison with what was the case a year and a half ago, the awakening and the results are striking enough, but old Dissent on one side, and especially the old Dissenting ministers, whom the new awakening has laid aside, are jealous, and are bestirring themselves. We have no other difficulty, except this jealous spirit of the ministers. They have taken the ground solemnly in a conference lately, that the Church was not responsible for the condition in which it then was. I feel myself much more, or rather altogether apart, from all official connection with their system; as to individuals, I hope that love will be only the more easy in its exercise; but it appears to me a principle of rebellion against God.[19]

> They had what they called a *Conference Fraternelle*, to judge the expressions of my tracts . . . At the meeting which I had declined attending, but went afterwards, at the demand of many who were come from far, they admitted the ruined state of the Church, which they had denied hitherto, but denied our responsibility, saying that we were not answerable for the evil of our forefathers. I told the two I was most intimate with, that after that I could not go on with their *Dissidence* any longer, though I was in charity with all. I am much freer and happier since, and blessing is manifest.[20]

As, according to Neatby, Darby's replies to Rochat and Olivier made it clear "that it was of the Church as the company of the elect that Darby predicated the ruin,"[21] his own account of the controversy is misleading, to say the least. The ruin of the organized church structures might have been a doctrine which would have been acceptable to Rochat and Olivier: but Darby's doctrine, to quote Neatby again, "was at least startling."

Nevertheless, it is probable that the dispute did not lead immediately to open division in Vaud. The allusive style of Darby's letters makes it difficult to determine when he is referring to a new congregation, gathered as a result of his own teachings, and when he is referring to one of the existing congregations, or whether and to what extent he differentiated between the two. The probability is that separate congregations of Darby's supporters formed alongside the existing congregations of *L'Ancienne Dissidence*, without a definite breach. In Geneva, on the other hand, there had been an open breach (if the editor of his *Spiritual Songs* is not confused in his dating, it was for the second time). Darby was absent at this time, but was in touch with the congregation. Concerning 3rd March 1842, a member of the original congregation (which had moved in 1839 from Bourg-de-Four to la Pélisserie), wrote sadly:

> About sixty brothers and sisters suddenly broke off their brotherly fellowship with us, without any sort of previous warning.[22]

Yet even here, Darby seems to have refrained from taking sides, for he wrote in a letter of 11th April 1844:

> As to Geneva, it has been said to me, Will you judge and condemn those brethren who have separated themselves? and this has been put to me as a test. I have replied, that if I judged those who separated themselves, I must judge others also, and I did not pretend to do either the one or the other: that if I were at Geneva I should act according to my conscience, and should endeavour to walk individually in peace.[23]

It was probably an outbreak of violence from a new quarter which for a time prevented further disintegration. Darby left for London in 1843, arriving in the "vast and horrible town" (as he called it) at the beginning of August. He paid a further visit to France and Switzerland early in 1844, and after a year left again for Plymouth in March 1845 – a journey which, as we shall see later, was fateful for the movement. Shortly after he had gone, revolution broke out in Lausanne, and Jesuit-inspired riots of considerable violence were directed against the Darbyite and dissenting bodies.*

* Neatby suggests that Darby left because his life was in danger. Whether events had in fact reached such a dramatic point by the time Darby left Lausanne is uncertain: news of riots reached him *after* his return to England. It is plain that events in Plymouth played a considerable part in calling him back to England.

The dispute, nevertheless, left its scars, and when ten years later the aftermath of the breach in England reached the Continent, the Darbyist groups broke away to form their own tightly-organized body which has remained numerous to this day. They left behind them a group of assemblies which has also remained strong in Switzerland, contributing considerably to the missionary outreach of Open Brethren, and to its Continental development of later years. These assemblies have their own training centre at the Institut Emmaüs, Lausanne. Auguste Rochat died in 1847, before the breach was fully accomplished, but François Olivier continued a respected leader until his death in 1888. This group of churches can look back in its traditions to the gatherings of *L'Ancienne Dissidence** and to roots which antedate Darbyism and the movement in Britain.

* Ainsi donc, comme à Genève, les assemblées de frères dits "larges" dans le Canton de Vaud, le Canton de Neuchâtel et le Jura Bernois sont comme prolongation des assemblées qui constituaient *l'Ancienne Dissidence*." (Paul Perret, *Coup d'oeil sur l'Histoire et les Principes des frères appelés "Frères Larges"* – Institut Emmaüs, Lausanne – duplicated, undated, p. 21.)

Quotation References – Chapter 6.

1. *Letters,* Vol. I, p. 17 (letter from Ireland 30 April 1833).
2. *Interesting Reminiscences, etc.,* p. 21 (quoting from reminiscences of J. B. Stoney, dated 12th July 1871.)
3. *Letters,* Vol. I, p. 9 (letter from Granard, 15 October 1832).
4. Ibid., p. 13 (letter from Limerick 1832).
5. Ibid., p. 15 (letter of 1833).
6. Ibid., p. 18 (letter from Ireland 30 April 1833).
7. Ibid., *ad loc.*
8. Ibid., p. 23 (letter from Limerick, received in Plymouth 19 August 1833).
9. Ibid., p. 22 (same letter).
10. See *Søren Kierkegaard,* Johannes Hohlenberg (Engl. tr. 1954), pp. 232–75.
11. *Letters,* Vol. I, p. 64 (letter from London 3 August 1843).
11a. *Letters,* p. 147.
12. Ibid., Vol. III, p. 234 (letter from Hereford, "not before 1837").
13. Ibid., p. 230 (letter from Plymouth 10 August 1837).
14. *The Christian Witness,* Vol. IV, pp. 394–7.
15. *Letters,* Vol. I, p. 55 (letter from Lausanne, 21 January 1843).
16. Ibid., Vol. III, p. 294 (letter from Elberfeld, 1855).
17. Ibid., p. 303 (letter to Prof. Tholuck, 185–).
18. Ibid., Vol. I, p. 37 (letter from Lausanne, 23 March 1840).
19. Ibid., p. 53 (letter from Lausanne, 11 October 1842).
20. Ibid., pp. 54–55 (letter from Lausanne, 21 January 1843).
21. *History of the Plymouth Brethren,* p. 88.
22. Quoted *Coup d'oeil sur l'Histoire et les Principes des frères appelés "Frères Larges."* Paul Perret, Institut Emmaüs, Lausanne, undated, p. 15.
23. *Letters,* Vol. I, p. 74 (letter from St. Hippolyte du Fort, 11 April 1844).

CHAPTER 7

A PROVISIONAL ASSESSMENT
AND A LOOK BACKWARDS

> ... a continuing strain in Christianity which had been present from the
> very beginning and which before and since the Reformation has expressed
> itself in many forms ... There is that in the Christian Gospel which stirs the
> consciences of men to be ill content with anything short of full conformity
> with the ethical standards set forth in the teachings of Jesus and which
> awakens the hope and the faith that, seemingly impossible of attainment
> though they are, progress towards them can be made and that they must be
> sought in communities of those who have committed themselves fully to the
> Christian ideal.
>
> K. S. Latourette, *A History of Christianity* (on the Anabaptists).

IN 1863 HENRY SOLTAU, FORMERLY OF PLYMOUTH, ATTEMPTED
to give an account of the movement in which he had played a prominent part. He was inclined to the grandiloquent phrase, and opened his
lecture with a bold assertion:

> ... it has no parallel in the whole history of the Church of God, because in no
> other instance has the Word of God (freed from all tradition) been taken as the
> guide of those who have sought a revival in the Church of God.[1]

It was seventy years later that another brother published a book based
upon extensive study of British and Continental sources, many of which
were not available when Soltau spoke. By his *Pilgrim Church*, published
in 1931, E. H. Broadbent showed that the Brethren movement was one
event within a constant movement within Christianity: the element of
radical dissent and spirituality. An interest in earlier movements had
already been encouraged among Brethren in the previous century by
the writings and translations of Mrs. Frances Bevan, a talented lady belonging to the ex-Quaker group among them. Mrs. Bevan published
attractively written popular lives of several of the Continental reformers,
and had popularized the spirituality of the medieval Friends of God such
as Mechtild of Hellfde and Heinrich Suso, and of more modern mystics
as Paul Gerhardt, Gerhardt Tersteegen and others.

Broadbent, for his part, showed the kinship of the Brethren movement
with other movements dating from apostolic times, and in so doing
provided Brethrenism with an enthralling account of a continuous
spiritual heritage, and with a sense of continuity hardly less than that of the
episcopal churches. If he was inclined to minimize the eccentricities of
doctrine and behaviour which had occurred among many of the groups

whose stories he told, Broadbent could at least have pleaded that he was introducing a corrective bias to traditional views, and not before it was due. Indeed, a later exponent of a similar approach has openly pleaded this:

> ... the time seems to have come to reverse the derogatory treatment to which these Stepchildren of the Reformation have been traditionally subjected. One can speak very well of them indeed before he becomes guilty of a bias as pronounced as that of those who have so long spoken evil of them; one can let these Stepchildren play the role of the hero and he will be at least as near to historic truth as is the tradition that has so long assigned to them the role of the rogue.[2]

Yet Soltau's over-emphatic boast serves to emphasize that, if the early Brethren were treading in paths which had already been well worn by earlier radical spirits, they did so in ignorance of their predecessors. The movement was another spontaneous outbreak of a continuous element in Christianity which, to this day, is largely ignored by the more powerful spokesmen of Christian authoritarianism. It is doubtful whether any attempts to express Christian unity – least of all the amalgamations of diverse denominations – will succeed in avoiding the tyrannies of authoritarianism, until they have learned to recognize and give full play to this radical element within Christian belief. The centuries have shown that it will always assert itself, however it is repressed: and, indeed, it is from this element that, time and again, revivals of Christian life and spirituality have sprung. Oddly enough, Roman Catholicism, for all its depressing authoritarianism, has often succeeded in coming to terms with such radical movements within its own discipline far better than the established Protestant Churches – if only because Catholicism, in the last resort, if it does use the civil power for its own ends, does so as its master and will protect its own minorities; while traditional Protestantism often becomes the servant of the political world and the catspaw of its oppressive whims. Yet the Reformation itself is evidence enough of the ultimate failure of Roman Catholicism to face the deepest aspirations of radical reform.

The New Testament is often the inspiration of such radical movements. The more short-sighted among established leaders are often content to meet this fact today by sneering at "fundamentalism", but to do so is to miss the plain fact that, whatever opinions we may hold concerning the inspiration and authority of the Bible, the foundation documents of the Christian faith stand in blatant contrast to many of the most prominent later developments within the Christian Church. An established church which meets by repression men who try honestly to take account of this fact is simply creating secession, and is sowing the seeds of its own ultimate discomfiture. However blind the political state may be, there is a limit to the amount of denigration and ill-treatment of otherwise harmless (if eccentric) dissenters that public opinion will condone: ultimately the use of the secular arm will be refused in the support of mere ecclesiastical dignity.

For our present purposes we need not go back with Broadbent to the earlier centuries of the Christian Church, but can join the story of radical dissent with the teachings of John Wycliffe (*c.* 1330–1384). During a lifetime of involvement in secular affairs, Wycliffe developed a doctrine of authority and possessions which carried revolutionary implications. Wycliffe took up the doctrine that true dominion belonged only to those who enjoyed the grace of God, a doctrine which had earlier been used to support extreme papal claims, but he shifted its whole significance by giving a moral colouring to the definition of a "state of grace," in place of the sacramental definition which the papal claimants had used. To Wycliffe, "lordship could be possessed, along with God's other gifts, only by the righteous man, the man in a state of grace."[3] Wycliffe went further in undercutting sacramental claims. Despite a man's sacramental authorization, he taught, mortal sin could deprive him of his claim to exercise lordship or possess property. Moreover, Wycliffe denied the right of the clergy, and particularly of the orders, to hold possessions.

This doctrine, at first used for overtly political ends against papal demands, was applied to more directly spiritual ends after Wycliffe's withdrawal from public life in 1378, and during his few remaining years. Three basic doctrines came under review. The Church was defined, not as the organized body which men knew, whose limits were demarcated by its sacraments, but as "the predestined body of the elect": thus Christ alone was the Head of the Church, while the distinction between clergy and laity was broken down. "More comprehensively, Wycliffe put forward the primitive organization of the apostolic Church as the ideal for membership and behaviour."[4] Second, turning to the Lord's Supper, he rejected the doctrine of transubstantiation: "the determining factor to validate Christ's presence and reception in the Eucharist was the faith of the individual participant."[5] Third, the Scriptures became the final and only justification for any conclusion in matters of belief and life: this was the doctrine which lay behind his Bible translation work and his use of lay evangelists alongside the clergy.

Wycliffe's ideas seemed to have been suppressed with the Lollard movement after his death, but in fact they passed into two lasting channels. On the Continent, they were taken up and absorbed by the Bohemian Brethren and by other radical reformers; while in Britain they continued as a hidden ferment which was to burst into life after the break with Rome in the 1530s.

When Martin Luther posted his challenge to debate on the castle church door at Wittenberg on 31st October 1517, he could not have foreseen that Europe itself would be changed beyond recognition by the forces he had unleashed. Yet some of those who read the poster might have realized dimly that here was moving the spirit of a new age, and of questionings and challenges that would change the lives of all men.

Luther's challenge to the abuses of his day went deeper than he realized. Gross abuses had led him to rebel against the authority of centuries: and in doing so he appealed, as men will, to a yet higher authority. Luther, like Wycliffe before him, appealed from the Church and the Pope to an authority which neither could gainsay – the authority of the foundation documents of the faith. "My conscience is captive to the Word of God," he was to exclaim. "I cannot and I will not recant anything, for to go against conscience is neither right nor safe. God help me. Amen."

The Bible has been one of the great creative influences in the development of human thinking. Luther and those who followed him were appealing to an authority more dangerous and radical than they could have foreseen. In their different ways, both Luther and the Anglican theologians turned to the Bible to reform their doctrine; and in doing so they rediscovered the great source of the power of the Christian Gospel. Justification by faith, and the freedom of the human soul before its Maker, with no mediator other than Christ Himself: these were the basic doctrines which touched the innermost soul of every man. But the cutting edge of the New Testament examples was to be felt yet more deeply. As other men read the Bible, it was inevitable that they should look askance at the ritual and usages of the churches, and challenge the basis of their hierarchy and government.

So it was that another school of reformers arose, with the penetrating mind of John Calvin (1509–1564) to systematize their thought. The example of the early Church, as recorded in the New Testament, demanded in their view a reformation in the Church's polity and structure. The Presbyterian system of church government developed by them reverted to the twofold ministry of elder-"bishops" and deacons which they believed to be portrayed in the New Testament. The authority of the ministry was envisaged as something arising from the inner gift of God, and recognized and ratified by the consent of His people, rather than as something imposed from without by sacramental succession.

Both of these classes of reformers were united in their appeal to the secular power. The sheer political power of the papal system drove them to seek protection where it could be found, in those countries where the rising spirit of nationalism led men to chafe at the exactions of a foreign Pope. This in turn helped to shape their conceptions of the Church. The idea of the established national Church was one which appealed alike to the generous ideals of Christian men, and to those rulers who looked to the Protestantism of their subjects as a bulwark of national independence. From the ministrations of this Church all could benefit without distinction or favour, and within its shelter the Christian graces could flourish and purify the national life. The parallel with the national community of the Old Testament was close, and became a cardinal feature of the reformed doctrine of the Church. This Church, the people of God, they saw developing from the covenant with Abraham, the father of the faithful, carried through the days of the national Church of Israel, with its initiatory circumcision of its male infants, and now expanded by the new covenant in Christ to form the international new community of the Christian Church. The natural token of admission to this Church was the rite of infant baptism, for the promise remained, as in the days of the old covenant, "to you, and to your children."[6] It was a large and generous vision, and in days when Christian belief was almost universally acknowledged, a plausible doctrine.

Yet, plausible as the doctrine might be, a candid study of the New Testament indicated a tension even in this system. The Reformed Gospel stressed the New Testament experience of personal salvation, of personal faith and committal, as essential to true membership of Christ. Whatever the theory of the national Church, it was plain that many of the recipients of baptism as infants were not sharers of this essential experience. Indeed, they might be outright rejecters of the Faith itself. Accordingly, whatever their membership of the outward Church, they could not be deemed true members of the Church of Christ. To meet this difficulty, Protestant Christians developed a distinction between the "visible" Church and the "invisible" Church. The first was the Church of outward adherents, comprising those who professed the faith and their children – that is, those who had received baptism. The second was the true Church, known only to God, of the truly elect: the Church, in fact, of which Wycliffe had taught. This distinction was to pervade Protestant theology, although challenged in our day by so great an authority as Emil Brunner.[7]

It was soon apparent that the revolution inherent in the appeal to Scripture was not yet complete. Plausible though the theory of the national Church might be, and attractive as was its appeal to the whole sweep of Biblical history, it seemed to many that the Church which it conceived was something very different from the primitive Church of the New Testament. The primitive Church, far from partaking of the character of a national establishment, was often in open friction with the authorities. Instead, to many readers of the New Testament it seemed rather to be a body of men and women called out into a distinct and separate community. Such a conception harmonized with the individual experience of personal salvation, and carried with it more of the New Testament atmosphere of a communion of common life in Christ. It harmonized, too, with the suggestion that the old covenant itself had been narrower than many had assumed: that they were not all Israel who were of Israel,[8] and that the true Church was a faithful remnant within the nation.

Thus it was that a third class of reformers continued in a separate course from either Lutheran or Reformed Churches. For that very reason, they appealed to the more fiery and undisciplined spirits, and ran foul of the suspicions of the authorities. They included good men and fanatics, a host of disparate dissenting tendencies. Many of their ideas were inherited from Wycliffite influences. On the Continent, such tendencies found expression among the anabaptists and those who were popularly associated with them. Drawing their members largely from the humbler elements of society, these groups were maltreated by secular authorities, both Protestant and Catholic, and drew on themselves sufferings and persecutions unparalleled even in that cruel time. Many of their leaders were done to death at a very early age by the cruellest means available; while popular repute, tending as always to attribute fanaticism to those minorities who are in any way different from the common run of mankind, gladly classed them all with the lunatic fringe, and especially with the crazed extremists who for a brief period in 1534 turned Münster into a polygamous "New Israel." It is only in very recent years that historical research has begun to do justice to these, Verduin's "Stepchildren of the Reformation."*

In England this third tendency was more successful than abroad. The brief triumph of radical reform under Cromwell from 1649 to 1660, with its accompaniment of bitter dissension among the smaller and more extreme sects, ironically ensured by the reaction that it provoked that dissent itself should settle down to a more moderate course than was often the experience on the Continent. The Anglican Church, on the other hand, by accommodating much of the Calvinist theology in its articles, while retaining episcopal order and many of the older usages, took a middle course which was later to stamp religious tolerance on the whole of British theology. During its brief dalliance with Presbyterian ideals, Anglicanism also succeeded in giving to English-speaking Presbyterianism its classic statement of doctrine in the Westminster Confession of Faith (1646) and its two catechisms.

Nevertheless, even in this country the more radical reformers knew bitter hardship before a measure of liberty was given to them. They had not suffered the extremity of cruelty practised on the Continental anabaptists, or any repetition of the fires endured by all Protestants during Mary's reign (1553–1558), but, like Catholics on the other wing, several had been put to death for dissemination of their views during the latter half of the sixteenth century, and many more had been imprisoned under the worst conditions, so that not a few had died under their privations. The shadow of Roman political power lay over the land, and deviations to right or left were not to be tolerated by the authorities. Violent pamphleteering, such as the *Martin Marprelate* tracts of which the authorship was attributed to the unhappy John Penry, hanged as a result in 1593, served only to confirm the authorities in their views. Persecution continued until well into the following century, and instances of mutilation and other cruelties short of death were not infrequent.

* *The Reformers and Their Stepchildren*. British edition, The Paternoster Press 1965.

These English dissenters were influenced by the Continental radicals, but they took their origins from native influences. At the back of their actions there lay a deep dissatisfaction with the progress of reform, and a desire to return closer to the New Testament ideals. In the words of John Robinson at Delft Haven (1620):

> If God reveal anything to you by any other instrument of His, be as ready to receive it as ever you were to receive any truth by my ministry; for I am verily persuaded the Lord has more truth yet to break forth out of his holy word. For my part, I cannot sufficiently bewail the condition of the Reformed Churches, who are come to a period in religion, and will go at present no further than the instruments of their reformation. The Lutherans cannot be drawn to go beyond what Luther saw; whatever part of his will our good God has revealed to Calvin they will die rather than embrace it. And the Calvinists, you see, stick fast where they were left by that great man of God, who yet saw not all things.[9]

Harried by the authorities, or at best suffered to exist, they sought to meet in simple communities, sharing the common life which they had experienced in Christ. As they read the New Testament, they were conscious of a kinship with the communities of primitive times, which its pages portrayed. The early Christians had required no authority to meet together as churches of Christ, beyond that provided by their common love and the common attractive power of their one life in one Lord. Why then should these reformers require more?

In these circumstances another Protestant conception of church order developed – the independent or congregational concept of the "gathered church": that is, of a local community of believing men gathered into the fellowship of Christ. Its roots lay far back in the dim centuries which had preceded the Reformation: back, indeed, in the New Testament Church itself. Traditions of ancient communities, albeit some were heretical in doctrine (if the violent opponents who were their only chroniclers can be trusted), survived to indicate that there had always been Christians who had shared similar ideals, and the Waldensian Church of Italy remained as a living example.

> There have been those, indeed, who have asserted for them unbroken continuity from the Christians of the first century, a kind of apostolic succession different from that claimed by the Catholics. This, however, has not been incontestably proved. If continuity existed there was great diversity in its manifestations.[10]

Within these groups of independents, yet another reform soon showed itself. Many of them retained the practice of infant baptism; but with the rejection of the idea of the national Church, and the substitution of that of the gathered church, membership of which depended upon a personal confession of faith, many preconceptions which had coloured the reading of the Scriptures lost their force. Looking afresh at the New Testament explanations of the meaning of the rite of Christian baptism, some of the more radical reformers found that they pointed to the practice of believers' baptism: that is, of the baptism only of those who had made a responsible and voluntary confession of faith in Christ. It was true that New Testament examples of baptism were all concerned with first generation converts, and were silent on the position of the children of those converts: nevertheless, the New Testament evidence, taken afresh, appeared decidedly in favour of an understanding of baptism as a public expression of a personal commitment already undertaken, rather than as a prospective portrayal of a commitment which might never be made. Still less (apart from a few ambiguous verses) did it portray baptism as Catholics saw it, as a rite which itself conveyed some sacramental and quasi-magical change in the relationship of its subject to God: a change which in many of its subjects would later in life be evidenced by no obvious allegiance at all.

Those Independents who continued to practise the baptism of infants were to be the forerunners of modern Congregational Churches, while those who abandoned infant baptism for the baptism of believers developed into the modern Baptist Churches. On the Continent a similar development took place, the Baptist Churches there being named in some cases "anabaptists," or re-baptizers.

By the end of the seventeenth century, therefore, we find three conceptions of the Church, each firmly established in English religious life. Two of these existed among those who retained episcopacy as a mode of church government, and therefore remained within the Established Church. First, some retained the idea of a sacramental ministry, which derived its rights and authority from the apostolic succession of bishops: to them the Church existed as an entity apart from those who formed its members, a "mother" through whose sacraments her children received grace in mystic fashion. Secondly, there were others who retained the episcopal discipline, but sympathized with the conception of the national Church. To them, the Church was identical with the covenant people of God, and they looked back with assurance on the long history of God's dealings with His people throughout the Biblical record; a history of which the Church as they understood it was the true successor and inheritor.

Outside the Anglican communion were the dissenters, later to be known as the Free Churches. Among them, the Presbyterians retained the second concept of the covenant Church, and thus found much in common with the second of the two Anglican groups just mentioned. For a time, indeed, it had appeared possible that they could have been comprehended within the Anglican establishment together with some of the other dissenters; but the Act of Uniformity of 1662 ejected from their livings nearly two thousand clergy who had been unable to declare their wholehearted acceptance of everything contained in the Book of Common Prayer, and thus expelled them from the established Church. Ironically, this attempt to suppress Non-conformity probably had the effect of rendering it sufficiently strong to ensure its ultimate emancipation.[11]

The remaining dissenting bodies – the Independents and Baptists – held firmly to the third concept: that of the gathered church. To them also the Church was identical with the covenant people of God, but they could find no justification for that further identification with the national community which the Calvinist theology had made. The local church was a gathering to the name of Christ by those who by personal commitment were His. All such were members of the Universal Church of Christ, and a local church was a gathering of such believers, with a proper discipline and ordinances:

> Where the word of God is rightly preached, and the sacraments truly administered, according to Christ's institution, and the practice of the primitive Church; having discipline and government duly executed, by ministers or pastors of God's appointing and the Church's election, that is a true constituted church.[12]

Among Independents and some Baptists the church-hood of such a local congregation was expressed by the members taking a mutual covenant among themselves:

> The visible church is a visible communion of saints (that is) two, three or more saints joined together by covenant with God and themselves, freely to use all the holy things of God, according to the word, for their mutual edification and God's glory.[13]

Others among the Baptists (including, at a later stage of his life, the author of the extract just quoted) insisted upon believer's baptism in addition.

Those who held to the concept of the gathered church did not claim that there was an identity between the whole body of members of such local churches and the Church Universal. There were members even of such a local community who might be there insincerely, and thus were not members of the Universal Church. On the other hand, they recognized membership of the Universal Church in large numbers of Christians who were not members of any such local community. Thus they also had their distinction between the "visible", or professing, Church, and the "invisible", or true, Church: but it was a different conception from that which the reformed theologians had developed. Perhaps they would have avoided confusion by refraining from the use of the terms "visible" and "invisible", and limiting themselves to the distinction between the local and the Universal Church.

At first sight the conception of the gathered church seemed more restrictive than either of the other two conceptions. On further understanding, however, it becomes plain that it contains the seed of an ecumenicity to which neither of the other two conceptions can attain, although few of its early adherents recognized this. Neither a sacramentanor a national Church can give any account of those independent communities which have, throughout history, shown evident tokens of the genuine approval and blessing of God, and thus they fail to account for all the facts. The concept of the gathered community, on the other hand, is able to embrace every other form of Christian congregation. It asks only that Christians should meet together in formal association for the ministry of the Word of God and the observance of the sacraments of baptism and the Lord's Supper: where the blessing of God rests on such a congregation, there it recognizes a true church, whatever else in that congregation's arrangements or teachings may be disapproved. In its broadest application it must recognize the true church-hood of every congregation, of whatever denomination, in which the tokens of God's presence rest. Some few of the early Baptist congregations did recognize this: but it is part of the achievement of that element among the early Brethren which derived from Groves to have put this recognition into effect, even while other elements among them were rejecting every existing form of the Church. When unchurched by other systems, such men might have replied in words like this: "We claim no credentials, other than those which the earliest churches themselves claimed and possessed: the evident presence of the living Word of God in a community of His people. If thus enchurched by the living Lord Himself, we have no anxiety or care for any other recognition. Those same credentials we are glad to recognize in you, as we recognize them among ourselves; and we hold out a hand of fellowship and of brotherly love to every congregation in which the living Lord is evidently present." To those who have thought through the principle of the gathered church, the "problem" of intercommunion has ceased to exist.

This reformation in understanding of the nature of the Church inevitably touched ideas concerning its officers and ministry. The most distinct cleavage was again between those who retained a conception of ministry deriving from sacramental succession, the validity of which existed apart from the individual on whom it rested, and which bestowed upon its recipient a priesthood apart from that of the laity: and on the other hand those (both Anglican and dissenters) who adhered to the Protestant conception of the ministry. These last held that the right and duty to exercise any service within the Church derived from the gift that God had given to an individual. This gift the Church as a whole was called upon to acknowledge: but it bestowed on its possessor no status inherently different from that of other believers.

Again, these ideas went back to Wycliffe, and on this point both reformed and dissenting Churches were in agreement. The doctrine of the priesthood of all believers was an essential article of the Reformation, for the reformers had had too close an experience of the abuses to which a privileged priesthood could give rise to neglect this most explicit insight of the New Testament.* But the expression of this doctrine gave rise to a sharp division between the reformed and the dissenting Churches. To the reformed theologians, and particularly to the Presbyterians, the minister of a congregation was one of the group of elders, but if one among equals, he was distinctly the first among equals. The minister was the organ of the priesthood of the whole congregation.[14] This in turn led to the restriction of many functions to the minister, and particularly that of the administration of the Lord's Supper. Among early Independents and Baptists, however, practice differed. The presence of a recognized minister was by no means invariably considered essential: and where there was one minister, he was often in a secular occupation as well.[15] The holding of an extempore service of worship, at which any gifted brother might lead the worship, was known among them – if, indeed, it was not the common form of their worship.[16] The Baptists provided by the appointment of a district messenger for an office which extended to a group of churches: thus differing sharply from the strictly independent practice of their fellows among the Independents.

The rejection of the appointed ministry was carried yet further by another group, the Friends or Quakers, who arose from the teachings of George Fox (1624–1691). The Society of Friends developed a form of ministry, which derived from the individual's immediate personal experience of God, that Fox made the cornerstone of his theology, and which thus explicitly rejected the whole idea of a separate ministry.[17] Of this type of development we shall later have much to say. It is of interest, however, to note that modern Quakerism in America has established a wide system of pastoral leadership, and has reconciled this with the basic Quaker position.[18]

Such, then, was the position in England at the start of the eighteenth century. That century was, for many of the bodies which we have already considered, a period of declining vitality. It was the Age of Reason, and all forms of religious fervour were considered dangerous and degrading. Within the dissenting Churches Arian ideas gained ground steadily, developing into full unitarianism by the end of the century. The Presbyterian churches became almost entirely unitarian (the modern English Presbyterian Church is of separate origin, having been founded in 1876), and so did many of the General Baptists. The Independents and the Particular or Calvinist Baptists, however, remained for the most part orthodox in doctrine.

* See Rev. 1: 6 and 1 Peter 2: 5 and 9. Bishop J. B. Lightfoot writes: "Thus St Paul's language expresses the fundamental idea of the Christian Church, in which a universal priesthood has supplanted the exclusive ministrations of a select tribe or class." (On Phil. 2: 17, from *St. Paul's Epistle to the Philippians* (1908 edn.), p. 119.)

Within the Anglican Church, orthodoxy was maintained, but it was unemotional and wedded to pure reason. It was the age of Bishop Butler's *Analogy* (1736) and later of Paley's *Evidences* (1794). Still more ponderous in erudition were men such as Bishop Warburton, author of the massive *Divine Legation* (1738) which set out to prove the divine authority of Moses and of the Jewish religion and society, from the fact that Moses instituted both without any doctrine of a future state of reward or punishment. Warburton's argument ran that as a religion and society must have such a doctrine for their support, its absence from the Jewish dispensation was evidence of the divine Providence supporting that nation! To achieve this end, his work ran into six books, and is said to have ranged over an encyclopaedic area of human learning. It was not an age to find an easy kinship with the faith of the common man.

Into this atmosphere the Methodist revival was born, when John Wesley, listening to the Preface to Luther's *Commentary on Romans* being read in the evening of 24th May 1738, felt his heart "strangely warmed." Wesley and his associates did a second time for England what Luther had done for Europe, raising from obscurity those vital Gospel doctrines which could penetrate and transform the lives of men. Wesley, as is well known, remained a loyal member of the Church of England: but he was forced by circumstances into an act which made inevitable a breach between his Methodist societies and the Church of England, when in 1784 he himself appointed ministers in the societies in America for the administration of the sacraments. For some years before this he had recognized the validity of lay preachers among the societies, and the striking development of this system among the Methodists is a further interesting step in the direction of the theory of the ministry which was later to characterize Brethren.

From the impetus of Methodism sprang also the very different evangelical movement in the Church of England, which under Wilberforce was to transform English life in the space of a generation, between 1790 and 1820. Unlike Methodism, this movement penetrated the highest social circles of the land, and by sheer force of energy worked an unparalleled revolution in social manners. It is the influence of this movement that we can trace in many of the early members of the Brethren.

The turn of the eighteenth and nineteenth centuries was a period of turmoil. Politically, in the American and French Revolutions; economically, in the Industrial Revolution; in the arts, in the Romantic Movement; that process of change was beginning which has continued at accelerating pace ever since. In the Church, no less than outside it, the same influences were to be seen at work in Schleiermacher and Coleridge and the beginnings of German Biblical criticism, as also in the social and missionary thrusts of the evangelical revival. The fragmentation of parts of the Church into many little separating bodies, including among them some of the forerunners of Brethren whom we have already met in this book, was symptomatic both of radical dissatisfaction with the Church's structure, and also of reactionary disturbance over new thought.

The Brethren were children of this atmosphere, and inheritors of the happenings among their forebears. In many respects they were a reaction against the new tendencies: some of Groves's thinking, and certainly much of Newton's and Darby's, represented a retreat into the shelter of a spiritual monasticism from the adverse new winds which were blowing.*
Yet, paradoxically, the Brethren were in another sense in the forefront of radical reform. Their movement, crystallizing around leaders of personality and influence, gave focus to several of the tendencies which had been present in all the developments since Wycliffe. It brought together an insistence upon high standards of personal conduct and asceticism, with the direct appeal to the Scriptures over the head of all existing authority; the rejection of ministerial prerogatives with the freeing of the gifts of all members of the congregation (or, at least, of all male members – they were children of their day); and the concept of the Church as a fellowship and unity of all believers, to which outward forms were, as to its essence, irrelevant.

But, in saying all this, we have expressed only part of the story of the Brethren movement. There was another factor – a factor which gave it originality and character, and which was to bring it close to disaster. That factor was the extraordinary personality and genius of John Nelson Darby.

* On the other hand, Darby's own writings show that he kept himself well informed on current ideas.

Quotation References – Chapter 7.

1. *The Brethren, Who are They? What are their Doctrines?* H. W. Soltau (1863), pp. 6, 7.
2. *The Reformers and their Stepchildren*, L. Verduin (1964), from the postscript to the U.S.A. edition, p. 276.
3. *The Morning Star: Wycliffe and the Dawn of the Reformation*, G. H. W. Parker (1965), p. 25.
4. Ibid., p. 38.
5. Ibid., p. 41.
6. *Acts.* 2: 39. (R.S.V.)
7. *The Misunderstanding of the Church* (Engl. edn., 1952).
8. *Romans* 9: 6. (A.V.)
9. Quoted in *The Pilgrim Fathers*, Daniel Wilson (1851), p. 358.
10. *A History of Christianity*, K. S. Latourette (1954), p. 780.
11. *History of England*, G. M. Trevelyan (3rd edn., Oct. 1947 impn.), p. 450.
12. From the "Orthodox Confession of 1678." Quoted *The Gathered Community*, Walton (1946), p. 80.
13. From John Smyth, *Principles and Inferences concerning the Visible Church* (1607), quoted ibid., p. 81.
14. John Oman on "The Presbyterian Churches" from *Evangelical Christianity, Its History and Witness*, ed. W. B. Selbie (1911), p. 68.

15. *English Dissent Under the Early Hanoverians,* Duncan Coomer (1946), p. 23.
16. *The Gathered Community,* p. 135.
17. Edward Grubb on "The Society of Friends" from *Evangelical Christianity, Its History and Witness,* p. 188.
18. See "The Paradox of the Quaker Ministry," D. Elton Trueblood in *The Friends Quarterly* for April 1961, pp. 437–47.

CHAPTER 8

DOCTRINAL TURBULENCE

> THOUGH I have met with abundant individual kindness, and many dear children of God, yet I have not met the children of God dwelling together so much in unity, but have been a man of contentions rather. God is my witness whether I loved it or not.
>
> J. N. Darby, in a letter of 1832.

FRANCIS NEWMAN, AFTER HIS ABANDONMENT OF HIS EARLY evangelical faith, looked back with disillusion on "the Irish clergyman" who had for a time so dominated him:

In his after-course (which I may not indicate) this gentleman has everywhere displayed a wonderful power of bending other minds to his own, and even stamping upon them the tones of his voice and all sorts of slavish imitation. Over the general results of his action I have long deeply mourned, as blunting his natural tenderness and sacrificing his wisdom to the Letter, dwarfing men's understandings, contracting their hearts, crushing their moral sensibilities, and setting those at variance who ought to love.[1]

Another opponent wrote of Darby's arrival in Lausanne:

People spoke in glowing terms of the devotion of a man who, from love for Christ and for souls, had renounced almost the whole of his fine fortune; and who displayed in his whole conduct a simplicity and a frugality that recalled the primitive times of the Church. It was also said in his favour that, sacrificing the delights of family life, he spent his life in journeying from place to place to gain souls for the kingdom of God.[2]

After Darby's death, W. B. Neatby summed up the impression he had made:

Not often have men been called to mark the passing of a stranger or more complex personality. The saint of patient, tranquil contemplation, the theologian of deep, mystical insight, the apostle of tireless energy and total self-devotion, the ecclesiastic of restless ambition and stormy strifes – all were withdrawn from us in John Nelson Darby. . . . If Darby had occupied Abraham's position, he might have left behind him hardly less than Abraham's fame. It is easy to picture him dwelling in the land of promise as in a strange country, the contented heir of the promises of the world to come . . . But his lot denied him circumstances so favourable to the exercise of his virtues and to the repression of his one great vice, and cast him on the evil days of the turmoil of sects of the nineteenth century.[3]

There are few men of whom, nearly a century after their death, their disciples still speak with a devotion approaching awe, and whose writings they study with an appetite scarcely given to Holy Writ. Such a man was J. N. Darby. Because the story of his life inexorably emphasizes the disruptions which he brought about, it is the more important that we should also recall the immensity of Darby's positive character and achievements.

His energy was prodigious, and his gifts scarcely less so. When he died, he left behind him some fifteen hundred churches – in Britain and on the Continent, in North America and the West Indies, in New Zealand and Australia – who looked to him as their founder or their guide. His writings fill over forty ample volumes, and include comments and controversy over most of the great ecclesiastical events occurring during his long lifetime (1800–1882). In addition to a five volume *Synopsis of the Books of the Bible*, his individual commentaries cover the larger part of the Bible. His linguistic gifts were of no mean order, and he translated the whole Bible not only into English (a somewhat eccentric translation by reason of his odd style and excessive literalism, yet described by Weymouth as often giving a better literal rendering than the Revised Version itself[4]), but also into French and German, and the New Testament into Italian. His travels were world-wide, and, in a century when means of travel had vastly improved, must have greatly exceeded those of John Wesley in extent, and have equalled them in ardour. His hymns include much of profound insight, while "in his expository writings," wrote Neatby, "he often drops a half-hint that sets in strong light a passage that great commentators have left obscure."[5] His correspondence was enormous in volume, and always weighty in content.

Darby's English style was often slovenly, tortuous and obscure, and his thought was rarely systematized – "to analyse his position is often to refute it."[6] Yet few who have remarked on this trait have noticed the semi-hypnotic effect of his involved prose: an effect which has permeated the customary language and imagery of his most extreme followers until they have become almost incomprehensible to the uninitiated. Darby was essentially a mystic: he felt rather than thought his way through a problem. Indeed, he himself remarked of his own central doctrine of the ruin of the Church – "the theory came for me after the consciousness of it, and even now, the theory is but a small thing to my mind; it is the burden which one bears . . ."[7]

Allied to these gifts was a personality that could enslave by its sheer attractiveness. Winsome and deeply sympathetic, he could be of remarkable humility. On the one hand, those who were his social or intellectual equals, if they opposed him, often received from him treatment which remains a hideous stain on his memory: on the other, he had an instinctive sympathy with the poor and the weak. In his travels, he would seek out the humbler and more ignorant members of his flocks, and would prefer to stay with them rather than with the more affluent. With children he had an especial sympathy.

> In the act of addressing a meeting he would roll up his greatcoat as a pillow for a sleeping child whose uncomfortable attitude had struck him. I have heard that, on one of his numerous voyages, he might have been seen pacing the deck all night with a restless child in his arms, in order to afford the worn-out mother an opportunity of rest; and I doubt whether many children were more tenderly nursed that night.[8]

On another occasion a poor family in the United States, anxious to provide the best for their visitor, took one of their children's tame rabbits to provide a meal for him.

> Whilst the dinner was in process of serving, Mr. Darby noticed the little lad's downcast demeanour, inquired the reason; and the little fellow (contrary to previous instructions) blurted out the whole truth . . . Declining to eat any of the little fellow's pet, as soon as the meal was over Darby took him to where there was a large tank of water, and producing some mechanical toy ducks from his pocket . . . played with the little boy for an hour or so.[9]

It is said that in the early days at Plymouth, Darby went along to the barber's shop of a sick member of the church, and served there so far as he was able. On another occasion, an old woman, a candidate for admission to an assembly in Darby's fellowship, was interviewed first by two of its leaders, and then by Darby himself.

> She afterwards said that she had no doubt that the two were very clever and learned, but she could not understand them; and she could get on best with the simple old gentleman that came.[10]

Darby was in many respects as high a Tory as his background would indicate, yet his sympathies were by nature with the deprived, as a caustic comment on sabbatarian practices indicated:

> If in Parliament the proposition was made to shut up the London parks on Sunday (that is the foot-gates, leaving the carriage-gates perhaps open for the sick), I should have moved as an amendment (did I meddle with such things) to shut the carriage-gates, and open the foot ones; the rich could get out every day, and if sick could drive elsewhere. That a poor man, the one day he has with his family, should be able to breathe, is a delight.[11]

On another occasion (but not without ulterior motive, for he had been annoyed that some of his well-to-do acquaintances preferred his opponents in controversy) he wrote:

> Christ preferred the poor; ever since I have been converted so have I. Let those who like society better have it. If I ever get into it, and it has crossed my path in London, I return sick at heart. I go to the poor; I find the same evil nature as in the rich, but I find this difference: the rich, and those who keep their comforts and their society, judge and measure how much of Christ they can take and keep

without committing themselves; the poor, how much of Christ they can have to comfort them in their sorrows.[12]

Until the culminating crisis in 1848, it is this great and turbulent personality which we find, wherever we investigate Brethren history. Without understanding the driving forces of Darby's personality, we cannot understand, even today, the nature of many of the currents which run beneath the surface of the diverse expressions of the movement, whether those expressions are Darbyite or otherwise.

To understand them, we must go back some years to investigate more closely the formative events which pressed on Darby during the critical period which saw him moving away from the Established Church.

Many men in those days believed that the prophetic sections of the Bible were intended to provide a divine summary of future human history, from which it would be possible for the enlightened of later ages to draw firm information on the course of current historical events. It was not a new idea. Study of the prophetic Scriptures had in earlier centuries fascinated minds as diverse and gifted as those of the explorer Columbus, of Napier the mathematician, and of the great Sir Isaac Newton. Such studies had reached a point of great excitement in the years following the French Revolution, largely because, about a century before, several expositors had made prophecies on the basis of Biblical statements, which were taken to have foretold the French Revolution and its aftermath.* Earnest British preachers and teachers of many denominations were convinced that the world they knew was shortly to see dramatic and direct divine intervention, and several went so far as to date these happenings for the middle decades of the nineteenth century. Alongside such wild expectations, new ideas on the interpretation of the Biblical prophecies were abroad.

As a result of this ferment of excitement, various meetings were held for the study of prophecy. One series, held annually from 1826 to 1830 at the Albury, Surrey, home of the banker Henry Drummond, became the centre of wild speculation, and from them developed the pentecostalist movement of Irving's Catholic and Apostolic Church. It was this movement which swept Bulteel off his feet at Oxford, not long after his secession from the Church of England had received the support of Darby and of B. W. Newton. Darby wrote:

> What is poor — doing at Oxford? I love that man, much erred as I think he has. Oh, how little have we of the Spirit, to baffle the plans and devices and snares of Satan! The Church ought to be not only in possession of truth, but so possessed with the Spirit as, though tried, to baffle all his snares. . . . But the positive work

* For a full account of the predictions referred to in this paragraph see LeRoy E. Froom, *The Prophetic Faith of our Fathers* (1950), Vol. 2, pp. 642–730 and Vol. 3, pp. 338–409, 461–529 and 617–22. See also F. R. Coad, *Prophetic Developments, with particular reference to the early Brethren Movement* (1966), pp. 17–27.

of the enemy I do think most manifest at Irving's, but where was the energy to keep it out?[13]

Similar prophetic studies had been followed, on a more sober basis, by a group which was sponsored near Dublin by Lady Powerscourt and the Rector of Powerscourt, the Rev. Robert Daly, who later became Bishop of Cashel. After a year or two of meetings for study, three large conferences were held at Powerscourt in the years 1831 to 1833, to which leading Bible students from all over Britain were invited. The group who were forming the Brethren meeting in Dublin at that time were closely connected with these conferences, and Darby in particular took a very prominent part in them. It is of interest that the 1833 conference was attended by Darby and Bellett, by Newton and Hall from Plymouth, and (at the invitation of Craik's old sponsor John Synge) by Müller and Craik from Bristol. In addition, Henry Soltau, J. L. Harris, Sir Edward Denny, W. G. Rhind and G. V. Wigram have all been variously reported as present.

Darby threw himself wholeheartedly into this fervour of prophetic expectation and discussion. It was precisely the time when, on the one hand, he was going through his dramatic and painful conflict with the ecclesiastical authorities, and on the other he had established his deeply-felt ties with men of like mind in Plymouth. We can sense the pressures which were beginning to bear upon him and to develop in him those convictions concerning the apostasy of the professing Churches which we have already remarked. They were not the only pressures to which he was subject. It is said that at this time he was contemplating marriage to the widowed Lady Powerscourt: but that the engagement was broken off by mutual agreement when his commitment to a travelling ministry became obvious.

Then one of the Powerscourt conferences culminated in open dissension between the group sympathizing with the Brethren ideals, and those who remained with the regular Churches.* Lady Powerscourt was not able to use Powerscourt Castle after 1833 (apparently because her stepson, the

---

* In an account of the 1832 Conference (24–28 September), appearing in the Dublin *Christian Herald* and reproduced as a footnote to a letter of 15th October 1832 in the first volume of Darby's letters, there is a slight hint of dissension at that conference. Mrs. Hamilton Madden in her *Memoir of the Late Right Rev. Robert Daly* (1875) quotes from a speech by Daly (who presided at the conference) referring to differences of opinion and prospective divisions, and records from another correspondent a reference to Lady Powerscourt having spent most of a night in tears, at distress over what Daly must have felt (pp. 151–6). According to the notes of Miss Stoney (see Note 9 to Chap. 2) the dissension developed into open breach in the 1833 (23–27 September) Conference, which was chaired not by Daly but by a layman, John Synge, and as we have seen was "packed" with Brethren. Miss Stoney refers to Lady Powerscourt's distress, but Lady Powerscourt also joined the Brethren at Aungier Street (Mrs. Madden, op. cit., pp. 157–8).

heir to the title, had come of age), but she held later conferences in Dublin until her death in December 1836, and these seem to have been largely controlled by the Brethren.

These prophetic speculations merged with Darby's forebodings concerning the Established Church. He felt himself an instrument of God, burdened with an urgent call to His people to come out of associations doomed to judgment. In a letter of 1833, after referring to a Powerscourt meeting "which took a very marked and decided character, and where evil and good came into great conflict, the Lord holding the reins," he wrote:

> I feel as if I had lived two years since I came to Ireland, in the development of the Lord's work, and seeing that there is nothing, nothing else to live for. The Lord always gave me different work to do from what I lay out for myself almost, and puts me into positions I little seek. This meeting has done so here.[14]

This call to separation became the burden of Darby's ministry. But the pressures of those years affected his character deeply in other ways. As that character emerges from his contemporary letters, we see the shadow of approaching events. Darby was a prophet, with a prophet's characteristics. His approach to truth was subjective, and a matter of insight rather than logic. We have already quoted (p. 107) his own remark on the origins of his cardinal doctrine of the ruin of the Church. He felt that he possessed an insight into the trend of events before that trend was apparent to reason, and his letters are full of forebodings of dire events about to happen. In April 1833, he had written:

> I do feel that the ignorance and narrowness of the Church of England will be what will be judged for all this, and the judgment is at hand, lingereth not. The Lord have mercy on many in it – dear saints.[15]

Of Ireland, he wrote later in the same year:

> . . . there will be an entirely new state of things in a year or two. This country will, I doubt not, be practically separated from England, probably entirely.[16]

> That we are in the closing scene of revolution, moral as well as political, no person of any perception can doubt. Not closing as to judgment, *that* in God's own time; but closing in its principles – in its moral character – the ripening of the tares and wheat for harvest.[17]

So he wrote in the revised ending of his *On the Nature and Unity of the Church of Christ* in late 1833, and he added a little later:

> I have no doubt at all in saying that the present arrangements (ecclesiastical I mean) of the country, will not last a year, and that the result of the arrangements which will follow, will be to put the country under the direct dominion of Infidelity and Popery, and of the Pope or Primate of Rome *in the close*.[18]

Ten years later, it was the same:

> I am deeply convinced that it is a moment that the testimony is urgently

demanded in England, and I think that I must return to work here, that at least a testimony may be borne by the grace of God, before Puseyism possess the country, and whilst religious liberty remains to us, which I do not think will last too long.[19]

Yet, in some of his forebodings, there is that foreshortening of perspective which is characteristic of true prophetic insight.

Together with these forebodings, Darby early developed a theory of the workings of heresy which coloured his actions for the whole of his life. Heresy was to him a real and evil thing, working secretly and deviously beneath the surface, until it broke out in its full development, to the ruin of churches. On the other hand, he himself worked with total self-abandonment, not only as to physical comfort, but even in planning his very course of action, and he felt that he was personally and immediately over-ruled by God's leading. As we have seen, he had spoken of God continually putting him into positions which were different from those he sought.

> We must be the Lord's ministers if we were to beg our daily bread; at least, I feel so, but I equally feel how constantly we must wholly depend upon God's spirit, to guide and lead one in the path He has ordered for blessing . . .[20]

> I only await the signal to leave this, to be up in London. The Lord is working. I do not like leaving uncared for the sign of His hand; but I have learned enough of my own ways and to trust His, not to be anxious to anticipate His plans, nor to press beyond my measure.[21]

> . . . if I undertook to do such and such a thing, all that I have might fail me through the providence of God, or a more pressing need might present itself, and I, already bound, should fail, either as to the will of God or my engagements . . .[22]

> . . . I turn into a lodging alone tomorrow, knowing none here but those who now are almost all a weight, and that I have a sort of responsibility for drawing after me. But this is all well: it is my lot, and I bless God with all my soul for it too . . .[23]

The combination of these convictions brought with them dangers which became only too plain as events unfolded. Darby thought in terms of a direct personal call from God, and of a subtle hidden evil, constantly working against the task he had been given. There was a frightening absence of any sign of willingness to stand with the other man, and consciously to understand why he thought as he did. Darby was characterized by all the arrogance of the man who has no doubt of his own rightness. The corollary to his sense of divine leading, and his theory of the subtle workings of heresy in opposition to that leading, was that those who opposed him were the enemies of God: and he did not hesitate to say so plainly when the occasion arose, whether in the clergy in England and Ireland, the Wesleyanism of Lausanne, or the ministers of *L'Ancienne*

Dissidence in Vaud and Geneva. Did his sense of the hidden workings of heresy betray, as so often our fears do betray, something of which he was uneasy in himself? Certainly, his own actions in Lausanne, and later in Plymouth, closely resembled what he feared from others; and the theory is frighteningly mirrored in advice which he gave to a friend in Plymouth in 1834:

> As to work, I do trust the Lord is surely working there: as to the *Witness*, I think we ought to have something more of direct testimony as to the Lord's coming, and its bearing also on the state of the Church: ordinarily, it would not be well to have it so clear, as it frightens people. We must pursue it steadily; it works like leaven, and its fruit is by no means seen yet; I do not mean leaven as ill, but the thoughts are new, and people's minds work on them, and all the old habits are against their feelings – all the gain of situation, and every worldly motive; we must not be surprised at its effect being slow on the mass, the ordinary instruments of acting upon others having been trained in most opposite habits.[24]

It is startling that in 1845 he went straight from the storms which his own teaching had raised in Vaud to accuse Newton of a deliberate course of party-forming at Plymouth.

Yet, small as were his powers of self-analysis, Darby's personal counselling had about it something of those deeper insights into human nature which in a later day were to characterize the psycho-analyst.* His letters carried with them an apostolic style and fervour, until at times he wrote in the idiom of St. Paul. There was no pose in this: his mind was soaked in the wording of the Bible, and his whole life and personality were sunk in the work which lay at his hand.

> For me, the near coming of the Saviour, the gathering together of His own, and the sanctification and joy of those who are manifested, are always the thoughts predominant in my soul. There is every appearance that the Lord is hastening the time; for the rest, our duty is certain.[25]

Such a man cannot be accepted by objective standards. He must be taken on trust – and those who do so find themselves dominated by his immensity.

The characters of the other leading men of the movement stood in marked contrast to that of Darby. Groves shared Darby's devotion and something of his mystical insight, but there was with him nothing of Darby's harsh condemnation of all who opposed him. He had moved from Bagdad to India in 1833, writing:

> There are two or three objects in going, which I cannot detail, and feel it impossible to write about. One, however, very especial one, is to become united

* See, for example, his letter from Yverdon of 25th March 1843. (*Letters*, Vol. I, pp. 59–63.)

more truly in heart with all the missionary band there, and show that, notwith-standing all differences, we are one in Christ; sympathizing in their sorrows, and rejoicing in their prosperity.[26]

But Groves soon found himself involved in controversy which was not of his making. With the appointment of bishops in India, the Church Missionary Society had begun to insist upon episcopal ordination of Indian catechists, and this had led to differences with the German Lutheran missionaries working in connexion with the Society. Groves's attitude to this problem will easily be guessed. It was a fateful step, therefore, when in 1833 some Anglican friends invited him to intervene with the leading personality among the Germans, Rhenius of Tinnevelly (now Tirunelveli). He persuaded Rhenius to stay, but his sympathies were all with Rhenius, and as the controversy dragged its weary way for several years, Groves found himself blamed for accomplishing the very thing which he had been asked to do. He became the focus of unpleasant recriminations. Darby's reactions in such circumstances would have been plain. He would have denounced his opponents as enemies of the work of God, and within a few years would have established a chain of separatist congregations by the sheer force of his personality. Groves's own reactions are best por-trayed by extracts from his diary during this period.

Tell our dear friend Mr. E — that I have not forgotten his deep reproof. I trust it only came to strengthen what the Lord had done, and in this I had the reason given me. I cannot think on all the Lord's gentleness towards me without almost tears of thankfulness. I do so well know what it is to be corrected by Him in *measure*. If ever you needed to be proved and tried, what need have I had![27]

The chaplain has been up here, endeavouring to get things back again. He is a good man: he says, I have turned everything here upside down; but it was not I that did it, for I am as much surprised at the effect as he is. . . . I never felt so much the need of prayer, not only that I may not lead any wrong, seeing how kindly they receive me, and how willingly they listen, but that I may not even clothe truth in any other garment than the meekness and gentleness of Christ.[28]

I feel assured that all attempts to increase the *exclusive* spirit of the Church of England will do injury . . . I was told I was the greatest enemy the Church of England ever had in India, because no one could help loving my spirit, and thus the evil sank ten-fold deeper; but, indeed, I do not wish to injure, but to help her, by taking from her all her false confidences. . . . If I feel able, I go tomorrow to dine with the chaplain, with whom this controversy occurred. I believe he loves me. Whether I am weak or strong, alone or supported, I cannot give up the truth: it is that which has made me free, and by that I must, and, the Lord help-ing me, will stand.[29]

The chaplain is most kind in many respects: he says, "they cannot have too much of my spirit, or too little of my judgment."[30]

My first great object is to promote the publication of the testimony of Jesus, far

and near: and that which I feel to be of the next importance, is contending against
sectarianism in the East. . . . I do not object to anyone's enjoying the forms he
holds to be most scriptural, but I do absolutely object to his imposing his yoke on
the neck of his fellows.[31]

It is plain which of the two reactions would have had the most immediate
success: we may have a different opinion as to which would be the more
truly successful.

Müller and Craik were equally positive and much more practical.
Starting from a position that may, as a result of their convictions on
baptism, have been more exclusive than that which Darby then occupied,
their sympathies steadily broadened. Their pastoral work at Bristol concentrated on building up the churches under their care, and on working
for the relief of the needy people around them, and they spared little
time for the luxury of theological debate. They were glad to recognize
the kinship of all whose hearts were with them in their concern for the
work of God: the apocalyptic presages of disaster that loom so large in
Darby's thinking are absent from their work. Above all, in Müller and
Craik there was nothing of the mystical vagueness which blurred Darby's
teachings, and which was a fruitful source of confusion and misunderstandings in the face of the immediate practicalities of life. There can hardly
be a greater contrast than existed between the obscure half-suggestions of
Darby's writings, and the methodical and careful weighing of circumstances by which the Bristol pair dealt with each problem as it arose.

In Newton at Plymouth we find a different mind again. In some ways
his thinking was closer to Darby's, but in others he was even more sharply
contrasted. He shared much of Darby's sense of the apocalyptic, and his
attitude towards other Christians rapidly became more exclusive than that
of Darby himself: but Newton's mind was of the kind that is motivated
almost entirely by abstract principles. Little appears in Newton of that
warm-hearted impulsiveness and championing of the downtrodden,
which appears in Darby at his finest: but equally there is nothing in Newton of Darby's viciousness in debate. Newton was the austere scholar. His
thinking was clear and precise, and at the opposite pole from the stormy
chaos of Darby's mind.

The interaction of these different temperaments forms a vital part of the
history of the movement during the fifteen years which ended in 1848.

Groves had formed a deep regard for Darby when he had first met him
in Dublin years before: but he soon became conscious of the divergent
tendencies in their personalities. He wrote in 1833:

Mr. D. urged me years ago, not to preach on baptism, saying, I should thereby
become a sectarian; as well might our dear brother H. have been told not to
publish his tract against war, lest he should be identified with the Society of
Friends. Surely, if we are not free to follow all, where they follow Christ and His
will, we have only changed one kind of bondage for another. I do not think we

ought to propose to be modelled *unlike* every sect, but simply to be like Christ; let us neither seek nor fear a name. I wish rather to have from every sect what every sect may have from Christ.[32]

Although Groves was so far away from England, he was in constant touch with Plymouth and with other groups in England, and developments there began to distress him. In the following April he wrote:

Dear — 's letter, which left on my mind the impression of a Jehu-like zeal which neither pitied nor spared, led me to write the brief letter which will, I hope, accompany this: some wished to have copies of it, and therefore I had it printed. Surely it does become us, surrounded and eaten up with errors as we are, to touch those of our brother gently.[33]

The letter to which he referred was important as it threw into relief the divergency of view which was developing. He titled it *On the Principles of Union and Communion in the Church of Christ*, and set out at the beginning his leading principle: "to preserve the Christian alike from being chargeable with countenancing error on the one hand, or breaking the holy, heavenly bond of brotherly love on the other." He continued:

Then what are these principles of heavenly communion? *Loving all whom Christ loves* because they bear His impress; let this same rule then decide the question as to the subjects of our communion here on earth; all whom Christ loves, who bear His impress, or whom we ourselves acknowledge as Christians. Should we be asked how are these to be distinguished? we might hope the Holy Ghost will help us here; but at all events, not so much by agreement in those points which are the subjects of intellectual perception, as those which are embraced by a hearty and generous affection towards the Father for His love; towards the Son, for His unspeakable self-sacrificing humiliation; and to the Holy Spirit, for His aid and helps along our arduous, tottering course, till we are presented faultless before the Son of Man, at His appearing. Should it be asked what are to be done with errors? are they not to bar our communion? No; unless they bar Christ from the temple of the erring brother's heart. While we hope Christ lingers, let us linger; and rather be behind than before to quit, in pitiful remembrance of our own iniquities and unnumbered errors. So long as we judge Christ to be dwelling with a man, that is our warrant for receiving him; and for the charity of that judgment that declares Him not there, we are responsible.

From relations with individuals, he turned to relations with congregations:

The first duty to ourselves is in selecting the congregation with whom we should statedly worship; it should be where the form is most scriptural in our persuasion, and the ministrations most spiritual; where there is the sweetest savour of Christ; where our own souls are most edified; where the Lord is most manifestly present with those who minister and those who hear. This is what we owe the Lord, the Church of God, and our own souls. Considering, however, agreement in what we think best as to form of worship altogether secondary to heart-agreement in the mystery of Christ and of godliness. These, then, appear the principles that ought to govern our selection, as individuals, of the place where we statedly worship, since personally we cannot be with all. Yet as to our liberty in Christ to worship with any congregation under heaven where He manifests Himself to bless and to save, can there be in any Christian mind a doubt? If my Lord should say to me, in any congregation of the almost unnumbered sections of the Church, "What dost thou here?" I would reply, "Seeing Thou wert here to save and sanctify, I felt it safe to be with Thee." If He again said, as perhaps He may among most of us, "Didst thou not see abominations here, an admixture of that which was unscriptural, and in some points error, at least in your judgment?" my answer would be, "Yea, Lord, but I dared not call that place unholy where Thou wert present to bless, nor by refusing communion in worship reject those as unholy whom Thou hadst by Thy saving power evidently sanctified and set apart for Thine own." Our reason for rejecting the congregations of apostate bodies is, that Christ doth not manifest Himself among them in their public character, though He may save some individuals as brands plucked from the burning. To these churches we cry, standing on the outside, "Come out of her, my people; come out of her."

He concluded:

To the question, Are we not countenancing error by this plan? our answer is, that if we must appear to countenance error, or discountenance brotherly love, and the visible union of the Church of God, we prefer the former, hoping that our lives and our tongues may be allowed by the Lord so intelligibly to speak that at last our righteousness shall be allowed to appear . . . so long as Christ dwells in an individual, or walks in the midst of a congregation, blessing the ministrations to the conversion and edification of souls, we dare not denounce and formally withdraw from either, for fear of the awful sin of schism, of sin against Christ and His mystical body.[34]

Groves was maturing an outlook totally different from that which was developing at Plymouth at the same time. Both outlooks were agreed as to reception of individuals to their own congregations, and welcomed every Christian sound in faith and conduct: but papers which were appearing in *The Christian Witness* were eloquent of how differently the Plymouth leaders regarded the congregations of other churches. We have already quoted at some length both from Borlase and from Darby (pages 64f and 31ff). To Darby, both Establishment and Dissent had compromised irrevocably with "the world." In the amended edition of his *On the Nature and Unity of the Church of Christ*, written late in 1833 and appearing in the January 1834 issue, he wrote concerning both the Established and Dissenting Churches:

. . . does anybody doubt they are seeking worldly power as others to keep it? The path of the saints is most simple; their portion is heavenly; to be not of the world, as Christ is not of the world; to be clear from all their plans . . . If the saint knows *his* intrinsically, his path is very clear, to wit the spirit of separation from the world, through the knowledge of death, and power, and glory, and coming of the Lord Jesus Christ. . . . and hence growing *positive separation from them all*[35] [the italics are Darby's].

Shortly after, in reference to "the direct and undoubted title of Christians to meet together and break bread" he writes:

> it then ceases to be schism and is schism only from what is worldly, which is a Christian's duty.[36]

The words are echoed in Borlase's contention, contained in the title of his paper in the July 1834 issue, from which we have previously quoted at some length, "Separation from Apostacy not Schism." When national churches become churches of the nation, he contended, then they cease to be churches:

> For what is a Church – *the* Church of God? Scripture testifies of what it once was – a gathering together of believers upon the ground of *the common salvation* (for this was the simple bond of union which knit them together), and ordered by the power of the Holy Ghost. . . . To this corresponds the Church of England's own definition of the visible Church (often urged and as often disregarded), as "a congregation of *faithful* men, in which the pure word of God is preached," etc., a definition by which she utterly destroys her own title to be considered a Church . . .[37] (Borlase's italics)

In this Borlase had much in common with a long line of earlier reformers, but he rejected the possibility of any recovery.

> . . . a body which has become apostate, cannot restore itself, for the plain reason that the world *has* gained the majority. . . . For a Christian mind therefore, not taking for granted that things are as they should be, but judging by the plain truth of God, there is but one course, and that is to separate from the evil.[38]

Darby, with his High Church roots, shrank from the implications of secession, but found refuge in a verbal ploy. It was with reluctance that he used the term "church" in relation to the early congregations of Brethren.* Christians should meet together "not leaning upon ministry or assuming any thing, or pretending to set up churches, but simply (upon the ground that 'where two or three are gathered together, there is Christ in the midst of them,') as individuals, merely separating from present evil."[39] The suggestion must have seemed a distinction without a difference. It begged the question of what precisely constituted a local church,

---

* See his usages in his early letters. In May 1832, from Dublin, he refers to "the church here" (*Letters*, Vol. I, p. 4), but concerning Limerick, a year later, he writes, "a little church has been formed, or rather, body, like the one at Plymouth" (p. 15); on 30th April 1833 he writes, "I hear the north is dotted with little bodies, meeting as you do" (p. 17), but it is "the church at Limerick" (p. 18). In July 1834, "Bellett has just returned from visiting the churches or little bodies" (p. 26): to Geneva in 1837 or after, "a body assembled under the direction of the Lord, a church body" (Vol. III, p. 232). It is of interest that a resolution from the French Reformed Taizé community recommending the setting up of meetings "of Christians from all denominations who would try to go as far as possible in applying to themselves what is known from the Scriptures of the first Christian community in Jerusalem" (quoting Acts. 2: 42–46; 4: 32), uses precisely the same distinction, referring to these groups as "provisional communities." (*One in Christ*, 1967–2, p. 193.)

and Borlase's definition quoted on p. 65, that "a church consists not in rites and ceremonies, but 'where two or three are gathered together in His Name, there is He in the midst of them'," cut the ground from under Darby's feet. But Darby's view was not based on a mere quibble. As we shall see later, a local church could only, for him, be the sum total of believers in any locality, and it was therefore presumptuous for one congregation to claim that title. This definition itself raised yet more difficulties of definition, for what precisely constituted the locality? Anglican teachers could point to the parochial system, but Darby rejected that system violently in another paper, appearing in the July 1834 *Christian Witness*, entitled "Parochial Arrangement destructive of Order in the Church" (though he rejected its results, not its geography).

The *ad hoc* position which Darby envisaged was plainly an impossible position for a congregation to hold for any length of time. It is significant that at this time the question of the enduring position of his little bodies did not arise for Darby. His doctrine of the Church was built up under expectations of the imminent Advent of Christ which he dated on one occasion to 1842.[*] It may well be that this expectation is the key to the vagueness of his doctrine of the Church which many have noticed and pondered.

In the Plymouth teachers on the one hand and in Groves on the other, we have then two sharply contrasted positions. The Plymouth leaders gave a simple and easily-grasped call to separate from other churches: but their teaching suffered from two serious weaknesses. The first was that while it built upon a generalized and extreme image of existing church organizations, it overlooked the individual facts. It was easy for those early Plymouth leaders to show that existing church structures were not compatible with the Church depicted in the New Testament. It was easy also for them to lay their finger upon anomalies and corruptions within the historic churches. From that it was but a short step to the call to separate from apostasy, a word of frightening implications which they developed to the full. But, in the letter from which we have quoted, Groves laid his finger upon the weakness of this position. It ignored the fact that God *did* still work within those structures, and that men and women were still brought within them to a personal experience of God and to acknowledgement of the Lordship of Christ. So Groves's definition of apostasy was a

---

[*] According to a quotation from Darby's *Etudes sur l'Epitre aux Hébreux* (published in Switzerland), which appears on p. 142 of H. St. John's *Analysis of the Gospel of Mark*. In his *Studies on the Book of Daniel (Collected Writings*, Vol. V [Prophetic II], Morrish edn. p. 316) Darby disclaims date-fixing, but adds: "Some have indicated 1844, and some 1847; *I have made them myself in my time*. It is not, then, to blame others, that I say I do not think there is any basis for a true calculation." (My italics: it is with gratitude that I mention that my attention was drawn to this quotation by a moderate exclusive brother, who could have been forgiven for not wishing to produce it – F.R.C.)

very different one. For Groves, apostasy existed only when Christ Himself had withdrawn: "the apostate churches, where no souls are converted under the public ministrations,"[40] where "Christ doth not manifest Himself among them in their public character."[41]

The Plymouth conception was dogmatic and, ironically, attached determining importance to the very organizational structures which its exponents rejected. Groves also had rejected those structures – but his conception was pragmatic, and emphasized the immediate spiritual realities of the congregation.* Moreover, Groves's definition was capable of a salutary turn: it could be applied as rigorously to each of their own congregations as to any of those of the historic bodies.

This brings us to the second weakness of the Plymouth conception. It was essentially outward-looking, and could only lead to growing estrangement and hostility. Like all generalizations, it created a bogey in people's minds, which made them incapable of giving due weight to particular facts. To exhort Christians to separate from evil was excellent, until they took the outrageous step of attaching the word to matters of sincere conviction. To encourage men to believe that this separation could be achieved by a change in their church associations was to overlook the fact that not one of us can separate, ultimately, from the real roots of evil, for evil is within us. Again, Groves laid his finger on the spot. He wrote on 20th September 1834:

> I have been thinking to *whom* it was said, when they asked "shall we pluck up the tares? Let them grow together till the harvest, lest, while ye pluck up the tares, ye root up also the wheat with them." Surely the least this means is, "judge nothing before the time"; or, that we should be very wary in the exercise of this dangerous power, in which there is so much room for self-righteousness and pride, under the garb of zeal for what really may be the truth; but there may be a spirit of error, with much truth; and a spirit of truth, with much error. Besides, the Lord has said, "Vengeance belongeth unto me"; every kind and every degree of it. Some think this is sacrificing truth; but surely if you proclaim the truth, and condemn error by words of truth and by a life of truth, this would meet the precept, "ye should earnestly contend for the faith." Consider the Church at Jerusalem; consider the Church at Corinth, how much to be questioned, how much to be condemned, yet the Apostles *bore* with and reproved, but separated not. Indeed, the more my soul searches into this matter, the more I feel I cannot *formally* separate from, or *openly denounce* those, whom I do not feel are *separated* from Christ, and denounced by Him as His enemies. If I were to give up this principle, I know of none to guide me, but that which I have always seen fail, and which engenders a spirit more hurtful than could arise from a readiness to endure contradiction to your *own* views; this looks more like crucifixion of self, than casting out as *evil*, those who, with whatever faults, we cannot but believe are children of the kingdom.[42]

* Groves applied the same pragmatic test to Pentecostal claims that it was presumptuous to engage in Christian service without the prior reception of the "miraculous gifts" – *Memoir*, pp. 270, 313–14.

The two attitudes led directly to two distinct doctrines of the Church. Darby's conception left the definition of the Church vague, but it regarded all outward manifestations of the Church as corrupt and discarded. Whether or not the precise words "the ruin of the Church" had yet been used, the essence of the teaching was clearly present. In rejecting the outward, he could be left only with the idea of the purely spiritual, the "invisible" Church. Yet, paradoxically (and one despairs of ever finding a clear logical progression in Darby), he was later to reject that idea also (see p. 127 of this book).

Darby's teaching left a vacuum which could only be filled, at a later date, by his own bodies arrogating to themselves the position, if not the title, of the only valid churches (see p. 127 n.). It is significant that Wigram's suggestion of a centralized control of the congregations should have been made at about this time (see p. 76).

Groves, on the other hand, found his solution in the traditional "congregational" idea of the gathered church:* but he applied that idea in a startling new way. Borlase understood the idea, as most of the earlier dissenters would have understood it: in their hands it remained a separatist doctrine. Groves's use makes of it, when understood, an instrument of Christian unity. Groves rejected as vigorously as the Plymouth teachers the outward corruptions and anomalies of existing church systems, but to him those defects in denominational structure were irrelevant to the recognition of the spiritual realities of the individual congregations. If the true spirituality was there, then the outward forms were of secondary importance: there was a true church. Essentially, it was the conception of Ignatius: "Where Christ is, there is the Catholic Church;" and of Irenaeus: "*ubi Spiritus, ibi ecclesia.*"

That this became Groves's permanent position is plain from his widow's words after his death:

Though not himself connected with any society, he could not bear sweeping condemnations of religious institutions, believing they had answered important ends, and were, in many cases, owned of God. He looked on the Established Church as a system containing many and various congregations, some of which,

---

* Notice that it is the *congregations* of apostate bodies who are rejected (letter, p. 117 above). His full account of his "congregational" position is contained in the *Memoir*, pp. 441–2. In an article in the April 1840 *Christian Witness* (Vol. VII, pp. 127–41), which is apparently from Groves's pen, appear the words: "Now believing as we do, that the constitution of the family of God was a collection of several households of the faithful, all united by the bond of a common life to a common head – the Lord Jesus Christ," and the article goes on to extend this principle to the strategy of missions, believing that each individual church should send out its own missionaries, responsible to itself, in contrast to the contemporary organization of societies. These views were later taken up by James van Sommer of Hackney in the first issue of *The Missionary Reporter* (1853). The editor of *The Christian Witness* makes it plain that he approved of neither alternative, but regarded each missionary as directly responsible to God.

he owned, verged towards Popery; while in others, he rejoiced to feel, were many of a different character enjoying God's blessing and presence, both as regards the people and the minister. With such he felt quite at liberty, under certain circumstances, to unite in worship; and when asked why he had, at times, heard a faithful minister preach in the Establishment, which he himself had left, he often said, he felt it a *higher* and more important duty to own a true servant of God in the office that God had given him, for the edifying of His people, than to witness against forms which, it was well known, he had personally relinquished. He was also wont to say, "People must come to my house if they wish to know the kind of discipline I adopt in my own family. No one would make another responsible for the evils in a house, in which he was only a visitor."[43]

If Groves sensed the diverging views, so did the Plymouth group. In the April 1834 issue of *The Christian Witness* they printed extracts of correspondence from Groves, in which he spoke of his hopes for a restoration of the Church, but they prefaced it by a disclaimer:

It may be well to add, that as the extracts are made *verbatim* the thoughts are those of the writer, and as to any expectation of glory to be restored to the Church, it is to be considered solely his own.[44]

At the end of 1834, Groves returned to Europe to obtain new workers for his mission, arriving at the end of December. He visited many of the new congregations, and his widow described his reactions:

The year Mr. Groves spent at home was a chequered one. He had great sympathy and communion with the people of God in Bristol, and in the North of Devon, and thankfully ministered among them; and he visited, for a short time, the brethren at Plymouth. Here he found less comfort, feeling that their original bond of union in the truth as it is in Jesus, had been *changed* for a united testimony against all who differed from them. What this change amounted to in his mind may be gathered from a letter he wrote, on leaving England, to a brother whom he highly esteemed and loved, and who had formed one of their original number in Dublin, and had been mainly instrumental in organizing a meeting of a similar kind in Plymouth.[45]

The "brother whom he highly esteemed and loved" was, of course, Darby himself, and the letter is one of the most perceptive documents of the movement. It is reproduced in full in Appendix A of this book.

"I would infinitely rather bear with all their evils, than separate from their good." In these words, in his letter, Groves summarized his position: as Darby summarized his in the title of a pamphlet which was issued about this time: *Separation from evil God's principle of unity.* Which of them was answering the other may not now be clear: but the two slogans aptly crystallized the differences between them. Both of them used the term "evil" not in its normal sense, but in relation to theological opinions and ecclesiastical practices. Groves used it in this sense to make a point: but Darby used it with its full meaning. He seemed indeed to regard doctrinal evil as gross moral contamination – a notion which he passed to his successors, with frightening consequences. Francis Newman had already felt the edge of this attitude:

> Mysterious aspersions were made even against my moral character – I afterwards learned that some of those gentlemen esteemed boldness of thought "a lust of the mind," and as such, an immorality. This enables them to persuade themselves that they do not reject a "heretic" for a matter of *opinion*, but for that which they have a right to call *immoral*.[46]

The immediate effect of Groves's letter seems to have been nil. From India he watched developments in England with growing distaste, and (as friends whom he loved became victims of increasing intolerance) with indignation. In July 1837, after he had been in India again for a year, he wrote to a friend:

> You ask me to give you my opinion about separating from evil. I as fully admit as you can desire, that *in my own person*, it is my *bounden* duty to depart from *every* evil thing; but the judgment of *others*, and consequent separation from them, I am daily more satisfied is *not of God*. The blessing of God rests on those who are separated *by others* from their company, and it is a mark of apostasy to be of those who "separate themselves" from God's own redeemed ones; moreover, if ever there was a witness for God on earth, that witness was Jesus, and He never separated Himself from the synagogues; and this, if it proves nothing more, proves that *separation* is not the *only* way of witness, and yet He was emphatically "separate from sinners," not from their persons nor assemblies, but separate from their sins.[47]

He was turning the cry of "apostasy" back on those who had raised it. As differences developed within the group at Plymouth to the point of open conflict, Groves found himself less and less in sympathy with their intolerance. In 1845 he wrote to a friend in Teignmouth who was directly involved in the disputes arising at Plymouth:

> One point only is fixed on my mind; to receive all, as Christ receives them, to the glory of God the Father. . . . I am so glad to hear so pleasant an account of your brother's ministry; may he ever hate strifes, divisions, separations, and all those tendencies of the heart which make a brother an offender for a word.
>
> Instead of this being a day in which love "THINKETH NO EVIL," it seems to me a day in which man glories in paradoxes; shows how love, not only exists, but that it is an eminent proof of it, to think nothing good, but everything evil of a brother; to diminish nought but exaggerate everything; to call nothing by a gentle name, but to designate the most ordinary acts by the most vituperative appellations; and that "separation" is God's principle of *unity*. I am sure, as man now uses it, it is the devil's main spring of confusion.[48]

Finally, he struck at the very heart of Darby's system:

> D — seems justified in rejecting all such helps as the way of obtaining proper subordination in the assembly of God's saints, by saying the "Church is in ruins"; this is his *theory*; but neither in the *Word*, nor in my own experience or judgment do I realize that this state of the Church, even though it existed to the full extent he declares, was to be met by the overthrow of God's order, and the substitution

of one so exceedingly spiritual (if I may so use the term), as it seemed not good to the Holy Spirit to institute, when all things were comparatively in order.[49]

It was June 1847. Events were already in train which would finally separate the two men in their church fellowship. Distressing though the breach must have been to Groves, it may yet have brought with it a certain relief. "It is ten times better to have to do with those who are catholic in a sectarian system," he wrote of two Anglican missionaries later that year, "than those who are sectarian with no system. Dear good men! I do so love them ..."[50]

The comments on the "ruin of the Church" theory which Groves made in June 1847, and which we have just quoted, arose from certain practical results of that theory in the ordering of congregations. It is in the working out of those results that the main differences between Darby and his followers on the one hand, and the Bristol/Barnstaple group on the other, arose. Müller, Craik and Chapman were too occupied by their own work to be distracted by academic controversy, and by temperament they shunned it: but as they developed their church order from their reading of the New Testament, they inevitably set themselves on a course which diverged from that of Darby.

The differences were characteristic of their approach to Scripture. The Bristol/Barnstaple leaders deduced their principles from Scripture, and seemed able to do so with the minimum of pre-conception. Darby, for all his attempt to do the same, seems perpetually to be imposing on Scripture a pre-conceived system of interpretation.

At first Darby found their views to be much narrower than his own, as his letter quoted on p. 45 indicates. Müller later admitted:

> When I began, thirty-four years ago, as a young servant of Christ, to labour in this country in the Word, having just received certain blessed truths – as the coming of the Lord, etc. – my natural tendency was to look down upon those who did not see them. ... The mind of the young servant of Christ was to say, "Stand aloof!" – to esteem them as very little instructed. What was the result? Was it peace and joy in the Holy Ghost? Did I imitate Him Who bore with the ignorance of His disciples? No; it was anything but imitation of Jesus, and the result was anything but peace and joy in the Holy Ghost.[51]

Darby never adopted Baptist views, and to this day his more extreme followers practise a modified form of infant baptism. For Müller and Craik, on the other hand, believer's baptism soon became a cardinal point in their church practice. They had both been baptized as adult believers at some personal cost. In 1837 they took a step which was partially in Darby's direction, when, after long consideration and consultation with Robert Chapman, they ceased to make baptism a condition of fellowship at Bethesda. Their decision was based on II Thess. 3:6; the example of the apostles, in Müller's view, "would be an unsurmountable difficulty had not the truth been mingled with error for so long a time, so that it does not prove wilful disobedience if any one in our day should refuse to be baptized after believing."[52] This was the greatest extent of their move towards Darby's position, and would have permitted compromise agreement with him, as a later comment of his shows:

> While deeply convinced of it, and believing that I have the light of God thereupon, I would as much avoid being an anti-baptist as a baptist. I *really* desire the union of all Christians in the unity of the body of Christ. If any one has the conviction that he has not been baptized, I think he does very well in getting himself baptized. My desire is that we should be one, as we are one in Christ.[53]

Believer's baptism continued to be taught by Müller and Craik as the duty of all disciples, and it has continued to be a cardinal point in the doctrine of Open (or independent) Brethren.

Other developments at Bristol took them in an opposite direction from Darby. In 1838 Müller and Craik went into retreat for a fortnight to consider over prayer and the Scriptures certain matters of church order which had arisen at Bethesda. Their decisions are given at more length in Chapter 10, and for the moment we need only notice that they affirmed the need for a recognized eldership and for ordered government within the church. They were decisions which directly contradicted theories which were being developed by Darby.

In the earliest days of the Plymouth church, there had been a considerable measure of recognized authority, although its scope was contained within defined limits:

> ... it was considered to be right *to appoint an Elder* for preserving order in the assemblies. Liberty of ministry was recognized amongst those who possessed any ability from God; but it was considered that ministry which was not to profit – which did not commend itself to the consciences of others – ought to be repressed.
>
> The appointment of an Elder was peculiarly, I believe, in connexion with ministry in the assembly; at least, when appointed he was expected to exercise an especial oversight in that particular.[54]

Two tendencies in Darby's mind were, however, causing him to retreat even from this limited position, which had originally had his approval.

The first of these tendencies was a concern with the preaching and teaching functions within the church. In his emphasis upon the liberty of all who were gifted in this manner to take part in public worship, Darby tended to disapprove any formal recognition of these gifts, fearing that this might set aside a select band of ministers, and might also cause men to overlook the need for other gifts of pastoral government.

The second tendency was a symptom of Darby's revulsion from the structure of the church he had left. Outward forms – the recognition of rulers and ministers and all that went with it – were regarded by him only in their negative aspect, as restrictions upon the free movement of the

Spirit of God. Darby came to draw a distinction between the actions of men and the actions of the Spirit. The arranged and formal became equated with that which was "of man," and the spontaneous and informal with that which was "of the Spirit." The distinction was a false one, but under the pressures which bore upon Darby in his disputes with ecclesiastical authority it was understandable. Darby and his fellows took little account of the personal self-discipline and order which their own years of schooling within a formal structure had developed within them. In their own self-discipline they saw nothing of the results of the influence upon them of years of outward order, but only the fruits of a spontaneous grace of the Spirit.

At the same time Darby was developing his characteristic contrast between the "earthly" hopes of the Jewish Church, and the "heavenly" hopes of the Christian Church, and with it his views on the "ruined" nature of the Christian Church. These views caused him increasingly to devalue the importance of the formal recognition of elders. Darby reacted violently against the patent abuses of the doctrine of apostolic succession, but in doing so he tended also to reject any form of transmission of office. He also rejected firmly the dissenting alternative of election by the church as a whole.

> I do not reject conferred authority from God where it can be shewn in the grace of its exercise; derived authority from man I believe to be most evil, and to have apostasy in its character and principle.[55]

So it was that Darby reached his matured doctrine, at about the same time as Bethesda moved in precisely the opposite direction: indeed, it seems that the retreat by Müller and Craik to consider these matters was provoked by the influence of teachings coming from Darby's circle. In 1840, while in Switzerland, Darby included in his series of controversial pamphlets his booklet *Reflections on the Ruined Condition of the Church, and on the Efforts Making [sic] by Churchmen and Dissenters to Restore It to Its Primitive Order* (otherwise known as *On The Formation of Churches*), and this was also published in London in 1841 by the Brethren publisher D. Walther. It was written with the churches of *L'Ancienne Dissidence* in mind, and was repudiated at their conference of the following year (the pamphlet was written from Rolle, where Darby's chief opponent Auguste Rochat resided). It cannot have escaped notice, however, that its argument struck equally forcibly at Bristol and Barnstaple.

In this pamphlet Darby denied altogether the competence of Christians today to form churches after the model of the primitive churches.

> . . . the project of making Churches is really the hindrance in the way of the accomplishment of what all desire, namely the union of the saints in one body – first, because those who have attempted it, having gone beyond the power given them by the Spirit, the flesh has been fostered in them; – and, secondly, because

those who were wearied with the evil of national systems, thinking themselves under the necessity of choosing between such evil, and that which meets their view in the Dissenting Congregations, remain where they are standing, despairing of any thing better.[56]

He firmly repudiated familiar attempts to define the Church. The distinction between the visible and the invisible Church Darby saw as the unsatisfactory fruit of the Reformers' attempts to justify their subservience to the State, and their habit of regarding all subjects of a country with an Established Church as Christians, and he remarked caustically:

> To escape from this anomaly, believers have sought to shelter themselves under a distinction between a visible and an invisible church; but I read in scripture – "Ye are the light of the world." Of what use is an invisible light?[57]

To say that the true church is now invisible, Darby continued, is an admission of its apostasy and departure from its true condition. He was equally firm in his repudiation of the gathered church idea, for two reasons which go to the heart of his thinking. First, he declared, the state of things pictured in the New Testament has ceased to exist, and no authority or power is given by God to restore the failed economy. The church is in ruins, and to attempt to re-establish pure churches is an act of presumption. Second, the local church is a gathering of all believers in a locality (an idea which we have already encountered in discussing the Plymouth conceptions which Groves contested), and for any body which is comprised of less than that totality to claim the title of "church" is arrogant and presumptuous.*

So, Darby wrote in this pamphlet:

> Before I can accede to your pretensions I must see not only that the Church was such in the beginning, but, moreover, that it is according to God's will that it be restored to its primitive glory, now that man's sin has blurred over and turned aside from the glory, and, furthermore, that an union of "two or three" or two or three and twenty are entitled to take the name of the Church of God, when that Church was an assemblage of *all* believers.[58]

---

* When the early expectations of the Advent had been disappointed, and the Darbyite churches found it necessary to justify their more permanent existence, they faced the dilemma which Darby had placed before them in these arguments. The solution was the theory that their gatherings were not "churches" but that they "represented" or "expressed" the Church in any locality. Thus, at least in theory, every consistent Christian in that locality had the right to be present with them. For the same reason they rejected the idea of "membership" of a local congregation, for every Christian was both a member of the Universal Church, and (by that fact) of the potential local church. For a congregation to define its own membership on a more limited basis denied this truth, in their view.

Whatever the theoretical distinctions, the practical results have not been very different from those attending the arrogant claim to be the only valid local church in a given district – such as was later advanced by the "Needed Truth" offshoot of the non-Darbyite Brethren.

Those engaged in the project of making churches, he alleged, have their thoughts so engaged in their churches that they have almost lost sight of the Church.

> According to Scripture the whole assembly of the Churches here on earth comprise the Church, and the Church in any given place was no other than the regular association together of whatever formed part of the entire body of the Church, that is to say, of the complete body of Christ here on earth; and he who was not a member of the Church in the place in which he dwelt, was no member of Christ's Church at all, and he who says that I am not a member of God's Church at Rolle has no right to acknowledge me as being any member of God's Church at all. There was no idea of any such distinction between the little Churches of God in any given place, and the Church as a whole. Each one was of some church and therefore in the Church, but no one imagined himself to be in the Church, if he was not a member of some Church. The practice of making churches has alone led to the separation of the two things, and almost obliterated the idea of God's Church, by making churches in different places.[59]

We are struck again by the deep insights which lie within Darby's thought, and again by the utter impracticality of his development of that thought. His apparent failure to grasp the idea of the gathered church, and the almost mystical conception of a locality which he substituted (for by rejecting the parochial system he had destroyed any definite content in the word), are difficult to explain except on the premise that there was in his mind some deep block to acceptance of the dissenting position. His writings read as though he had to find reason to differ from the classical dissenting concepts, in order to denounce them.

Darby concluded his pamphlet with his standard suggestions, which were so inadequate for continuing congregations. The present dispensation was fallen, and any who tried to remedy this state had failed to grasp the Divine will. The promise of the presence of Christ whenever two or three were present in His name was still valid. Christians should avail themselves of this promise, and so meet to wait upon God, but no more. There was promise and power for such meetings, but none at all for those who sought to set up churches. To choose presidents or pastors is to organize a church, and even the appointment of elders is now impossible. The only government of the church was the acknowledgment of the Spirit of God.

The abuses and tragedies to which congregations might be subject when left thus with all practical suggestions specifically contradicted, and only a mystical conception of the Spirit's working to which to adhere, are obvious enough. Darby's teaching was diametrically opposed to all that was being done at Bristol and at Barnstaple. It is not surprising that Groves, with his personal links and sympathy of heart with both places, should have written in 1847:

For myself I would join no Church permanently that had not some constituted rule. I have seen enough of that plan, of every one doing what is right in his own eyes, and then calling it the Spirit's order, to feel assured it is a delusion.[60]

The differences between Groves and Plymouth over relations with other churches, and between the Barnstaple/Bristol leaders and Darby over matters of church order, were fundamental and of practical importance, but they did not come into direct conflict for years. It is characteristic of human nature that the strain should first have appeared publicly in another place, and over teachings which were, to say the least, esoteric. But at Plymouth, where these differences broke out, they occurred within a single church fellowship, and were aggravated by a clash of temperament and personality.

In major matters the leaders at Plymouth were in agreement against both Groves and Bristol. Newton and Darby shared similar convictions concerning the ruined condition of the professing Churches, and the "apostasy" (as they termed it) of the Christian dispensation. They were united in their call to Christians to separate from existing systems and to meet in simple gatherings. Both were united in the central place they gave to the apocalyptic Scriptures, and in making eschatological views the central point of their systems. Only in matters of church government would Newton later find himself nearer to Bristol than to Darby.

Yet, beneath this outward agreement there lay a deep difference of opinion, arising from their respective prophetic systems. The tragedy of Bulteel at Oxford had sealed for Newton (if, indeed, it was not its cause) a violent antipathy to Irvingism, and with Irvingism everything that was connected with it. Notably, this rejection included a feature of prophetic interpretation which Darby had adopted, the doctrine of "the secret rapture of the saints."

Many able students of their generation (including some of the early Tractarians) had moved away from the traditional interpretation of the book of Revelation, which considered that book to give a symbolic outline of the history of the Church.* These men had been repelled by the sensational and wild results of those traditional teachings, exemplified in much that we have already noted at Albury. For the traditional view of the Revelation, another was substituted. This view had first been suggested by the Jesuit Francesco Ribera in the sixteenth century, and had been popularized in the early years of the nineteenth century by the translation into English of the work of another Jesuit, Manuel Lacunza, who (under the pen-name of Ben-Ezra) had written a long treatise, *The Coming of the Messiah in Glory and Majesty*. This was the futurist view, according to which the Revelation, except for the first few chapters, predicts the events

---

* At this time, the more modern view of *Revelation*, which considers it in relation to its contemporary setting, was hardly thought of as an alternative.

of a closing few years of Divine judgment on the earth. Many of them believed this era to be imminent. It would be inaugurated by the appearance of Antichrist, a violent persecutor of the Church, and would be closed by the Second Advent of Christ, when He would appear in glory to destroy the oppressor and to establish the millennial reign of peace and righteousness.

Into this system both Darby and Irving had injected a further refinement, based upon a detailed attempt to reconcile the different parts of the New Testament which they considered to be relevant. In their view, the Second Advent would take place in two stages: first, there would be a quiet appearance – the "presence" – of Christ, when all true Christians, the true Church, would be removed from the earth. This was the "rapture of the saints." Only then, when the restraining presence of the Holy Spirit in His own people had been removed from the world scene, would Antichrist arise. His rule would be brought to an end by the second stage of the Advent – the public "appearing" of Christ in glory.

There was plainly a problem in this interpretation, and it was around this problem that the differences between Darby and Newton crystallized. If the Church were to be removed before the persecutions of Antichrist started, who then would be the faithful ones who would suffer at his hands? Newton's objection was a forcible one: if they were not of the Church, it was necessary to postulate another people of God, apart from the Church. Since, by his definition, the Church included all who were redeemed by Christ, this remnant must therefore be the fruits of a redemptive act of God other than the redemption through Christ. Thus, in Newton's view, the idea struck at the very heart of the orthodox doctrine of salvation, and was perilously near to postulating another Gospel and incurring the condemnation pronounced in Paul's letter to the Galatians.

This step Darby (in Newton's view) seemed willing to take. He distinguished sharply between the Old Testament economy and the New. In his view the faithful of the Old Testament were not comprised in the Church, and the two dispensations were utterly distinct. Following out this distinction, he taught that the faithful remnant of the tribulation under Antichrist would be, in effect, a restoration of the Old Testament economy: they would be a remnant of Jews remaining faithful to God in the fires of persecution. In the millennial reign of Christ, all the Old Testament promises to the Jewish people would have a literal fulfilment, while the Church, the "saints" of the dispensation of grace, would have no part in that "earthly" reign.* In contrast to these "earthly" hopes of the Jewish remnant, the promises to the Church were essentially "heavenly" in character.

* Hence the full irony of the misstatement in *The Oxford Dictionary of the Christian Church* (see p. 231 of this book).

To Newton, this teaching struck at the fundamentals of Christian doctrine. He considered that it implied two distinct schemes of salvation. When Darby's followers proceeded to develop the distinction between Jewish and Christian hopes, dividing the Scriptures of both Testaments between them, and making numerous deductions which fundamentally changed traditional interpretations and doctrines, Newton concluded that he was faced with a full-blown heresy. He was probably unjust, for it is doubtful whether Darby in fact drew the conclusions from his teachings that Newton drew: but they were each working with the quite different conceptions of the Church which resulted from their very different theological backgrounds.

As early as 1834, Newton had clashed with Darby by arranging a prophetic conference in Plymouth at the same time as Lady Powerscourt's Dublin conference of that year. (It is possible, indeed, that a similar step had been taken in 1832, but the evidence is uncertain.) By 1837 the differences were a matter of public comment, and even Groves in India knew of them, for he wrote on 10th October 1837:

> The dissensions among many dear children of God in England make one long for the Lord's coming; for if those who are confessedly walking in so much grace and singleness of eye cannot walk in "unity and love, and by bearing one another's burthens, fulfil the law of Christ," who can be expected to do it?[61]

We today may well wonder at the fierceness of those controversies. Their subject seems unreal, and the story seems only to illustrate the odd propensity of mankind for fighting its fiercest verbal battles over those things of which it knows least. The points at issue are speculative and at best incidental to Christianity. But the study of prophecy had brought those men to a closer study of the Scriptures than ever before, and the Scriptures had worked a revolution in their outlook. It was natural that they should believe that the agent of their introduction to the Scriptures was a more essential part of the Scriptures' message than in fact it was. Something of this was expressed by an anonymous writer in the July 1834 issue of *The Christian Witness*, who, in a paper entitled "Retrospect and Present State of Prophetic Enquiry," made it plain that the whole spectrum of Christian doctrine had been enlivened and renewed for him by his prophetic study.

Dissension began to gather around the editorial policy of *The Christian Witness*. Darby accused Newton (who was never its editor) of controlling it in the interests of his own teachings. The modern reader might not find it easy to trace the dispute in the papers which were published, without prior knowledge of the issues involved, but it is plain that from an early date Newton and others were pre-occupied with the difficulties into which they saw Darby's system to lead, and that they were attempting to develop the convictions concerning the differences of the dispensations, concerning the ruin and apostasy of the present age, and its pending judgment, all of which they shared with Darby, in ways which would preserve the basic orthodoxies of Reformed theology.

Thus, in a paper in October 1835 ("Letter to a Friend on the Study of Prophecy") we find the suggestion that "the present dispensation commenced, *as regards the earth*, at the flood,"[62] and that the Jewish era was the first part of this one dispensation. This cut across Darby's view, but the paper went on to attempt a reconciliation by adopting a modification of Darby's teaching on the rapture of the Church before the Tribulation. According to this modification, a remnant both of faithful Jews and of Gentiles would survive the Tribulation, while some would be caught up before it to heavenly glories.*

In a "Second Letter to a Friend on Prophecy" in the next issue (January 1836) the same writer enlarged on the millennial kingdom, and wrote, in a further specific contradiction of the cardinal point of Darby's system:

> Accordingly, the resurrection glory of the saints is as distinctly connected with Israel and Jerusalem, as with the earth.[63]

He found confirmation of the Church's earthly hopes not only in Luke 22:28–30, but also (a few pages later) in Rom. 8:19–22:

> Such then being the appointed relation of the saints to the earthly system in its millennial blessedness, we can well understand the words of the Apostle, when he says "that all creation, groaning and travailing in pain together, waiteth for the MANIFESTATION of the sons of God."[64]

Newton and his fellows continued into later issues this struggle to maintain the integrity of their classical Reformed position, which maintained the unity of God's dealings with mankind, insisting that redemption was accomplished by the work of Christ on the basis of the covenant of faith which went back to Abraham. Against this, they felt, Darby was building a completely new structure of Biblical interpretation.

Darby's paper on "The Apostasy of the Successive Dispensations" appeared in the October 1836 issue. In the form it took there, it could not have been particularly objectionable to Newton, and an article attributed to Newton himself, "On the Apostasy of the Present Dispensation," which appeared in January 1838, took very similar ground. In July 1838, however, another paper (also attributed to Newton) appeared, called

---

* Those familiar with this bypath of theological speculation will recognize how close this view comes to that school of thought which was later known as the "partial rapture" view. It would be interesting to know more definitely who was the author of the articles concerned. The present author's copies of *The Christian Witness* have been annotated in manuscript by an earlier owner – apparently a member of a well-known family among Exclusive Brethren – with the initials of the men he considered to be the writers of the papers published (in the original print they are anonymous throughout). It is fascinating to see that he attributes this paper to Newton himself. Elsewhere his annotations are normally reliable where they can be checked, although there seems to be at least one known incorrect attribution.

simply "The Dispensations." In it there was put forward a fully-worked-out reconciliation with orthodox Reformed theology. In Abraham

> we for the first time find ostensibly and manifestly introduced that method of elective grace, which alone secures the perpetuity of blessing, because it is "not of him that willeth nor of him that runneth, but of God that sheweth mercy." And hence the call of Abraham, . . . Here was sovereign grace calling, and sovereign grace giving and multiplying, and this is the character of all the branches of the covenant to Abraham. And therefore nothing that could arise from man, no subsequent arrangement even of God Himself could possibly annul it, so as to make the promise of none effect. This covenant therefore must be everlasting, and all that ever will be effectually blessed either in earth or in heaven, hang upon it as a covenant of promise. Upon this covenant the natural seed of Abraham, Israel according to the flesh is secretly sustained now.[65]

The writer distinguished four dispensations of the present era: but the key to his interpretation is that they are largely concurrent, not consecutive as in Darby's view.

> We have thus from Noah to the second coming of the Lord, four periods of distinct dispensation, of which three are continuing to exist together, and one has entirely passed away.
>
> The first of these comprehends the whole period from Noah to the second coming of the Lord. The dispensational arrangements of the first six verses of the ninth chapter of Genesis, still continue.
>
> The second is the Sinai dispensation, which was the seeking of the Abrahamic blessings in the Hagar way. And this terminated when our Lord pronounced desolation on Jerusalem.
>
> The third is the committal of power to the Gentile image; it commenced with Nebuchadnezzar, continues still, and will be terminated by the ten kingdoms and Antichrist.
>
> The fourth is the New Covenant dispensation, which has began [sic] to bring in the Abrahamic blessings in the Sarah way, for the Church as citizens of Jerusalem which is above, have even at present, the Sarah character of blessing, though not in earthly things. And this commenced with the preaching of the Apostles, after the Lord gave them the cup of the New Covenant or Testament (for the word is the same in the original) in His blood.[66]

A footnote explained at length that "both the Hagar and Sarah dispensations are of course only the results of God's giving blessing through Abraham; on the covenant with him, these and the millennial and all future dispensations hang."

The millennial reign was not to the writer, as it was to Darby, an era of national glory for Israel, from which the Church was entirely excluded. Israel would be restored, but restored under the same covenant of faith as the Church itself, and the glories of the millennial reign would be the heading up of all the dispensations in Christ.

> John had lived to see the commencing failure even of our Church dispensation,

and he prophesied to the Churches of it, that their candlesticks would be removed. But he was taken up into heaven, and there he saw the rainbow of the Noachic dispensation; the lordship of the Adamic dispensation; the glory of Israel which Ezekiel had seen removed from Jerusalem; the title to Church blessing as indicated by the Lamb's taking the book: he saw all these things centred in Him, and preserved by Him, who is the Lamb in the midst of the throne, hidden with God.

But when He is manifested, He will come with this power, and then all dispensations will manifestly centre in Him. And the power dispensed will not fail of its end, for the end of the Millennium is this – "He must reign till He hath put all enemies under His feet"; and then all will be brought back to God and subjected in blessing for ever to Him.[67]

The Church, he considered, would have been removed (after the Tribulation) by the coming of Christ, but the remnant of Jews in Jerusalem would be converted and blessed.

Restored Israel in Jerusalem, will in many respects resemble the Church now. Not indeed, in suffering, for that is a privilege possessed by the Church of the first-born distinctly. But as it is now said of the Church, that they are a chosen generation, a royal Priesthood; so it is written of Israel in that day, that they shall be a kingdom of priests and an Holy nation.[68]

The definite line of contrast which Darby drew between the "heavenly" hopes of the Church and the "earthly" hopes of Israel, was removed by this interpretation.* The lines of blessing were not distinct and parallel, but converging. The basic covenant was the same for each, the covenant of faith with Abraham, and the millennium was the foretaste of the culmination of all things: "an abiding earnest of all that final change in which all things will be made new."[69]

Why should this clash of interpretation on such recondite matters have led to open dispute? There is little doubt that Newton and his party forwarded their views by aggressive propaganda, and with all the vigour which characterizes those who are convinced of the rightness of their own case, but find that they must press it upon an audience that is not willing to listen. Yet, we are still entitled to ask, why did Darby for his part not recognize the deep concern that moved Newton? If Newton's tactics were objectionable, could Darby not recognize that his concern was genuinely for truth, and that Newton sincerely considered that his colleagues were in danger of subverting Christian doctrine? For Newton or one of his party had, as we have seen, come part way to meet him. Once again, that

* An article in the April 1838 issue, attributed to Darby, had stated: "There are two great subjects which occupy the sphere of millennial prophecy and testimony – The Church and its glory in Christ, and the Jews and their glory as a redeemed nation in Christ – the heavenly people and the earthly people. The habitation and scene of the glory of the one being the heavens; of the other, the earth." (*Christian Witness* for April 1838, p. 164.)

curious strain in Darby's make-up appears: his inability to stand in the place of the other man, and his assurance that anything which opposed his own work was *ipso facto* born of evil.

Another of those unaccountable blocks in Darby's thinking appears in this dispute. The teaching that the Jews would be restored was common to Darby and to Newton: yet the former could apparently visualize this only as something entirely distinct from the Church. Not only was Newton's view, that the restoration would be within the covenant of the Church, absent from Darby's writings: it is difficult, on reading his polemics, to believe that the thought ever occurred to him, even though his opponents specifically advanced it.

We have remarked that the writer of the article of October 1835 (was it indeed Newton himself?) had come a long way to meet Darby's position: even the secret rapture being included in his scheme. Only the supposition of a mental block can explain Darby's total failure to acknowledge that what was proposed was a strengthening, not a weakening, of his own system. Not only did it bring his teaching back into accord with the basic Reformed orthodoxies, without denying anything essential in it, but it also cured the dangerous Docetic tendencies that were latent in Darby's own vivid distinction between the exclusively earthly hopes of Israel and the exclusively heavenly hopes of the Church. It is significant that a tendency to Docetism has always been a serious flaw in Darbyite thinking.★

By 1841 Darby was wearied by fourteen years of incessant controversy with numerous different opponents. In that year it faced him again in what he had hoped was the virgin soil of Switzerland. The teachings which Newton was denouncing were those which Darby elaborated and polished in his series of Swiss pamphlets, and which also raised such an outcry in Vaud. At first, he was still inclined to shrug off the Plymouth dispute. He wrote from Lausanne in February 1841, and his letter was pacific, except for one sinister hint that his mind was already looking for the hidden heresy he always feared:

> The Lord can speak the word of peace; a little love will smooth all this trouble. I was not united with the brethren for exact opinions on such or such a point, but by the love of Jesus, though truth be precious; and the Holy Ghost is able to and in love will order this. . . . I doubt not that a little love will soothe the spirit of —, and irritation on any side is not of the grace of the Spirit of God. If it were

★ It is not intended to suggest, of course, that Darby himself taught the Docetist heresy – although the developments referred to on pp. 160 and 210 show how near some of his early followers came to it, while many have traced even more explicit tendencies in his later followers in the most extreme branch of Exclusive Brethren. Darby himself was too sound a theologian to have fallen into such an elementary error. See an interesting article by Professor F. F. Bruce tracing the history of these ideas in Brethrenism, *The Humanity of Jesus Christ* (Christian Brethren Research Fellowship *Journal* No. 24, September 1973).

a foundation truth for the soul, no peace could be held with error: mistake in the interpretation of Revelation, one may exercise much patience with. These things are always the sign of some other evil; but God will turn it to good. Perhaps knowledge has been too much attended to at Plymouth.[70]

Two years later he was concerned, but not alarmed:

The anxiety of dear —'s followers to propagate his views, seems to me the flesh. . . . But I have never combated it much. My mind has opened out to many wider views and details. I find many more classes of saints and glory in the Apocalypse than heretofore, though all blessed. It may be some will pass through, but I am more than ever confirmed that it is not presented to our faith, but the contrary, and that the faithful will be kept from it . . .[71]

Darby's letter suggests that if the opponents could have taken part in a real meeting of minds at this point, harmony could yet have been restored. Letters preserved in the Fry collection show that there was an attempt to reconcile differences.[72] Newton, in those letters, was courteous and clear, and tried to bring Darby to a reasoned discussion of the disputed doctrines: but Darby's was a mind impossible to bring to objective debate. Both Newton's reminiscences and Darby's own later account of their quarrel indicate only too plainly that by now the wall of mistrust had grown too high to be surmounted. Darby in his *Narrative of Facts* stated that after one meeting Newton had told him that all friendship was at an end between them, and that he was soothed only with great difficulty. One of Newton's letters seems to refer to a similar incident, and to apologize for it:

It was under this impression that I said "Do not let us for the future converse on prophetic and dispensational subjects" – not at all as implying separation from yourself, but simply in the desire that no additional pain might be added to what must be exquisitely painful to us both.[73]

Soon it became too late for reconciliation. In 1843, Newton published his *Thoughts on the Apocalypse*, and Darby publicly attacked it. Tragically and fatally Darby struck back at his opponents in their own kind:

And it is precisely on this point, much more clear than heretofore in my mind, that I feel that Plymouth has lost, or for the most part never has attained, the idea which seems to me essential to the Church – that is, which essentially distinguishes it in its privileges. I knew that the system which prevails there placed the Church on the same ground as Israel in the millennium, and it was one of the things which convinced me that the notion of the Church was *entirely wanting* . . . But my answer to your question, Has the church any spiritual things which it has not received through Israel? is – ALL *that is properly essential to it as the Church.* I admit the truth of what is stated at Plymouth. The evil is this, that all the higher part of truth is left out, and everything which expresses it *reduced* to this level. Does "To us a son is born, to us a king is given" satisfy the desires of your heart in your knowledge of Christ?

But union with a Saviour hid in God, the Son one with the Father Himself, so that we are one body with Him, of His flesh and of His bones, is of the essence of the Church: and I cannot see that this forms a part of Israel's privileges in the millennium . . . In a word, all that is distinctive to the Church is lost in this system, for that which is distinctive to it is not the subject of promise . . .[74]

Newton, to Darby, was depriving the Church of its glories in Christ. The simple thought that Newton's system did nothing of the kind, but that it rather added the glories of a redeemed Israel to the glories of the redeemed Church, seems never to have entered Darby's mind.

In the meantime, another cause of friction had grown at Plymouth. Darby, as we have already seen, had abandoned his original practices as to formal government within the Church. Plymouth, like Bristol, had in the face of the practical demands of the life of a very large church, developed its own marked structure of authority and discipline. In some ways it was at Plymouth a severe one. To Darby, as his thinking was now developing, it committed the worst of sins: it put the "rule of man" (and that man Darby's chief doctrinal opponent) in the place of the "rule of the Holy Spirit."

It was on this point that the storm broke.

Quotation References – Chapter 8.

1. *Phases of Faith*, pp. 33–34.
2. *History of the Plymouth Brethren*, W. B. Neatby, p. 78.
3. Ibid., pp. 308–9.
4. *The New Testament in Modern Speech* (1905 edn.), preface, p. xi.
5. Neatby, op. cit., p. 332.
6. Neatby, op. cit., p. 332.
7. *Letters*, Vol. I, p. 42 (letter of 8th October 1840).
8. Neatby, op. cit., p. 195.
9. *John Nelson Darby*, W. G. Turner (1944), p. 36.
10. Neatby, op. cit., p. 198.
11. Quoted Turner, op. cit., p. 37.
12. *Letters*, Vol. I, p. 205 (letter of 15 May 1852).
13. Ibid., p. 23 (letter of 19 August 1833).
14. Ibid., p. 16 (letter of 1833).
15. Ibid., p. 19 (letter of 30 April 1833).
16. Ibid., p. 23 (letter of 19 August 1833).
17. *The Christian Witness*, 1834, p. 27.
18. Ibid., p. 28.
19. *Letters*, Vol. I, p. 66 (letter of November 1843).
20. Ibid., p. 26 (letter of 24 July 1834).
21. Ibid., p. 30 (letter of 31 January 1839).
22. Ibid., p. 32 (letter of 22 November 1839).
23. Ibid., p. 37 (letter of 23 March 1840).
24. Ibid., pp. 25–26 (letter of 24 July 1834).
25. Ibid., pp. 31–32 (letter of 22 November 1839).
26. *Memoir*, p. 226.
27. Ibid., p. 251.
28. Ibid., p. 310.
29. Ibid., p. 314–15.
30. Ibid., p. 320.

31. Ibid., p. 321.
32. Ibid., p. 231.
33. Ibid., p. 287.
34. Ibid., the letter is reproduced in full in the Appendix, pp. 533–5.
35. *The Christian Witness*, 1834, p. 29.
36. Ibid., loc. cit.
37. Ibid., p. 339.
38. Ibid., pp. 339, 340.
39. Ibid., p. 29.
40. *Memoir*, p. 534.
41. Ibid., p. 535.
42. Ibid., pp. 339–40.
43. Ibid., pp. 36–37.
44. *The Christian Witness*, 1834, p. 196.
45. *Memoir*, pp. 356–7.
46. *Phases of Faith*, pp. 67–68 (including footnote).
47. *Memoir*, pp. 373–4.
48. Ibid., pp. 409–10.
49. Ibid., p. 412.
50. Ibid., p. 435.
51. From an address at Clifton, Oct. 1863. *Jehovah Magnified*, Geo. Müller (1876), pp. 28–29.
52. Quoted in *George Müller of Bristol*, A. T. Pierson, 6th edn. 1901, Appdx. L., p. 416.
53. *Letters*, Vol. I, p. 198 (letter of 12 September 1851).
54. *Three Letters*, S. P. Tregelles, pp. 6, 7.
55. *The Christian Witness*, 1835, p. 110 (from *Character of Office in the Present Dispensation*).
56. *Reflections on the Ruined Condition of the Church*, pp. 2, 3.
57. Ibid., p. 5.
58. Ibid., p. 9.
59. Ibid., pp. 9, 10.
60. *Memoir*, p. 420.
61. Ibid., p. 376.
62. *The Christian Witness*, 1835, p. 344.
63. Ibid., 1836, p. 45.
64. Ibid., p. 49.
65. Ibid., 1838, p. 290.
66. Ibid., p. 298.
67. Ibid., pp. 302–3.
68. Ibid., p. 306.
69. Ibid., p. 307.
70. *Letters*, Vol. I, pp. 45–46 (letter of 3 February 1841).
71. Ibid., p. 58 (letter of 1843).
72. *Fry MS book*, letters copied, pp. 320–8.
73. Ibid.
74. *Letters*, Vol. III, pp. 240–2 (letter of 14 November 1844). Note also the previous letter in this volume dated "1844."

CHAPTER 9

THE INEVITABLE HAPPENS

There's a great text in Galatians,
Once you trip on it, entails
Twenty-nine distinct damnations,
One sure, if another fails.
Robert Browning, *Soliloquy of the Spanish Cloister*

BRETHRENISM is the worst of all "isms," for it takes the sublimest truths and makes them the tools of party strife.

Frank Holmes, *Brother Indeed*

THERE IS LITTLE DOUBT THAT NEWTON'S CONTROL OF THE church at Ebrington Street, Plymouth, was severe and autocratic. Such was the character of the man who had written at the age of twenty-one from Oxford to his widowed mother that, if he were to spend the Long Vacation at his home, he must "stipulate for a few indulgences, of which the most important is *that the servants should be read to by me morning and evening*."[1]

Newton had been the precocious only son of a widowed mother, and his life had seen only brilliant and repeated successes. His autocracy was not reduced by the fact that that life had been one of deliberately chosen self-denial. Well before he was thirty he had become the leading figure out of many gifted figures in a very large and fast-growing congregation, in the building of which he had played a major part.

Yet there was another side to his autocracy, of which little notice has been taken. The Plymouth church soon numbered nearly seven hundred persons, and its building at Ebrington Street could hold several hundred more hearers. This church adopted the new principles of freedom for every gifted man to exercise his talents of preaching and teaching. That a strict control of participants was essential if proceedings were not to degenerate into chaos was obvious, and the firm control of Newton's strong personality must have been an essential element in its success. Tregelles, in his account of the Plymouth troubles, pertinently remarks that Darby himself at first recognized this fact:

> . . . and to this end it was considered to be right *to appoint an Elder* for preserving order in the assemblies. Liberty of ministry was recognized amongst those who possessed any ability from God; but it was considered that ministry which was not to profit – which did not commend itself to the consciences of others – ought to be repressed.[2]

Tregelles added in a footnote:

> Mr. J. N. Darby requested Mr. Newton to sit where he could conveniently take
> the oversight of ministry, and that he would hinder that which was manifestly
> unprofitable and unedifying.[3]

If Newton was later to interpret his position narrowly, Darby for his
part amended his views in a contrary direction. After a time he began to
oppose Newton's actions with vigour, reasoning that Newton's strict
control of proceedings was usurping the prerogative of the Holy Spirit
within the church. This reasoning was symptomatic of a radical development in Darby's own views, both as to the nature and distribution of gift,
and as to the mode of the Spirit's working.

We may trace this development of Darby's thinking back to his bitter
experiences within the episcopal churches from 1827 to 1835. It was the
reverse side of that coin whose obverse had been the writing of *The Notion
of a Clergyman Dispensationally the Sin Against the Holy Ghost*. Darby
became bitterly and emotionally anti-clerical, and his Swiss experiences
sealed his views. In relation to events there, he wrote in April 1844:

> ... you must be a very slight observer of the hand and of the ways of God, not to
> see that there are, although the flesh may mix with it, two principles which are in
> conflict, and that those who like clericalism, have done all that they could to put
> into bad odour the principles of those who do not believe this clericalism to be of
> God. I have seen the fruits in those who have subjected themselves to this yoke,
> and in those who have not, and I cannot say that the result has weakened my con-
> victions.[4]

In the same year another long letter made direct reference to the prophetic views being expounded at Plymouth: the church there (he feared)
was departing from the truth, yet Darby consoled himself:

> My soul is in singular peace as to all this, though not without grave and serious
> thoughts; for we are in serious times. I trust my love is not diminished but
> increased, but I feel more and more the Lord's servant, and so of the brethren.
> He that is nearest to Christ will best serve Him, and there is no serving Him
> without it. The principle of anticlericalism is making way in and through all
> that is active for the truth, even where there is notable opposition to them that
> have been in testimony to it.[5]

The admission of anticlericalism was specific enough, as was the fore-
warning of the line that the attack on Newton would take.

Nevertheless, Darby may never have taken up this cudgel, if he had not
been first irritated beyond endurance by persistent attacks from Plymouth
on his doctrinal system. For nearly twenty years Darby had been the
centre of continuous controversy: from the events of 1827 in Dublin, on
through the further disputes at Oxford, then with Whately, then at
Powerscourt and at Westport – and finally in Geneva and Lausanne. He

was frayed in temper by controversy, and wearied in body by constant travelling and super-human exertions.

> . . . for these seventeen years I have had to undergo the consequences, painful and trying to my heart, of the convictions and of the faith that God Himself has wrought in my heart by His word.[6]

Now, from the most brilliant of Brethren churches itself came the same story of opposition. Darby was never a man to brook opposition lightly – and events by now had made him dangerously unbalanced. But, oh, if only those two great men could have dared to face the possibility that they themselves might be wrong!

The brushwood was piled, and the striking of a match would set it violently ablaze.

The church at Plymouth was at peace. Darby admitted as much in his *Narrative of Facts* (though the circumstance was characteristically turned against his opponent by a taunt: "When they make a solitude around them, they call it peace"). There had been irritation in several places against Newton for his continual raising of the alarm over Darby's teachings; but a visit by the judicious Henry Craik to Plymouth had helped to calm Newton himself. Craik was far from sharing Newton's pugnacity, but his quiet and clear, scholarly mind, and the moderate Calvinist background of his education, would have made him, of all the early leaders, the one to whom Newton would listen with respect. Newton was later to write to Harris:

> I believe it was a happy period in Plymouth. There was much unity of judgment among the brethren who were engaged in teaching here, and a unity that the like could not be shown anywhere else among those similarly engaged, and brethren elsewhere began to look upon Plymouth with more confidence. Craik's visit was an evidence of this. It was at this moment Mr. Darby came.[7]

This calm struck one young man who joined the church in 1843. W. H. Cole was conscious in it only of the simplicity of his first love:

> I breathed what appeared to me the pure element of love; I was in the enjoyment of the liberty of home; I was enlightened by its teachings, cheered by its joys, comforted by its hallowed fellowship, strengthened by godly companionship, and encouraged by those who were over me in the Lord. Those were delightful times, so sweet for their simplicity. The fruits of the Spirit (Galatians 5: 22) were in evidence. Whatever undercurrents were at work they threw nothing to the surface.[8]

Early in 1845, Darby wrote to Harris in Plymouth. He had long regarded Harris, who was fourteen years older than Newton, and Newton's intellectual equal, as the restraining influence on the tendencies he deplored. But, this time, Harris in his reply firmly but temperately resisted Darby's charges. Darby felt his own supporters to be prevaricating. To a correspondent in 1844 he had written:

> Lately I have received more than one letter speaking to me of the propagation of Plymouth views, one adding that you had yielded.[9]

Harris's letter had, however, suggested a visit by Darby to Plymouth, and Darby immediately availed himself of that suggestion, feeling (in his own words), "that conflict and trial awaited me, though I knew not what.[10]

In March 1845 he arrived in Plymouth, and immediately started his own teaching sessions, attacking Newton's doctrines (and, it would seem, Newton himself). Newton had received Darby coldly, and this new development alarmed him. On 30th March Newton wrote to his fellow-elders, Harris, Soltau and Batten. After referring to their unity of feeling for some time past, he asked for their decisive intervention with Darby:

> I do not ask you to act ungraciously. I do not wish you to discredit his gifts, but I do entreat you to express openly and unequivocally your united disapproval of the course which he has thought fit to pursue. It might be for his incalculable advantage personally – and for the welfare of the saints thro' the kingdom.

Then, after setting out a summary of the "strange system of dispensational doctrines" which, he alleged, Darby was teaching, he concluded:

> If Mr Darby is once permitted to establish himself in the place he wishes, you will not only find the supremacy of one mind – that were comparatively a little evil – but the supremacy of a mind that has wandered from the orthodox truth of God and has ceased to be in subjection to His Word.[11]*

Harris and Batten saw Darby, and apparently were satisfied by him that he had no antagonistic intentions. The result was a letter from Newton to Darby on 1st April, apologizing for having assumed that such was Darby's purpose.

This innocent letter struck the match. The tone of Darby's reply was plainly the product of long-suppressed emotion. Picking up Newton's use of the words "antagonistic position" and "us," he brought out his long-nurtured accusation. Newton had "acted very badly towards many beloved brethren and in the sight of God."[12] Darby laid stress only on this point: in the letter he dismissed their doctrinal differences as "comparatively immaterial."

Darby's tactics were disingenuous. He must have realized that it was alarm at the doctrinal differences which was the root cause of Newton's obstreperousness. If he had wished deliberately to demolish Newton, he could not have planned his attack more skilfully, as the sequel was to show. By avoiding a contest on the doctrinal grounds (where he was undoubtedly weak, and where his own involved arguments were no

---

* It is significant of the impermeability of mind of the two contestants that Darby in his *Narrative of Facts* made an almost identical point concerning Newton!

match for Newton's incisive intellect), and by concentrating on Newton's practices towards others, Darby was choosing his opponent's weakest spot, and the one point on which he might isolate him from his colleagues.

Five more letters followed in quick succession. Newton was indignant but courteous, Darby too characteristically ready to score points. Newton asked for names and circumstances to substantiate the charge: Darby replied that he would give them "whenever the brethren who have been interested required it," or if Newton demanded it of them. Newton replied that Darby, in effect, wished him to assemble a meeting in order that Darby might accuse him before it, and he insisted on his Scriptural right to hear the charges himself alone. Darby replied that he charged him with "a systematic effort to form a sect and the discrediting and denouncing those who do not adopt the opinions which form its base." This, replied Newton, was a new charge, and it implied that others were involved. He would lay the letter before his colleagues and they would act together.

The result was that Newton and Darby met before thirteen other men. It was an unequal confrontation between Darby, hardened by long years of controversy, and his much younger opponent, who had always had things his own way. Fatally, Newton lost his self-control, and declared heatedly (according to Darby's account) "that he did seek to make a focus of Plymouth, and that his object was to have union in testimony there against the other brethren (that is, as explained and is evident, their teaching), and that he trusted to have at least Devonshire and Somersetshire under his influence for the purpose; and that it was not the first time that I had thwarted and spoiled his plans."[13]

In all these events Darby persisted in his disingenuous tactics. He deliberately made light of those doctrinal differences which were the cause of Newton's obsession, and by brushing them on one side prevented their being brought into the light of reasoned discussion. Instead, he concentrated on actions of Newton's which were the result of Newton's doctrinal anxiety, for Newton genuinely believed that Darby's teachings were disruptive of foundational Christian doctrine.

Newton's loss of self-control proved to be disastrous. From that time his own colleagues, and more particularly Harris, began to lose confidence in him. Newton, for his part, refused to move from his position of extreme antagonism to Darby's teachings, while Darby, with his theory of the secret workings of heresy, seized upon the clue his mind was instinctively seeking. He thought that he now detected the "evil" at work in Plymouth. For the moment, however, he bided his time, writing to a friend after the meeting:

My mind did pass through the same process of anxiety as that of which you speak, as far as anxiety went; a qualm crossing my mind that some work of the enemy, more thorough than I knew how to judge of, was at the bottom.[14]

The effect on the church was tragic. Tregelles later wrote:

> I was myself at Plymouth for the first nine or ten weeks of 1845; during this
> time I was in frequent intercourse with Mr. J. L. Harris, and he appeared to be
> particularly happy in his fellowship of labour in the service of the Lord with Mr.
> Newton. He showed then no feeling of opposition on Ministry But the arrival
> of Mr. J. N. Darby in March of that year, and his assaults on Mr. Newton wrought
> a great difference on Mr. Harris as well as on others. Mr. J. N. Darby possessed a
> paramount influence over many minds in this place, and of this he was himself
> perfectly conscious.[15]

Cole, from among the rank and file, was even more vivid in his reminis-
cence:

> But no account, gathered merely from pamphlets, could describe the distress of
> mind, the poignant sorrow and heart-grief produced by Mr. D. as he ruthlessly
> pursued his course against his former friend. There was no question of evil
> doctrine in this antagonism, but only of ecclesiastical practice. I deeply regret to
> have to record that strifes, jealousies, wraths, factions, parties, works of the flesh,
> took the place, in great measure, of the fruit of the Spirit and loving fellowship
> of the saints.[16]

Of those factions, Darby later made full use, in his *Narrative of Facts*, to
discredit Newton. Although he indignantly repudiated the suggestions
that the differences only arose with his coming, it is plain from his own
account that the arrival on the scene of such a powerful opponent of
Newton's autocracy gave the cue to every element of discontent within
the church.

Darby, for a time, left Plymouth. Others worked for a reconciliation,
but both antagonists stood aloof. As Darby travelled he found traces of
Newton's influence widespread in the West of England. Eventually he
descended again on Plymouth; "my conscience," he wrote later, "allowing me no longer to stay."[17] He arrived on 18th October 1845, and this
time no holds were to be barred. His attack was launched directly at
Newton's personal integrity.

Harris had left Plymouth a little time before this, following his second
marriage (he had lost his first wife some years earlier). He wrote to Newton
from Lynton on 8th October 1845, announcing that he had decided to
withdraw from ministering at Plymouth. He pleaded the recent unhappy
condition of things there, the closing of the Friday meeting of elders
(which Newton had proscribed and as adamantly refused to reconvene),
and changes which had been made in the diaconal department without
consulting him. He felt that he had lost the confidence of others. Newton
replied (as Harris had written) in an affectionate but sad spirit. He would
himself have left Plymouth if he had not believed "the whole system of
Divine truth to be affected by the system promulgated by Mr. Darby."[18]
Harris saw Tregelles on 19th October and told him "that his reason for

leaving Plymouth was, that he would not take any part with Newton against Darby or with Darby against Newton."[19]

Then followed Darby's attack on Newton. On 26th October, he announced to the assembled church at Ebrington Street that he was withdrawing from their communion: "I felt God was practically displaced." He was asked to attend a meeting to explain the reasons for his action more fully, and there he launched his public attack on Newton's personal honesty. If his previous tactics were disingenuous, he had now descended to the disreputable.

The charges were based on two incidents. Following the April meeting, Newton had been asked by a friend for an account of what had taken place there. This he gave, and the letter was later printed and circulated. Newton professed to give "the substance" of what he had said, and made plain his intention to oppose "the evil" of Darby's system, but he did not include in his summary any reference to his own outburst. This published account, Darby claimed, was therefore untrue and deliberately deceptive.

The second charge was similar. During the same period, Newton had republished a letter he had written some years before, and which had been widely circulated in manuscript. In the reprint he deleted one paragraph and added explanatory matter, both alterations being made to meet charges Darby was levelling at him, and he added to the letter a prefix to the effect that it was "now published with some omissions and alterations; but in substance it remains the same." Darby, in a better frame of mind, might have welcomed the changes as a sign of a willingness to listen. Instead, he was furious at what he construed as a deliberate attempt to cut the ground from under his feet, and accused Newton of deliberate falsification of evidence.

On such evidence, Darby based the weight of his attack. We may wonder why Newton did not take an obvious course. On this point, Neatby may be quoted with effect:

> We cannot choose but admire the rigid adherence to the principle that forbade all appeal to a secular tribunal. This constancy was not peculiar to Newton. Probably all his leading opponents would have done just the same in his place. . . . It is at all events pretty certain that if Newton had sent Darby a lawyer's letter on the first publication of the charges of lying, there would have been an end of the whole matter, and the Church of Christ would have been saved a very great scandal.[20]

Once the charges had been made, Darby did not restrain his language. His letters of the time are full of indignant accounts of the "mass of evil"[21] at Plymouth.

> The evil was both in the assembly and in individuals, and in individuals leading and taking a prominent part – I judge positive actual evil, and it seems to me of a very sad tendency.[22]

Other men, with a keener sense of propriety, intervened. Four men, with Lord Congleton at their head, asked Darby to meet Newton, with four men nominated by each party, to investigate the charges. Darby refused to appear before "a mere worldly tribunal," insisting on a full church meeting (he seems to have held the view that what a supporter later called the "worldly principle of arbitration" . . . "would be taking the case out of the hands of God and His Church, as well as making himself the head of a party.")[23] The reply of the four was firm. In December, therefore, a group of at least ten men,* in addition to Darby and Newton, met to investigate the charges. Wigram and another apparently attended un-invited. The proceedings were abortive. The majority acquitted Newton of any intention to deceive, a document which exculpated Newton being signed by five of them, including four of the most influential (Congleton, Campbell, Code and Rhind), while two others, Morris and Rickard, as well as Congleton and Rhind, later gave Newton individual testimonials to the same effect.[24] But Wigram vigorously disagreed, and Newton himself rejected the findings, feeling that they were not suffic-iently in his favour. The fact was that neither rival would be content with anything less than the condemnation of the other – and ultimately Darby, as the more widely influential and the more ruthless, was to win.

Newton's refusal to compromise was again his undoing – this time leading to the forfeiture of the confidence of the powerful friends who had reached a decision in his favour. A further attempt to convene a church meeting to discuss the charges being refused, Darby, for his part, waited no longer. On Sunday 28th December he set up a rival congrega-tion in the Raleigh Street chapel, fifty or sixty joining him on the first Sunday, and a considerable further number later.

The miserable affair could not rest, and the division soon took on a wider aspect. Wigram and Lord Congleton were leaders of London congrega-tions, and Congleton, who was always noted for an intense sense of that which was honourable, clearly felt that Wigram's partisanship had been an aggravating factor in the dispute. He went twice to Wigram in private, but Wigram refused his protests. Congleton therefore charged Wigram in his own congregation at Rawstorne Street with helping Darby to make a division at Plymouth, and he later laid a complaint concerning Darby's attacks on Newton's integrity. Unlike Darby's charges against Newton, neither of these charges was taken up.

---

* There are at least twelve names which occur in connexion with these proceed-ings, although Neatby states categorically that only ten were present at the initial meeting, apart from Darby and Newton. The twelve names were: Lord Congleton, Sir Alexander Campbell (who later withdrew his acquittal of Newton), Potter, Code, Rhind, Wigram, Naylor, Rickard, Morris, Walker, Mosely and Chapman. Embley ("The Plymouth Brethren" in *Patterns of Sectarianism*, p. 233) mentions yet a thir-teenth, McAdam, as being one of "the ten."

The Plymouth leaders who remained maintained such dignity as was possible to them under the circumstances, although some of Newton's personal partisans were less wise, and continued bitter pamphleteering and the Plymouth community at large was rent by party spirit. Darby and Wigram for their part consulted neither peace nor dignity. In the early summer of 1846 Darby published his *Narrative of the Facts, Connected with the Separation of the Writer from the Congregation meeting in Ebrington Street*. It was a partisan statement of his case, no better and no worse than a thousand other similar productions of squalid ecclesiastical quarrels.* It was followed in the autumn by a bitter printed attack by Wigram upon Newton, which aroused a firm but unavailing protest from Tregelles, who was then in London. Ebrington Street maintained its ground, but when meetings were convened in London, its representatives repeatedly refused to attend. They probably had unhappy memories of Newton's loss of self-control at the earlier confrontation, and possibly they also hoped to avoid aggravation of the quarrel. If so, their hopes were vain. Their refusals in themselves tended to alienate other leaders, who were by now being involved on a national scale by the London group. Eventually, as Darby was about to leave again for the Continent, an invitation was sent to Newton to meet him at Rawstorne Street at a public meeting, the invitation being repeated under the hand of W. H. Dorman. Newton (not unjustifiably) claimed that as the investigators of the previous year had largely exonerated him, he should not be expected to appear again. Accordingly, the Rawstorne Street congregation, in December 1846, high-handedly sent Newton a note excluding Newton from communion there, an action against which Tregelles protested in vain.

To these proceedings there was a tragic personal footnote. On 18th May 1846, Newton's wife had died. In January of that year Darby had written a lengthy letter from Plymouth setting out with some heat his version of the dispute up to that point. He had added a postscript:

> Poor dear Mrs. N. is very ill – I suppose dying off, but peaceful. But there is nothing now to distress her. She is now quite peaceful, I hear.[25]

Darby's habit (or that of his editor) of using initials does not enable us to identify this lady definitely as Mrs. Newton (Newton himself is "N" or "Mr. N." in most of the letter, but Mrs. Newton's death is referred to in the *Narrative of Facts*). Comment seems superfluous.

As we have said, if Darby's campaign to discredit his rival had been deliberately planned, it could not have been more skilfully executed. Newton and the remnant of the Ebrington Street church were by now effectively isolated from all Brethren elsewhere. In February 1847, while Darby was on the Continent, another meeting, of men from widely

* Lord Congleton, in a letter of 5th November 1846 announcing his withdrawal from association with Newton and Ebrington Street, added a description of Darby's *Narrative of Facts* as "a shameful misrepresentation" (*Fry MS Book*, p. 374).

different places, took place at Rawstorne Street, and heard denunciations of "the evil system which had grown up at Plymouth"[26] (as one of Darby's party described it) from a number of well-known leaders, including Harris and Hall; whether these two gentlemen would have wholly approved of this description of the purport of their accounts we have no means of knowing. Newton retained only those who remained faithful to him at Ebrington Street. Events were soon to complete their discomfiture.

A month or two later a lady in Exeter, who was a keen hearer of Newton's teachings, lent to Mrs. Harris, for her edification, notes which she had taken of an address by Newton. Mrs. Harris, puzzled by certain statements in the notes, asked her husband to explain them. Harris was shocked at the implications of some of their contents.

What had happened was that Newton, in developing the truth of the Incarnation, seemed to have passed acceptable limits of doctrine. He was teaching that some of the sufferings of Christ arose to Him because, in his identification with mankind and with Israel, He had Himself become subject to the wrath of God and to the penalties laid on Israel, but not by direct voluntary submission to judgment, but as the necessary result of the relationship to God which He had assumed.* Newton insisted upon the absolute sinlessness of Christ, but went on to suggest that, as a result of the relation to God which He had undertaken in His identification with men, it became necessary for Him to emerge from His condition of liability to judgment, by His own obedience. The teaching hardly touched orthodox doctrine concerning Christ's Person, but it was considered by many to have dangerous results in relation to the doctrine of the atonement, while its implications could be deeply offensive to men with a warm devotion to Christ. Müller later summed up this point of view, by remarking that the teaching implied that Christ Himself needed a saviour.

Nevertheless, the narrowness of the error becomes clearer as the teachings are analysed. It is one of the cardinal truths of Christianity that God, in Christ, took human flesh: that He took to Himself the full burden of the penalty of man's sin, and that He identified Himself in incarnation with the human condition.† It is doubtful whether Newton in intention ever went beyond strict orthodoxy; but it is equally clear, from the conse-

---

* Newton later in life spoke of a confusion between the instrumental causes of the sufferings of Christ, and the procuring causes, as being at the root of the errors.

† "That he experienced our condition here, every true Christian believes ... Christ's being obnoxious to wrath along with the people, and so being glad at John's message [i.e. Newton's teaching] is precisely the opposite to his identifying himself entirely with the condition of His people: His being baptized was taking their place. So in His really entering into the circumstances of man's condition. Blessed be God, He did. But Mr. N. distinguishes this from what he means, namely, inflictions by reason of the relation of God to Him who did so enter." [J. N. Darby in "Observations on a Tract entitled 'Remarks on the Sufferings of the Lord Jesus'" – Coll. Writings, Stow Hill edn., Vol. 15, p. 36.]

quences which he and others were drawing from his teaching, that (whatever the logic of their position) their minds had crossed the frontier which lay between Christ's voluntary atoning assumption of sin's penalty, and an involuntary subjection to that penalty.

Harris's judgment failed him at this moment. He was in possession, not of a first-hand writing of Newton's, but of notes taken by a non-technical listener. Common courtesy – to put the matter no higher – should have suggested a reference back to Newton himself. Instead, he took steps which were disastrous. The notes were sent to a supporter of Darby's, accompanied by a long letter of criticism, and Harris gave him permission to print them. They were published in July 1847.

Newton made no direct reply at this point, but instead published a tract entitled *Remarks on the Sufferings of the Lord Jesus*, in which he set out his views for himself. Darby had all that he needed. He intervened with a long and viciously worded attack, not only on the doctrines, but on Newton himself. Newton did not reply directly to Darby, but published in September a dignified reply to Harris. Again it was Darby who responded. Newton's two tracts were to become of prime importance in the controversy which followed.

At last Newton's analysis of his own teachings caused him to realize the error into which his thinking had led him, and on 26th November 1847 he published a retractation: *A Statement and Acknowledgment Respecting Certain Doctrinal Errors*. On 8th December he left Plymouth.

There, in common charity, the dispute should have rested. Newton's *Acknowledgment* was a long and detailed confession and withdrawal of erroneous teachings. Because of its importance to the history it is printed in full in Appendix B, and from it the reader may judge for himself as to Newton's sincerity. It was carefully and fully worded. He traced back the beginning of the teachings to some writings of his own in 1835 over the Irvingite controversy, in which, in opposing Irving's teachings on the peccability of Christ, Newton had suggested that Christ, while sinless, had taken certain of the consequences of sin upon Himself through the "federal headship" of Adam.

Newton had clearly thought more deeply into his teachings than any of his opponents, and his intention was to deal with his offence at its root. He may also have thought that, by showing that the root of the teachings had been freely circulating for twelve years, some of his attackers might well pause to consider whether, if they themselves had not noticed them, Newton himself was really as deliberately culpable as they alleged. In this his judgment was at fault.

His judgment was at fault in another respect also. He failed to reckon with Darby's theories on the secret working of heresy. Darby was now certain that he had at last reached the root of all the long developing "evils" at Plymouth, and that his justification was plain for all to see. The damaging consequences of the earlier attacks on Newton's personal integrity now became plain. The unbridled language of Wigram and Darby over many months, combined with Newton's own silence, had sufficed to sow sufficient doubts concerning Newton's integrity in the minds of men at large, to allow Darby's prompt dismissal of the *Statement and Acknowledgment* as a trick* to seem just credible. Developments at Ebrington Street itself sealed the tragedy.

Thoroughly alarmed by the implications of the teachings they had embraced, and which they now found denounced by their author, Soltau, Batten and Dyer, the three leading teachers remaining at Ebrington Street, called a meeting for Monday, 13th December. It was an emotional occasion. Anxiously they with others pictured the deductions which might have been drawn from the teachings, renounced them, and also announced their withdrawal from Ebrington Street. Their confessions (unlike Newton's) were acceptable to Darby.

> One of his (Soltau's) auditors who was pained by what he had said, addressed him, "Oh! Mr. Soltau, if I had known that you had held such views as you expressed last night, I could not have remained in communion with you." To this he replied, "I never held these things *in my conscience*." To this was rejoined, "But surely you gave us that idea last night!" To this he said, "I held what *might have led* to them."[27]

Those who remained at Ebrington Street issued *A Statement from Christians Assembling in the Name of the Lord, in Ebrington Street, Plymouth,* on 10th January 1848. With Tregelles at their head, they explicitly disclaimed every statement of doctrine which would impute the guilt of Adam or the curse of the broken law to Christ, and re-affirmed the traditional orthodox teachings. It was too late, for no Darbyite was now listening. Newton was received at Ebrington Street, if ever he visited Plymouth, and that sufficed. It would be a cardinal principle of Darbyism thereafter that both Newton and Ebrington Street were actively and cunningly continuing to propagate the doctrines they had disclaimed, and other darker things (it would be implied) beside. Every disclaimer would be dismissed as mere deceit. To doubt this thesis would be to court the charge of Newtonianism for oneself.

Batten, in his confession, listed eight points of error which could be deduced from the teachings as he understood them. Each of these was a direct consequence of the theory concerning the federal headship of Adam which Newton had put forward those years before. In a letter written at a later date to explain his rejection of Newton's confession,

---

* This description is used advisedly. Darby's *Notice of the Statement and Acknowledgment of Error Circulated by Mr. Newton* (Coll. Writings Vol. 15) is a lengthy attempt to show, by semantic and doctrinal juggling, that Newton had not renounced his errors despite his clear profession to have done so.

Darby listed Batten's eight points (which were drawn up after the confession had been published), and pleaded that "the second article is the one, and the only one, to which Mr. Newton's retractation of 1847 applies."[28] The second point was the only one in which Batten in so many words traced back his deduction to the views on Adam's federal headship, but even so Darby's statement was untrue on the face of it. Not only did Newton withdraw "all statements of mine, whether in print or in any other form, in which this error, or any of its fruits may be found," but the most vital of the remaining seven points listed by Batten, "That the Lord Jesus extricated Himself from these inflictions by keeping the law," had been renounced in precise terms in Newton's *Statement*. This is significant. Batten's other points are simply repetitive of the main theme which Newton had renounced, but it was this seventh conclusion which most plainly showed that their thinking had crossed the fatal boundary between Christ's voluntary and the involuntary assumption of sin's penalties.

Newton's withdrawal of "all statements of mine, whether in print or in any other form" was surely embracing enough. A few sentences later, however, in listing his writings, he stated that his two recent tracts were withdrawn "for reconsideration." To his opponents, who considered that the tracts repeated the heresy, if in less objectionable form, this seemed to be a deliberately partial confession; but Newton (academic to the end) was in fact reserving his judgment as to whether those tracts contained the heresy at all.

It is here that the crucial matter of these two tracts calls for further comment. Newton plainly did not consider that they set out the heresy, and his opponents as plainly thought that they did (an opinion, it should be added, which was not only held by Darby's followers, but was later expressed by the Bethesda leaders when they were called upon to pronounce on the matter). The reason for this difference in opinion lay in the fineness of the distinctions which we have already noticed. Newton read his remarks in the light of his own intentions, and to him they therefore clarified his earlier misunderstandings, and remained on the orthodox side of the fatal boundary. Others read them in the light of the conclusions which had been drawn from them, and to them they seemed to be mere repetitions, though in guarded form, of the error. Newton, who had analysed his position much more closely than his accusers, was probably conscious of this ambiguity, and his action in withdrawing the tracts, rather than disclaiming them, was the precise and somewhat pedantic course which was characteristic of the man.

As late as 1885 Newton stated that "I have never thought, even in my unconverted days, the heresy charged on me. Indeed, I have laboured all my life against it."[29] In his remarks, which were occasioned by the publication of E. K. Groves's *Bethesda Family Matters*, and were taken down by

a friend, Newton repeated his view that he adhered to the tracts as substantially sound, but added:

> These two tracts are indeed open to criticism and I disapprove of some things in
> them, things in which I was not correct. But, curiously, those are not noticed by
> my assailants; perhaps they would agree with them and praise them, for there
> was a great deal of latent Brethrenism in the two tracts. What are the faults?
> Well, chiefly the statement that certain things in the Lord's life were *huper* and not
> *anti* as regards His people.[30]

Newton was too contemptuous of his opponents, for the doctrine of
which they complained was closely related to this very distinction between
sufferings "on behalf of" and sufferings "in place of" His people.* His
observation is not without pertinence, however. That Christ's sufferings
during life were not in themselves part of His atoning work was an element
of Darby's teaching, in contrast to the Calvinist scheme to which Newton
adhered. Developments later in Darby's life, to which reference is made
at the end of the next chapter, were to underline the acuteness of Newton's
comment.

In later years Newton published several further booklets on the subject
of the sufferings of Christ. Although his opponents denounced each one,
the judgment of objective readers has invariably agreed that the erroneous
teachings had disappeared. Certain high Calvinist theologians, indeed, later
regarded him as a champion of orthodoxy against Darbyite error! Nor
was the conflict without farce: Neatby mentions an incident when a
violent onslaught was made by one of Darby's partisans upon a certain
statement in one of the two original tracts: only for it to transpire that
Newton was quoting Darby himself![31]

The consequences of the debate for Darbyism were serious. It is plain
from the details of Newton's teachings that in principle he (like Irving
before him) had been following up a real and proper concern with the
doctrine of the Incarnation. This concern in itself was healthy and important, and its pastoral and devotional implications badly needed development. Reaction against Newton's errors, when combined with the intense
emphasis upon the "spiritual" and the "heavenly" which characterized
Darby's theology, and with his "impulsive" doctrine of the Holy Spirit's
activities, has invariably caused Darbyite thinking to be shy of the full
implications of the Incarnation, and has forced it into Gnostic and Docetic
trends. Its later exponents have not always been successful in avoiding
error as a result.†

---

* In this connexion, Neatby's analysis of Newton's position (*A History of the Plymouth Brethren*, pp. 136–8) is interestingly confirmed by Newton's own comments,
to which Neatby did not, apparently, have access.

† It is to be gratefully acknowledged that that section of exclusive Brethren which
later rejected the teachings of F. E. Raven has, in reaction to Raven's Gnosticism,
always laid great stress on the orthodox doctrine of the true humanity of Christ. It

Newton's connexion with the Brethren ceased from this time. He lived until 1899, retreating into a little circle of two or three churches of his own, and leaving a devoted following, mainly among Strict Baptists. The result of Darby's campaign in Plymouth had been to destroy one of the most flourishing churches of the movement, and to drive into the wilderness one of its most brilliant teachers.

As to Newton himself, we can do no better than to quote Neatby's tribute to him:

The execrations of his adversaries pursued him to his distant grave, but not once in half a century did they avail to provoke retaliation. His name to this day is regarded with absolute loathing by thousands who have never troubled to read a single tract of all that he has written; and there are certainly hundreds, scarcely a bit better informed, who have made it one of their chief objects to perpetuate the frantic prejudice. But none of the leaders of the campaign of calumny, and none of their dupes, have ever, so far as I can learn from an extensive inquiry, been assailed by Newton with one angry word of a personal character,* or with one uncharitable imputation. With Newton's ecclesiastical course I have no sympathy. He contracted the limits of orthodoxy till there can scarcely have been five hundred sound Christians in the world, and he taught principles of church-fellowship that were actually narrower than those of Darby himself. . . . If theological animosity could still restrain me from recognizing the grace of God in his conduct, I should feel that words were poor to express my admiration either of the dignity with which his path was chosen, or of the steadfastness of self-control with which it was pursued through all its bitter length. It seems to me that Newton ignored, all unwittingly, some of the most sacred principles of Holy Scripture; but the light of one text at least shone steadily on his path. When he was reviled, he reviled not again; when he was persecuted, he threatened not: but committed himself to Him that judgeth righteously.[32]

Quotation References – Chapter 9.

1. *Fry MS book*, p. 171. (The underlining is Newton's own.)
2. *Three Letters*, S. P. Tregelles, p. 6.
3. Ibid., p. 7 n.
4. *Letters*, Vol. I, p. 74 (letter of 11th April 1844).
5. Ibid., Vol. III, p. 239 (letter dated 1844).
6. Ibid., Vol. I, p. 73 (letter of 11th April 1844).
7. *Fry MS book*, p. 341. References are given to the MS book into which the letters

---

may still be doubted whether they have fully appreciated the more distant effects of Darbyite thinking. (See F. F. Bruce, *The Humanity of Jesus Christ*, in CBRF Journal 24 [1973].)

* The Fry records of Newton's private conversations do little to modify this judgment. Some of the leaders of Brethren came in for strictures in those conversations, but they are records of a man's private talks to his friends: the present author has no wish to withdraw anything from the force of Neatby's belated act of justice to this shockingly ill-used man.

are transcribed, but the original letters (or Newton's copies of those from him to other men) are also in the Fry collection. This letter is dated July 1845.

8. Quoted *Anthony Norris Groves*, G. H. Lang, p. 327.

9. *Letters*, Vol. III, p. 237 (letter dated 1844).

10. *Narrative of the Facts Connected with the Separation of the Writer from the Congregation meeting in Ebrington Street*. (1886). J. N. Darby (*Coll. Writings*, Vol. 20. Stow Hill edn., p. 20).

11. *Fry MS book*, pp. 328–31 (letter dated 30th March 1845).

12. This and other unreferenced quotations in the next two paragraphs are from the letters in the Fry collection. Darby's own *Narrative of Facts* contains a fairly full summary of the correspondence.

13. *Narrative of Facts*, op. cit., p. 30.

14. *Letters*, Vol. I, p. 79 (letter of 21st April 1845).

15. *Three Letters*, p. 21.

16. Quoted *Anthony Norris Groves*, p. 328.

17. *Narrative of Facts*, op. cit. p. 40.

18. *Fry MS book*, pp. 346–7. The copy is of an undated draft.

19. *Three Letters*, pp. 21–22.

20. *History of the Plymouth Brethren*, p. 155.

21. *Letters*, Vol. I, p. 85 (letter of 12th November 1845).

22. Ibid., Vol. III, p. 244 (letter of 10th November 1845).

23. *The Whole Case of Plymouth and Bethesda*, W. Trotter (1849) pp. 11, 12 (this open letter exists in a number of different reprints, with different paging; quotations are from a pamphlet reprint under the title of *The Origin of (so-called) Open Brethrenism*).

24. They are preserved in the Fry collection.

25. *Letters*, Vol. I., p. 91 (letter of 20th January 1846).

26. Trotter, op. cit., p. 14.

27. *Three Letters*, S. P. Tregelles, p. 28 n.

28. *Letter to the Rev. Mr. Guers*. J. N. Darby (1853) (*Coll. Writings*, Vol. 15. Stow Hill edn., p. 189).

29. *Fry MS book*, p. 376. See also the letter from Newton to a Mr. Lake quoted in Fromow, *Teachers of the Faith and Future* (1959), p. 158 – the letter is dated 1st June 1885.

30. Ibid.

31. *History of the Plymouth Brethren*, pp. 150–1.

32. Ibid., pp. 151–3.

CHAPTER 10

DEVELOPMENTS IN BRISTOL

FOR the disease of sin is separating, and God is uniting, for He is love.
J. N. Darby, *Letter of May 1832.*

THE Jansenists long before had been willing to condemn the "five propositions"; but this was not sufficient; the Pope required that they should also
declare that the five propositions were to be found in Jansenius.
W. B. Neatby, *A History of the Plymouth Brethren.*

IN ALL THE UPHEAVALS OVER PLYMOUTH, ONE NOTABLE
church had remained content to pursue its own course in quietness.
Even Chapman had become involved in the Plymouth disputes, but
Bethesda seems not to have been brought into the conflict by either party.
Both Müller and Craik were occupied enough by the pressure of work at
the Orphan Homes and by the flourishing churches under their care,
while Müller had paid an extended visit to Stuttgart in the latter half of
1843, and again from July to October 1845.

As we have already noticed, Bethesda's course had been purposeful, and
based throughout on its understanding of Scripture. Although at Gideon
they had joined an existing Independent church – albeit one with a
distinctly individualistic history – at Bethesda Müller and Craik had
started a new work in an empty chapel, building their fellowship step by
step in accordance with the guidance they found from the New Testament.
The result had eventually been that they had left Gideon altogether, in
April 1840, rather than enforce the relinquishment of customs which had
been in existence before they joined the congregation, and which they
now felt to be wrong.

We have also seen how they had moved from making believer's
baptism a condition of fellowship to a more open position, a move made
directly under the influence of Robert Chapman, and thus through Chapman from Harington Evans.

Then, in 1838, and apparently disturbed by the trend elsewhere to
renounce all formal government within the churches, Müller and Craik
had withdrawn into retreat from Bristol for two weeks to give themselves
to prayer and meditation concerning matters of church structure. They
had returned with carefully matured convictions on eldership and discipline. They considered that it was the mind of God that there should be
recognized elders within the church. These elders were the appointment
of the Holy Spirit, their call being a personal call of the Spirit, but con-

firmed by possession of appropriate qualifications and by God's blessing upon their work. These elders were to be acknowledged and their judgment submitted to, but acts of discipline were to be settled finally in the presence of the church, as an act of the whole body. Each of these conclusions was backed by its own Scriptural references.

Finally, as to ministry within the church, on 7th July 1841 they removed the boxes placed in the chapel to receive gifts for their support. In their statement of that date to the church they recited their original conviction as to declining a regular salary, and continued:

> We did not act thus because we thought it wrong that those who were ministered unto in spiritual things should minister unto us in temporal things; but (1) because we would not have the liberality of the brethren to be a matter of constraint, but willingly; (2) because on the ground of James ii. 1-6, we objected to seat-rents.[1]

They now felt that the boxes were inconsistent with their developing convictions, and set out four reasons:

1. They appeared to set Müller and Craik above all the other brethren, and to indicate some office as being held by them.

2. They hindered other brethren from being fully recognized as equal to themselves in the tasks of ruling and teaching.

3. They gave an impression "that we were seeking to keep our place in the church by some outward title."

4. They caused some to look on them as exclusively "the ministers," and this led to a feeling of neglect if others than themselves visited members of the congregation. "The notion that two individuals should be able to exercise pastoral inspection over about five hundred and fifty believers, we consider to be very unsound; but for ourselves we feel that it is a responsibility which we dare not take."[2]

Darby would have whole-heartedly approved of their relinquishment of the strict rule as to baptism, and the convictions which they expressed on ministry would have pleased him: but their position as to elders was one which was, as we have seen, directly opposed to a central development of his own views – and, moreover, was closely allied to the Plymouth practices. The Bristol leaders shared neither his militant anti-clericalism, nor his dramatic expectations concerning the Second Advent. On the contrary, they were glad to recognize the gifts of God shown by men with whose church order and position they disagreed; and on the second matter, despite their expectations as to the Second Advent, the intense apocalyptic note was almost entirely absent from their teaching. They certainly held the probability of the near return of Christ, but equally certainly they did not make that expectation a foundation of their teaching. Craik was too sound a theologian to do so, while Müller shared Newton's view, that the appearance of "Antichrist" would precede the Advent, and continued to hold that view throughout his life.

There was one other factor which set them apart from Darby's thinking. Craik in particular was concerned with the proper development of the doctrine of the Incarnation, and its very important pastoral implications, and had expounded them in his *Pastoral Letters* of 1835. He was never guilty of the speculations which had eventually discredited both Irving and Newton, but his teachings were opposed in this most important respect to the dangerous Docetic tendencies in the Darbyite system.

There is no indication of any earlier irritants in the relationship between Darby and Bristol. It may well be that Darby never regarded Bethesda as being wholly "with us" (he certainly firmly alleged this later). If by that, he referred narrowly to his own scheme of doctrine, he was certainly correct: but the extent to which he was correct in later referring to Bethesda as a "mere dissenting congregation," as distinct from Brethrenism in general, plainly depended on his own definition of Brethrenism. We have the assurance of William Trotter, Darby's own follower, that Bethesda had "links of connexion with almost every gathering throughout the country."[3]

In May 1848 there was held at Bath a meeting of some hundred Brethren, to discuss the aftermath of the Plymouth upheaval. Men were present from all over the country: William Dyer from Plymouth, Chapman from Barnstaple, Dorman, Congleton and Robert Howard from London, Bellett from Dublin, Robert Nelson from Edinburgh, and Jukes from Hull. The results were inconclusive. According to Darby's Yorkshire supporter William Trotter (who was not present) Darby's *Narrative of Facts* and other publications were triumphantly vindicated (Trotter is silent as to Wigram's contributions to the controversy), but others gave different versions.[4]

Even while this conference was taking place, events nearby in Bristol were shaping for the final *dénouement*. Two members of the Ebrington Street congregation (which about this time moved to Compton Street in Plymouth) came to Bristol and applied for communion at Bethesda. They were a Captain Woodfall and his brother. By this time Newton's *Statement and Acknowledgment* had been in circulation for several months, and the Ebrington Street congregation had also issued its own forthright disclaimer of the erroneous doctrines in the previous January. Captain Woodfall, who had been on the Continent at the time of the Plymouth troubles, was admitted, but his brother's application was held for consideration. Objections were raised within the church at Bethesda by certain of Darby's supporters there, and on Craik's suggestion the objectors were therefore appointed to examine the Woodfalls, who were pronounced clear of the heresy. Darby also referred to a lady follower of Newton who was similarly admitted after examination by Craik.

Darby had visited Bristol at the end of April 1848, and called on Müller as was his usual custom. He was asked to preach the following Sunday at

Bethesda, but declined on the grounds of a previous engagement. A few days later Darby announced publicly in a meeting at Exeter that he could never go to Bethesda again because of their reception of Newton's followers. This he later confirmed in a letter to Müller: the first intimation that gentleman had had of these proceedings.

Darby later alleged that the followers of Newton had begun to circulate Newton's writings in the church at Bethesda. Darby obviously wrote from hearsay, but it is possible that this was so. The impugned tracts, after all, were not in circulation, and Newton's other writings were common currency among Brethren. Darby's own partisans within Bethesda were no less vigorous than those of Newton, and, despite the clearance of the Woodfalls by some of their own number, began to press for a formal church investigation into the erroneous teachings (teachings, it must be remembered, that had already been condemned by their own author). Eventually, in June, one of Darby's followers seceded from Bethesda. The elders, feeling their hands forced by this action, summoned a church meeting at the end of June, at which a statement signed by ten of the elders was read and sanctioned by the majority of the church. At this, others of Darby's sympathizers promptly left the church fellowship.

"If this document," wrote Neatby, "had been a concise subscription to all the heresies of Christendom from the days of Cerinthus downward, it could hardly have raised a greater tumult of execration."[5] That the reader might better judge of the merits of this execration, the *Letter of the Ten* (as the document came to be known) is printed in full in Appendix C to this book. It will be noted that in it the authors of the letter specifically denounced the teachings attributed to Newton, and they read it to the church with appropriate explanations.

Later William Trotter commented on this letter.

That is, they severally and jointly disclaim Mr Newton's published views on these subjects. And yet it is well known that one of those who signed the paper agrees with Mr. Newton on these points; and in the very last tract I have seen, written by Mr. Groves, brother-in-law to Mr. Müller, and an active agent and zealous advocate of Bethesda, Mr. and Mrs Aitchison are named as among the known friends of Mr. Newton, and Mr. Aitchison is one of the ten who signed the paper. The simplest saint can see the want of uprightness in a course like this. Ten men sign a paper, in which they disclaim views held, and known to be held, by at least one of those who signed it.[6]

A "saint" who was a little less simple than the simplest might have remembered that both Newton himself and the Ebrington Street congregation had long since disclaimed the teachings, and might have been prepared to assume that Aitchison was simply telling the truth as to his own views. But by now the followers of Darby were incapable of objectivity. If someone alleged to be a friend of Newton did not denounce the doctrines, he was held to be an active supporter and propagator of them: if he did denounce them, his denunciation was condemned as fraudulent.

The final tragedy was not long in maturing. Darby visited Yorkshire, and found that churches there were sympathizing with Bethesda. Urged on by Trotter, who was alarmed at this, he issued from Leeds, on 26th August 1848, a circular excommunicating Bethesda *en bloc*. "Members of Ebrington Street, active and unceasing agents of Mr. Newton, holding and justifying his views, are received at Bethesda," he wrote (a statement which, if it was intended to relate to the heresies of which Darby was in context writing, was plainly untrue both in relation to the members of Ebrington Street and of the Bethesda elders). "Woe be to (Brethren) if they love the Brethren Müller and Craik or their own ease more than the souls of saints dear to Christ!"[7]

Bethesda, faced with the circular, eventually decided to take firmer action. On 31st October 1848, Müller publicly announced his personal condemnation of Newton's teachings (in a letter to Deck he stated that he had in any case made his views public in June and July). Seven church meetings were held in November and December to the same end, and the judgment announced that no one defending, maintaining or upholding Mr. Newton's views or tracts should be received into communion. The result was to lose them several of Newton's sympathizers, including the Woodfalls, but the action was otherwise ineffective. Like Ebrington Street a year before, Bethesda found that Darbyism was not listening.* Darbyite Churches everywhere must henceforth, first and foremost of their duties, "judge the Bethesda question."

In October 1848 Wigram took up the invitation in the *Letter of the Ten* to examine Craik's *Pastoral Letters* of 1835, and charged Craik with "blasphemous and heretical" statements in them. The objects of Wigram's

* To this statement there might be a significant qualification. It was later recorded with Müller's approval that in July 1849 Darby had called upon Müller at the Orphan House and told him that, as he had judged the tracts, there was no longer any reason for their separation. Müller replied that he only had ten minutes remaining before an important engagement, and "as you have acted so wickedly in this matter, I cannot *now* enter upon it, as I have no time."

Some of Darby's followers later strenuously denied that this interview took place. Neatby (op. cit., p. 176) considered that "of all the incidents in Darby's chequered career, this is distinctly the most damaging to his reputation, for he left Müller's presence only to enforce to the last letter the decree that he had just declared obsolete." We may dissent from this view, and hope for the sake of Darby's reputation that the interview did take place, for it would be the one clear sign of personal compunction on Darby's part during the whole weary history of the Plymouth and Bristol disputes, while Müller's rebuff (humanly understandable as it was) would at least provide a human, if still regrettable, excuse for Darby's intransigence.

(A full examination of the evidence for and against the interview is preserved, for those who wish to see it, in G. H. Lang's *Anthony Norris Groves*, pp. 333–41. Darby's later odd actions as to the "withdrawal" of the Bethesda circular (see next chapter) are also in point.)

attack were certain perfectly orthodox statements concerning the true humanity of Christ, and his denunciation of Craik was elaborated by various pieces of hearsay. Wigram, in his blind loyalty to Darby, was now prepared to leap with both feet into Docetism. Not only Craik, but Bellett also, was momentarily under attack. Even Darby had had enough, and declined to enter into the matters.[8] He is reported as saying later "that Mr. Wigram sent him his tracts, and that he put them at the back of the fire."[9]

Darbyism had over-reached itself. Müller and Craik were men deeply and widely respected for their outstanding Christian work, and the culmination of the campaign against Bethesda alienated some of the most influential men in the movement from Darby. The sheer power of Darby's personality, coupled with the fact that his travels had made him a personal friend of men to whom Müller was only a name, may well have meant that the Darbyite party (henceforth known as "Exclusive Brethren") was the larger in the division which followed: but the names of those who refused to apply his decree against Bethesda,* and who in consequence suffered the same excommunication, show eloquently enough that Darbyism was not to be an enduring force.

Chapman and those under his influence in North Devon remained with Müller and Craik: so did Groves, who, being in England at the time, himself suffered from personal attacks by Darby's party. These adherents were to have been expected. Lord Congleton broke with Darby: as did Rhind, Harris, Soltau and the Dyers. Many of the ex-Quaker element broke with Darby, including its two most influential men, Wakefield of Kendal and John Eliot Howard of Tottenham. In London, Orchard Street, Hackney and Tottenham were lost to Darby, and the Tottenham church put out a concise statement of its position, which is still exhibited in Brook Street chapel, and is reproduced in Appendix D. Even more significantly, Code and Hargrove, Darby's old associates from Westport, and Maunsell (then still in Limerick) remained in fellowship with Bethesda. So did Jukes at Hull, in so far as he retained his links with Brethren. The powerful church at Hereford remained aloof from the controversy for a time, until a division in 1850 led to a secession under Hall, the seceders then adopting Darby's position. Even the saintly Bellett, deeply attached by long personal friendship to Darby, while applying Darby's discipline against Bethesda, yet remained, in Neatby's words, "a strange Darbyite" and would scandalize his fellow "exclusives" by walking arm in arm in the streets of

---

* Commonly called "Open Brethren," but in this book referred to hereafter by the more accurate description of independent Brethren. The name "Christian Brethren," which is increasingly used, in fact ante-dates the division, appearing in a tract of 1839 (*Reply to an Article in the* Eclectic Review *for May last entitled "The Plymouth Brethren,"* p. 24). It is also used (of "Open Brethren") in an official letter of the Registrar-General for Scotland quoted at pp. 143, 144 of Vol. XVIII of *The Witness* (1888).

Dublin with men from the other party.[10] In his simple graciousness he was far removed from the bitter aftermath of controversy.

History had written its own ironical judgment upon this movement that had proclaimed its separation from "the world" and its evils: for it was the year 1848, the European "Year of Revolutions," when virtually every capital in Europe was convulsed by revolt; the year, also, in which Methodism found itself split in two.

Two important men remained with Darby for a few further years. Dorman and Hall had both supported him vigorously in the Plymouth controversy – although Hall at least was apparently unhappy over the Bristol developments, and did not openly take sides until the Hereford division took place. Their attachment to Darby was to lead to a strange sequel.

It will be remembered that differences in prophetic interpretation had been an original cause of the dispute between Darby and Newton, and the principal irritant in their relations. Darby had minimized these differences in the early stages of the Plymouth quarrel, but once the breach was made he took the opportunity to discredit Newton's prophetic scheme. After Newton's erroneous teachings had been disclosed, he even made the ludicrous assertion:

> I have not the least doubt (from circumstances I have heard lately of the authenticity of which I have not the smallest question) that Mr. Newton received his prophetic system by direct inspiration from Satan, analogous to the Irvingite delusion.[11]★

The gravamen of Darby's attack was this. Newton's error was considered to lie in the suggestion that Christ's subjection to the displeasure of God was caused, not by His voluntary atoning submission to the penalties of mankind's sin, but rather because He was necessarily identified by birth with the sin of mankind, and more particularly with that of the nation of Israel. Darby, in attempting to use this to discredit Newton's prophetic system, put forward the virtues of his own system:

> I believe that what has been the instrument of ripening this terrible doctrine as to Christ . . . is really the prophetic system of the writer. And in this way: he does not admit the existence of a Jewish remnant which has life, and which is consequently within the reach, and the immediate object, of the sympathies of Christ. Hence he is obliged to associate Christ in His condition with the sinful and rebellious nation (and the consequence follows immediately), instead of His being the gracious vessel of feeling, thought, and faith, for the believing remnant, in the position of which He did put Himself.[12]

In point of fact, Newton's teaching was no more than incidentally concerned with his prophetic system: it arose from his doctrine of the

★ Absurdity is double-edged. Modern supporters of Newton have made precisely the same charge against Darby!

incarnation rather than from any eschatological views. Yet there was a measure of justice in Darby's charge. In the *Christian Witness* for July 1838 Newton (or a member of his school) had written while expounding his prophetic ideas:

> One only had been a righteous Servant; but whilst on earth He could not be blessed, because He had voluntarily identified Himself with Israel's circumstances and Israel's sin. He died for that nation.[13]

In itself this was unobjectionable, but it is plain how easily it was extended to the errors which Newton later renounced.

What Darby himself overlooked was that, in this argument, he was shifting much of the offence of Newton's teaching to his own. He was retaining the offensive positional subjection of Christ to judgment, and with it the imputation of His sufferings to His position in incarnation, rather than to His voluntary act of atonement. Darby pleaded that his identification was with an assumed "elect remnant" rather than with the nation at large; but the principle remained, and the weakness of his position would surely have been apparent to him if his mind had not been distorted by prejudice. Instead, he began to work out this line of speculation in relation to his own system of thought.

It was in 1858 that Darby began contributing a series of articles to *The Bible Treasury*, an excellent periodical which had been started by the good William Kelly, the most erudite of his younger followers. In these papers Darby set out his development of this line of thought. When he did so, a number of readers noticed the weakness, and the result was a minor storm, lasting some years, within Darbyism itself. Darby, indignant at finding himself accused of Newtonianism, denied his intention to attribute to Christ anything other than a voluntary identification with the remnant, and was formally cleared of the charge of heresy by an investigating group of nine of his leading followers, who showed him more mercy than he had been prepared to show Newton. Yet, as a direct result, he lost among others, in 1866, both Hall and Dorman, who followed the logic of their position and rejected the whole Bethesda discipline. Another who left Darbyism at this time was one, Joseph Stancomb, who had been one of the first trustees of Müller's orphan buildings, but had taken a leading part in the agitation within Bethesda eighteen years before.

Darby was a complicated and immense personality. Psychologically, he was obviously abnormal: but so have been many geniuses. It would be trite to see his deplorable actions only as the fruit of a subconscious drive for power: but such power as he sought would bring him little fame and less fortune. Somehow, beneath it all, there was also the force of a genuine and intense devotion to Christ. Darby's tragedy was that his actions, in their result, could only bring dishonour on the Name he loved.

Yet a better man sometimes burst out surprisingly from behind the storm clouds. When Craik was on his death-bed in 1866, Darby wrote affectionately to him, regretting his "ecclesiastical separation."[14] On another occasion, it is reported, Darby overheard some of his followers speaking slightingly of Robert Chapman, and broke in abruptly with: "Leave Robert Chapman alone: we talk about the heavenly places, but he lives in them."[15] Most unexpected of all, and quite incredible if this trait in Darby's character were not well attested, was an incident from near the end of Darby's long life. The incident was recounted by Dr. Robert Cameron of New York in the magazine *Perilous Times* for April 1917:

> Over forty years ago, at my own table in New York City, Mr. Darby called Mr. Newton "dear brother Newton". I expressed my deep surprise at the use of such an endearing term concerning the one who had been freely called "that danger-ous man," "the arch enemy," "the fearful blasphemer," and other equally harsh terms. At once Mr. Darby replied: "Mr. Newton is the most godly man I ever knew." I said, "Well, then, what was all this trouble and condemnation about, if Mr. Newton is such a godly man?" He answered promptly, "Oh, but Mr. Newton had taught blasphemous doctrines about the person of our blessed Lord, and these had to be dealt with."[16]

As the years went by, it is plain that Darby himself grew confused over the events of his first stormy fifty years. We have several times met his gift for coining the telling controversial slogan. Like many men with that facility, he too easily became the victim of his own inventions. Against Bethesda he had raised the cry of "neutrality," of "indifference to Christ": and that slogan worked upon his mind. On 19th February 1864, writing on a matter of discipline within his own community, he could write:

> The evil at Bethesda is the most unprincipled admission of blasphemers against Christ: the coldest contempt for Him I ever came across.[17]

Again, in 1867:

> I reject Bethesda as wickedness, as I ever did ... When the blasphemous doctrine of Mr. Newton ... came out, Bethesda deliberately sheltered and accredited it.[18]

Both remarks are their own condemnation. Neatby well characterized the latter as "not merely untrue, but ... simply destitute of the remotest connexion with truth." Yet Darby passionately believed that he was speaking the truth.

The final comment comes from Darby's own pen, near the end of his life. He died at Bournemouth on 29th April 1882. Three-and-a-half years before his death, a supporter had written to him concerning the Bethesda discipline, and in November 1878 he had replied:

> I have no wish to keep up the Bethesda question, not that I judge the evil as less than I thought it, but that from the length of time many there are mere dis-senters, and know nothing of the doctrine; so that they are really in conscience innocent, though gone in there as they would into any dissenting place. If this

brother had never had anything to do with B. as such, I should have asked him nothing about it, as happens every day. But your account is that his separation was on account of looseness in discipline. What I think I should do would be not to discuss B. but shew him, say J. E. Batten's confession, where he states what they taught, and ask him simply if he held any of these, as they were the things that made the difficulty. I should not ask anything about B. If he does not hold them I should not make any difficulty.[19]

The casual reader would be excused for supposing from this reference that Batten's confession related to the teachings of Bethesda itself. It is possible that by this time Darby himself thought so. The extract has a more telling feature than this, however. The course the old man was advocating was scarcely distinguishable from that for which he had excommunicated Bethesda and its friends thirty years before, and for which he had ruthlessly destroyed churches, friendships and the common courtesy of dealing of man with man.

Quotation References – Chapter 10.

1. *Autobiography of George Muller*, p. 155.
2. Ibid., p. 156.
3. *The Whole Case of Plymouth and Bethesda*, p. 34.
4. *A History of the Plymouth Brethren*, W. B. Neatby pp. 146–9.
5. Ibid., p. 159.
6. *The Whole Case, etc.*, pp. 29, 30.
7. *The Bethesda Circular (Coll. Writings*, Vol. 15. Stow Hill edn., pp. 165–6).
8. *Letters*, Vol. III, p. 262 (letter of 25th July 1851).
9. Neatby, op. cit., p. 171.
10. Ibid., p. 240.
11. *A Plain Statement of the Doctrine on the Sufferings of our Blessed Lord (Coll. Writings*, Vol. 15, Stow Hill edn., p. 109 note).
12. *Observations on a Tract Entitled "Remarks on the Sufferings of the Lord Jesus." (Coll. Writings*, Vol. 15. Stow Hill edn., p. 42).
13. *The Christian Witness*, 1838, p. 293.
14. Neatby, op. cit., p. 172.
15. *An Ordered Life*, G. H. Lang (1959), p. 15.
16. Quoted G. H. Lang, *The Local Assembly* (1929), pp. 16–17.
17. *Letters*, Vol. II, p. 216.
18. Quoted W. B. Neatby, op. cit., p. 257. (From introduction to 1867 edition of *The Sufferings of Christ*.)
19. *Letters*, Vol. III, pp. 474–5.

CHAPTER 11

OUTREACH AND EXPANSION

Undenominational
But still the church of God
He stood in his conventicle
And ruled it with a rod

Revival ran along the hedge
And made my spirit whole
When steam was on the window-panes
And glory in my soul.

John Betjeman, *Undenominational*

BY 1850 THE MOVEMENT WAS IRREMEDIABLY DIVIDED, AND its two sections were to go their own way, with opposed ideals and conflicting doctrines. The "exclusive" Darbyites became more and more introverted and mystical as the years passed. Retreating behind the fences of the Bethesda discipline, they remained relatively serene while their leader lived, but afterwards reaped to the full the fruits of that morbid fear of evil and of the disastrous methods of controversy which were his tragic legacies to them. Darbyism had a worm at its heart: a worm bred in self-deceit and injustice.

The independent Brethren by contrast had no such powerful central leadership, and as adamantly as Darbyism adopted its centralized discipline, they adopted the opposite principle of extreme independency. Thus, they were to become the happy hunting-ground of the individualist. Each local church would be shaped by its local leaders: where they were wise and tolerant, the spirit of the church would be the same, but elsewhere churches were to be at the mercy of men whose intense sincerity was matched only by the narrowness of their sympathies. It was one of the greatest of their missionary pioneers who expressed concerning the Nonconformist missionaries of his own field something which was only too true of their own churches at home:

Many a little Protestant Pope in the lonely bush is forced by his self-imposed isolation to be prophet, priest, and king rolled into one – really a very big duck he, in his own private pond. Caesar was not the only man who said he would rather be first in a village than second in Rome.[1]

A few years after the division, there was one half-hearted attempt to repair the breach – if in fact it was an attempt at all, which is far from clear.

On several occasions since the beginning of the troubles in Plymouth various groups had met for meetings of "humiliation and prayer." It is to be feared that they fell into a familiar trap. Humiliation and prayer are of little value if they are not accompanied by a resolution to remedy those causes of the humiliation which are within one's power to remedy. Without both correct diagnosis of the sickness, and firm action to cure it, they simply become high-sounding means of self-deceit.

In July 1852 such a meeting was called in Taunton. Darby had been on the Continent again, but he was now back in England, and was involved in the preparations. He declared:

> If any in Bethesda desire really to join in humiliation, it is not desired to exclude them, and means would be taken to afford them the opportunity in such a way as would not involve any one in any sanction or acceptance of what they judge to be evil.[2]

Despite this declaration, the meeting hardly started under favourable auspices, for Darby also declared firmly that he was not proposing to alter his judgment concerning Bethesda,[3] and himself selected the persons to whom invitations were sent. Even so, sufficient dissatisfaction with Darby's actions was voiced to impress him. Another meeting in Bristol followed immediately, and at it Darby made a startling declaration: he had withdrawn his original circular as to Bethesda. The result was a consternation among his followers to which his contemporary letters bear eloquent witness. Darby, like many another in his position, found himself a victim of the prejudices he had created. During his absence from the country, matters had developed beyond his control. Hastily he retreated and explained himself:

> At the meeting at Bristol, I declared that I had withdrawn my original circular as to Bethesda. This took a stumbling-block out of the way of others, and left the ground entirely on its own merits, putting me entirely out of the question. I was questioned on it and cross-questioned: I only resumed all my liberty, that is, position of duty to Christ for my future path; so that Bethesda stands on its own merits, and the discussion on it and its relationship with Brethren I am totally free from, as that is the only act I ever had to say to.[4]

> Is it that my judgment is altered as to the cause of B.? Not at all. But I am outside and beyond that question. I am upon my own evil before God – humbled because we have not maintained His glory.[5]

What precisely had Darby intended? If it had meant anything at all, his statement at Bristol had surely indicated a genuine effort to retrace his tragic steps – perhaps even to effect a belated fulfilment of his words to Müller at that last sad meeting between them (if Müller's version of that incident is accepted). But, as he tried to explain it to his followers, he made it seem nothing but a rather despicable controversial stratagem.

One minor good resulted from the farcical proceedings. Darby wrote as a postcript to a letter of 26th July 1852:

> W. (presumably Wigram) writes me word he has withdrawn his printed papers from circulation and thinks of something else.[6]

Freed from the incubus of Darbyite ecclesiology, the churches of the independent Brethren were now open to their own destiny. The churches described in Chapter 5 continued their natural healthy development, although in some places they had to pass through their own crisis of division in the aftermath of the Bethesda troubles.

The beginnings of an extensive work overseas had already been laid, with work in India and in British Guiana, and with visits by Chapman and others to Spain, as well as the developments in Germany and Switzerland of which we have already learned. This aspect of the story is to be considered in the next chapter. Two of the more important centres in England were closely involved in these efforts overseas. Müller's Scriptural Knowledge Institution in Bristol was already a considerable channel through which financial support was sent to workers in many different parts of the world, particularly to those connected with their own churches. At the same time, the churches to the north of London (which were in direct personal touch with Bethesda*) began to develop their interest in these missionaries. Hackney was then a fashionable residential suburban village, and had long been an important centre of nonconformity. James van Sommer, a solicitor in the Hackney congregation, started in 1853 the Brethren's first missionary journal, *The Missionary Reporter*, while others from the Hackney and Tottenham churches were in touch with men (including James Hudson Taylor and Benjamin Broomhall) who later were to form the nucleus of the China Inland Mission. George Pearse and William Berger, both later home leaders of the China missions, were of this Hackney group: Pearse himself later became a missionary in North Africa.

The decade which followed the Bethesda controversy was one of quiet consolidation. Early in 1853, the movement lost Anthony Norris Groves, one of the first of its leading pioneers to be removed by death. His health already undermined in the East, he had returned to England in March 1848, only to find his strength still further drained by the Bethesda controversy. Nevertheless, he had been able to visit extensively while in England, and had included the North London groups in his journeys. He returned to India in June 1849, but his stay there was short, and it was as a seriously sick man that he reached England for the last time in September 1852. Despite failing health, he was able once more to visit his friends in

---

* Edmund Gosse, when referring to his father's joining the Hackney group in 1847, said that "their central meeting was at Bristol," and did not even know that the Plymouth Church existed! (*The Life of Philip Henry Gosse, F.R.S.* (1890), p. 213.)

Devonshire and London, to encourage them to support the growing work in India, and to meet men who brought him news of wider developments. At Orchard Street he met a notable Italian from Florence, Count Guicciardini, a link with an interesting movement in Italy of which more will be said later, while in Torquay he met a pioneer from yet another part of the world. This was Leonard Strong, a former Anglican clergyman, who had founded the Brethren work in British Guiana. Numbers of men and women who had been influenced by Groves in India, among them several retired army officers who provided a natural source of leadership, were returning to this country and joining with the Brethren churches, and Groves was also able to meet some of the earliest of these accessions to the home churches.

These contacts all brought relief to Groves's last months of intense physical suffering. He died at the Bristol home of his brother-in-law, George Müller, on 20th May 1853, with the exclamation, "Precious Jesus." The work in which his influence had been so positive was now firmly rooted and growing in widely different places. Less known, but surely no less significant, was his personal influence on two of the great shapers of the modern missionary movement: Alexander Duff* and (indirectly through his writings and his influence at Tottenham) James Hudson Taylor.

As in the early years of the movement, small independent churches were still being formed by spontaneous local action in widely separated places. It was almost inevitable that such churches should soon come into contact with the growing movement. In the 1840s and 1850s the birth of such churches in Northern Ireland and in Lanarkshire in Scotland (the latter in some cases among working men in the mining districts) foreshadowed extensive later development in those areas. The formation of such churches in those parts was no new phenomenon, as the New York correspondence of 1818 (see p. 82) had shown. In England, work in the Suffolk villages was also beginning quietly, and attracted the pastoral care of men who proved themselves to be genuine builders of churches. It was to the village of Woolpit in this county that Chapman's protégé Henry Heath moved in 1870, after he had spent twenty constructive years in Hackney. In Liverpool, where there had been groups from the earliest days of the movement, a stable church had been formed in 1844 around a group of men who included William Collingwood, an artist and later a Fellow of the Royal Water-Colour Society, who was born in Greenwich in 1819.

Then, in 1859, the extraordinary religious revival which had started in North America in the previous year reached Britain. In a few years it had transformed the religious life both of North America and of Britain.

---

* For Groves's influence on Duff see his *Memoir*, pp. 323–7, and particularly Duff's letter at Appdx. G. (pp. 536–8). Groves was his companion during his severe illness and journey home in 1834.

Churches of all denominations were filled, and not only churches, but hired halls and theatres and great open-air spaces. Converts were numbered in hundreds of thousands,[*] and great but often eccentric preachers of the Gospel, both working men and men from the upper classes of society, began to attract large crowds of hearers throughout the country.

The effect of this movement upon the independent Brethren was even more fundamental than on other bodies, great though that was. During the years between 1860 and 1870, many of those other bodies experienced an unprecedented increase in membership. The Baptists added two thirds to their strength in England,[†] with more churches founded than in any other single decade of their history, while Congregationalists, Methodists, and to a smaller proportionate extent the Established Churches of each constituent country of the British Isles, all benefited to an extent which in total could have been little, if any, less than in the evangelical revival of the previous century. For their own part, the independent Brethren received an impetus from the revival movement that within two decades transformed both their character and their influence. The impact upon Darby's followers, the exclusives, was probably smaller, and yet they too benefited from the revival. At this period exclusivism numbered among its members many of the more intellectual men among Brethren, and by their prolific writings they gave back to evangelicalism in general some flavour of Darbyite thinking, particularly in matters of eschatology. Their "other-wordly" teachings also reinforced the tendencies towards pietism that evangelicalism had already absorbed from parts of Methodism.

Many of the early revival preachers mixed freely with the congregations of Brethren that were then in existence, and men who were prominent in its earliest days, like Richard Weaver, ex-miner and prize-fighter, on one hand, and Brownlow North, grand-nephew of the great Lord North and grandson of a Bishop of Winchester, on the other, left a lasting influence on them, although not themselves Brethren (Brownlow North was a life-long Anglican, who was also an accredited lay evangelist of the Free Church of Scotland[6a]). To the independent Brethren, the revival came not so much as a means of increase in their existing strength, as a definite formative influence in its own right. Many men who were brought to faith during the revival found the restrictions and inhibitions of the older churches intolerable. Some of them left the older churches of their own will, while others from the start were working independently of existing bodies, and yet others were forced out by clerical opposition. Many of these found a natural home in the uninhibited atmosphere of the informal

[*] See Orr, J. E., *The Second Evangelical Awakening in Britain* (1949), p. 207, and preface, p. 5. Was it a reaction in the next decade which led to the "alarming" religious censuses, of which Gladstone wrote to Samuel Morley in 1881? (*Life of Samuel Morley*, p. 417.)

[†] Ibid., pp. 270-1. Orr computes 100,000 of the 250,000 1865 membership as products of the revival years. See also his *Light of the Nations* (1965), pp. 166 ff.

congregations of Brethren, although the evangelists themselves rarely confined their work within the limits of any one fellowship.

So it was that the second generation of revival preachers included many notable men who threw their lot in fully with Brethren: men such as Joseph Denham Smith, at first a Congregational minister in Dublin; Gordon Forlong, Aberdeen solicitor and at first an episcopal layman; John Hambleton, ex-actor and adventurer; Henry Moorhouse, the "boy evangelist"; and Charles Russell Hurditch, an intense young Devonian. They brought outstanding personality and energy to the service of a simple clear-cut message, which made up by its direct appeal to the crowds who came to hear them, for all it might have lacked in theological finesse. There was a joyous abandon in their revivalism which added a colour and zest to life that more than compensated for that which their Puritan ethic was accused of destroying.

On this side of the Atlantic the revival first broke out in Northern Ireland, and the circumstances marked also the beginning of the main growth of independent Brethren churches there. A certain Mrs. Colville from Gateshead was living near Ballymena, Co. Antrim, in 1856 and 1857, and spent her time visiting the cottages of the district and speaking to the people about a personal knowledge of salvation. One day she met a young man, James M'Quilkin, who had been somewhat antagonistic to her.

> At a tea-table where they met he asked, "Are you a Calvinist, Mrs. C?" "I would not wish," she answered, "to be more or less of a Calvinist than our Lord and His apostles. But I do not care to talk on mere points of doctrine. I would rather speak of the experience of salvation in the soul." She added: "If one were to tell me what he knows of the state of his heart with God I think I could tell him whether he knows the Lord Jesus savingly." This at once closed James's mouth. He felt that his heart was not right, and he dreaded exposing its true state if he spoke further.
>
> As God so ordered it, a lady present began to unbosom herself to Mrs. C.: and had the Holy Spirit been revealing the state of James's heart, he himself told me that it could not have been more exactly described than in the words this lady used. "I waited," he said, "with breathless expectation to hear what Mrs. C. would answer. After a brief pause she said solemnly, My dear, you have never known the Lord Jesus. I knew that she spoke what was true of *me*. I felt as if the ground were about to open beneath me and let me sink into hell. As soon as I could, I left the company. For two weeks I had no peace day or night. At the end of that time I found it by trusting the Lord Jesus."[7]

M'Quilkin immediately began to meet for private prayer with one or two like-minded men, his first convert being one Jeremiah Meneely.*

* This account of the relationship of M'Quilkin and Meneely follows that given by J. G. M'Vicker (*Memoir and Letters* (1902), pp. 31–34). This account is closer to the events and more circumstantial than that appearing in George Müller's *Autobiography* (pp. 448–9).

They had been inspired by reading of George Müller's experience of answered prayer, and soon they were praying for an outpouring of the Holy Spirit on their district. On 14th March 1859, one of a series of meetings convened by these men in Ahoghill, three miles from Ballymena, saw the first of the remarkable mass movements which characterized the revival. The crowds were so great that the indoor meeting, in the First Presbyterian Church, was abandoned, and outside in chilling rain hundreds, moved by the speakers, were falling on their knees in the streets. Soon the movement had reached Belfast, and was affecting churches of all denominations.

Near Ballymena, at the village of Cullybackey, a Presbyterian minister, John Galway M'Vicker, a man of thirty-three, welcomed the revival preachers. He was deeply discontented with his own spiritual life, and was moved by the revival experiences. One night, returning home with his wife, he prayed: "Lord, if we are already Christians make us sure of it; and if we are not, Lord, make us Christians."[8] Within a few weeks he was himself moved by the same experience. M'Vicker's convictions were developing rapidly in the same direction as those of Groves and Müller thirty years before, when he came into contact with M'Quilkin. A short time afterwards he was baptized by Meneely in the nearby river Main, and was immediately disowned by his church. After a brief period with Baptists, M'Vicker threw in his lot with Brethren. Of these men, Meneely became an evangelist who was instrumental in establishing the work of Brethren in Northern Ireland, and he also visited Scotland.* M'Vicker became a Bible teacher known among Brethren throughout the British Isles, and in 1879 he settled in North London.

The revival in Dublin brought into the movement another man who became one of its leaders. This was Joseph Denham Smith, who had been pastor of a Congregational Church in Dun Laoghaire (then Kingstown) since 1848. He became a leading evangelist of the revival and left his pastorate to engage in this wider ministry. Meeting some of the Brethren in Dublin, he threw in his lot with them, and with him one of his converts, T. Shuldham Henry, a barrister and the son of a President of Queen's College, Belfast, who became another leading evangelist of the revival, preaching throughout Britain and in Paris. By the initiative of William Fry,† a Dublin solicitor, Merrion Hall was built in the centre of Dublin in 1863, and in time became one of the largest centres of independent Brethren. Denham Smith (like M'Vicker) later settled in London, and became a nationally-known preacher and teacher. Another influential founder member of the Merrion Hall congregation was the Hon.

* His son, W. J. Meneely, was also an evangelist who moved widely among Brethren in Northern Ireland and Scotland.

† An Alexander Fry of Dublin had been in touch with the North London *Missionary Reporter* in 1854.

Somerset Maxwell, later the eighth Lord Farnham, who became a leader of Irish Protestantism.

From Dublin also came an influence which led through James Patton, a Newtownards watchmaker, to the beginning of a growing work in the Ards Peninsula of Northern Ireland. This work was forwarded by John Walbron, a Scottish evangelist whom Patton invited to settle in the district. Many independent churches were thrown up by the revival in the villages and towns of Ulster, and numerous further foundings took place in the years after 1870, particularly around Belfast. Two teachers who were responsible for much of the pioneer work were Dr. W. J. Matthews, a Belfast medical man, and James Campbell: churches were also visited and built up by evangelists and teachers from the growing Brethren movement in Scotland, among them William McLean, James Smith, John Halyburton, and David Rea, while another man converted in America, John Boal, also returned to his native Northern Ireland to help the churches there.

The result of the efforts of these men and of a long line of their successors has been to make Ulster one of the stronger centres of Brethren work. It must be added that some of the "open" Brethrenism of Northern Ireland has adopted a generally rigid attitude towards other Christians, although these separatist attitudes are not universal, and where they exist they have not been entirely without a cause in some particularly unpleasant opposition from other churches. There is current a wry joke which Brethren tell against themselves, to the effect that there are few "exclusive" assemblies in Northern Ireland, as there are enough rigid "open" assemblies to fulfil that need!

The revival in Britain threw up two distinct classes of evangelist, moulded to the needs of different audiences, and both classes contained men who identified themselves more or less fully with Brethren, although the evangelists seldom confined themselves within strict barriers, but moved wherever opportunity presented itself. It is a fact that many Brethren churches owed their origins and their increase to the work of such evangelists. On the one hand, there were the popular "preachers from the people," men hard in experience and direct in speech, whose lives had often been colourful and dramatic. Of this type there were several noted men among those who mixed freely with Brethren. Henry Moorhouse, son of a Manchester Methodist family, ran wild as a profligate gambler and drinker, but after a brief enlistment (from which he was bought out by his father) he was converted after he had attended revival meetings in December 1861. He went on to become an internationally-known evangelist. John Hambleton was a travelling actor, adventurer and gold-prospector, who had "knocked about" both America and Australia before his conversion in Liverpool, as the revival was beginning: his most notable convert was Thomas John Barnardo. Another man who appears constantly in the records of the period was Joshua Poole, popularly known as "Fiddler Joss," who was converted in Wakefield Prison through Seth Tait, a prison officer, after he had destroyed two families of his own children by drunken neglect, and had scarcely been prevented from murdering his second wife. The story of his rescue from the most degrading and sordid conditions to become a leader of the revival was an evangelical classic.

In sharp contrast to men of this type were the "gentlemen evangelists," often men from the upper classes of society. Three of these men who were of particular importance to the expansion in Ireland were the "Three Kerry Landlords," William Talbot Crosbie of Ardfert Abbey, Richard J. Mahony of Dromore Castle, and F. C. Bland of Derriquin. They were for a time joined in South-West Ireland by two men who had just graduated from Trinity College, Dublin: Robert Anderson (who later became Sir Robert Anderson, for fourteen years head of the Criminal Investigation Department of Scotland Yard), and G. F. Trench, who later married into the Crosbie family and settled at Ardfert. The preaching of these men was by no means confined to Ireland. In Ireland itself the results of their work could not be consolidated amid the contemporary political and religious upheavals, and the extensive emigration which was the feature of those bitter years in Ireland. Crosbie and Mahony both spent some time in Italy, and the influence of all three men was felt throughout Britain. Other unusual leaders among Brethren produced by the later influences of the revival included the Earls of Cavan and Carrick, both of whom became active and influential preachers and teachers.

James Turner, a fish-curer of Peterhead in North-East Scotland, was another man to be powerfully affected by the 1859 revival. Like M'Quilkin in Northern Ireland, he began to hold meetings for prayer, and a considerable movement of God broke out among the hardy fishermen of the district. Turner, praying one day, in his enthusiasm, for the conversion of all the unconverted ministers and elders of Peterhead, was promptly excommunicated by the Kirk. The excommunication merely freed the energies of these enthusiastic men, and a powerful evangelistic movement sprang up along the coasts of the Moray Firth. An ordinary fish-curing shed was used for the early meetings, and here Gordon Forlong the lawyer and "gentleman evangelist" from Aberdeen, and other leading evangelists, preached under lighted oil-lamps to an audience seated on rough planks of wood supported on fish barrels. The work in Peterhead was consolidated, and there grew up there some of the largest Brethren churches of Scotland; although the ubiquitous "exclusive" division reached out to divide even this flourishing community.

In 1860, at about the same time as the events in Peterhead, a new secretary of the North-East Coast Mission had been appointed in Aberdeen. Donald Ross had formerly been a Free Church missionary among the Lanarkshire miners. His work was highly successful, and he was soon in the full tide of the revival movement. Eventually he became dissatisfied with the restrictions of his position, and in 1870 resigned to take the Gallowgate Chapel in Aberdeen for an independent evangelistic work. At that time, he wrote, he had heard of Brethren "as bad, bad people, and we resolved to have nothing to do with them."[9] Within a short time, however, his study of the Bible caused him to join forces with a tiny Brethren congregation in Castle Street. It was the beginning of a considerable work, Donald Ross proving himself to be a pioneer of the first rank. Later he worked in Edinburgh, and afterwards, from 1879 until his death in 1903, built up churches in a number of centres in North America, including Chicago, San Francisco and Kansas City. He established periodicals both in Britain and America, the British *Northern Evangelist and Intelligencer* later becoming the *Northern Witness* and from 1887 *The Witness*, which has proved to be one of the most enduring of all Brethren journals.

Farther south, in Lanarkshire, there were already some scattered congregations, the result of spontaneous actions on the part of groups of individuals in the pre-revival years. The influence of the revival greatly increased the movement both in that county and in the adjoining county of Ayrshire. In Dalry, in Ayrshire, there was direct influence from the Northern Irish Movement. The leading figure there, a blind man named Samuel Dodds, had been a Free Church missioner: he was gifted as a Bible teacher, and his influence led to the formation of a church which was visited by men from his native Ireland, including Jeremiah Meneely and John G. M'Vicker. Much of the movement in those counties was spontaneous in character. It spread rapidly in the 1860s and 1870s, and was eventually to form another of the strong areas of Brethren influence. In the city of Glasgow itself, the work was more directly the result of preaching by the more notable evangelists of the revival, in particular of Gordon Forlong. It is possible that earlier groups had been in existence there, but the first group which is still surviving dates back to about 1860. From that date the movement took firm root, and the number of churches in the city and its environs increased quickly, so that Glasgow became one of the chief cities of the independent Brethren movement.

There had been groups in Edinburgh from the earlier days of the movement. Darby had known of a group there very early in the movement's history,[*] and Robert Nelson of that city had been one of the main challengers of Darby's actions at the Bath meeting which followed the Plymouth troubles. In the late 1860s the church in Edinburgh was strengthened by the coming of Robert Mitchell, an Ayrshire man who had been influenced by Lord Congleton and others in London. Mitchell was a scholarly man, and his influence in Edinburgh was a wholesome one. The churches in Edinburgh and district were later increased through evangelistic work by Donald Ross and his colleagues.

[*] See page 85 of this book.

In England the movement had already become numerous well before the revival broke. A common pattern of growth followed the example of the early churches in Plymouth, Bristol and Barton Hall, Hereford, where strong central churches established groups of churches in their own districts. This tendency was greatly accelerated in the atmosphere created by the revival. Several districts in the London area experienced this type of development, the earliest growth being in the suburbs and villages to the north. The two early groups at Tottenham and Hackney (both of which were then separate villages in the countryside), were in close touch with each other, and became vigorous opponents of the Darbyite Bethesda discipline. They were strengthened by the arrival of Henry Heath from North Devon in 1848, and later when James Wright from Bristol lived there for a period of some years in the mid-fifties. The most powerful factor in the growth in this district was, however, the accession to the movement of John Morley, the wealthy senior partner of the noted textile firm of I. and R. Morley. Morley came from a Hackney Nonconformist family of considerable influence, his younger brother being the Congregational leader and political reformer Samuel Morley (who later became Liberal member of Parliament for Bristol). John Morley retired from business in 1855, at the age of forty-eight, and thereafter gave the whole of his time to development of Christian work. He was responsible for bringing many of the more noted of the revival preachers to visit North London, and for introducing leading men of the movement and of evangelical circles in general to each other. He also brought to settle in London men such as Denham Smith and John G. M'Vicker. In 1867 Morley set up an "iron room" in Clapton, not far from Hackney, where there had not previously been a Brethren assembly. The church there flourished under the influence of such strong personalities as Denham Smith, Shuldham Henry, and Russell Hurditch. Starting with a membership of eleven, the numbers increased to more than four hundred within twelve years, and accommodation in the little mission hall (the Victorian equivalent of the modern prefabricated building) became impossibly strained. Accordingly, Morley built Clapton Hall in Alkham Road, Stoke Newington, one of the largest buildings which Brethren have built for themselves. J. G. M'Vicker was preacher on the first Sunday, 1st February 1880, and remained as a pastor of the church until, on 5th January 1900, he passed quietly into the presence of God in the evening of a long day spent visiting members of the church. The church reached its greatest membership in 1888, when over seven hundred were in fellowship there. Other churches were formed as offshoots from Clapton Hall in the growing outer suburbs of London to the north-east.

The influence of the three active churches at Clapton Hall, Hackney and Tottenham has led to the establishment of a strong body of churches throughout the north and north-eastern parts of the London area, although the movements of population of later years have long deprived the original churches themselves of much of their former strength.*

John Morley's youngest brother Samuel did not join with the Brethren, but remained a leading Congregationalist and social reformer. It is of interest, however, that his oldest daughter, Rebekah Hope Morley, took an active part in her uncle's work while living nearby at Stamford Hill, and sympathized with her uncle's views.*

> She had long devoted herself to Christian work, and at Stamford Hill, and elsewhere, her labours had been attended with remarkable success. She had the rare gift of speaking straight to the hearts of people in simple but stirring language, and winning them into paths of righteousness. Moreover, she had considerable literary skill, and carried on an important "ministry" by means of her pen.[10]

When Samuel Morley moved to Hall Place at Leigh, near Tonbridge in Kent, in 1870, a tent mission was immediately arranged in the village, and it was conducted by Russell Hurditch. Samuel Morley then built an "undenominational chapel" in Leigh, a Brethren evangelist named Maxted being invited to settle there in a cottage which was built to adjoin the chapel, and Rebekah Morley threw herself "heart and soul"[11] into the work of the chapel. Samuel Morley himself, though, in his biographer's words, "not in any sense or degree an Open or a Plymouth Brother,"[12] attended the services at this chapel, and occasionally the communion. His reply to inquirers was: "Why? because I like the simplicity of the meeting, that is all."[13]

The semi-apologetic tone of Morley's biographer over this part of his life is amusing:

> And so it came to pass that, although, to all intents and purposes, the chapel was undenominational, the Sacraments were administered in a manner identical with those of the "Open Brethren".[14]

– a pretty apt description of virtually every congregation of the independent Brethren at that time!

On 16th May 1872, Rebekah Morley married Herbert Wilbraham Taylor, a Brethren "gentleman evangelist" who had accompanied Henry Moorhouse on an evangelistic tour of America in 1869–70, and whose

---

* Although much smaller than in their prime, two of these three churches still survive as active works. Tottenham and Clapton still use their nineteenth-century buildings, but the Hackney assembly long since lost its separate identity, and is continued in several other churches in the inner suburbs of North London.

* "Her views on religious questions, if not entirely identical, were very nearly in accordance with those held by the religious community known as Plymouth Brethren." (*The Life of Samuel Morley*, Edwin Hodder, 1887, p. 376. Hodder is throughout rather amusingly sensitive on the Morley family's connexions with Brethren, and makes virtually no reference to John Morley's extensive Christian work.)

father had been Gentleman Usher to Queen Victoria. She died as a result of childbirth after only five-and-a-half years of marriage. Edwin Hodder wrote of her:

In all parts of the country there were those who traced the beginning of new life to her loving ministrations.[15]

Under her married name of Mrs. Herbert W. Taylor she published devotional works which had a considerable vogue.

After her death, Samuel Morley founded several similar "undenominational chapels" in local villages in Kent. Later, in 1879, the veteran Nonconformist missionary Robert Moffatt settled in Leigh in a house belonging to Morley, and regularly attended the chapel until his death in 1883. Only a few days before his death he had written to Henry Groves acknowledging with pleasure the receipt of the first part of the diary of the first great missionary journey of the Brethren pioneer missionary F. S. Arnot.[15a]

Brethren congregations were established in other parts of the London suburbs somewhat later than in the north and centre. In South London the movement received an impetus after the secession from the Anglican ministry in 1862 of William Lincoln, who had been curate at St. George's, Southwark, but had later become minister of Beresford Chapel, Walworth. The lease of the building was in the minister's name, and the congregation (or as many as followed him) continued to use it after his accession to Brethren. Lincoln published an explanation of his disagreement with the Church of England under the title of *The Javelin of Phinehas* – a book which plainly had a considerable vogue, for it could only have been a few months after its publication that Edmund Gosse, then a boy of thirteen, remembered finding in his father's secluded home in St. Marychurch

. . . a perfectly excruciating work ambiguously styled *The Javelin of Phineas* [sic], which lay smouldering in a dull red cover on the drawing-room table.[16]

(But, then, the work was hardly intended for light juvenile reading, however precocious.)

Lincoln associated with Brethren from the time of his secession, bringing his church practices only gradually into line with those customary among them over a period of years. He always retained a close personal control of the preaching, most of which he undertook himself, and as a result some men who desired to see a more whole-hearted acceptance of characteristic Brethren practice moved from his church to form other congregations. These new churches, however, retained their communion with Beresford Chapel: an interesting example of the working of independent tolerance. In this way differences of practice produced multiplication, rather than the division being caused by exclusive practices – an important factor in judging the viability of the two systems.

Shortly after this, Gordon Forlong began a settled evangelistic work in the inner western suburbs, while on the outer western fringes of London congregations were established during the 1860s in Hampton and Kingston on the south-west and in St. Albans in the north-west. By now the movement, carried on the flood-tide of the evangelical awakening, was spreading into practically every corner of the country. London itself was soon circled with meetings. In the Midlands widespread evangelistic work was undertaken by Frederick Bannister, a former Anglican clergyman, and by John Hambleton, while the industrial districts of Lancashire and Yorkshire saw the evangelistic campaigns of Richard Weaver and Henry Moorhouse. The older groups of churches in East Anglia and in the West Country continued to grow, the movement also spreading strongly into South Wales. New ground was also broken in the south-east corner of England, with a strong work at Eastbourne in the early 1870s, while at the other end of England, in Carlisle on the Scottish border, a successful Presbyterian minister, William Reid, left that church in 1875 to found a congregation which became another strong regional centre. Like nearby Kendal, the churches of the Carlisle district owed much to a man of Quaker background, Jonathan Carr of the famous biscuit manufacturers. Carlisle more recently gave to the movement another of its greatest benefactors in Sir John Laing, of the well-known building and civil engineering concern, who later moved to North London.

The movement, with its complete lack of any formal organization, has nevertheless benefited from a number of other well-to-do men who have generously financed its work. Other men who emulated Morley and Carr in this respect were Huntingdon Stone of Greenwich (like Carr, a biscuit manufacturer, of Peek Frean & Co.), Charles A. Aitchison, of a well-known Glasgow bakery, and P. W. Petter, engineer of Yeovil, the inventor of the well-known Petter engine.

Developments in one obscure district of the West Country during the latter part of the nineteenth century showed the characteristics of the movement at its best. On the borders of Devon and Somerset there is an area of rural upland known as the Blackdown Hills. The district adjoins those parts which had been evangelized during the first half of the century by the sturdy Robert Gribble, but the Blackdowns themselves were not touched by this movement. In 1863 there arrived on the hills, at the village of Clayhidon, a shoemaker from Exeter, George Brealey, and his wife.* Brealey was a man of great physical courage, who had achieved some local celebrity in his earlier years by two exploits, in which he had rescued a woman from drowning in a river in the full spate of flood, and later when he had entered a burning house and rescued two children. This physical courage had stood him in good stead in the revival years when, encouraged by the evangelist Reginald Radcliffe, he had engaged in open-air preaching and tract distribution around Exeter, in the face of frequent

* *Strength of the Hills*, by Roland H. White, 1964.

threats of physical violence. He was planning to go as a missionary to the West Indies, when the needs of the Blackdown Hill country were brought home to him.

During the remaining twenty-five years of his life, George Brealey remained in the Blackdowns, building village chapels or re-opening older ones, in the six or seven hill villages, and maintaining a steady pastoral work which also included day-schools for the elementary education of the children. Brealey himself was a poor man, and his congregations were no better off, but they put up several buildings of their own, and he was able to install resident colleagues in some of the villages. He avoided clashes with the parish clergy, sometimes winning their co-operation, and succeeded largely in gaining the confidence of local authorities. Much of his financial support was provided through the Scriptural Knowledge Institution in Bristol. Two of the Mission's earliest converts became prominent in the Brethren movement, Ephraim Venn as an evangelist, and Alfred Redwood as a missionary in India. Redwood was only the first of a succession of missionaries from the hills: he and his sons after him have made a notable contribution to Brethren missions in India.

The work of the Blackdown Hills Mission was continued after George Brealey's death in 1888 by numbers of helpers who came to reside on the hills, and especially by his son Walter, and then by his grandson Douglas Brealey, who became one of the most venerable and generally respected leaders of Brethren. It is interesting that educational work continued until as late as 1947, when the last of the day-schools, at Bishopswood, was closed, the growth of the State education services having at last made it redundant.

The social features of Brealey's work introduce an interesting side of the activity of the revival years. We have already seen how Müller and Chapman had succeeded in identifying themselves with the needs of the community around them, in ways which certainly did not suggest any carelessness of the material needs of the people. In their limited and individualistic manner, not a few of the Brethren of the mid-century period also showed a proper consciousness of the requirements of Christian compassion. Because aspects of their teaching, particularly where it was influenced by Darbyism, were "other-worldly" and inclined to decry "mere philanthropy," it by no means followed that all of them drew the false conclusion that philanthropy was not a part of genuine Christian action. It is indicative of the more outgoing of them that James van Sommer's *The Missionary Reporter* included home social problems within the range of its interests.[17]

So it was that many of the revival preachers committed themselves whole-heartedly to spells of enthusiastic, if amateur, effort for the relief of some of the victims of crying poverty and *laissez-faire* economics. In London, Charles Russell Hurditch, who at the time of his marriage on 11th May 1865 to Mary Holmes (the daughter of a well-to-do London stationer and cricket enthusiast, who was also linked with Brethren), was secretary of the Young Men's Christian Association at the Stafford Rooms, Edgware Road, threw himself with his helpers into relief work. They organized soup kitchens and coal and food tickets, and tried amateur efforts at organizing employment, in the face of overwhelming needs whose cure was so far beyond the capacity of small groups of well-meaning men. He had by then resigned his appointment with the Y.M.C.A. to engage in wider work, and something of the immense energy of men like Hurditch can be gauged from his daughter's description of the evangelistic activities which were accompanied by his social work:

> He published in succession five magazines, changing their character and style according to the needs of the day. Thirteen million Gospel papers and tracts, of which he was the editor, had been issued from his office in sixteen years. He compiled two hymn-books – and was himself the composer of thirty of the hymns – which reached a circulation of over half a million. Then there were his constant preaching tours throughout England, Ireland, Scotland and Wales.[18]

> Keen young men and women started night-schools where working people were taught to read and write, where factory girls learnt to sew and cook; street urchins and hooligans were gathered into clubs where they were given free instruction in trades and hobbies. And all this ten years before the first Education Act, with its ultimate train of technical schools and evening-classes.[19]

Lord Congleton defied a deeply felt prejudice against "engaging in worldly politics" to support Lord Shaftesbury's reforms in the House of Lords, and in this connexion it is of interest that another leading man, Somerset Maxwell, Lord Farnham, also served in Parliament for some years. In the remote Island of Achill, Co. Mayo, in West Ireland, Lord Cavan made strenuous efforts to improve the economy and livelihood of the islanders, even while the Irish troubles were at their height.

A few of them (like Müller in earlier years) broke through into large-scale organized work. William Stokes, the early pioneer of the movement in Dublin, was responsible for starting orphan work and rescue work in that city. In England, J. W. C. Fegan, brought up an "exclusive," but himself an independent, was inspired by a visit to Deptford Ragged School to devote his life to "rescue" work among poor lads, and opened his first boys' home in 1872. The work grew into a full-scale orphan and training programme and still continues. Fegan's work gained the sympathetic interest of the Darwin family at Down in Kent, to which village his parents had moved their home, and it was through Darwin's goodwill that Fegan was able to obtain the use of the village Reading Room for services. Members of the Darwin household attended his services, in which the family itself maintained a sympathetic if distant interest. They were apparently particularly struck by Fegan's success in reforming alcoholics. Not only did Charles Darwin himself comment on this, but Mrs. Darwin wrote in the course of her family correspondence:

Hurrah for Mr. Fegan! Mrs. Evans attended a prayer meeting in which old M. made "as nice a prayer as ever you heard in your life" (Mrs. Litchfield added the note: "'Old M.' was a notable old drunkard in the village of Down, converted by Mr. Fegan.")[20]

From a Brethren background also came the greatest name of them all in orphan work, Thomas John Barnardo. Barnardo was converted under John Hambleton in Dublin in 1862, and joined the Brethren there. At first he intended to join the party who were going with Hudson Taylor to China, but the story of how in 1866 he was diverted, while still a medical student, into rescue work in the bitter surroundings of London's East End is now a classic of Christian social action. During the early years of his work, Barnardo attended the Brethren meeting in Sidney Street, Stepney, and it was from among the Brethren, then in the full flush of the revival enthusiasm, that he found a large proportion of his early helpers. When, in those early years, he was met by opposition and slander from men who included representatives and ministers of the older churches, it was in the freedom which he had learned from Brethren church practices that (like Brealey in the Blackdown Hills) he found liberty to baptize his converts and to consolidate their faith in the communion of the Lord's Supper. Barnardo remained with Brethren throughout the formative years of his great orphan work, and it was not until the late 1880s that he eventually left Brethren for the Church of England. A few years earlier, on 27th November 1882, he had written in his diary:

> Attended Lord's Supper; very happy, although much I don't like. Am less and less impressed by propriety of "open" Table. Am sure *not* God's order; but congregation not prepared for any change.[21]

(By the "open" order to which he objected he apparently referred to freedom for participation in the leading of the worship, not to the free admission of all true Christians to partake of the communion.)

It is interesting, too, that Wilson Carlile, the founder of the Church Army, was converted through the instrumentality of his aunt, a member of the Brethren, with whom he had his early Christian experience.

To many a man in the street, the name of the Plymouth Brethren conjures up a picture of unrelieved gloom that rivals that of the Presbyterianism of Holy Willie. An example of this reflex reaction is seen in the comment by Lord Haldane's biographer on Haldane's grandfather, Richard Burdon-Sanderson: "the narrow Evangelicalism which he finally embraced cast a deep shadow over an otherwise happy home. He had joined the Plymouth Brethren in 1837."[22] It is perhaps inevitable that the memories of ecclesiastical equivalents of Cold Comfort Farm should survive (particularly as many of them make first-class anecdotes), while the far more numerous examples of happy family life are passed over. The childhood experiences of the talented Edmund Gosse, shut up in his most formative years to share the recluse life of his widowed father, are all too often and inaccurately assumed to be typical of Brethren family life (and even Edmund Gosse enjoyed the companionship and love of his eccentric but noble father to an extent which thousands would envy).

Sometimes, indeed, the truth could be sad and dark, particularly where a narrow-minded bigotry reigned: but in what circle cannot that be said? The very fact that so many of the large families of those days remained loyal to the churches of their childhood, in the face of their uninviting meeting-rooms and the eccentricities which inevitably accompany the extreme democracy of Brethren worship, tells its own story. There were many others also, who found the intellectual bondage of an extreme evangelicalism intolerable and had not the patience or the insight to find their own way through to the broader pastures beyond, but who nevertheless took with them to other fellowships the stable Christian faith they had learned among Brethren. Life was puritan, and many amusements normally regarded as an ordinary part of life were regarded as almost morally wrong: but life had many compensations to offer. As the youngest daughter of Russell Hurditch wrote:

> I write from childhood's memories of those conferences, so it is not to be expected that I can render an account of their spiritual portent. To me they assumed the character of a delightful indoor picnic. There were miles of tea-tables – so it seemed to my infant gaze – covered with unbleached linen cloths and adorned with pink spiraea plants, endless rows of pink-bordered delf tea-cups and saucers, on which were inscribed the words "Jesus Only" in a circle of pink. There were plates piled with new bread and butter and penny buns, the buttering of which had occupied all the morning hours of my mother and other sainted women. There was the High Table at which we were privileged to sit with the speakers – who from the platform heights had seemed such awesome persons, but who were now benevolence and fun personified. I was fascinated by an eyeglass that continually jumped from its precarious holding in the twinkling eye of General Sir Robert Phayre and the long pointed "nannygoat" beard of Dr. McKilliam that waggled as he ate and talked.[*] I would watch the ferret-like eyes of a notorious gaol-bird – whom the Revival had transformed into a popular preacher – which sparkled with humour or glinted like steel as he regaled us with stories of his prison life . . .

> Lord Congleton was there – a long lean, graceful-figured man with a face of peculiar melancholy, who to judge from his correspondence with my father was chief arbitrator in the Brethren's quarrels; the Earl of Shaftesbury, who had pondered on the cruelties inflicted on the little boys who were made to climb and clean London's foul chimneys, and from which by a Parliamentary measure he had them all released; Sir Robert Anderson, of Scotland Yard, who knocked down his Biblical opponents like ninepins, and the aesthetic young Campbell

* The beard is in evidence in his photograph contained in *Chief Men Among the Brethren*.

Morgan with high cheek-bones and an abnormally high forehead, from which long hair was thrown back, who appeared at the conference with a red rose in his buttonhole. (He was then in his twenties.) A buttonhole was considered worldly by the Brethren, so my father had it "blocked out" when reproducing his photograph and thereby incurred his displeasure.[23]

Nor were they without social life:

Sundays, far from being the gloomy days usually associated with that epoch, were especially bright and cheerful; for then it was that my father's thoughts turned to the lonely young business men and women of London, with whom his earlier work at Stafford Rooms had bought him into contact.

Family friends would be the guests at Sunday suppers, when practical jokes – which were such a feature of those days – would convulse the family with laughter . . . Such hilarity, however, was reserved for those times when my father was on his evangelistic tours and mother taking the waters at Harrogate.[24]

Christmas in its religious sense may have been written off by some of them (as by Philip Gosse) as a "heathen festival" (which may not have been without an element of historical truth), but the more down-to-earth drew from it a conclusion which was the opposite of the dismal one which Gosse drew – if it was not a religious festival, then festivities were not, after all to be inhibited by religious scruples![25]

Those were days of great conference meetings, when Brethren from all over the country would meet, and the links between the unorganized and scattered congregations would be cemented by personal contacts. At the larger of these, attendance was by no means always limited to members of their own churches, as the account already quoted shows plainly enough. Impressions and reports of some of these conferences survive. One of the most celebrated, because of its subsequent appearance in one of literature's minor classics, was held at the Freemason's Hall in London from 9th to 12th May 1864. Speakers included J. L. Harris, Leonard Strong, H. W. Soltau, the Hon. W. Wellesley, J. M. Code, the Earl of Cavan, Robert Howard, William Lincoln, John Hambleton and also Philip Henry Gosse, who had been persuaded out of his seclusion in Devon for one of his then rare visits to London (perhaps by his neighbour, Leonard Strong). Edmund Gosse, not yet fifteen, accompanied his father, and from a speaker there fell one of those fatuous remarks which tend to escape from the best of men on such occasions, and which hammered yet one more nail into the coffin of Edmund Gosse's evangelical beliefs:

The interminable ritual of prayers, hymns and addresses left no impression on my memory, but my attention was suddenly stung into life by a remark. An elderly man, fat and greasy, with a voice like a bassoon, and an imperturbable assurance, was denouncing the spread of infidelity, and the lukewarmness of professing Christians, who refrained from battling the wickedness at their doors. They were like the Laodiceans, whom the Angel of the Apocalypse spewed out of his mouth. For instance, who, the orator asked, is now rising to check the outburst of idolatry in our midst? "At this very moment," he went on, "there is proceeding, unreproved, a blasphemous celebration of the birth of Shakespeare, a lost soul now suffering for his sins in hell!" My sensation was that of one who has suddenly been struck on the head; stars and sparks beat round me. If some person I loved had been grossly insulted in my presence, I could not have felt more powerless in anguish. No one in that vast audience raised a word of protest, and my spirits fell to their nadir.[26]

Perhaps Gosse's wandering attention had over-dramatized the occasion. If no protest was raised in public, the offence of the remark was at least removed in the printed report of the conference. For the "elderly man, fat and greasy, with a voice like a bassoon" (whose identity is plain from the report, but is not disclosed here for charity's sake, for he was a man loved and honoured for his work) was in fact making a protest, not unnatural to a pious Christian devotion,* against the performance of a sacred oratorio during the Shakespeare tercentenary – "the groans of Christ set to music, and sung as a kind of introduction to a festival held in honour of Shakspeare [sic]"[27]

A formative series of conferences was held for many years at Leominster in Herefordshire. William Yapp, who had been one of the early members of the Hereford church, had moved to London in 1853, where he set up a Bible Depot in Welbeck Street and acted as a publisher of many of the Brethren writings. He was joined in this venture by a partner, James E. Hawkins, in 1861, and was therefore able to return to Leominster in 1863. There he later established a conference centre in Waterloo House, which was much used by Brethren, the series of conferences beginning in 1874, the year of his death.[27a] John G. M'Vicker was a leading mover in some of these conferences, and his impressions of two successive days of one such conference give an indication of their value to leading men in the loosely-knit fellowship of churches:

Leominster, 24-8-81.
I keep well, and on the whole am enjoying the meetings. My want of enjoyment in them is as useful perhaps as the highest enjoyment of them would be. One gets used to pull in single harness, and is in danger of losing the capacity of running comfortably in a team. The discomfort that may be experienced when trying to get on with others shows the bad habits that one has been forming, and the need of being helped on that point.
At the same time I must not leave on you the impression that I am not enjoying these conference meetings now. For I am, and in part greatly, and hope today and tomorrow to enjoy them still more, and from them all to get great good. And the private intercourse with brethren is exceedingly pleasant.

Leominster, 25-8-81.
I am enjoying the meetings increasingly, and also greatly enjoying the private

* A similar protest is voiced less directly by the Rev. John Macpherson in his life of Henry Moorhouse.

fellowship with brethren for which the brief intervals and the meal times give opportunity. I have seldom been in a better meeting than we had last night. Mr. Groves* surpassed himself in speaking on the sovereignty of the grace of God; a brother followed briefly and well; then Mr. Dyer wisely and most ably and profitably filled up and guarded and strengthened what Mr. Groves had so well said. Robt. Chapman closed with the weighty words which only he of all men I have known or heard seems given to use. We all felt it good to be there, and to worship in the power of the truths we had been listening to. After supper I read David's words to God in 1 Chron. xvii. as the best expression of our hearts in contemplating the great things which God had opened up to us.[28]

It is interesting that the printed report of a similar conference at Leominster in October 1884 shows that the Lord's Supper was celebrated on the Tuesday evening.[29]

The expansion during the later part of the nineteenth century altered the character of the independent Brethren movement. One enemy of the movement, in the 1880s, quoted with approval an earlier scornful gibe at the

> knot of high Tory gentlemen and ladies, unable to endure either the corruptions of Anglicanism or the vulgarity of Dissent, and so establishing a sort of Madeira climate for their delicate lungs,[30]

but even when he repeated the gibe, it was already out of date. The revival turned the independent Brethren very largely into a "gospel mission" movement, and many of the difficulties which they have since encountered, as well as their considerable pre-occupation with church doctrine (sometimes referred to tendentiously as "assembly truth"), have arisen from attempts to restore the intense insight into the essential nature of the Church which characterized the early movement.

The revival preachers used temporary accommodation for their missions – large tents and, where the work took root, the ubiquitous Victorian pre-fabricated hut or "iron room." This habit coincided with a deliberate indifference to any form of outward show, and with the sentimental attachment of many of the survivors of the first generation to the makeshift accommodation in which they had seen their early spiritual visions; and the overall effect upon the architecture of Brethren halls has been disastrous. Few among them have paid any attention to the subtle influence of surroundings upon the worship and thinking of those who frequent them week after week. We may also attribute to the revival influences the common use of the title of "Gospel Hall" for those buildings – a use, it should be added, which is now almost discarded in the cities, but which is still common in rural districts: it is not of course confined to Brethren meeting-places. In cities it is more usual today to find one of their buildings

* Henry Groves, the eldest son of Anthony Norris Groves.

known by a geographical definition (often the name of the street in which it stands) and described as a "Hall" or "Chapel": very occasionally a building will be called a "Church," but this is not generally favoured because it is held to lead to confusion with the correct use of that word for the fellowship of Christian believers themselves. It should also be added that it is most unusual to find any denominational description added: we shall make reference to Brethren's quixotic relationship to their name in a later chapter – it is necessary only to remark here that it derives from a sentiment that is important and praiseworthy, namely a reluctance to take any distinctive label which would seem to deny the basic principle that every true Christian is an equal member of the Church of God.

To the revival influence we may probably look also for an explanation for the almost universal use of two separate hymnbooks in their services; a devotional book, containing many of their own distinctive hymns of adoration, for the communion, and an evangelistic or more general book for the other services. The "Sankey" hymnbook was itself in very common use until about the time of the Second World War.

By the time of the First World War, according to A. Rendle Short, there were about twelve hundred churches of independent Brethren in the British Isles.[31] If this figure is accurate,* there would seem to have been further expansion in the following half-century, for a recent address book lists about seventeen hundred churches in 1959. These figures can only be approximations, not only because the lists themselves are inaccurate and incomplete, but also because the line of distinction between Brethren churches and other independent congregations and missions has always been one which it has been impossible to draw with any clarity, and Brethren themselves would feel that any attempt to draw such a line would be contrary to their own basic principles of church fellowship. The figures indicate that the total membership of independent Brethren churches (excluding those of "exclusives") in the British Isles may be between 75,000 and 100,000, or about one quarter the size of the Baptist and Congregationalist denominations, and comparable, in England alone, with the Presbyterian Church of England, as it existed before its union with the Congregational Church.

Quotation References – Chapter 11.

1. *Thinking Black,* Dan Crawford (1912), pp. 324–5.
2. *Letters,* Vol. I, p. 211 (letter of July 1852).

* All statistics relating to Brethren churches must be treated with a measure of reserve, as with no denominational organization in existence no accurate figures have ever been compiled. Some indication of the number of churches can be obtained from a published U.K. address book, but this itself is very approximate as notification of the existence of churches and of changes depends entirely upon local initiative. Figures of actual membership are necessarily subjective estimates, based on the number of churches.

3. Ibid., pp. 212–14 (letter of 16th July 1852).
4. Ibid., Vol. III, pp. 280–1 (letter undated).
5. Ibid., Vol. I, p. 219 (letter of 30th July 1852).
6. Ibid., p. 216.
6a. *Brownlow North: the Story of his Life and Work*, K. Moody-Stuart (1904), pp. 107 and 110–16.
7. *Selected Letters with Brief Memoir of J. G. M'Vicker*. "Echoes of Service" (1902), pp. 31–32.
8. Ibid., p. 9.
9. Quoted, David J. Beattie, *Brethren, the Story of a Great Recovery* (1940), p. 266; and James Cordiner, *Fragments from the Past* (1961), p. 18.
10. *The Life of Samuel Morley*, Edwin Hodder (1887), p. 375.
11. Ibid., p. 376.
12. Ibid., p. 377.
13. Ibid.
14. Ibid.
15. Ibid., p. 386.
15a. Reproduced in the preface to Arnot's *Garenganze* (1889).
16. *Father and Son*, p. 145.
17. "James van Sommer, an undenominational Christian and man of prayer," T. C. F. Stunt, *Journal* of the Christian Brethren Research Fellowship, August 1967, No. 16, p. 80.
18. *Peculiar People*, "Septima" (1935), p. 30. (The book is written anonymously, but the identification has been verified by comparison of details of the marriage on p. 20 of the book with the relevant Marriage Register.) "Septima" was the second wife of Henry Grattan Guinness.
19. Ibid., p. 13.
20. *Emma Darwin: A Century of Family Letters*, Mrs. Henrietta Litchfield (1915), Vol. II, p. 244 (letter dated February 1881).
21. Quoted Norman Wymer, *Father of Nobody's Children* (1955), Arrow edn., p. 121.
22. *Haldane of Cloan*, Dudley Sommer (1960), p. 39.
23. *Peculiar People*, pp. 45–47.
24. Ibid., pp. 81–82.
25. Ibid., pp. 43–45.
26. *Father and Son*, p. 167.
27. *Report of Three Days' Meetings for Prayer and Addresses on the "Sure Word of Prophecy"* held in Freemasons' Hall, May 9th, 10th and 12th, 1864, p. 70.
27a. The date is given on p. 19 of Robt. Chapman's *Letters*.
28. *Selected Letters*, op. cit., pp. 108–9.
29. *Notes of Conference Held at Leominster No. 4 – October 6th–10th, 1884*.
30. *Plymouth Brethrenism Unveiled and Refuted*, William Reid (3rd. edn. 1880), p. 37. (The original remark was made in 1842 by J. C. Philpot, a High Calvinist seceder from the Church of England who was contemporary with the beginning of the Brethren movement.)
31. *The Principles of Open Brethren*, A. R. Short (1913), p. 94. Short adds that the list from which he took his figures is "very incomplete," and the increase referred to in the text might therefore be partly accounted for by the inclusion in later editions of previously omitted addresses. The book is not dated, but I am indebted to Professor F. F. Bruce for the publication date.

CHAPTER 12

WORLDWIDE GROWTH

> Boom ye church timbers!
> Flash forth ye curses of the councils!
> Crush with eternal anathemas,
> The outcast race of Stundists!
>
> Dark and gloomy, demon-like,
> He shuns the flock, the Orthodox,
> He skulks in nooks and corners dark,
> God's foe, the damnèd Stundist.
> > from an Orthodox attack on Nonconformists, quoted in
> > R. S. Latimer, *Dr. Baedeker and his Apostolic Work in
> > Russia* (1907), p. 192

> I AM de-nationalized – a brother to all men; Arab, African, Mongol, Aryan,
> Jew; seeing in the Incarnation a link that binds us up with all men.
> > Dan Crawford, quoted in *Dan Crawford of Central Africa*, p. 431

IN 1867 DWIGHT L. MOODY VISITED GREAT BRITAIN FOR THE first time. He did not come, as in later years, as the leader of a great evangelistic campaign, but for a more private reason:

There were two men in England whom Mr. Moody had a great desire to hear and meet – Charles H. Spurgeon and George Müller, and with the twofold purpose of affording a beneficial trip for Mrs. Moody and making the acquaintance of these leaders in Christian work, he went abroad.[1]

While in Britain, he visited Dublin. There he was accosted by a young man.

He introduced himself to me and said he would like to come to Chicago to preach. He was a beardless boy – he didn't look more than seventeen – and I said to myself, "He can't preach." He wanted me to let him know what boat I was going to America on, as he would like to go on the boat with me. Well, I thought he couldn't preach, and I didn't let him know.[2]

The young man was Henry Moorhouse, now aged twenty-seven, and a veteran preacher of the revival. A year later Moody received a letter in Chicago, saying that Moorhouse was in America, and wished to preach in his church in Chicago, if he would have him. Moody was not enthusiastic, but Moorhouse persisted. Reluctantly, Moody and his elders gave him the pulpit on a Thursday evening, when Moody was away from Chicago. Returning on the Saturday, Moody was surprised to hear that the young preacher had electrified his audiences with two addresses on John 3:16, and that he would be preaching again on Sunday. On the

Sunday evening Moorhouse again announced the same text, and, said Moody, "preached the most extraordinary sermon from that verse."[3] So it continued for four more nights, the same text serving on each occasion. At the end of it, Dwight L. Moody's own speaking methods and message had been changed for good.

> Mr. Moorhouse taught Moody to draw his sword full length, to fling the scabbard away, and enter the battle with the naked blade.[4]*

This influence on Moody – vital to his later evangelistic preaching – was perhaps the most spectacular indirect result of the work of a Brethren evangelist, and Moorhouse by that week of sermons on one verse of Scripture probably accomplished indirectly a greater work than that which resulted from the remarkable campaigns of his own short life (he died in 1880 at the early age of forty).

If this influence on Moody was the most spectacular incident in the indirect influence of Brethren overseas, the direct results, in the growth of Brethren-type churches, were as remarkable as in the British Isles.[18]

With the possible exception of British Guiana, the earliest extensive expansion in another country had come about after J. N. Darby had linked and clashed with the churches of *L'Ancienne Dissidence* in Switzerland in the closing years of the 1830s. The later development of the churches there has been covered in Chapter Six. As we have seen, Darby also established his own chain of churches through French-speaking Switzerland and southern France. W. H. Dorman also knew of groups in Holland in 1837. In the nature of the case, most of the churches which Darby founded went with him in the later division. The independent Brethren, for their part, had already made contacts on the Continent, not only with the Swiss churches that opposed Darby, but also with Stuttgart and other parts of Germany, both through Müller and through Groves's contacts with Rhenius and other German Lutheran missionaries in India. Groves was instrumental in encouraging several groups of German missionaries to sail for India in the later 1830s. Chapman, too, had contributed to expan-

---

* To this week of sermons there was an interesting sequel, which we will give in the words of Moorhouse's own biographer:

"In his enthusiasm Moody went and hired the Farwell Hall, and covered every space in the great city with huge posters, announcing in flaming capitals the celebrated, the wonderful English Boy Preacher. The vast building was crowded, and Moorhouse preached. The preaching was a complete failure, his tongue was tied. The audience waited in vain for something wonderful; there was nothing to be wondered at, unless it were the wonderful collapse. Moody was confounded. Not so Moorhouse, who, noticing on the way home one of the grand bills, exclaimed, "Ah, here is the explanation of our failure! Exalting man so! God could not bless that!" It says not a little for the moral courage of Moorhouse that instead of hastening away from the scene of so humiliating a failure, he went on calmly and hopefully with his work."

John Macpherson, *Henry Moorhouse, the English Evangelist* (undated) pp. 65-6.

sion on the Continent by an evangelistic tour of Spain during 1838. This work was followed up later in the century by teachers who settled there, the first being Gould and Lawrence, who went out with Chapman in 1862. Chapman himself paid several further visits to Spain.

After 1869 the work in Spain developed in the districts of Barcelona, in Madrid, and in the north-west corner of the country, under the care of a number of able leaders from Britain, and there are today some sixty to seventy churches in Spain. The growth of the work has been much restricted by the attitude of the Roman Catholic hierarchy, which has led in turn to considerable losses of promising Spanish leaders by emigration to South America.

The movement developed in Portugal also after 1876, and has become one of the largest Protestants group in that country, with over 100 churches, although it is probably second in membership to the more recent Pentecostal churches.

The Iberian work has had to face bitter opposition, sometimes leading to outright persecution of the converts, but it has continued to be sturdy and well-instructed, with able leadership. Something of the atmosphere in which it has matured is indicated by a realistic comment in a missionary booklet concerning North-West Spain (c. 1920):

> In past years it was impossible to sell (Bibles and tracts) in the cathedral towns, of which there are five in Galicia, but patience and appeal have worn down this illegal opposition. We know what *we* think of Mormon or Millennial Dawn propaganda at home. *We* are looked on as much worse here, as "deceivers," "heretics," "wolves in sheep's clothing," and blasphemers of their goddess; therefore violence and riot are necessary and lawful arguments.[5]

An interesting, and completely indigenous, development took place in Italy.[19] For some years Count Piero Guicciardini, head of one of the most ancient families of Florence, had been reading his Bible privately, at first with his caretaker, and later with other secret evangelicals, many of them of the working classes. Then, in 1848, came the brief triumph of the first stage of the *Risorgimento*, and in 1849 open evangelical meetings were started. In the following year the revolution was put down by foreign arms. The *evangelici* were especial objects of suspicion in the subsequent repression: and unfortunately the authorities were in possession of many names and addresses as a result of naïve publicity in England.*

* "Some English Christians exhibited a want of discretion in the publicity which they gave to *names* and *particulars* in connexion with the reception of the Gospel in Tuscany . . . observe the results: such publications find their way to Italy, for every English religious periodical of any value, is there read for the purpose of obtaining information to be used against Protestantism; and thus the Popishly-inclined authorities had brought before them, as Protestants, not only well-known persons, such as Count Guicciardini, but shoemakers, tailors, and other mechanics, whose names and abodes were printed in England in full."
S. P. Tregelles, in his introduction to *Prisoners of Hope* (1852), pp. 7, 8 n.

On 3rd May 1851, Count Guicciardini prepared a statement of his belief for publication, intending to leave thereafter for voluntary exile, but on 7th May 1851 he and six others were surprised by the police while reading the Gospel of John at a farewell meeting, and imprisoned. Guicciardini rejected an offer of personal exemption from the religious repression, and on 17th May he and his companions were sentenced to six months' imprisonment, this being later commuted to exile, for most of them. Guicciardini's statement was later printed clandestinely and widely circulated.

Numerous arrests of evangelicals followed in Florence, in some cases acquittal by the courts being followed by re-arrest and by banishment or imprisonment by police edict. A great outcry was raised in England by the arrest and imprisonment without trial, in August 1851, of two of them, Francesco and Rosa Madiai, for no reason other than the profession of evangelical faith, and for holding private Bible readings in their home.* They were not brought to trial until June 1852. A most able and eloquent defence was made by their lawyer, Odoardo Maggiorani, his speech later being published with considerable sensation, but the full and savage sentences demanded by the prosecutor were awarded by the Court: to Francesco, four years and eight months solitary imprisonment and hard labour, and to Rosa three years nine months of the same, to be followed in each case by three years' police surveillance. In October 1852, a deputation from England left to plead with the Grand Duke of Tuscany, one of its members being the Earl of Cavan, and it was joined by Continental Protestants as a result of a request from the Evangelical Alliance of Geneva, contained in a letter over the honoured signature of Louis Gaussen. It is pleasant to record that the editor of the English report of the proceedings in the Madiai case was B. W. Newton's relative and supporter, S. P. Tregelles. As a result of the deputation's visit, the Madiai were later released and exiled, although Francesco never fully recovered from the effects of his imprisonment.

Count Guicciardini eventually came to England, and there made contact with leaders of Brethren, including (as we have seen) Anthony Norris Groves. By an odd coincidence, it was in the town of Teignmouth, where Müller and Craik had met some twenty years before, that Guicciardini himself had a meeting which was, to the movement in Italy, of equal importance to that of Craik and Müller to the English movement. This was with Teodoro Pietrocola Rossetti, who had been forced into political exile from Naples, and reached England in 1851. He was welcomed by his uncle, Gabriele Rossetti (father of the poets Dante and Christina), himself

---

* At the eventual trial, the prosecutor admitted in his speech: "that of direct political elements, the cause of the Madiai offers no trace." The charge was based on an allegation of proselytism.

Prisoners of Hope, p. 97. ("Speech of the Public Minister.")

a political exile and a professor at King's College, London. Later, Teodoro Rossetti was converted to evangelical faith through Guicciardini, and was brought into contact with the Orchard Street congregation of Brethren.

When, after a few years, the Grand Duke was forced out of Tuscany, Guicciardini and Rossetti were able to return to Italy, and through their efforts a chain of congregations was established in Northern Italy, centred on Florence, and on Alessandria in the more liberal Piedmont, and reaching into Liguria and Lombardy.

Of Rossetti, Ruskin's biographer W. G. Collingwood later wrote: "It is hardly too much to say that he did for evangelical religion in Italy what Gabriel Rossetti did for poetical art in England: he showed the path to sincerity and simplicity."[6] Collingwood records a later interesting incident. When Ruskin was sixty-three, in October 1882, he visited Florence, and was there introduced by an American artist whom he had met at Coniston to an American lady artist, Miss Alexander, in whose art he took a close interest. He goes on to describe another interest which they came to share:

> In religious matters her American common sense saw through her neighbours – saw the good in them as well as the weakness – and she was as friendly, not only in society but in spiritual things, with the worthy village-priest as with T. P. Rossetti, the leader of the Protestant "Brethren," whom she called her pastor. And Mr. Ruskin, who had been driven away from Protestantism by the Waldensian at Turin and had wandered through many realms of doubt and voyaged through strange seas of thought, alone, found harbour at last with the disciple of a modern evangelist, the frequenter of the poor little meeting-house of outcast Italian Protestants.[7]*

Rossetti died in the year after Ruskin's visit.

Italy has thus had a strong indigenous movement for a century. In the north, this is by now old and established, while in the south the vigour of the movement continues to show itself by pioneering expansion, which has led to the continued establishment of churches since the Second World War, the total now being some 200 churches.

The movement was soon carried to the English-speaking lands, in the wake of the extensive emigration of the later part of the nineteenth century. While exclusivism experienced a parallel expansion, as evidenced by Darby's travels, the independent Brethren also grew overseas as a direct result of the British revival movement. The leading preachers and church builders were conscious of their responsibilities to those who had left this

---

* It is of interest that W. G. Collingwood himself accompanied Ruskin on this journey. I am indebted to a member of their family for the information that he was the son of the water colourist William Collingwood, who was an early member of the Brethren in Liverpool and remained with the movement until his death in 1903, latterly living in Bristol as a member of the Bethesda congregation. W. G. Collingwood himself was the father of R. G. Collingwood, the philosopher.

country, and in the 1870s numbers of them left to settle in the developing new lands. Henry Groves, Norris Groves's oldest son, had already visited the United States between 1857 and 1863. In 1871 Richard W. Owens, a member of the Merrion Hall congregation in Dublin, settled in New York, and joined the small church there. He exercised a strong pastoral influence on the thirty-odd churches which formed around that city during the next fifty years. In 1879 Donald Ross settled in Chicago, having toured the United States three years before. After building up churches in Chicago, he then moved in 1887 to San Francisco, and in 1894 to Kansas City, before returning to Chicago shortly before his death in 1903. From each of these centres he actively evangelized the district around. About the same time as Ross moved to the U.S.A., another pioneer, Alexander Marshall, settled in Canada, where he worked until 1896. Brethren in North America are not relatively numerous, but their work is often progressive and forward-looking. There are some eleven hundred congregations (in addition to about three hundred exclusive churches) in the U.S.A. and Canada,[8] where a particularly vigorous growth area centres on Vancouver. Although other areas have a greater number of churches. Vancouver is particularly notable for the foundation in 1968, largely under Brethren influence, of the inter-denominational Regent College, now an affiliated college of the University of British Columbia. Several of its first teaching staff are drawn from Brethren, including the first Principal, Dr. J. M. Houston, formerly of Hertford College, Oxford.

In both countries there is a marked contrast between more conservative and traditionalist groups, who are strongly marked with the characteristics of their founders from Scotland and Northern Ireland, and other groups which are less inhibited in their activities than is the general run of the movement in the United Kingdom. On the whole both groups have drawn on the British churches for teachers: more recent years have, however, seen the beginnings of an indigenous movement of true Biblical scholarship among North American Brethren.

There has been vigorous growth in Australia and New Zealand, and in New Zealand Brethren probably form a larger proportion of the Christian churches than in the United Kingdom. The hymnwriter J. G. Deck emigrated to New Zealand in 1853, and the North London *Missionary Reporter* had been in touch with an ex-clergyman from Dublin, J. C. Courtney, in that country since 1854. The year 1876, which saw the first visit of Donald Ross to the U.S.A., also saw two significant pioneers moving to Australasia. Gordon Forlong moved to New Zealand in that year; while Harrison Ord, an engineer who had been converted under Spurgeon and had become a successful evangelist of the revival, moved to Melbourne, whence he continued his evangelization in Victoria and Tasmania, and also visited New Zealand and other parts of Australia. Later, in 1879, came another year of notable accessions for the work in the

English-speaking countries, with the movement of Alexander Marshall to Canada, of John Hambleton to Australia, and Charles Hillam Hinman, who became a convert of Forlong's, to New Zealand. Emigration from Scotland and Ireland, and from parts of England (the Blackdown Hills Mission saw numbers of its converts emigrating during this period) led to a continual building up of the overseas churches during the remainder of the century.

Meanwhile, to return to the European area, the growth which had strongly affected the north-east Scottish fishing communities, was soon extended to other fishing communities in the islands to the north and north-west of Scotland. In addition to Orkney and Shetland, the influence of Brethren reached the Danish Färoe Islands, about midway between Scotland and Iceland. A Scots worker, William Gibson Sloan, visited the islands first in 1865, and settled there in the 1870's, his work being continued after his death in 1914 by his son, Andrew William Sloan. The most significant name in Faroese Brethrenism was however the islander Victor Danielson. The Brethren community in those islands today amounts to a considerable proportion (in some districts approaching ten per cent) of the population. In the other Danish dependency (as it was then) of Iceland, a pioneering work was undertaken for many years by the late Arthur Gook, a man who became legendary among the isolated farms and settlements of the island, and numbered among his converts one who later became one of the most prominent Lutheran churchmen of Iceland. Gook attempted to use radio in his evangelism when the medium was still in its infancy and ranks as one of the pioneers of this form of evangelism.

In Denmark itself the movement has taken little root, although there is a church in Copenhagen and recent years have seen the growth of a very similar movement, the Christian Fellowship, which has close personal links with Brethren workers. Sweden also has had little attention from Brethren, and only a handful of churches exist there, but areas of Norway have more congregations, established largely under Scottish influence.

One of the most remarkable stories attached to the Slav countries of Eastern Europe. Protestantism has always been stubbornly persistent in those lands, although the religious climate has rarely been favourable, and Baptist or Brethren-type movements (their description often depends upon one's point of view!) like the Stundists and the Mennonites have found a widespread following. The basic ideals of such movements are almost indistinguishable from those of Brethren, and a natural link of kinship has formed between many such congregations and teachers from Brethren churches in Britain and Germany.

One of the earliest and most noteworthy of such travellers was Friedrich Wilhelm Baedeker. Born on 3rd August 1823, the son of a Westphalian naturalist, Baedeker lived a roving life for his first thirty-five years, wandering about Tasmania and Australia and then returning to Europe. He later became a Doctor of Philosophy of Freiburg University. He visited England and married in Weston-super-Mare in 1862. In 1866 Baedeker was converted in evangelistic meetings arranged by Lord Cavan in Weston-super-Mare, at which the preacher was Lord Radstock, an evangelical Anglican layman who mixed freely with Brethren and was a favourite speaker at many of their meetings. Lord Radstock shortly after this engaged in a remarkable evangelistic work among aristocratic circles in Russia and Eastern Europe, and introduced Baedeker to his friends in those countries. Despite the persecution of evangelical groups, Baedeker succeeded in winning the confidence of many of the highest officials, and in obtaining a prison visitor's permit valid throughout Russia. He held this permit through bi-annual renewals for eighteen years, and used it valiantly in evangelistic work. Although the work of men like Baedeker and Radstock was somewhat unsympathetically portrayed by Tolstoy, from his different viewpoint, in *Resurrection*,[8a] it is difficult to over-emphasize the self-denying ardour of Baedeker's travels. These took him throughout Russia, and right across Siberia into Sakhalin Island. His work became increasingly important and dangerous after Pobiedonostsev, the Procurator of the Holy Synod, had issued his edict of 1891:

> The rapid increase of these sects is a serious danger to the State. Let all sectarians be forbidden to leave their own villages . . . Let all offenders against the faith be tried, not by a jury, but by ecclesiastical judges. Let their passports be marked, so that they shall be neither employed nor harboured, and residence in Russia shall become impossible for them. Let them be held to be legally incapable of renting, purchasing, or holding real property. Let their children be removed from their control, and educated in the orthodox faith.[9]

This edict resulted in widespread bitter persecution of dissenting groups throughout Russia, and in the course of his journeys Baedeker was also able surreptitiously to visit and encourage many of these groups of Christians. He died on 9th October 1906 in Weston-super-Mare.

Although the men who followed Baedeker have not had the advantage of his gifts or social opportunities, they have included several noteworthy travelling pioneers who have carried out a sterling work among the simple Christian communities of the Slav lands. Another noteworthy German, Johannes Warns, will be more fully referred to shortly. From Suffolk in England, Edmund Hamer Broadbent, in the early years of the twentieth century, travelled widely in Eastern Europe, and in Russia. He was followed by James Lees, an Ayrshire miner, who started on a travelling ministry to Scandinavia in 1912, at the age of thirty-three, which took him into the Baltic States and then to the Slav countries. There he visited the consider-able number of scattered communities among which several other Brethren teachers from Britain were already living and working. Lees's travels also took him into the Balkans. After the holocaust of the Second World War he was able to continue his visitations, together with others of the Brethren workers. Encouragement and material relief was taken by these workers to many of the little communities in lands which had been left in desperate straits by the disasters of the war, and several relief funds were operated from Britain and the United States, including one particularly well-run organization under the Bresnen brothers at Bebington in Cheshire. Lees himself died in Vienna in 1958.

The work of such men, and of a number of others who settled with their families among the peoples of eastern Europe, has encouraged a persistent growth of Brethren-type churches there, which persevere against all the post-war difficulties. Governmental attitudes have varied over the years, and such independent churches are sometimes forced into formal union with Baptist and similar denominational organizations, as happened in eastern Czechoslovakia during the war.* Denominational distinctions thus become indistinct.

In south-west Poland some of these churches were known as "Followers of the First Christians" or as "Free Evangelical Churches," and had become fairly numerous by the outbreak of the Second World War. These churches were not suppressed by the Soviet authorities (as were many formal denominations) when that part of Poland was occupied in 1939. In other parts of Poland such churches joined later with similar groups to form the United Evangelical Church.

In those areas of south-east Poland and eastern Czechoslovakia which were incorporated into the Soviet Union after the Second World War, a vigorous indigenous work grew up between the wars. It was furthered by three English couples who had settled there, D. T. Griffiths, S. K. Hine and A. C. MacGregor and their wives. This work centred on the town of Lublin (Lvov). In Czechoslovakia itself, and extending into Yugoslavia, the most extensive expansion in the Slav countries took place. Numbering some 150 churches, it largely owes its origins to another English couple, Mr. and Mrs. Frederick Butcher, who lived for most of forty years from 1900 in Bratislava. In near-by Hungary, a vigorous indigenous growth owes an immense debt to the influence of the late Ferenc Kiss, for fifty years Professor of Anatomy in Budapest University.

In Rumania a group of churches was established in the early years of the twentieth century, the Brethren churches among them being influenced by evangelists from the French-speaking Swiss congregations. There are said to be several hundred congregations of Brethren in Rumania, and two

* H. L. Ellison gave several examples of such forced union in his address at the Swanwick Conference of Brethren in June 1964 – see Christian Unity (the report of the Conference, 1964), pp. 44–45. He remarked of the Russian churches: "that is why according to the ecclesiastical background of the foreign visitors they are referred to as Baptists or Brethren" (p. 44).

somewhat kindred groups, the Baptists and Pentecostalists, are even larger. †
All three groups have been greatly reduced by persistent administrative
eroding of their liberties by the authorities, in some cases accompanied by
physical torture and ill-treatment of their members, which extends back
to the pre-war Fascist régime, as well as since the war. (The Seventh Day
Adventists are also reported to have several hundred congregations, which
had been similarly reduced in number.)[10]

The indigenous Continental movements in French-speaking Switzerland and Germany have themselves influenced considerably the growth
of Brethren-type movements in Europe. As in Rumania, the Swiss
churches have also contributed to work in Belgium and in Italy, and to a
lesser degree in the neighbouring parts of France, where the largest independent congregation in that country is situated in the near-by city of
Lyons. In both France and Germany the Darbyite movement has been
stronger than the independents and, indeed, has probably retained the
essence of Darby's teachings with far less corruption than British and
American "exclusives." It is of interest that Evelyne Sullerot, the French
feminist, was born on her mother's side of a Darbyite family. France,
indeed, has been largely overlooked by independents until recent years,
and their churches there number only some sixty congregations. In
Germany, however, a strong indigenous movement developed with
Mennonite influence behind it and today numbers some three hundred
churches.* A work of considerable intellectual and practical vigour was
associated with the name of Fräulein Toni von Blücher, a descendant of
Wellington's ally in arms. Influenced by a visit of Baedeker to Berlin in
1875, she was responsible for a mission work in that city during the next
thirty years, itself associated with a new wave of Pietism, the *Gemein-
schaftsbewegung*, which swept Germany at that time under the influence
of the English-speaking revival movement and is still influential in all
denominations. In 1905, at the height of the Russian persecution of
evangelicals, a group of aristocrats associated with Fräulein von Blücher,
among them General Georg von Viebahn, founded a Bible School, the
Allianz-Bibelschule, in Berlin for the preparation of evangelists for eastern
Europe: this school was also connected with Mennonite work. The first
teachers at this school were two scholarly men, who had each renounced

---

† An article in *Echoes of Service* for April 1968, p. 64, states that the work in
Rumania was started in 1905 by a French missionary from Switzerland, M. Berney.
In July 1967, according to this article, there were some 350 assemblies with 25,000
members (of which 6 with 2,000 members are in Bucharest). This article puts the
Baptists at 100,000 and the Pentecostals (dating from 1922/23) at 80,000: it also
says that the Pentecostals have *increased* from only 18,000 in 1939. (The article is by
a Polish visitor to Rumania. See also note 10.

* The German list is almost certainly most incomplete and the true number of
churches much greater than 300. The situation is complicated by the existence of unofficial groupings, with inter-communion among the groups.

positions with the Lutheran State Church on grounds akin to those of the founders of the British Brethren movement: Christoph Köhler and his son-in-law Johannes Warns. Warns later travelled widely throughout Eastern Europe, and strongly influenced the churches there by his teaching and his writings.

The Bible School has been responsible for the training of many teachers and evangelists, including in the early days many Russians, not a few of whom died for their faith in Siberian prisons. In 1919† the school was transferred to Wiedenest, near Gummersbach, in the Rhineland, where forebears of Warns had been pastors. Later the school became the teaching centre of the honoured Erich Sauer. Government restrictions imposed on the independent churches of Germany during the Nazi régime led to a forced union of Darbyite, Baptist and independent Brethren churches in a *Bund*, together with some other minor groups. Out of that appalling phase of modern history there has survived something of the co-operation learned in the *Bund*, although a few churches, chiefly Darbyite, reverted after the war to their earlier position. In this continuing co-operation, the Wiedenest Bible School has played a not inconsiderable part.

The Wiedenest Bible School has since the Second World War played a prominent part, both in forwarding and greatly extending the missionary outreach of the German Brethren churches, which the Darbyite or *Elberfelder Brüder* had initiated about 1860, and also in the production, in conjunction with the formerly Darbyite publishing house of Brockhaus in Wuppertal, of a wide range of scholarly Christian literature. In its main lecture-room hang the portraits of Groves, Müller and Baedeker, alongside those of Comenius, Paschkow (a leader of the Russian evangelical movement), Zinzendorf, Schwenkfeld, Menno Simons and George Fox.

The beginnings of Brethren work in South America and the West Indies go back to the earliest days of the movement: in fact there was a spontaneous movement at Georgetown in Guyana (then British Guiana) which was contemporary with the beginnings of the movement in Britain. The leading personality in this movement was Leonard Strong, an ex-naval officer turned clergyman who went out in 1826 as rector of an Anglican parish. His work among the plantation slaves enraged the slave owners, and he was moved for his protection to Georgetown, where he later left the Anglican Church and started meetings for worship on the lines which characterized Brethren. He was put in touch with early Brethren (he came from Herefordshire and had been curate at Ross-on-Wye), for whom British Guiana (or "Demerara") and the West Indian Islands soon became a prominent interest, fostered by Müller's Scriptural Knowledge Institution. Numbers of missionaries were sponsored by the

† Not 1918, as given by Ernst Crous in his article on *German Mennonites* in *The Recovery of the Anabaptist Vision* (ed. Guy F. Hershberger, 1957), p. 246.

home churches from 1840 onwards, some of them going to an early death. The earliest and one of the most remarkable of these men was John Meyer, a Swiss who had been connected with Brook Street Chapel, Tottenham. He sailed in 1848. Rendle Short wrote of him:

> Some of the missionaries, notably Meyer and Gardiner, have left a most extraordinary record behind them. The former endured awful privations in his journeys through the untrodden forest, preaching to the Indians, living amongst them in the most primitive fashion. For simple faith, devotion and self-sacrifice he and his wife have few equals in missionary annals. He died as he lived, by the river-side in the forest, surrounded by his Indian brethren.[11]

Although Strong returned to Britain shortly before 1850, the growth of the work in the West Indies, both in Guyana and in the English-speaking islands, continued unhindered, and the revival movement also affected some of the islands. On the mainland, Alexander Henderson, who had been with a Baptist Missionary Society in British Honduras since the early 1830s, was brought into the growing movement and was supported from North London and from Bristol. This work later lapsed, and it was only in 1911 that Brethren workers re-entered British Honduras (there were a few "exclusive" missionaries there shortly before that date). Brethren teaching, with its certain inherent *gravitas*, has not had quite the same astonishing success with the West Indians as has Pentecostalism, but it has none the less prospered greatly, and the churches on some of the West Indian Islands are as large and active as anywhere in the world.

After his return to Britain, Leonard Strong settled in Torquay, where we have already met him. It was at Torquay in 1860 that he was responsible for introducing to Philip Gosse the "sympathetic Quakerish lady," "with a soft pink cheek and a sparkling hazel eye"[12] who became Gosse's second wife:

> One morning in March, the late Mr. Leonard Strong came into the Cottage and said, "I am just come from the cemetery, where I have been conducting the funeral service over Mr. Gosse's mother, who had lived with him ever since he left London about two years ago." I at once asked, "What Mr. Gosse? Is he the noted naturalist?" "Yes," said Mr. Strong; "and he lives in St. Marychurch, close by you. The name 'Sandhurst,' in plain letters, is on his gate. He is the minister of a small church at the east end of that village."[13]

In the republics of South and Central America, the greatest development of independent Brethren has been in Argentina, where a succession of able leaders from English-speaking countries has encouraged a considerable indigenous growth of churches since the first of them, J. H. L. Ewen, arrived there in 1882. There are nearly 300 churches in that country, and some 200 in neighbouring Brazil. Mexico has numerous churches,

Guatemala over 100, Honduras about 30, and Venezuela over 50. There are active movements in most of the other republics also, with New Zealand and North American teachers taking a considerable part. The story of the recent successful approach, after initial tragedy and martyrdom, to the Auca tribe of Ecuador, which was largely pioneered by Brethren missionaries, has already become a classic of missionary endeavour.

Missionary expansion in the East also goes back to the very beginning of the movement. As we have seen, missionary ambitions were a leading motive of Groves's early spiritual development. The story of his own initial venture in Bagdad was a tragic one. He arrived there early in December 1829, but in March 1831 plague entered the city. Within two months more than half the population of the city perished. The plague seemed to be passing, when suddenly, on 7th May, Mrs. Groves sickened, and within a week was dead. The plague was followed by civil war and the horrors of famine. Groves's infant daughter died in August, and he himself and his two sons barely survived. When the relief party from Britain arrived in 1832, they too had lost the ladies of their party en route. The party did not find itself of one mind, and in 1833 Groves moved to India, to which country he gave the remainder of his life. Groves was highly critical of the organizing of existing missionary work, and particularly of the dependence of so many of the converts upon European help, and he was greatly attracted by the idea of self-supporting enterprise, which could provide employment and economic stability for the local communities. He himself started two projects of this nature, a silk farm and a sugar refinery, but he was ill-equipped as an entrepreneur and both projects were failures, the latter leaving his two older sons with a substantial burden after his death. Nevertheless, in matters of missionary strategy Groves was a man in advance of his time, and he foresaw clearly many of the problems which recent political changes have brought about.

Groves brought Swiss and British missionaries with him when he returned to India from his visit to Europe in 1836, some of these missionaries joining an independent missionary named Start with whom Groves had established close fellowship. Start had a substantial work, including several schools, in Bihar state in the north-east of India, and the Bethesda group of churches continued to take a close interest in his work. Other missionaries from Brethren congregations in Britain started work in Bihar in 1870.

William Bowden and George Beer, the two Barnstaple men, went to Masulipatam on the western coast, accompanied by John Parnell (he was not yet Lord Congleton). Parnell, as we know, did not stay, but the work of Bowden and Beer was the beginning of a considerable outreach in the Godaveri delta, which flourishes to this day with numerous churches. In the very southern extremity of India, around Rhenius's field at Tinnevelly (Tirunelveli) another considerable work was established by an

Indian Christian who had grown up under Rhenius and later joined Groves, John Christian Aroolappen.* Churches descended from his work still survive. Other noted leaders were the late Handley Bird, and the Indian poet K. V. Simon, who founded a strong movement in Kerala. A Bible school movement has fostered Indian leadership throughout the land. There are over 800 churches in India,[13a] and a very active and extensive indigenous literature work. There are also numbers of Brethren churches in Pakistan. In several places on the sub-continent the missionaries have established excellent hospitals and other medical work, as well as educational work. At Bangalore in particular, a successful school, the Clarence High School, was founded by the Redwood family. In India, as in other fields, the missionary force has been drawn from New Zealand, Australia, Canada and the United States, as well as from the United Kingdom and in Pakistan there are German workers.

Malaysia (as it now is) saw a spontaneous development about the year 1860, when two Presbyterians, a missionary, Alexander Grant, and a minister named Chapman, together founded a congregation in Penang which later linked with Brethren missionaries from Britain, and (more recently) from Australia and New Zealand. Grant was later in Singapore, where he was a scholarly and able leader. The movement in Singapore and Malaysia has drawn some vigorous men, and churches have been established in most of the main cities. There are now some fifty churches in the country, the majority among the Chinese population, who have from the start provided leaders for the work. There is a large and notable school in Kuala Lumpur, and medical work is also carried on, especially among sufferers from leprosy. Missionaries from Switzerland have worked in near-by Laos since 1902, and the Philippines have received missionaries from the United States since 1919. Work in Thailand dates from 1886, but it is only in the post-Second World War years that it has developed beyond tiny proportions.

In addition to the work of the China Inland Mission, so much of which in its earliest days sprang from a Brethren background, independent Brethren missionaries also penetrated China during the century before the Communist régime was established. Work in Shantung started in 1888, and later developed in Manchuria, Kiangsi and other areas. The movement had its own martyrs during the Boxer uprising. The work was hard and often discouraging, but steady progress was made until the Japanese war. Even more interesting was the entirely indigenous and independent movement of the "Little Flock," a Brethren-type movement which grew up in China between the wars under the leadership of the saintly Watchman Nee (Nee To-sheng). Despite its similarities to the Brethren move-

* The recent "Brethren type" indigenous church movement associated with the Indian evangelist Bakht Singh is also said to have drawn on work descending from Aroolappen.

ment, this movement remained a separate entity from European missions but Nee was influenced by Darby's writings and adopted his view that there could be only one local church in any one town, comprising all believers there. Since the Communists gained power in China, Watchman Nee has been imprisoned, and his churches suppressed.

Immediately after the Second World War a considerable impetus was given to the work in China by the arrival of numbers of young men and women from Europe and America, and an attempt was made to penetrate Tibet – only for the work to be cut off suddenly, except in Hong Kong and Taiwan (Formosa), by the Communist accession to power. It was out of the abortive attempt to reach Tibet, and his subsequent imprisonment by the Communists, that Geoffrey Bull's well-known *When Iron Gates Yield* was born: as indeed was also the work by his companion George Patterson (who escaped to India), *Tibetan Journey*. In Hong Kong, the recent work of the "Peace Clinic" among refugees deserves notice.

Brethren work in Japan dates from the two later decades of the nineteenth century, after W. G. Smith had settled in Tokyo in 1888 as Professor of English at the Imperial University, but it has only expanded considerably since the Second World War. Full-time missionaries settled there first about 1930, although an "exclusive" worker had started a publishing work before then. From "exclusive" influences there has also developed a circle of indigenous independent churches in Korea.

We have left until the end reference to the continent which has produced the most prominent pioneers among Brethren missionaries: that of Africa. The northern Muslim countries have all had workers, and Egypt had an extensive "exclusive" work. Mention should be made here of the remarkable work of the late Capt. E. G. Fisk. After building up a substantial medical and church work in Morocco – almost unique in Western North Africa – he translated the whole Bible into colloquial Arabic in the 1960s, completing it after reaching the age of 70. It should be added that he battled against constant ill health, the result of First World War wound and gassing. Farther south, the Saharan country of Chad (then a French possession) was the field of the remarkable twentieth-century pioneer, John Remeses Olley. Born in London, Olley went to sea in 1902 at the age of fifteen, and after sailing to many parts of the world and seeing service in several different ships, including an Italian wind-jammer, he settled in New Zealand in 1905. Picking up a training in surveying during the course of railway building in the undeveloped centre of the North Island, he later qualified as a schoolmaster, and it was at this time that he taught himself French. Converted in 1917, he shortly afterwards linked with Brethren. Late in 1919 he sailed as a missionary for North Africa, teaching himself Arabic in Tunis, and reaching Kano in Northern Nigeria in 1925. He entered Chad the following year, and eventually made his centre at Fort Lamy.

Olley remained in Chad for thirty more years without a break. Pioneering throughout the country, he saw some eighty churches established. He himself undertook extensive translation work, translating *inter alia* the New Testament into two local languages, and he also taught himself medicine, obtaining an American medical degree. His biographer writes:

> He never made medical work a spearhead for the Gospel believing that the Gospel itself needed none as it is itself a two-edged sword which pierces even to the dividing asunder of soul and spirit. He used it as a means of expressing his Christian compassion to those in need.[14]

Olley died in Sydney in 1956, on his way back to New Zealand for his first furlough since he had left the country thirty-seven years before. The Chad churches continued to increase, and French missionaries also work there.

In South Africa the work of the brothers James and Joseph Fish among the lepers of Robben Island was of some note. The development of churches in South Africa dates from the 1850s. The movement there has been small, the total churches numbering less than one hundred, but in addition to these churches there is a vigorous outreach in the African areas of Natal, Pondoland and the Transvaal, with medical and educational work.

The main development of Brethren work in Africa has been in a strip of Central Africa reaching from the Angola coast to the Zambia border with Mozambique, and including areas of Angola, Zaire, Zambia and Rhodesia. So many of the early pioneers were buried there as a result of premature death by disease and privation that this section of Africa has become known to Brethren as "The Beloved Strip." "Septima," in writing of the great Exeter Hall meetings of mid-Victorian times, spoke of the "new recruits – heroes every one – who would rise and tell how the Call had come to them."[15] They were heroes indeed, for acceptance of a "call" to Africa in those days meant giving oneself to an even likelihood of death or invalidism within weeks of arrival.

One of the great pioneers of African missionary work was the Brethren missionary Frederick Stanley Arnot. As a boy he lived in Hamilton in Scotland, where he was a neighbour and friend of Livingstone's family. The example of the great missionary explorer fired Arnot with an ambition to follow in his steps, and from an early age he set himself to learn all the practical skills he would need in primitive conditions. On 19th July 1881, two months before his twenty-third birthday, he sailed for Africa in the *Dublin Castle*. He went on to Durban from Capetown in a coastal steamer, arriving at Durban on 20th August 1881. For the next seven years he was lost to civilization in Central Africa. After a short time with the christianized Bamangwato of Bechuanaland, he set off alone on foot for the interior. Several times he was near death from fever, lack of water, or other dangers, but eventually he reached Lealui, the capital of the powerful chief of the Barotse people in the Zambesi valley, where he was detained by king Liwanika for eighteen months. After the arrival of a

Portuguese trader, Arnot was allowed to leave Lealui, and eventually reached the west coast of Africa at Benguela.

During his travels he had heard rumours of a powerful native empire in the far interior, under a mighty chief Msiri (Msidi). In June 1885, therefore, he left Benguela again for the interior, and reached Msiri's capital in Katanga (a country which Arnot named Garenganze) after eight months, the first white man to do so. Little did he know it, but Msiri (whose villages were surrounded by stakes and tables piled high with skulls) had in his capital a stake specially sharpened for the head of the first white man to enter his territory, for years before a prophecy had been given of a power which would come from the east and rob him of his empire. He had been persuaded by Arab traders from the east that this prophecy referred to white men. Happily for Arnot, he arrived from the west, and succeeded in winning the chief's confidence. After two years Arnot was relieved by two more missionaries from Brethren in Britain, Messrs. C. A. Swan and W. L. Faulknor, and in September 1888 he arrived back in Britain, just over seven years after his departure. Six months later, married to Miss Harriet Jane Fisher, he left again for Africa with a large party, after a great send-off meeting at Exeter Hall, which had been addressed among others by Lord Radstock and Henry Groves, who had become a moving force behind the growing missionary interest in the British churches of Brethren.

Arnot never returned to Msiri's capital during the chief's lifetime, but spent the remainder of his life establishing a chain of mission stations along the track from Benguela to Katanga. His health had been seriously under-mined by the privations of his first solitary journey, and he died in May, 1914, aged fifty-five. Arnot, more than any other man, was the architect of Brethren missionary work in the Beloved Strip. He also helped other missionary work in Central Africa, including that of the Paris (Huguenot) Missionary Society, the South Africa Baptist Missionary Society, and the South Africa General Mission.

Three in particular of Arnot's colleagues in those early days were men who were themselves to make a deep mark on the Beloved Strip. C. A. Swan, who was one of the two men who relieved Arnot at Msiri's capital, was a man of intense honesty and moral courage. He alienated Alfred Sharpe, the British envoy who visited Msiri on embassage in 1890, by refusing to persuade Msiri to sign a treaty until he had first read it over in full to Msiri (who then declined to sign). After many years of work in Africa Swan moved to Portugal in 1903, where he built up the work of the Brethren churches there. In 1908 he was asked to return to Angola by a well-known English cocoa manufacturer to investigate reports that slave labour was being used on the cocoa plantations on the islands of San Tomé and Principe; previous investigations had been unable to find evi-dence, although it was fairly well known that the practice (though strictly forbidden by Portuguese law) was rife. Swan spent six months in Angola, and with his intimate knowledge of the country was able to produce a report, *The Slavery of Today*, which accumulated a mass of damning evidence and caused some sensation when it was released. It led to a measure of reform. Swan died in 1934, aged 73.

Dan Crawford, one of the party which accompanied Arnot to Africa when he made his second journey there in 1889, attained no small fame in his own right. Still a lad of 18 when he arrived in Africa, he went directly to Msiri's capital from Benguela with two companions, Lane and Thompson, to relieve Swan and Faulknor. He arrived there in November 1890. Sickness and circumstance took three of the five white men away from Msiri's within a short time, and Crawford and Lane were left alone. In the two years following their arrival, they were unwilling observers of the intrigue and counter-intrigue by successive British and Belgian expeditions to Msiri, that ended with the killing of Msiri on 20th December 1891 by a Belgian officer of the Congo Free State expedition led by the Englishman Captain Stairs. There followed the annexation of Katanga by the Belgian-sponsored Congo Free State.

In the upheavals which followed Msiri's death, Crawford was able to move to the shores of Lake Mweru. There his stations became a place of refuge in the disturbed countryside, and he eventually built a permanent station at the lakeside at Luanza. Despite scanty education, Crawford proved to be a linguist of no mean order, teaching himself Greek and Hebrew, and translating the Bible into the Luba language. He read extremely widely (as his famous books *Thinking Black* and *Back to the Long Grass* show) and was altogether an original, with a marked sense of impish humour. His identification with African ways did not always endear him to his European fellows, and his character is well expressed in two famous remarks of his own. One of these stands at the head of this chapter: the other was a daring misquotation of Scripture – "What shall it profit a man if he gain the whole world, and lose his own smile." Crawford, like Arnot, died at the age of 55, on 3rd June 1926, the victim of blood-poisoning from a trivial domestic injury.

Another member of the party which left England with Arnot in 1889 was Arnot's brother-in-law, Dr. Walter Fisher. After spending many years in the Zambesi valley, Fisher opened a medical station in 1906 on a hill near the source of the Zambesi which Arnot had noticed on his first lone journey to Msiri's capital and had marked on his map as "Border Craig." This was Kaleñe Hill, situated in that corner of Zambia where the country meets Angola and Zaire. Within a few years he made Kaleñe, in the words of a recent American writer, "a major centre of curative medicine,"[16] with Fisher himself as "Northern Rhodesia's foremost medical evangelist."[17] Kaleñe itself is today only one of a considerable number of Brethren medical missionary stations in Africa, and about one-fifth of medical missionary work in Zambia is in Brethren hands, with some seven hundred hospital beds.

In their missionary work in Central Africa, Brethren's inhibitions against any form of political involvement served them well in the early days,* but their principle of extreme independency has brought with it other disadvantages. Moreover, the very structure of an entirely lay and autonomous congregational church life means that inevitably it will often reflect the full prejudices of its members, and will be the least accessible to constructive adaptation to those social changes which affect the prejudices of those members.

There are today probably some five hundred churches of Brethren in Zambia, Zaire, Angola and Rhodesia. The missionary workers have included the doyen of twentieth-century Brethren missionaries, Mr. William Lammond of Johnstone Falls in Zambia, who went to Africa as long ago as 1900, living there until past his ninetieth year, and attaining there an honoured place not only in his missionary work, but also in the affections of many of his Zambian countrymen.

We leave the story of the expansion of the movement overseas unfinished. Since the Second World War, new areas have been penetrated by Brethren missionaries, particularly in East and West Africa (expansion in which the German churches have shared), and (mainly by New Zealand missionaries) in New Guinea. Brethren missions are known in many areas under the name of *Christian Missions to Many Lands*. There are today some 650 missionaries from the United Kingdom on the prayer-list of the magazine *Echoes of Service*: when missionaries from other countries are added, this number is probably doubled.† To the 650 men and women from the United Kingdom listed by *Echoes of Service* must also be added an unknown number of men and women serving with inter-denominational societies. If we also take into account those who are engaged in full-time evangelism and Bible teaching at home, it seems possible that as high

---

* Professor Rotberg suggests (*Christian Missionaries and the Creation of Northern Rhodesia 1880–1924* [1965] pp. 68–70), that intrigues by "the Brethren" were responsible for inspiring a punitive expedition which deposed one chieftain, Kazembe, in 1900. No source is given for his suggestion, and it is therefore fair to state that the surviving correspondence at the office of *Echoes of Service*, the Brethren missionary clearing-house, in Bath, not only gives no support to this suggestion, but shows plainly that the missionaries who wrote home were sympathetic to Kazembe, and that some of them were his personal friends: indeed, he took refuge with two of them, Mr. and Mrs. Anderson at Johnston Falls, after his deposition. The full letters, from which extracts are quoted in the book, when read in total, give a very different impression from the extracts by themselves: indeed, their tenor is almost the opposite of that implied. Whether any individual might have engaged in personal intrigue is, of course, another matter, but Rotberg gives no hint of his sources in this respect. The general neutrality of the Brethren at this time is well attested in Ruth M. Slade's *English-Speaking Missions in the Congo Independent State* (1959).

† *Echoes* list about 500, but overseas lists include names omitted by *Echoes*.

a proportion as one in fifty Brethren adherents from the United Kingdom may be engaged in full-time religious service, the large majority overseas.

In tracing our story we have in fact touched only a part of Brethren missionary activity. As suggested in the last paragraph, a very considerable number of men and women are serving with inter-denominational societies, a tendency which has increased considerably since the last war, in the generally changing pattern of missionary activity. Brethren are not welcomed by all inter-denominational societies, for their habit of independency can sometimes be a disturbing factor, and free celebration of the Lord's Supper (their most prized and persistent liberty) is still embarrassing to many societies.

Other missionary works have owed much to Brethren influence. Groves exercised personal influence on a number of outstanding men, including Alexander, the first Anglican Bishop of Jerusalem, Morrison of China, and Alexander Duff of India. We have already spoken of the even more direct influence of Brethren on the China Inland Mission in its earliest days. The North Africa Mission and the Royal National Mission to Deep Sea Fishermen also had Brethren influence in their founding. Another noted missionary from a Brethren background was Dame Edith Brown of Ludhiana fame, who was a grand-daughter of David Walther, the early Brethren publisher.

The growth of the independent Brethren has been noteworthy by any standards, particularly as it has been carried out under no closely-knit organization or powerful leadership, as was the much greater Methodist movement of the previous century. In places, it has been eclipsed by the even more startling growth of Pentecostal-type churches. In principle, the two have much in common, both being examples of that spontaneous "grassroots" Christianity which is probably the spring of a major part of true renewal within the Church: but Brethren are the more sedate of the two movements, tending to be more intellectual in their approach to the faith, and freer (apart from the aberrant tendencies within Darbyism) from the doctrinal eccentricities of so much Pentecostalism.

Older churches are often suspicious and resentful of these energetic and spontaneous movements, regarding them as threats to order and challenges to their authority. Where such movements carry fundamental heresy, as with some of the popular cults, they may indeed sap the life of Christianity, but the attitude of suspicion is generally foolish and narrow-minded. Not only do some of these older churches forget that their own origins were from similar movements of the past, but a broad sense of Christian history and of the dynamic character of the Church should suffice to show that such movements are the very stuff of the Church's continual self-renewal. The independent churches among them – and in this the Brethren movement is of more importance than the much more numerous Pentecostal churches – also retain a feature of vital importance to the life of the

Church as a whole. It is well recognized that every form of organization ultimately creates its own power-structure, and has inherent in it the inevitable corruptions of power. Not least is this so in the modern trend to an organized unity of the churches. There is little ultimate hope for the peace and unity of the Church until the "antiseptic" function of the independent movements in relation to this power-corruption is recognized. No one would deny that abuses of power can arise as tragically within an individual independent church as in an organized body of churches as a whole: but the independent churches have an inbuilt barrier to the wider development of such abuses.

Quotation References – Chapter 12.

1. *The Life of Dwight L. Moody*, W. R. Moody (undated *c.* 1897), p. 119.
2. Ibid., p. 125.
3. Ibid., p. 127.
4. Ibid., p. 128.
5. *Galicia, North West Spain* (*Echoes* Manuals, No. 7), H. S. Turrall and B. L. White undated – *c.* 1920), pp. 15–16.
6. *The Life and Work of John Ruskin*, W. G. Collingwood (1893), Vol. II, p. 218 n.
7. Ibid., pp. 217–18.
8. "Plymouth Brethren (Christian Brethren), a brief study," A. C. Piepkorn, in *Concordia Theological Monthly*, March 1970, puts the figures at 700 "Open" congregations in the U.S.A. and over 350 in Canada, with an estimate of 300 "exclusive" congregations in the two countries.
8a. See Malcolm V. Jones, "Some notes on Dostoyevsky, Tolstoy and the 'Redstokisty'" in *Slavonica*, University of Nottingham Dept. of Slavonic Studies, May 1968.
9. Quoted R. S. Latimer, *Dr. Baedeker and His Apostolic Work in Russia* (1907), p. 190.
10. Alan Scarfe (*Religion in Communist Lands*, Nov.-Dec. 1975, "The Evangelical Wing of the Orthodox Church in Romania") traces the present Brethren Movement in Rumania to three sources: Berney's work (which he dates to 1903–4), an indigenous evangelical movement from within the Orthodox Church under a former priest Tudor Popescu, and a breakaway from Popescu's movement, later reunited to it. Scarfe suggests as many as 120,000 members for the combined group.
12. *Father and Son*, p. 129.
13. *The Life of Philip Henry Gosse*, Edmund Gosse (1890), p. 353.
13a. Preface to *Brethren Missionary Work in Mysore State*, K. J. Newton (1971).
14. *John Olley: Pioneer Missionary to the Chad*, J. W. Clapham and N. J. Taylor (1966), p. 131.
15. *Peculiar People*, p. 92.
16. *Christian Missionaries and the Creation of Northern Rhodesia, 1880–1924*, R. I. Rotberg (1965), p. 95.
17. Ibid., p. 76.
18. An essential source book on Brethren missionary work, so far as sponsored through *Echoes of Service* is now available in the *Echoes* centenary history *Turning the World Upside Down* (Bath, 1972).
19. For Italy to 1886 see *Tra Risveglio e Millennio* by D. Maselli (Turin, 1974).

CHAPTER 13

THE DISINTEGRATION OF EXCLUSIVISM AND LATER DEVELOPMENTS AMONG INDEPENDENTS

WHEN Lady Powerscourt told Mr. Daly that she had determined on joining the Plymouth church, which at that time held its meetings in Aungier Street, he said to her: "You expect to meet with perfection, and you will be disappointed; it is not to be met with among any body of Christians in this sinful world. After a little time you will separate yourself from some whom you will find not to be as perfect as you thought them to be; others will be added to the number; at last you will be left alone; and when you look into yourself, you will not find perfection there."

Mrs. Hamilton Madden, *Memoir of the Rev. Robert Daly*

But revolutions are made by fanatical men of action with one-track minds, men who are narrow-minded to the point of genius. They overturn the old order in a few hours or days; the whole upheaval takes a few weeks or at most years, but for decades thereafter, for centuries, the spirit of narrowness which led to the upheaval is worshipped as holy.

Boris Pasternak, *Doctor Zhivago*

WHILE DARBY LIVED, EXCLUSIVISM SEEMED TO PROSPER. At the division of 1848 a large body of churches went with him, and their number continued to increase, not least as a result of his own near apostolic exertions. By about 1880 an exclusive writer could claim eleven monthly magazines circulating from London, several with a circulation of forty or fifty thousand. In the United Kingdom, he said, were about 750 meetings, 101 in Canada, 91 in the U.S.A., 39 in Holland, 189 in Germany, 146 in France, and 72 in Switzerland, with scattered congregations in twenty-two other countries.[1] Darby's own travels took him regularly to the Continent, where he travelled widely. Between 1862 and 1868 he made three extended visits to North America, and at the end of 1868 was in the West Indies. Further visits to North America followed in 1870, 1872-3 and 1874-5. From there he went – following Wigram – to New Zealand, before returning to the United States and Canada, where he remained until 1877. An attempt to establish exclusivism in Italy met with little success, although he visited that country. In Dublin, on the other hand, he met with greater response, and some of the revival workers joined him. Throughout these years, Darby was also keeping in touch with the world-wide development of the exclusive meetings by a voluminous correspondence.

Exclusivism's great strength lay in the literature it produced. Andrew Miller, in the book quoted, was able rather complacently to contrast the output of exclusive writers with the much smaller production from the independent Brethren, and quoted a contemporary American Methodist:

> The Society, or Order of Christian Men, usually styled the Plymouth Brethren, has already, and almost without observation, spread over the face of the civilized world. It seems, in fact, to have stolen a march on Christendom, and must now, whether for good or for evil, be acknowledged as a power in the present awful crisis in the world's history, or tremendous conflict between the powers of light and of darkness. That it is felt to be such a power, is evident from the fact of the controversy about Plymouth Brethren coming up all over the Protestant world just now, and by the innumerable articles, pamphlets, and volumes which this wide-spread controversy has called forth.[2]

Some of these exclusive writings were of no mean order. J. G. Bellett's little volumes of devotional literature, particularly his *Short Meditation on the Moral Glory of the Lord Jesus Christ*, were classics of their genre, written in a prose of delightful simplicity. William Kelly, twenty years younger than Darby, and like Darby a classical graduate of Trinity College, Dublin, was the greatest of them all. He was of as deep learning as Darby, with nothing either of Darby's warped bitterness in controversy, or of his tortured thinking, and soon became the chief interpreter of Darby's theology. His literary production almost equalled that of his chief in extent, and was of forbidding calibre. In addition to a long series of doctrinal works and commentaries, he issued a journal, *The Prospect*, in 1849 and 1850, and followed this from 1856 until his death fifty years later with *The Bible Treasury*, an erudite monthly which had a considerable acceptance well outside his own ecclesiastical circles. In addition, he also collated and edited the *Collected Writings* and *Letters* of Darby. It is to Kelly, as much as to Darby, that the student must turn if he wishes to study the authoritative texts of developed Darbyism.

Another popular writer among exclusives was an Irish schoolmaster, Charles Henry Mackintosh, who preached extensively in the revival movement. The initials "C.H.M." became familiar in many pious evangelical households of the later Victorian and Edwardian years. No critical scholar, Mackintosh nevertheless had a marked gift for simple Biblical exposition, and his works on the Pentateuch had an enormous vogue as simple aids to devotional interpretation of the first five books of the Bible. He was, however, no theologian, and certain isolated sentences in those books which referred to "the heavenly humanity" of Christ (and thus verged on formal heresy), brought him much hostile notice from the more prejudiced opponents of Brethren (who took his writings as being far more significant and representative than they deserved). He later withdrew the expressions, on Darby's insistence.

Andrew Miller, a London Scottish merchant, became another popular writer, producing among other works a readable outline of Church History, written from his own eschatological viewpoint. Miller also co-operated for many years with Mackintosh in issuing another periodical popular among exclusives, *Things New and Old*. Charles Stanley, a Yorkshire businessman, became a successful evangelist and issued a long series of evangelistic tracts, *The C.S. Tracts*, which had a wide circulation (and which were probably the originals of the "CRS Tracts" which afforded so much surreptitious amusement to the students of the Catholic seminary in A. J. Cronin's *The Keys of the Kingdom*).

Yet, despite this activity, the marks of exclusivism's decay appear in Darby's own letters. Increasingly suspicious of all outside his own circle, and morbidly pre-occupied with the "evil" and "worldliness" around him, he set his followers on a course of systematic estrangement from the common life of men and women that could lead only to disaster.

The first act of the dissolution took place just before the end of Darby's long life. The conflict came to a head in a clash between the more mystical introspectives and those who through their evangelism or their scholarship still retained windows upon the outside world. The storm broke over the head of the veteran Dr. Edward Cronin, Darby's companion from the earliest days in Dublin. Cronin died in February 1882, in his eighty-first year, three years after exclusivism had broken his heart by cruelly rejecting him, on little more than a pretext, from the fellowship to which he had given his life. In the controversy which had followed Cronin's rejection in 1879, Darby had showed that in his old age he had lost his once sure command over his followers. Exclusivism was divided from top to bottom by the quarrel, and Darby died on 29th April 1882, knowing that William Kelly, his greatest follower, was in the opposing faction from himself. "He had survived precisely to the tragic moment," wrote Neatby, "just long enough to see his work go to pieces by his own act."[3] Wistfully, he had been personally reconciled to Cronin at the end: had sent daily to inquire of the health of Andrew Miller, now divided from him by the rift, and lying seriously ill in the same town of Bournemouth: and had exclaimed pathetically on his deathbed. "I should particularly object to any attack being made on William Kelly."[4] His dying wish was vain.

With Darby's strong hand no longer in control, disintegration followed, although the Kelly section, still under strong leadership, did retain its vigour and unity during the further quarter century of its own leader's life, except when a few churches under W. W. Fereday rejoined the independent movement shortly before Kelly's death. Kelly died, universally respected, in 1906, at the Exeter home of his friend Dr. Heyman Wreford. He had not met Darby until 1845, when he was twenty-four, and had thus scarcely been identified with the most damaging episodes of the older man's career. Perhaps the aptest comment on Kelly was contained in Spurgeon's often quoted *mot*, that he had a mind made for the universe, but narrowed by Darbyism.

Disaster in the other and stricter section of exclusivism was violent and rapid. Leadership passed after Darby's death, first to J. B. Stoney, a survivor of the early Dublin days, and then to F. E. Raven, a civil servant whose descendants (largely outside the movement) have produced a marked collection of talent, including a senior Cabinet minister. Nevertheless, further major divisions took place in 1884, 1885, 1890 and 1908, and there were other minor quarrels. The first of these major divisions saw most of the American churches in a separate camp from the hard central core of exclusivism, and the 1890 quarrel lost to them most of the Continental churches. In 1885 they parted company with one of their remaining leaders of genuine scholarship, Clarence Esme Stuart of Reading, and a few congregations who adhered to him. Stuart, of aristocratic lineage, had been educated at Eton and St. John's College, Cambridge, where he had been a Tyrwhitt Hebrew Scholar. He had joined with exclusive Brethren under Dorman's influence in 1860. Stuart's expulsion took place over mystical teachings which he had put forward concerning the continuing propitiatory work of Christ as High Priest "in the Heavenlies:" this teaching closely foreshadowed similar teachings which were later put forward by Bishop Gore in his *Body of Christ* in 1901,* and have been followed by other men in the Anglo-Catholic tradition.

The 1908 division saw the final rejection of the evangelistic and outward-looking elements among the extremer exclusives. One evangelist of note remained among them in George Cutting, author of a celebrated evangelistic pamphlet *Safety, Certainty and Enjoyment*. Cutting's influence was largely behind the consolidation of a considerable number of exclusive congregations in the rural areas of the East Midlands, which had been only sparsely touched by the movement as a whole. Most of these congregations were doomed to become extinct in the collapse which resulted from the exclusive developments of the third quarter of the twentieth century. For, after the "Glanton" division of 1908, what was left of the extreme core of exclusivism degenerated under the American leadership of the two James Taylors, father and son, into an introspective and mystical group whose esoteric teachings, and completely closed outlook, eventually brought it to the much publicised débâcle and public opprobrium of the 1950s and 1960s: and at that point to the loss of a large proportion of its remaining membership to all Christian denominations (including independent Brethren.) The most morbid strains of Darby's teachings, isolated and exaggerated, reached their over-ripe maturity in

---

* See D. M. Baillie, *God Was in Christ* (1961 edn.), pp. 194–7. The teaching had been partially anticipated within exclusivism on a more popular level, by Charles Stanley's slogan of "justification in a Risen Christ."

those developments, which took the teaching of this exclusive group far from the paths of normal Christian orthodoxy.†

The last and most pathetic contact with an outside group of Christians had occurred in 1932–35, when they came into touch with Watchman Nee and the "Little Flock" movement in China. Nee was welcomed to their congregations in this country in 1933. Alas, the good man visited and broke bread with a congregation of another Christian body in Britain, and the connexion was abruptly broken off in 1935 by the Taylor group of exclusives. Their letter rejecting the "Little Flock" contained an innuendo redolent of Darbyite controversial methods at their most despicable:

> In this connexion we feel sorrowfully obliged to refer to a lack of uprightness which has marked Mr. Nee, particularly in some of his movements, while amongst us.[5]

The complaint was that he had not allowed his itinerary to be, in effect, completely within their own circle: this was "lack of uprightness"!

The Kelly group and other groups rejected by the hard core of exclusives, both in Britain and abroad, have retained their basic doctrinal balance, and have of recent years made several attempts at reunion, with a fair measure of success. Their decay has been mainly by slower natural processes. They have in fact forced themselves into a blind alley. Rigid central control is rejected because of abuses made obvious under the Taylors and their forerunners; complete independency is rejected because it is like the independent Brethren; while the only apparent compromise – a loose federal structure involving automatic acceptance by all churches of the judgment of a local church – is also rejected because of their own experiences of the injustices to which it gives rise. It is little wonder that the basis of their "church principles" has become so rarified that few can understand it!*

Their surviving churches are tending to find themselves in a position which is indistinguishable from that of the independent Brethren: a position which normally leads in course of time to full inter-communion with the independents.

Not a few individuals among the moderate exclusives had long since anticipated this result, and the independents have throughout the twentieth century been strengthened by able preachers and teachers from their ranks. Men who have taken this decisive step have often proved, ironically, to be a moderate and broadening influence, although others have brought

† See the extremely detailed and well informed article "The Exclusive Brethren: A Case Study in the Evolution of a Sectarian Ideology" by B. R. Wilson in *Patterns of Sectarianism* (ed. Bryan R. Wilson) (1967).

* This summary is not a caricature, but is based on a recent publication put out privately by one of their members, *The Brethren Since 1870* (c. 1966).

with them a leavening of the more eccentric parts of the Darbyite theological system.

The independent Brethren have always found parts of the Darbyite thought to be strangely pervasive. In the years of great expansion on the floodtide of the revival the exclusives provided more intellectual satisfaction than the more thoughtful among the independents could find among most of the ardent evangelists of their own churches. Attempts by men like J. G. M'Vicker to call their attention to the rich heritage of earlier Christian writings, were not always successful. M'Vicker himself appreciated deeply the devotional writings of men like Bellett, but had his own opinion of other "exclusive" influences. He wrote, while visiting Ballymena in 1881:

> Some young men have been hashing up things they have picked up out of Kelly's and Darby's tracts and books about having life before faith or forgiveness, etc., and one or two heady ones, who ought to be at the Cross learning to subdue their temper and pride, are in danger of being taken up with these speculations, and are trying to get the rest to argue about them, fancying themselves ever so much more enlightened than the poor brethren who cannot take in the "new light." Of the many evil spirits which have gone out in these last days, the proud and lying spirit which has seduced the poor "Darbyites," is one of the most dangerous.[6]

The next year, from London, he wrote with his Irish humour:

> I am glad you like Hawker, and that all the high things you have heard in brethren's addresses and read in their tracts have not spoiled your taste for the old-fashioned manna, small indeed as coriander seed, but sweet as wafers made with honey, which abounds in Hawker, Romaine, M'Cheyne, and other such "old masters" in Israel. Of course there are giants who can swallow a whole shoulder at a mouthful, and can afford to despise such children's fare. I remember one such Goliath almost extinguishing me with his scorn, for quoting such a poor bat or owl of a writer as Bunyan, to a saint like him, who could look at the sun any day without winking. I dare say he could, like the prophet, have contracted himself to the dimensions of such a baby as Bunyan, but it would have cost him a great effort, and he didn't make it, but stood up to every cubit of his height and scoffed at poor little Bunyan and poor little me. I fancy he owed a good deal of his size to gas which he had swallowed out of tracts, and which had swelled him up. Let us keep small, dear brother, and we shall keep safe, and retain our taste for the children's fare.[7]

Something of the depth of the penetration of Darbyite ideas among the independents may be gathered from a statement in Müller's own church at Bethesda, made in May 1917, less than twenty years after Müller's death, when one of its own leaders had to appeal for a fresh recognition of the office of elder:

> We still have the apostles with us in their teaching, and we are responsible to act in accordance therewith. Although we have no officially appointed elders among

us, we are called to recognize those who do the work, and to esteem them highly in love for their work's sake.[8]

Although another leader indicated that this movement towards Darbyite views in Bethesda itself, in what had been one of the major issues between Bethesda and Darby, was more a matter of names than of fact,★ it is still significant that the actual name of "elder" had been dropped: for where an office is no longer recognized, the understanding of its importance and function cannot long continue. Happily, this particular departure from Scriptural principles of church order has not been permanent among Bethesda's successors; but it is not uncommon in other congregations of independent Brethren.

In one respect, however, Darbyite views made no penetration, and that was in relation to the independent status of each local church. Exclusivism directed some of its main criticisms at this feature: the independents, it insisted, had no idea of the unity of the Church; independency destroyed the truth of the one Body. The criticism was indicative more of the nature of the critics' own thinking than of the real position of those criticized. It could only be valid both if outward conformity was considered to be essential to unity, and if that outward unity already existed – which it plainly does not. Exclusivism has always shared with other High Church systems a narrow mechanical view of visible unity, and the result has been a perpetual rending of the Body of Christ in the name of the Body's one-ness. There was more justice in another part of exclusivism's criticism of the independents, namely, that they had little concern for "church truth." The aggressive "gospel" character which the revival influences gave to many of the independent churches did not care much, or think deeply, concerning the deeper aspects of the nature of the Church. But where the independents did concern themselves with these deeper aspects, they clung to independency (as we have already seen from Groves's writings) as a result of a deeper and a more realistic concern for true Christian unity than exclusivism has ever shown. It was from the independent position that they could recognize the true action of God wherever it took place, and could be free to acknowledge unity and kinship with every man and every congregation which showed the signs of God's grace. Human shortsightedness and weakness has kept them back, in general, from a full expression of their ideal; but in the present broken state of the Christian confession, it is difficult to visualize any stance from which a man's outlook could more satisfactorily embrace every other one of his brethren in Christ. If independents have deprecated attempts towards forcing an outward organizational unity (whether of evangelicals

★ "Mr. Davies remarked that although we have not now officially appointed elders, yet we still have men in the Church who are evidently qualified of God, and are actually doing the work of elders." (P. 23 of book quoted.)

alone or of all professing Christians), it is because they have seen that Christian unity is something deeper than its outward shell: and it is also because they have understood the very real evils which can arise from the power structure of an outward organization, directed to creating a unity which it identifies with itself.

Yet independency brings its own problems. First, it can lead to carelessness over succession, because it lacks co-ordinated arrangements for the selection and training of an adequate leadership. Darbyite mysticism, which had always drawn a contrast between the supposed invariable spontaneity of the Holy Spirit's working and "human arrangement," seriously tainted their thinking at this point: so that they seemed to imagine that this lack would be mystically supplied. Secondly, concern for a more widely demonstrated unity of the Church of God results in a broad tolerance of the beliefs of others, and the more ardent and narrow enthusiasts have never reconciled themselves to this. They are not able to distinguish tolerance from indifference and from lack of principle, and fail to recognize that tolerance itself is a principle of over-riding importance.

Concern over this lack of effective leadership and over faulty co-ordination of discipline, both results of independency, led to the only secession from the independent Brethren which has occurred since the "exclusives" separated into their own fellowship. Apart from this one minor instance, independent Brethren have been spared the continual fragmentation which has destroyed the exclusives: their loosely connected churches have retained an overall unity of fellowship and of witness, which embraces a wide variety of opinion. It is emphatically not true, as opponents have alleged, that a proper act of discipline in one church will automatically be ignored and over-ridden by a neighbouring congregation. Of course there are instances, as in every communion, where foolishness and wilfulness prevail; but, where there is sound local leadership, one local church will give proper respect and regard to the decisions of another, while reserving its right to make its own final decision in direct responsibility to God. In this way the tragic despotism which has accompanied the exclusive view of the authority of "the assembly" is avoided. A foolish or an oppressive act by one congregation is not taken up, as it is so easily in exclusivism, into the system of the churches as a whole.

The difference between the two views is the result of two different attitudes of mind. Exclusive principle, for all its protestations as to the unity of the Body, must be based upon the drawing of a line of fellowship narrower than that of the whole Church of God. On the other hand, beneath the thinking of the independent congregations, however narrow or rigid that may be, there lies a sense of a wider unity of the Body of Christ which extends far beyond the congregations for which they are responsible. The "unity" of an entity consisting only of their own congregations is, ultimately, a meaningless conception to them (as, indeed, is the idea of a group of "their own" congregations in itself): the only unity which they can recognize, above that of the local congregation, is that of the whole Church of God.

The contrast was plainly seen in the one secession from independent Brethren, to which reference has been made. Concern for an effective leadership and discipline led to secession only when the preserving sense of the wider unity of the whole Body was made subservient to the very conception against which Groves had struggled in earlier days – the conception of "separation" in protest against the alleged corruptions of others. Protest is a continuous element in the history of the Church, and often arises from a genuine divine initiative. But if protest is often a part of the divine movement in the continually reforming Church, it can also be dangerous and divisive, when it is allied to restricted vision and to suspicion of others. The way in which matters were developing was shown by a letter to *The Witness* in 1888:

> About ten or eleven years ago I was what is called a Baptist, but several Christian friends pointed out to me the sin of being in any way mixed up with any sect, and that it was wrong for a Christian to attend any sectarian meeting for any purpose whatever, or in fact any meeting except those of believers gathered out to "The Name." I then turned my back on sects once and for all, and broke bread with those who professed to be obedient believers, thinking that all those who met on the first day of the week around the Lord, really were gathered-out ones. Gradually I was undeceived, and, to my horror, found out that a large majority of those I met with, went in and out among the sects, and that they denied the truth of separation, and were angry at same being mentioned. [*sic*]. In the town where I live we have a small meeting, and (would you believe it?) those in fellowship go to the following meetings, and in some cases take part in same

and then there followed a list of most of the churches of the district, ranging from the Congregational Chapel ("where the minister holds the doctrine of non-eternity of punishment") to "the (so-called) Church of England" (which apparently required no other indication of its iniquity).

In itself the letter is plainly trivial – but it was an indication of a trend. We may smile at its naïveté, and wonder how the writer expected to avoid "sectarianism" by establishing yet another fragment of the Church. Plainly, he could do so only on one of two alternatives: either on the premise that his group alone constituted the one pure Church, or by evacuating the word "sect" of all meaning, and using it as a simple term of abuse. (By a delightful irony, it is in a precise combination of these two alternatives that the word has often been used by the representatives of the more imperialist of the older churches, and is today commonly used by some of the more ardent advocates of organized ecumenism.)

The first indication of the coming secession had been given in 1887, when a quarterly magazine appeared under the title *Needed Truth*, becoming a monthly in 1891. A conference at Windermere in 1891, at which the seventy-year-old Henry Dyer spoke for the moderates, attempted a reconciliation of the irreconcilable. The extreme section were intent on forcing their point of view, and open secession soon followed. In the years from 1892 onwards a number of congregations formed themselves into a close fellowship which adopted a strict Presbyterian polity, with national and district oversights controlling the local groups of elders. The new group disclaimed strongly any connexion with either the exclusives or the independents, and were nicknamed by the name of their magazine, *Needed Truth*. They have remained small in numbers, with some ninety congregations in Britain, and are extreme (though orthodox) in both doctrine and discipline. They unashamedly reserve to themselves the title of "the Churches of God." Inevitably, a narrow exclusivism and a rigid discipline has led them (as it led the exclusives) to in-breeding of thought and to division among themselves. This followed in 1901–04 over one of their teachers, the evangelist Frank Vernal.*

The *Needed Truth* outburst left its marks on the independents. The extremist point of view characteristic of the seceders has continued to find advocates among them, and one of the first editors of *Needed Truth* became influential among the independent congregations of the Manchester district. This was William Henry Hunter, an Irishman from Tyneside who was chief assistant to Sir Edward Leader Williams in the building of the Manchester Ship Canal, and later its consulting engineer. Hunter was a dominating character, and impressed his personality on many of the local congregations. Although he died in 1917, his influence is still felt in the district, where the shadow of a "central oversight" still exists as a link between the separate congregations. Another early editor of the journal also returned to the independents, but L. W. G. Alexander, unlike Hunter, also cast off his exclusive tendencies to become an influential and moderate leader.

On the other hand, reaction against *Needed Truth* ideas has in general further strengthened the movement's commitment to independency.

* For an extremely detailed study of the *Needed Truth* churches see "The Churches of God: Pattern and Practice" by G. Willis and B. R. Wilson in *Patterns of Sectarianism* (ed. Bryan R. Wilson, 1967). The *Needed Truth* group adopted the "exclusive" view that the local church comprised all the faithful in one town, and not each local congregation. But they went one step further than the exclusives – who at least retained the theory that all the local Christians were in principle members of this local church. To the *Needed Truth* view, their members alone constituted this true church. The difference between the *Needed Truth* outlook and that of the independents who are not influenced by it has been neatly expressed in an unpublished paper by Mr. Kingsley Melling. He points out that it substitutes for the classic concept adopted by the independents – "where Christ is, there the Church is" (see p. 121) – the precisely opposite idea – "where the Church is, there Christ is."

Today independency has largely ceased to be a reasoned position adopted from conviction as to its advantages, and with due regard to its weaknesses; instead, it has tended to become a matter of dogma, and its divine right would be championed by many of the independents as strongly as by any of their predecessors of the seventeenth century. This is to be regretted, for when a movement turns its guiding principles (however sound they may be) into dogmatic tradition, it ceases to be capable of a realistic assessment of its own shortcomings. We may be deeply convinced that independency is the right and proper course for a movement like the Brethren, in their particular circumstances, and yet still be able to regret that even a proper course should be followed blindly. Just as the *Needed Truth* seceders justified their actions by a selective appeal to Biblical authority, so the appeal of the independents to Scripture tends to be selective of its proof texts, and often its approach to Scripture is from positions already arrived at on other premises.

Later in this book we shall strongly advocate the maintenance of this independency. It is the more important therefore that we recognize that (like any other form of polity) independency is far from perfect. Practical weaknesses are inseparable from the extreme independent position. Any action which requires knowledge or resources beyond those commanded by the single local congregation is hindered or prevented by lack of means of communication and co-operation. The support of those who are engaged in full-time evangelistic, teaching or pastoral work tends to become dependent upon sporadic and disconnected giving. Arrangements for the training of future leadership and for the instruction of the membership in general – so vital to a movement which professes to use the talents of all its members – are at best improvised, and more often neglected altogether. More insidious, but no less disastrous, local leadership tends to become restricted in its outlook and narrowly concerned with its own preoccupations, sometimes with the preservation of its own position. The wider gifts of men whose abilities and outlook are strategic rather than tactical – the statesman, the scholar, the constructive thinker – are frustrated, with little outlet for their use, and with no means by which their possessors can be supported and freed to use their gifts full-time for the benefit of the churches. At the worst, such men are regarded suspiciously by those whose interests are more narrowly circumscribed. Too often, also, an unacknowledged rivalry can develop between individual congregations. The effect is somewhat similar to that which would result if the affairs of the nation were to be controlled entirely through the unorganized work of local councils.

One prominent example of co-operation among the independent congregations arose before this dogmatic attitude had hardened. If the work of the editors of *Echoes of Service* had not started when it did, it is difficult to believe that it could have developed much later.

James van Sommer started his *Missionary Reporter*[9] in 1862, and continued it until 1858, linking the home churches with the growing missionary work and helping to distribute gifts. William Yapp and Dr. John Lindsay MacLean also circulated notes of overseas workers, particularly concerning those in Italy, and Robert Mitchell of Edinburgh was also in touch with this group. In 1872, together with Henry Groves and Henry Dyer, Dr. MacLean, who shortly moved to Bath, started another journal, *The Missionary Echo*; the name being changed in 1885 to *Echoes of Service*. The editors of this journal undertook the distribution of gifts to missionaries, in this way supplementing the work of Müller's Scriptural Knowledge Institution. Both centres still continue their work, with similar centres in Scotland and in other countries, but the work of *Echoes of Service* rapidly grew to be the main channel by which monies were distributed to the increasing missionary force. For a period after the First World War a residential training centre for lady missionaries was established in Bath, under W. E. Vine, then an editor of *Echoes of Service*, and the saintly H. E. Marsom.

The editors of *Echoes* have consistently refused to regard themselves as a missionary society, and have insisted that they have no power or right of control over individual missionaries, but the mere existence of their highly efficient centre for distributing monies and information, and the issue by them of a list (entitled *A Prayer Guide*) of workers to whom they send money, together force them into continuous anomalies in this respect. They have also consistently refused to accept the guidance of any form of advisory committee, although if they had done so they might have spared themselves a great number of difficulties*: they are in the obviously difficult constitutional position of trying to combine both a *de facto* policy-making function and ordinary administrative functions.

The prominence of *Echoes of Service* should not be allowed to obscure the immense importance of Müller's Scriptural Knowledge Institution, particularly during the first fifty years of the movement's expansion. Its support was given liberally and widely at home and overseas, and its name constantly recurs in the records of the development years. The extent of its influence justifies the claim that Müller was, to a greater extent than any other single man, the architect of the growth of independent Brethren. The Institution still continues to distribute gifts to missionaries, on a substantial scale.

There are real weaknesses which have sprung from the highly fragmented nature of the movement; a hardening of tradition which occurs when the wider outlook of the constructive thinker is not present; local

---

* In very recent years there have been signs that this rigid position may be amended, and initial steps have been taken toward the establishment of such an advisory committee.

foolishnesses which result from lack of the statesman's moderating influence; a general shallowness of preaching and teaching (despite a wide popular knowledge of the Bible) which marks the absence of the scholar's understanding. There have been various attempts in the last fifty years to remedy the worst of these defects. The most successful has been the growth of the residential conference movement, arising largely out of the Missionary Study Class movement launched by the late Professor A. Rendle Short and others in the early decades of the twentieth century, and itself based on some of the earlier conferences to which reference has already been made. The conference movement now covers most of the country, and under different committees and a variety of different types of conference, attempts in short residential sessions to fill a little of the gaps which so often occur in the local churches themselves.

Despite the weaknesses mentioned, Bible teaching was by no means neglected between the wars. Certain Brethren writers, such as C. F. Hogg, W. W. Fereday, J. B. Watson and G. H. Lang produced expository works and commentaries which were widely useful, on a popular level, in their own churches, while William Edwy Vine,† who was for years one of the editors of *Echoes of Service*, not only wrote alone, and in co-operation with C. F. Hogg, a considerable series of commentaries on the Bible, but also put the Bible student permanently in his debt with his useful *Expository Dictionary of New Testament Words* (first published in 1939), as useful a work as any produced by Brethren since G. V. Wigram had sponsored the *Englishman's Concordances* to the Greek and Hebrew texts of the Bible a century before (it was upon Wigram's work that Thomas Newberry, another Brother, based his *Englishman's Bible*, which appeared at about the same time as the Revised Version). Other writers also have contributed to an extensive literature.

The post-war years have seen a growth of sound Biblical scholarship, much of it the result of the increased educational opportunities of recent years. Pre-eminent in this has been the influence and example of Frederick Fyvie Bruce, now Rylands Professor of Biblical Criticism and Exegesis in the University of Manchester, and of H. L. Ellison, formerly an Anglican clergyman, who became senior tutor at their Moorlands Bible College at Dawlish.★ There are a number of younger men in different universities who are beginning to make their mark on Biblical studies, and a much larger number who make use of the training which they have received within the British educational system as lecturers and teachers in Religious Knowledge, to the general well-being of their churches.

† Vine is "the chief of the elders, an erudite learned Greek scholar, with a vast knowledge of Biblical exegesis, a loving impetuous man . . ." who appears on p. 24 of Anne Arnott's *The Brethren*.

★ Founded by a Brethren evangelist, D. L. Clifford. Now in Dorset.

In one field above all the independent churches are always ready to further to their fullest powers any constructive work: that is in Bible distribution and in evangelism. Whatever deaf ears may be turned to other appeals for co-operation, this is a sphere in which others can always count upon a response. True to their revival background, the independents (and, indeed, many of the moderate exclusives) have contributed disproportionately of men and money to all the great evangelistic campaigns of the past seventy-five years, while many evangelical societies have owed a considerable part of their impetus and their growth to men from Brethren churches. Two names which were especially prominent in the years before and after the Second World War were the brothers George and Montague Goodman, but they are representative of a very large number of less well-known men, and of a multitude of the rank and file of the movement who are prepared to undertake any chore as the servants of evangelism. The British and Foreign Bible Society has also been enthusiastically supported by many Brethren, just as Brethren missions throughout the world have themselves benefited immeasurably from the unflinching generosity of this and its smaller sister Bible Societies.

Quotation References – Chapter 13.

1. *The Brethren: a Brief Sketch of their Origin, Progress and Testimony*, Andrew Miller (undated, *c.* 1880), p. 163.
2. "Plymouth Brethrenism," in *The Southern Review*, Baltimore, by Dr. Blescoe (quoted Miller, op. cit., p. 77).
3. *A History of the Plymouth Brethren*, p. 308.
4. *John Nelson Darby*, W. G. Turner (1944), p. 52.
5. *The Recovery and Maintenance of the Truth*. A. J. Gardiner. (1951), p. 220.
6. *Memoir and Letters*, pp. 110–11.
7. Ibid., pp. 116–17.
8. *Bethesda Church*, E. T. Davies and others (1917), p. 15.
9. See J. W. Forrest, "The Missionary Reporter," in *C.B.R.F. Journal*, No. 21, May 1971.

CHAPTER 14

ECCENTRICS, SAINTS, AND CRITICS

> But each has his own special gift from God, one of one kind and one of
> another.
>
> St. Paul, *First Letter to the Corinthians*

THIS CHAPTER IS AN UNASHAMED MISCELLANY. IN IT, WE shall consider the lives of several remarkable men who have been associated with Brethren, and to whom it has not been possible to do justice in the more general history. Afterwards we shall take the opportunity of a fairly light-hearted look at some of the criticisms which have been made of Brethren down the years.

The first of the biographical summaries is an act of belated justice. Philip Henry Gosse has suffered so deeply from the caricature which emerges from his son's brilliant and tragic study in *Father and Son*, and from the ridicule attaching to his unfortunate *Omphalos* contribution to the Darwinian debate, that the real attributes of a remarkable man have long been overlaid. Gosse senior is classed by Sacheverell Sitwell among poets and artists, and the Cambridge naturalist Dr. Geoffrey Lapage has written of him (dismissing T. H. Huxley's gibe of "the honest hodman of science") that he has well earned the respect of every naturalist.*

Edmund Gosse published an objective biography of his father in 1890, soon after the father's death in 1888. *The Life of Philip Henry Gosse* presents a very different picture from that given by *Father and Son*. It must be emphasized from the start that the father's failings portrayed in both books are essentially those of an intellectual widowed recluse, rather than those which are normally associated with religious narrowness. Edmund Gosse had a secluded and restricted childhood, but it was also a childhood lived in an atmosphere of true affection and security: it must be remembered that he was the only child of a father who was already thirty-nine at his birth, and that he lost his mother at the age of seven. Philip Gosse emerges from the two books as an eccentric, but nevertheless as a gifted and noble man.

Philip Gosse was born on 6th April 1810 in Worcester, the son of a travelling painter of miniatures, whose talents he inherited. He was possessed of a "photographic" memory, which stood him in good stead in his later scientific researches. He travelled about North America from

* See J. S. Andrews, "Philip Henry Gosse, F.R.S.," in the *Library Association Record* for June 1961, pp. 197–201, from which these quotations are taken.

1827 to 1838, and reached England again on 4th January 1839. He was reduced to starving penury when his book *The Canadian Naturalist* was accepted by a London publisher later in that year and rescued him from poverty. After a brief spell with Methodists he associated himself with the Hackney group of Brethren through William Berger, the brother-in-law of James van Sommer: there is a conflict of evidence as to whether this was in 1844 or 1847.* Between those two dates he visited Jamaica, and thereafter became for some twenty years a prolific and highly popular writer on naturalistic subjects, while devoting himself to detailed study of different forms of life, and pre-eminently of the marine invertebrates. Gosse married his first wife from the house of Robert Howard in Tottenham in 1848, and his son Edmund was born in September 1849. His first wife died in 1857, and he married again in 1860.

After several extended visits to Devon and Pembrokeshire, Gosse settled with his son in St. Marychurch, near Torquay, in 1857 after the death of his first wife, and he lived there until his death on 23rd August 1888. He did not make or retain friends easily: among the longest of his friendships were those with Charles Kingsley and with the Rev. J. E. Gladstone, the cousin of the Prime Minister. He became virtual pastor of a small assembly of Brethren which he founded at St. Marychurch, but his association with Brethren was individualist. His son wrote:

> In the middle life he had connected himself with the Plymouth Brethren, princi-
> pally, no doubt, because of their lack of systematic organization, their repudia-
> tion of all traditional authority, their belief that the Bible is the infallible and
> sufficient guide. But he soon lost confidence in the Plymouth Brethren also, and
> for the last thirty years of his life he was really unconnected with any Christian
> body whatever . . . In those thirty years he scarcely heard any preacher of his
> own reputed sect; I am confident that he never once attended the services of any
> unaffiliated minister.[1]

It should be observed against this that Gosse's widow refers to the congregation as "Brethren" without any qualification, although from her own description their proceedings were in some ways uncharacteristic. Edmund Gosse's own information concerning Brethren is inaccurate in matters of fact and at best sketchy although he was from 1868 to 1874 a member of the Brook Street, Tottenham, congregation.

The life of the second of the men to be described in this chapter was a dramatic one. Sir Robert Anderson was the son of the Crown Solicitor for Dublin, and was born there, of Scots-Irish descent, on 29th May 1841. He was educated at Trinity College, Dublin, after private schooling, and after graduating he spent some time evangelizing in Southern Ireland with his college friend George F. Trench. He was also associated with "the three Kerry landlords" in their evangelism. In 1863 Anderson was called to the

---

* Mr. Robert Boyd has shown conclusively that it was in 1843 or 1844 (*Broadsheet* of the Christian Brethren Research Fellowship, March/April 1969, p. 49).

Irish Bar, and became involved in government anti-Fenian investigations. His success led to his transfer to London, and to various government appointments there. Eventually, in 1888, he was appointed Assistant Commissioner of Police and head of the Criminal Investigation Department at Scotland Yard, at a time when the "Jack the Ripper" scare was at its height. He remained there until retirement in 1901, when he was appointed K.C.B. During his years at Scotland Yard, Anderson was closely concerned with the reform of police methods and of the penal system.

Anderson wrote prolifically on religious matters, earning the (slightly depreciatory) description from L. E. Elliott-Binns of "that doughty champion of popular Protestantism."[2] His books, which included a number of attacks on various aspects of Biblical Higher Criticism, were characterized by the application of a robust lay common sense, rather than by special expertise. Others of his more general books were very popular: *The Silence of God*, published in 1898, caused no little sensation on its appearance, and ran through three editions in a few weeks. In the preface he justified his main theme by a quotation from Froudes's *History of England*: "For the religion of Christ was substituted the Christian religion." Perhaps the most enduring of Anderson's books was also one of his earliest – *The Gospel and Its Ministry*. Anderson died on 15th November 1918.

At the time of his conversion, at the height of the revival movement in Dublin, Anderson associated with the Brethren there and attended Merrion Hall. After he moved to London, he associated with the Brethren at Camberwell and for twelve years at Walham Green, and he moved freely among them for the rest of his life, although his closing years were spent as a member of the Presbyterian Trinity Church at Notting Hill. He was a close friend of J. W. C. Fegan, as well as of other leading figures in the movement.

A notable "character" was Alfred T. Schofield,* who, after qualifying as a doctor somewhat late in life after a false start in business, became a popular and well-to-do Harley Street practitioner. At first an "exclusive," Schofield later moved to the independent fellowship. What his fellow medical-men thought of his flamboyance is not recorded: but in evangelical Christian life he was a prominent figure during the later nineteenth and early twentieth centuries (he lived from 1846 to 1929), and he travelled widely, preaching and lecturing. He published a number of books, several of which dealt with the Palestinian background of the New Testament, in which he took a special interest: one of the best of these was the useful *Journeys of Jesus Christ, the Son of God*. Others of his writings included some quaint but commonsense popular works on physical and mental well-being, including *Christian Sanity*, and a long list of books on nervous disorders. He published a volume of reminiscences, *Behind the Brass Plate*, in which

* Not to be confused with the American editor of the Scofield Bible.

he showed himself to be an amusing raconteur. There is one story in the book worthy of wider currency. It describes how a high official (plainly from the details given it was Sir Robert Anderson) summoned Northcliffe to answer for certain irreverent remarks in *The Daily Mail*, and Northcliffe's unanswerable retort that he was glad that it was the official who had seen it, and not his own mother.

Two interesting men of later years, of contrasting character, but each of wide spiritual influence among the independent assemblies, were George H. Lang (who married a sister of Douglas Brealey of the Blackdown Hills) and Harold St. John. Both came from an exclusive background and moved to the independents in early life. Lang, born in 1874, was an eccentric, and his writings (particularly his autobiography *An Ordered Life*) betray a strong streak of egocentricity. He became during his lifetime a highly controversial figure within the movement. Surrendering all regular support, he was from 1899 to 1909 pastor of Unity Chapel in St. Philip's, Bristol, an independent congregation which was an offshoot of Bethesda. He then went to Egypt and India, and spent the remainder of his life, until his death in 1958, in an extensive travelling ministry which took him through the Middle East, North Africa and Eastern Europe, as well as in the British Isles. Lang was a self-taught man of great originality, and his long list of writings contains, among some eccentric matter, a great deal which shows a breadth of vision and a readiness to challenge accepted ideas that is unusual in Brethren writings. His work may well prove to be more formative after his death than that of many men who were more generally approved.

Harold St. John left a reputation for a deep personal devotedness and holiness of life. He was born in 1876, the son of the Treasurer of Sarawak, and lived an expatriate childhood in the Far East and in Europe. A man of a mystical and scholarly cast of mind, he spent years in quiet study before he left his banking career in 1913 to go to South America as a missionary. Later he travelled world-wide as a Bible teacher, leaving a deep influence on those whom he taught. In Britain, he was particularly influential as a teacher within the conference movement that arose out of the missionary study class movement, and he was supported in his service by a wife of as remarkable character as himself. St. John died in 1957, leaving very little written work behind him: his little volume *An Analysis of the Gospel of St. Mark* is distinctive of the man. His character was well expressed in his memorable closing address to the formative High Leigh conference of Brethren in 1955:

> There are those with whom our consciences will not allow us to walk in church fellowship. I recognize that. There are many whose consciences will not allow them to walk with us. I recognize that. But have we ever acknowledged the incalculable debt of gratitude which we owe to the great historic churches? I think of the Church of Rome, scarlet in her sins, supreme in her saints, and strong

in the way that she has stood like a rock in early and medieval history. A score of times she has saved the framework of the Christian society in days of assault by the heathen and by heretics. I recall what we owe to our beloved national Church in this land, for having kept the faith alive for centuries in the towns and villages of England. I thank God for our brethren in the Salvation Army who have reminded us to consider the poor: and for our friends, the Friends, who have poured out their lives, their wealth, and their sympathies in the service of wretched refugees in scores of darkened lands. Should a man not lay his hand upon his mouth before he criticizes his brethren? When we pass swift, uninformed, unloving, and ungenerous judgments, surely we have forgotten that if we speak evil of them, at the same time we speak evil of the Lord Whose Name they bear.[3]

A man who played an important part in the movement during a period when there was little intellectual leadership within it, was Arthur Rendle Short, Professor of Surgery at Bristol University from 1933 to 1946. Short was born on 6th January 1880, and was brought up in the Stokes Croft congregation of Brethren, an offshoot of Bethesda. His father, Edward Short, was an elder and leading spiritual influence both there and in the city in general, as well as being an active worker in the "Ragged School" and other social movements of the day in Bristol. Rendle Short's grandfather William Short had been the first resident schoolmaster at Müller's Orphan Homes. Rendle Short spent his whole professional life in Bristol, except for periods of study in London at University College Hospital, St. Bartholomew's, Guy's and the London School of Tropical Medicine. He made considerable contributions to medical knowledge, and was a brilliant and original teacher.

Until his death on 14th September 1953 Rendle Short remained a mainstay of the Christian communities in which he had grown up, and, despite his professional eminence, was available to serve the humblest of them. His influence on the congregations of the Bristol district was strong and positive. At a time when the intellectual morale of the movement was at its lowest, he provided it with a centre of stability and strength by his writings and his teaching. His constructive and influential contribution to wider Christian witness, and particularly to the student work of the Inter-Varsity Fellowship, needs no introduction here. Within the Brethren movement itself, it is likely that the conference movement which has arisen out of the missionary study class movement which he pioneered, will prove to be one of the most constructive elements of the later part of the twentieth century.

If some independent Brethren churches, particularly in parts of Scotland and Northern Ireland, are alleged to adopt a rather more jaundiced view of other Christian bodies than is altogether good, either for Christian charity or for their own souls, they might plead a certain justification in

228 A HISTORY OF THE BRETHREN MOVEMENT

the account which now follows. No reader of this book, and least of all
one who continues through the chapters which follow this, will carry
away the impression that the movement is not in need of constructive
self-criticism. There are, however, other types of criticism which are of
more dubious value.

As exclusivism began to enter on the beginnings of its long death-agony,
the scandal of much that had happened within Darbyism began to be
public property. At about this same time, some twenty years after the
revival had broken on the British churches at large, the movement was
becoming, in the eyes of the more parochially minded, a menace to the
orthodox. That which was happening within the exclusive congregations,
with excommunications and counter-excommunications and narrow-
minded persecutions of each other beginning to present a picture of some
less bloodthirsty French Revolution, was a gift to the more violent critics.
They seized their opportunity with both hands. Not a few men who had
suffered under the scandalous "discipline" and the deplorable controversial methods of Darbyism, publicized their experiences. The accounts were
often colourful and (in retrospect) amusing. It mattered little to some
critics whether those against whom they used this convenient ammunition
had themselves been victims of the same scandal. With that lack of discrimination common to religious controversy, they found it convenient to
bundle all their dislikes into one generic sack labelled "Plymouth Brethren," and to belabour that sack in sublime disregard as to the identity or
the realities of those upon whom the blows fell.

The later 1870s saw the beginnings of this attack, largely from those
parts of Northern Ireland and Scotland which were in point of fact the
home of the new "revival" Brethrenism, rather than of the earlier Darbyite
tendencies. It became the custom in the more respectable Calvinist works
of erudition of this period to take the odd sniper's long-shot at the
Brethren. Some of the works of truly great men, such as Patrick Fairbairn
and George Smeaton, contained references to Darbyite teachings which
were scarcely well-informed in their application to Brethren as a whole;
but these men at least took the trouble to be reasonably objective.

The same could not be said of all their compatriots. The main target
of all these attacks was the theological system of Darbyism: there is not
one of these books which contains anything of moment that is really
relevant to Brethrenism as it has been pictured in this book. In 1875
appeared Mearns's *Christian Truth and Plymouthism*, to be followed in the
next year by a work delightfully entitled *Brethren in the Keelhowes*. 1877
saw the publication of a book which became enormously popular. Dr.
James C. L. Carson was a Northern Ireland medical man, the son of a
distinguished divine, who adopted a number of hobby-horses, which he
rode with vigour. Among them were the advocacy of phrenology (or the
study of cranial bumps), the abolition of capital punishment, and (although

he was a supporter of the revival) the baiting of the Brethren. This last he indulged in *The Heresies of the Plymouth Brethren*, a book which Neatby (himself no uncritical advocate for Brethren) dismissed with the aside – "... Dr. James Carson's book, which is much worse than [Reid's] own, and which I forbear to characterise."[4] The book makes amusing reading for the idler of today, but in its day it was vicious. No man who had had any connexion with Brethren could be spared: even Newton's withdrawn tracts were taken out of the limbo into which their author had consigned them, to be made the basis of a violent attack upon that ill-used man. Carson was plainly a compulsive controversialist: not only do the back pages of his book quote at great length all the adulatory reviews of his various writings, as was the custom of the time, but he also quoted extracts from adverse reviews and answered them at great length.

In 1879 the Rev. Thomas Croskery of Londonderry published *Plymouth Brethrenism: a Refutation of its Principles and Doctrines*. The best known of these books was also published about the same time, running quickly into its third edition, which appeared in 1880. This was the other book referred to by Neatby in the extract just quoted, *Plymouth Brethrenism Unveiled and Refuted*, by a Scottish Presbyterian minister, the Rev. William Reid, D.D. On all these books, it is sufficient to quote Neatby's comment:

> The writers that have made this subject their special province are generally extremely untrustworthy. They are commonly passionately prejudiced against the Brethren. For the most part they make the writings of altogether unrepresentative men the basis of their attack, and even these men they have misrepresented.[5]

Such substance as there was in the attacks was usually relevant only to peculiarities of the Darbyite theological system: but even then the critics were inclined to mix their targets. Croskery saw Brethrenism as a mixture of Romanism and rationalism (a remark which was not *quite* as silly as it sounds). Reid listed among the "heresies" of Brethren one truly shocking one – "The Lord's Day not the sabbath": but, unfortunately, Dr. Carson chose to bind up with his criticism a dissertation of his own entitled "The Lord's Day is not the Creation Sabbath."

Most of these attacks are now dead letters, but evidence that some of the corpses are paraded from time to time as living is given by the republication in 1967 of *Discussions: Evangelical and Theological*, by one Robert L. Dabney, of Virginia, published in 1891 and now disinterred from the obscurity into which they had fallen. In these two volumes of *miscellanea* of some 700 pages each is republished an attack on "The Theology of the Plymouth Brethren" which fails completely to differentiate between Darbyite exclusivism and the main stream of the movement. The same criticism might be made of Clarence B. Bass's *Backgrounds to Dispensationalism* (1960).

We may well wonder why it is necessary to disinter these trivia of another day. The answer lies in the significant fact that it was at this time, and in the districts from which these productions emanated, that the *Needed Truth* reaction was bred, to break out fully ten years later. Men, many of them working men, who had been spiritually moved to the depths of their being by the revival, tried to associate freely to express their new spirituality – only to meet this type of denunciation, much of it relating to doctrines which bore no relation to the circumstances from which their own enlightenment had come. Is it to be wondered at that many of them became fiercely separatist, and resentful of the established churches of their own districts? The iron entered the soul of many of the independents at that time, with results that are still not fully seen.

Happily, the Church of England restored something of a balance. In 1883 Prebendary J. S. Teulon, of Chichester Theological College, published his *The History and Teachings of the Plymouth Brethren*. Once again, most of its criticisms were applicable to the distinctive theology of Darby and his followers, and for that reason it is of little relevance today, but this defect (if inexcusable today) was unavoidable in the perspective of his day. (A similar distortion makes even W. B. Neatby's *History of the Plymouth Brethren* of 1901 quite unreliable for the modern reader.)

Teulon, however, contributed an objective and fair-minded discussion of his subject, and he corrected many of the wilder atttacks of earlier critics by characterizing as valuable theological insights several of the statements of Brethren writers to which they had taken objection – a judgment obviously deriving from the fact that he was writing from a very different background from the earlier critics' hyper-Calvinism. It is fair to say of Teulon's work that in so far as his criticism is valid in relation to non-Darbyite Brethrenism, it is more a critique of the evangelical scheme in general than of Brethrenism in particular.

Nevertheless, the criticisms of the more violent writers achieved much of their purpose. That often-remarked psychological quirk, that men will behave largely as they think they are expected to behave, was seen in the reactions of some of the independents in their own districts, and, as we have seen, the criticisms were followed within a few years by the *Needed Truth* outbreak. As to their non-Brethren readers – they were provided with a full enough excuse for not bothering their heads further with this strange new sect.

A book which appeared in 1890 was symptomatic of a change which was taking place. It was a reprint of a series of articles which had appeared in the *British Weekly*, and was entitled *Life Among The Close Brethren*. It was a readable account by a Scottish doctor of a year's association with exclusives in London, an association which had been abruptly severed when he had "broken bread" with "Open Brethren." The book showed one thing plainly: that Darbyism was no longer the formidable theological enemy which the critics of fifteen years before had thought it: it had become a curiosity, perhaps even a laughing-stock, and its effects on personal character were by no means of the best. The nadir of this descent was reached much later by a work from within exclusivism itself. In 1936 Napoleon Noel, an elderly exclusive, published two volumes in America. Misnamed *The History of the Brethren*, they were little more than a wearisome and emetic account of all the petty quarrels of exclusivism. Their shame was not only published to the world, but thrust upon it: the exclusive publishers, in a fit of enthusiasm, were said to have circulated copies to libraries on an international scale!

One of the purposes of the present book is to correct the perspective engendered by those writings of the past. The publication of many of the scandals of the exclusive spirit had brought the name of Brethren into contempt by the end of the century, and that contempt inevitably involved the independents, whatever the services to the Church that so many of them had rendered. It became noticeable that biographies of men who had spent years with Brethren, if written by persons who were of other persuasions, would often carefully cover up the fact of those associations. Brethren themselves, by refusing to accept the name, on the ground that it was wrong to adopt any distinctive potential barrier between themselves and other Christians, found that this refusal thickened the fog in which the impressions of their fellows were wrapped. It was not the generous motives behind the refusal that came across to others – instead, it seemed that they were adopting a subterfuge, covering up that of which they were ashamed. The position soon became ludicrous.

Just how ludicrous, three modern incidents must suffice to illustrate. The august *Oxford Dictionary of the Christian Church*, in the article on "Plymouth Brethren" which appeared in its 1957 edition, solemnly informed its readers that among Brethren "emphasis is laid on an expected millennium when the Brethren will reign," and added for good measure: "they renounce secular life generally, allowing their members to practise only medicine and a few handicraft trades." It requires a long experience among Brethren to savour the real bouquet of two flights of fancy, one of which has been only partially corrected in the second edition.

In 1961 a little book was issued by the Anglican Mothers' Union. It was written by Dr. Lilian Powles, and was entitled *The Faith and Practice of Heretical Sects*: no doubt its purpose was to instruct the united mothers the better, in their warfare against the hosts of Barbary. The Pentecostals made the grade for a full chapter, but the "Plymouth Brethren" (as not-quite-heretics) appeared in an Appendix, in the honourable company of (among others) the Quakers and the Salvation Army.★ The author informs her readers that among the Brethren "at one time some of them leaned

★ There was doubtless poetic justice in this. Brethren publishers have in their time given several similar works to the world. I have not ascertained whether there is one which includes Anglicans!

towards the Adventists' belief in the 'sinful' nature of Christ's humanity."
For all the subtleties of the Newtonian controversy, it is fair to say that
there is no doctrine which would have more greatly outraged every man
among them, or which could more easily have united them against the
world. Inevitably, *Father and Son* is also brought in, dragged in by the
back cover as it were, to illustrate Brethren practices.

This latter habit is a somewhat endearing trait of many latter-day
critics. A young man from a Brethren assembly attending a well-known
Anglican teachers' training college a few years ago, was well-meaningly
informed by his theological tutor that to learn more about Brethren he
should read *Father and Son*. Academically, the advice was about as respectable as to recommend an inquirer concerning the Anglican Church to
certain essays in Lytton Strachey's *Eminent Victorians*. Perhaps all persons
giving such advice should be prescribed a compulsory reading of A. T.
Schofield's *Behind the Brass Plate*. They might be bored (unless they have
a taste for after-dinner anecdotes *en masse*): but their ecclesiastical ideas
might be suitably revised.

Quotation References – Chapter 14.

1. *The Life of Philip Henry Gosse*, F.R.S., Edmund Gosse (1890), p. 330.
2. *English Thought 1860–1890, the Theological Aspect*, L. E. Elliott-Binns (1956),
   p. 320.
3. *A New Testament Church in 1955* (report of the High Leigh Conference of Brethren,
   16–19 September 1955), p. 91.
4. *History of the Plymouth Brethren*, p. 229 n.
5. Ibid., p. 229.

CHAPTER 15

HYMNOLOGY OF THE BRETHREN

IT has been said that the vitality of a movement, be it religious, social or political, is shown by its songs. If there is no singing the movement is unlikely to endure.

Hugh J. Schonfield, *The Jew of Tarsus*

THE SOUL OF A RELIGIOUS MOVEMENT IS TO BE FOUND IN its direct response to God: and that response is to be found at its most personal and direct in its prayers and its hymns. The practice of Brethren has meant that none of the prayers of the movement have been recorded: but of hymns it has produced a great number.

Brethren hymnology is little known outside the movement itself, apart from a few pieces which have reached general collections. For this there are two main reasons. One is the limited range of much Brethren hymnology. The revival produced a multitude of hymns which did yeoman service in the context of their origin, but are now best forgotten. Of the earlier hymns, a great deal of the extant material is morbid and pedestrian: one misses in most of it the robustness and breadth of thought of the really great hymnwriters. A characteristic theme is a too self-conscious renunciation of the world and its ways, that in ordinary congregational use strikes the ear with a note of insincere unsuitability. The second reason is that many of the really original and choice pieces are written with the distinctive communion service in view, and strike a note of personal adoration and of identification with the sorrows of Christ which is at once entirely suitable for that service, and also extremely difficult to blend harmoniously with other congregational activities. This difficulty has been felt by Brethren themselves, as is shown by the persistence of the habit of using a more general interdenominational hymnbook for services other than the communion service, which we have attributed to the revival influence.

Unexpectedly, Darby himself was one of the choicest of Brethren hymn writers, although most of his output is probably more accurately classified as devotional poetry. His tortured style of English disappears in his poetry, and we feel ourselves closer to the real aspirations of this man of so much good and so much else that was wrong. They are aspirations which show all the strengths and weaknesses of his thinking: a deep personal and self-abandoning devotion to God, combined with an "other-worldliness" that largely emasculates the present life and leaves the spirit wringing its hands by Babylonian rivers. There is a deep wistfulness in the longing for rest constantly expressed in the poetry of this man of turbulent spirit: but it is a rest not to be attained in this life. At its best, his poetry could rise clear above the basic morbidity of the system he fathered on his disciples. In 1837, it is said on a first visit to Switzerland, he wrote one of his most celebrated poems – a poem which it is interesting to compare with Newman's famous poem of four years before, *Lead Kindly Light*. The comparison is by no means entirely to Darby's disadvantage:

> Rise, my soul! Thy God directs thee;
>   Stranger hands no more impede:
> Pass thou on! His hand protects thee,
>   Strength that has the captive freed.
>
> Is the wilderness before thee,
>   Desert lands, where drought abides?
> Heavenly springs shall there refresh thee,
>   Fresh from God's exhaustless tides.
>
> Light Divine surrounds thy going;
>   God Himself shall mark thy way;
> Secret blessings, richly flowing,
>   Lead to everlasting day.
>
> Though thy way be long and dreary,
>   Eagle strength He'll still renew:
> Garments fresh and foot unweary
>   Tell how God hath brought thee through!
>
> When to Canaan's long-loved dwelling
>   Love divine thy foot shall bring,
> There, with shouts of triumph swelling,
>   Zion's songs, in rest, to sing,
>
> There, no stranger God shall meet thee,
>   Stranger thou in courts above!
> He, who to His rest shall greet thee,
>   Greets thee with a well-known love.

There are echoes in his poems of a sense of personal weakness that was rarely allowed to escape in his dealings with other men. In 1845, that year of bitter strife, he wrote:

> Yet, Lord, alas! what weakness
>   Within myself I find;
> No infant's changing pleasure
>   Is like my wandering mind.
>
> And yet, Thy love's unchanging!
>   And doth recall my heart
> To joy in all its brightness,
>   The peace its beams impart!

So, in serious illness in Canada in 1867, he composed an exquisite poem, *The Man of Sorrows*, which ran to forty-six verses:

> O ever homeless Stranger!
>   Thus dearest Friend to me;
> An outcast in a manger,
>   That Thou might'st with us be!
>
> . . . .
>
> Bless'd Babe! who lowly liest
>   In manger-cradle there;
> Descended from the highest,
>   Our sorrows all to share.
>
> Oh, suited now in nature
>   For Love's Divinest ways,
> To make the fallen creature
>   The vessel of Thy praise!
>
> O Love! all thought surpassing!
>   That Thou should'st with us be:
> Nor yet in triumph passing,
>   But – human infancy!
>
> We cling to Thee in weakness,
>   The manger and the cross;
> We gaze upon Thy meekness,
>   Through suffering, pain, and loss;
>
> There see the Godhead glory
>   Shine through that human veil;
> And willing, hear the story
>   Of love that's come to heal!

Darby's eyes were turned, perhaps too consistently, away from this life to the heavenly places. Yet, from his vision of heaven there was absent the maudlin insipidity that disfigures so many common hymns on the subject:

> Rest of the saints above,
>   Jerusalem of God!
> Who, in thy palaces of love,
>   Thy golden streets have trod,
>
> To me thy joy to tell?
>   Those courts secure from ill,
> Where God Himself vouchsafes to dwell
>   And every bosom fill!
>
> The Lamb is there, my soul!
>   There God Himself doth rest
> In love Divine, diffused through all
>   With Him supremely blest.

>   There on the hidden bread,
>   Of Christ once humbled here –
>   God's treasured store, for ever fed,
>   His love my soul shall cheer.
>
>   God and the Lamb shall there
>   The light and temple be,
>   And radiant hosts for ever share
>   The unveiled mystery!

That hymn, again, dated from 1845. From 1867 came another on the same subject:

>   And can I call my home,
>   My Father's house on high,
>   The Rest of God, my rest to come,
>   My place of liberty?
>
>   My God the centre is:
>   His presence fills that land;
>   And countless myriads, own'd as His,
>   Round Him adoring stand.

In 1872, the best-known of all his hymns on this subject appeared:

>   And is it so! I shall be like Thy Son!
>   Is this the grace which He for me has won?
>   Father of glory! Thought beyond all thought,
>   In glory, to His Own blest likeness brought!
>
>   Nor I alone; Thy loved ones all, complete
>   In glory, around Thee with joy shall meet!
>   All like Thee: for Thy glory like Thee, Lord!
>   Object supreme of all, by all adored!
>
>   The heart is satisfied, can ask no more;
>   All thought of self is now for ever o'er:
>   Christ, its unmingled Object, fills the heart
>   In blest adoring love, its endless part.

His ear uncharacteristically failed him in the second of those verses quoted. We may leave this man of the soaring vision and the tortured pathway to the longing he expressed as early as 1832:

>   O Rest! Ineffable, divine,
>   The Rest of God above:
>   Where Thou for ever shalt be mine,
>   My joy, eternal love!

One hymn from the earliest days of the movement stands out for an unusual serenity and breadth of worship. It was by the wife of Sir Alexander Campbell, Lady Margaret Cockburn-Campbell, who died in 1841 at the age of 33:

Praise ye Jehovah! Praise the Lord Most Holy,
    Who cheers the contrite, girds with strength the weak;
Praise Him who will with glory crown the lowly,
    And with salvation beautify the meek.

Among the hymnwriters of the earliest movement, were S. P. Tregelles, J. G. Deck, and Sir Edward Denny. Tregelles's hymns tend, as we might expect, to strike a note of broader worship than most of those of the early movement. Deck was deeply moved by the human experiences of Christ, and by the devotional meaning of His resurrection, and expressed his feelings in some lines of great beauty:

O Lord! when we the path retrace
    Which Thou on earth hast trod,
To man Thy wondrous love and grace,
    Thy faithfulness to God

O Lord! with sorrow and with shame,
    We meekly would confess,
How little we, who bear Thy Name,
    Thy mind and ways express.

Give us Thy meek, Thy lowly mind,
    We fain would like Thee be;
And all our rest and pleasure find
    In learning, Lord, of Thee.

Lamb of God! our souls adore Thee
    While upon Thy face we gaze;
There the Father's love and glory
    Shine in all their brightest rays;
Thine almighty power and wisdom
    All creation's works proclaim;
Heaven and earth alike confess Thee
    As the ever great "I AM."

Lamb of God! when we behold Thee
    Lowly in the manger laid,
Wandering as a homeless stranger
    In the world Thy hands had made;
When we see Thee in the garden,
    In Thine agony of blood,
At Thy grace we are confounded,
    Holy, spotless Lamb of God!

Lamb of God! Thou now art seated
    High upon Thy Father's throne;
All Thy gracious work completed,
    All Thy mighty victory won:

Every knee in heaven is bending
    To the Lamb for sinners slain;
Every voice with praise is swelling
    "Worthy is the Lamb to reign."

The veil is rent – lo! Jesus stands
    Before the throne of grace,
And clouds of incense from His hands
    Fill all that glorious place.

Lord Jesus, are we one with Thee?
    O height, O depth of love!
Once slain for us upon the tree,
    We're one with Thee above.

Such was Thy grace that for our sake
    Thou didst from heaven come down;
With us of flesh and blood partake,★
    In all our sorrow one.

Our sins, our guilt, in love divine
    Confessed and borne by Thee,
The gall, the curse, the wrath were Thine,
    To set Thy members free.

Ascended now in glory bright,
    Lord, one with us Thou art!
Nor life, nor death, nor depth, nor height,
    Thy saints from Thee can part!

Thou wast the image, in man's lowly guise
Of the invisible to mortal eyes;
Come from His bosom, from the heavens above
We see Thee (God) incarnate, "God is Love."

We are but strangers here, we do not crave
A home on earth, which gave Thee but a grave;
Thy cross has severed ties which bound us here,
Thyself our treasure in a brighter sphere.

Hymns by Deck's sister, Mrs. Mary Jane Walker, are included in many collections, and include the well-known "Jesus, I will trust Thee." Her husband was Rector of Cheltenham. The hymns of the wife of another Anglican clergyman, Mrs. Mary Peters, are also much used by Brethren.

Sir Edward Denny was pre-occupied with the study of unfulfilled prophecy, and the published collection of his hymns included a considerable section headed "millennial hymns." His hymns are by no means all

★ This line was originally "Our mortal flesh and blood partake," but in the aftermath of the Plymouth controversy it was altered to its published form. The change is to be regretted.

coloured by this preoccupation, and among his hymns of adoration are some which express the full intensity of the communion of the Lord's Supper:

> To Calvary, Lord, in spirit now,
>   Our weary souls repair,
> To dwell upon Thy dying love,
>   And taste its sweetness there.
> Sweet resting-place of every heart
>   That feels the plague of sin,
> Yet knows that deep mysterious joy,
>   Of peace with God within.

> O wondrous hour! when, Jesus, Thou,
>   Co-equal with th' eternal God,
> Beneath our sin vouchsafed to bow,
>   And in our nature bore the rod.

> Thy cross! Thy cross! there, Lord, we learn
>   What Thou, in all Thy fulness, art:
> There, through the dark'ning cloud, discern
>   The love of Thy devoted heart.

> Sweet feast of love divine!
>   'Tis grace that makes us free
> To feed upon this bread and wine,
>   In memory, Lord, of Thee.

> Here every welcome guest
>   Waits, Lord, from Thee to learn
> The secrets of Thy Father's breast,
>   And all Thy grace discern.

> Here conscience ends its strife,
>   And faith delights to prove
> The sweetness of the bread of life,
>   The fulness of Thy love.

> 'Tis past the dark and dreary night;
>   And, Lord, we hail Thee now,
> Our morning star, without a cloud
>   Of sadness on Thy brow.

> Thy path on earth, the cross, the grave,
>   Thy sorrows all are o'er,
> And, oh, sweet thought! Thine eye shall weep,
>   Thy heart shall break no more.

> Deep were those sorrows – deeper still
>   The love that brought Thee low,
> That bade the streams of life from Thee
>   A lifeless victim, flow.

> Light of the lonely pilgrim's heart,
>   Star of the coming day!
> Arise, and, with Thy morning beams,
>   Chase all our griefs away.
>
> Come blessed Lord! bid every shore
>   And answering island sing
> The praises of Thy royal name,
>   And own Thee as their King.
>
> Bid the whole earth, responsive now
>   To the bright world above,
> Break forth in rapturous strains of joy
>   In memory of Thy love.

In two lines of his poem, *The Vessel*, he seems to sum up this experience of communion:

> I, a deep vessel in the shoreless sea
>   Of thine own fulness, O eternal God!

Robert Chapman, too, could touch devotional heights with that absolute simplicity which seems to tread a narrow edge above bathos. Chapman, too, was pre-occupied with the meaning of the cross of Christ: but especially with the working out of its consequences within the Christian character:

> Show me thy wounds, exalted Lord!
>   Thou hast the power and skill divine,
> Since Justice smote Thee with the sword,
>   To make my heart resemble thine.
>
> Shew my Thy wounds, and by Thy skill
>   May I, my Saviour, be refined,
> To do, like Thee, the Father's will,
>   And serve Him with a perfect mind.
>
> ———
>
> O Jesus, Lord, whose hands and feet
>   Declare Thy power to save,
> Dominion o'er myself complete –
>   Full mastery I crave.
>
> May I in body, spirit, soul,
>   Thy holy vessel be!
> Do Thou my every wish control –
>   Thy sorrows let me see.
>
> ———
>
> O My Saviour, crucified!
>   Near Thy cross would I abide,
> There to look with steadfast eye
>   On Thy dying agony!

Jesus, bruised and put to shame,
    Tells me all Jehovah's name;
"God is Love," I surely know
    By the Saviour's depths of woe

Dwelling on Mount Calvary,
    Contrite shall my spirit be;
Rest and holiness shall find,
    Fashioned like my Saviour's mind.

Thy perfect image, Thy delight,
    He ever had beheld Thy face;
Thy bosom was, of native right,
    His proper, secret dwelling-place.

Yet was the Lord made flesh, and nailed
    By men, His creatures, to the tree;
By all the powers of hell assailed,
    And bruis'd and pierc'd and slain by Thee!

In His own majesty arrayed,
    He spake and built the universe;
Yet to redeem us He was made
    A dying outcast and a curse!

By threefold title I am Thine,
    Thou blessed Son of God!
The Father's choice, Thy blood divine,
Thy Holy Spirit's power combine
    To make me Thine abode.

Companion of my pilgrimage,
    Jesus! exalted Lord;
Thou art the same from age to age,
My strength, my joy, my heritage,
    My glory and reward.

The later experiences of the revival loosed the pens of a considerable number of hymnwriters. Many of these hymns served the joyful exuberance of their day, and are now most kindly interred: a few of more lasting merit found their way into general collections. Russell Hurditch is found in some books, but few of his hymns have endured. One of the better ones which is familiar to Brethren congregations is:

He dies! He dies! the lowly Man of Sorrows
On whom were laid our many griefs and woes.

Denham Smith also is represented by hymns such as "Rise, my soul, behold 'tis Jesus!" and "Jesus, Thy dying love I own." One writer from the moderate exclusives of this period also deserves mention. Albert Midlane was a prolific hymnwriter, who attained a considerable vogue in the later Victorian era, and whose hymns reflect the aesthetic deterioration of his day. Many of them were for children, the best known being "There's a Friend for little children." A hymn of Midlane's which is in many collections is "Revive Thy work, O Lord!"

A writer from this period of a completely different kind was Frances Bevan.* Born in 1827, Emma Frances Shuttleworth came of a well-known clerical family, her father becoming Bishop of Chichester. She married Robert Cooper Lee Bevan, the banker, in 1856, as his second wife. Bevan was one of that inter-connected web of talented Quaker and evangelical Anglican families who already had links within the Brethren, and they moved in the circles which included men such as Lord Shaftesbury and Lord Radstock. Mrs. Bevan, who associated with Brethren in Barnet after her marriage, read deeply in the German mystics and pietists (as did Wesley, of whom she wrote a biography), and she published volumes which included translations and free adaptations of their verses, and original compositions of her own. The best known of her collections is the two-volume *Hymns of Ter Steegen, Suso and Others*, first published in 1894 and 1897. Her original poems are often not distinguishable from the others, and as she signed many of her own compositions with the initials of the house in which she was staying at the time of composition, there has been much confusion over the authorship of the pieces which she introduced to the public – not least between those which she wrote at their London house in Princes Gate and the writings of the German Paul Gerhardt (of whose hymns, in point of fact, she translated only two). It is not possible to do justice to Mrs. Bevan's work by brief quotation. She found in the German piety a rich subjective vein ideally suited to the temper of the circles in which she moved (Tersteegen, of the eighteenth century, in particular had very much in common with the outlook of the independent Brethren), and her works were influential. One of her own verses from *The Gospel According to Paul* became an often-quoted theme verse for the expanding missionary outreach of the time:

> Christ, the Son of God, hath sent me
> Through the midnight lands;
> Mine the mighty ordination
> Of the piercèd Hands.

It is interesting that another lady translator of hymns from the German, Miss H. K. Burlingham, was also with Brethren.

Of later hymnwriters from among Brethren, Samuel Trevor Francis is perhaps the best known, from one or two hymns found in most collections. "Oh, the deep deep love of Jesus" is a favourite. Another of his

---

* See J. S. Andrews, "Frances Bevan, Translator of German Hymns" (*Evangelical Quarterly*, Oct/Dec 1962 and Jan/Mar 1963) and "The Recent History of the Bevan Family" (ibid., April/June 1961).

hymns is notable for striking a robust note unfamiliar in Brethren hymnology:

> Arise! ye warriors of the cross,
>   The Master's word obeying,
> Gird on the sword, count all things loss,
>   Go forth without delaying;
> Still forward, 'tis our Lord's command,
>   He will forsake us never;
> His mighty hand none can withstand,
>   And He is with us ever.

He also wrote another hymn familiar to Brethren – "Jesus! we remember Thee." Alexander Stewart (not to be confused with the founder member of the Stafford congregation) is also found in general collections, with his hymn "Lord Jesus Christ, we seek Thy face." Another hymnwriter of this period was Douglas Russell, author of a communion hymn much used by Brethren: "Gathered, Lord, around Thy table." Christiana Helene von Poseck, a German "Darbyist," is also to be found in Brethren collections; while Ada R. Habershon, another recent hymnwriter, was also with Brethren.

More recently, J. M. S. Tait, a Shetland solicitor, has published devotional verses which often strike a note of true poetry. His work has not included many hymns, although one which has not yet found its way into any collection is an admirable expression of the spiritual meaning of believer's baptism:

> Into death's dark waters faring,
>   Christ passed for me;
> Shame, reproach and sorrow bearing,
>   All, all for me.
> Now I spurn the sins that slew Him,
> Turn from scenes that never knew Him;
> Take my cross and hasten to Him –
>   He died for me!

The American poetess, Luci Shaw, a descendant of J. G. Deck, has recently produced some outstanding poetry in the modern idiom, while in the Orkneys, Robert Rendall, who died in 1967, also produced some volumes of poems (many of them of local inspiration) which have gained considerable appreciation. Two of his dialect poems appear in *The Oxford Book of Scottish Verse*, and he has a short poem in *The Oxford Book of Twentieth Century English Verse*.

Another Scottish writer who has produced true poetry is I. Y. Ewan, a somewhat eccentric Bible teacher, and it is a matter of regret that his work is not available to a wider public. It is also of interest that Stuart

K. Hine, the Brethren missionary to eastern Europe, translated and introduced to the western world the Slav hymn* which has attained world-wide popularity, largely through its adoption in the Billy Graham crusades: "How Great Thou Art."

Brethren writers have produced few hymns of the very first rank, but among their output there are hymns which would enrich any collection, and which are well above the abysmal standards of some popular hymnology. It is the Church's loss that many of them are not better known.

* Originally composed in Sweden by Carl Boberg, although it was the Slav version from which Hine adapted his English rendering. See Hine's own account of the hymn, *The Story of "How Great Thou Art"* (Nov. 1958) and hymnbook *Crusader Hymns and Hymn Stories.*

Quotations of hymns in Chapter 15 are taken from:

Spiritual Songs, the definitive collection of J. N. Darby's poetry.
The 1889 definitive edition of Sir Edward Denny's *Hymns and Poems.*
Hymns of Light and Love.
The *Mitchley Supplement* to *Hymns of Faith.*
The Present Testimony (Scotland. c. 1940) Vol. 8.

CHAPTER 16

SOME GUIDING THOUGHTS

FOR freedom Christ has set us free; stand fast therefore, and do not submit
again to a yoke of slavery.

St. Paul, *Letter to the Galatians* (R.S.V.)

THE BRETHREN MOVEMENT OWES ITS EXISTENCE TO NO
one distinctive tenet or dominating personality. If Darby was the
lodestone of many of the early adherents, and if Darby alone among
its leaders developed a distinctive system of Biblical interpretation, yet
events have shown that Darbyism was unable to harness whatever driving
force lay behind the movement. Darbyism dug its channels, but when the
revival floods rose, the water flowed strongly into other courses. If for
their part Müller and the Scriptural Knowledge Institution were in the
background of much of the movement's expansion, yet they were there
as useful and timely instruments of forces they neither originated nor
controlled.

The movement has lacked its co-ordinating genius. Men have arisen
with the strength of purpose to provide it with a cohesive force, but they
have been men of separatist ideals, and of narrow vision, and the basic
common good sense of the movement has ended by rejecting them. A
healthy body rejects that which is foreign to its own tissues: by some
such reaction Brethrenism, for all its inbuilt tendency to separatism,
ends by rejecting it. It is probably for this reason that the movement
proves to be intractable material for those who, sharing its conservative
theology, its Bible-based thinking, its ardent evangelicalism, think therefore
to find it malleable to their own conceptions of evangelical unity.
Somewhere within its nature there is an element of wider sympathy,
that cannot be restrained by the limits even of its own doctrinal
principles.

Yet, behind the spontaneity of the early movement there was a common
factor. That factor was later to forge into one fellowship many of the
ardent and individualist spirits of the revival. It was a factor which
appealed to the surprisingly young men who formed the movement's
leadership in 1830, and it also took up the youthful energies and high
spirits of the later revival years. That factor caused young men gladly to
abandon comfort and prospects for a vision, and to give themselves with
ardour to sacrifice and to self-denying ways of life. Young men are not
normally won by weight of unimaginative tradition, by oppressive and

sterile dogmas, by all the débris of enthusiasms grown stale, which are the features making up the popular image of much of later Brethrenism.

If we search for that factor, we end with a surprising conclusion. Those who live out in their own persons that popular image of which we have spoken are only too tragically common: yet the basic factor of the movement is precisely opposed to them. Essentially, that factor is an urge to freedom: freedom to express man's personal response to God fully and without restraint. Those early men looked for a community of men and women wholly committed to Christ, but within that community they were impatient of anything which would restrict the liberty of Christ to do what He wished with His own.

The working out of this urge in Groves's early development was characteristic of many others. To satisfy his thirst for God, he turned to the Bible, which he began to read with passion. What he read there reacted on him, to produce an intense devotedness to Christ that expressed itself in the surrender to the service of Christ of property and career, and then in a drawing together with others of like mind. From this developed a quest for the full fellowship of all like-minded men, and the abandonment of all those restrictions of denominational discipline which seemed to frustrate that quest. So there followed his desire for the full unity of the people of God, the free celebration of the Lord's Supper with all believing men and women, the replacement of ordination by the free exercise of the gifts God had given, the free response to whatever service was committed to them.

The place of the Bible in this development is important. The search for freedom of service and worship was not undisciplined, but was controlled by an over-riding awe of God. When the rules of the historic Churches were abandoned, they turned naturally to the Bible for guidance and inspiration. It was in the message of the Bible, as contained in its teaching and exemplified in the life of the apostolic Church, that they found liberation and broader horizons. Thus they struck the authentic note of all Protestant and evangelical revival; just as their contemporaries the Tractarians, in finding their inspiration in the ancient spirituality of the historic Church, touched the authentic note of Catholic revival. In fact, we can go further back: for the note struck by those early leaders of Brethren who were not bemused by a separatist spirit, was the authentic note which Paul had struck in his revolt from a narrow Judaism. The ideals both of evangelicalism and of Catholicism are capable, when the first freshness of vision is lost, of degeneration into a harsh and negative narrowness of mind. Because we today look back on the Brethren through so much of that narrowness, we must not forget the joyful freedom of their original inspiration.

Brethrenism came into existence, because existing church life seemed to its founders to be formal and lifeless. The churches they knew seemed too often to be governed by aspirations and motives which were merely worldly and carnal, while demanding little real spiritual experience of their adherents.* Yet, if in one sense those churches were too lax, in another they were too restrictive, for they provided no ready channels for the full expression of that spiritual experience where it appeared, but rather hampered and thwarted it by suspicion and by sheer formality both of worship and of office To the harsher spirits among them it seemed that those churches had lost the marks of true grace: they were apostate and to be rejected. To the milder spirits, and to those who retained a deeper sense of the realities of life in the churches they had left, the churches were backsliding victims of the long processes of history, to be loved and prayed for. These milder men rejected the structure of the churches, but not their fellowship, and they would work with them where possible, hoping for a birth within them of a larger liberty.

If the movement had not come into existence thirty years before the mid-century revival broke on the churches in 1859, something similar must have arisen from the revival enthusiasm: but, in 1859, the movement, loosed from the trammels of Darbyism, was young enough to welcome and absorb the energies of the independent spirits of the revival who broke loose from the older churches. Whether it would be flexible enough to react similarly today is another matter.

In other respects, the movement was of its own time. It could not have arisen in the form it did before the Bible had been for a long time readily and freely available, and Biblical ideals widely disseminated. We forget today that the greater part of the Church's history has been lived in days when the Bible could not be the property of the common man, simply because it was not generally to be obtained, in the absence of printing and general literacy. On the other hand, the movement arose while the

---

* "When the century dawned, it dawned upon a sleeping Church. There was little or no enthusiasm anywhere, and co-operation for great and good ends was only just beginning. Between the Church of England and the dissenters a great gulf was too often fixed: the former was commonly associated with all that was high and dry, cold and orthodox; the latter with vulgarity and ignorance. . . . The spiritual life of England was only just beginning to awaken from nearly a century of sleep. Teaching and preaching the gospel by laymen was undreamed of, except among the followers of Wesley" (Edwin Hodder, *The Life of Samuel Morley* (1887), pp. 51–53). Hodder goes on to refer to features which are of some significance in considering the background of the thirty years which preceded the beginnings of the Brethren movement:

Political antagonism embittered strife between dissenters and the establishment, until political freedom triumphed in 1832.

The evangelicals in the Church of England were increasing in numbers, and through their societies were beginning to join with dissenters in common good works.

There were signs of awakening life: 500 churches were built between 1801 and 1831, mostly in the later part of the period. Sunday schools were being widely organized. Preaching and music were both reviving. Much of this came to a head, not in evangelicals, but in the Tractarian movement, after the publication of Keble's *Christian Year* in 1827.

authority of the Bible was still largely unquestioned, and when it provided a common standard of appeal for all earnest Christian men. The effect on the basic ideals of the movement of the critical studies of the century and more which has passed since then, must be considered in our next chapter.

The character of most of the men of the early movement was in general cultured, even dilettante. Where it was harsh and ascetic, these were the eccentricities of men of cultivated sensibility. The revival movement overlaid this character with another element, particularly in those areas which had not been touched by the earlier movement. In considerable districts the revival movement brought a strong injection of rougher enthusiasm, without the deep spiritual instincts of the earlier pioneers, and often these new men were suffering from complexes engendered by rejection by other churches. This enthusiasm was less informed, less cultured, and with less understanding of others. The difference was exemplified in the contrast between the intellectualized exclusivism of Darbyism, and the coarser prejudice of the *Needed Truth* reaction. Early Darbyism, for all that it so fiercely rejected other churches, yet tried to keep its sympathies open to all Christians, and in theory at least welcomed to its own congregations all those who were sound in doctrine and conduct. The *Needed Truth* reaction (like Taylorite exclusivism) rejected even this wider sympathy, and looked uncompromisingly for a church "pure" by its own narrow standards.

Brethren chose to build their church life at the precise spot where the tension between the ideals of unity and of purity was felt the most severely. The *Needed Truth* reaction rejected unity altogether in the search for purity – a solution of the dilemma common to a hundred other seceding movements before and since: simple and attractive to all who can be persuaded to confine their sympathies within a narrow and rigid code of life and belief, but impossible to all others. Darbyite exclusivism was more sophisticated, and in practice proved too sophisticated to hold its position. As the years have gone by, it has slipped, against all resistance, either into full exclusivism, or into a position indistinguishable from the independents. The independents alone have developed (often, it seems, without any clear understanding of what they were doing) a stable middle course, and they have done so only because their strict independency has allowed the idealistic freedoms of the early movement to remain alive, despite oppressive beliefs and conduct in individual local churches.

Essential to this independent position is an instinct that truth is wider than the mind of man, and that therefore full unity cannot find expression within the restraints of any code, whether of church order or belief. Basic also is a realization that Christianity rests finally on the individual's personal response to God: that it cannot truly rest on an outward form of church order, or on mechanical sacramental transactions, for a sacrament is so much make-believe unless it answers to an inward spiritual reality. It is in the light of this basic premise of the personal response that they understand the Scriptural teaching that all who have been baptized into Christ have put on Christ, and are one in Him. Baptism is understood not in a mechanical or half-magical way, but as answering to the spiritual reality it symbolizes: the answer of a good conscience towards God.

Nevertheless, where rigidity of practice and doctrine becomes supreme, it is too easy for mere conformity to be confused with inward spiritual reality. Darbyite exclusivism facilitated this error by retaining the practice of infant baptism, which blunts the insistence upon a personal response to God, and makes it easy for those who have made no such response to be welcomed to the fellowship: a fact which may go far to explain many of the sheer unchristian developments of their discipline under the latter régime of James Taylor, junior. *Needed Truth* exclusivism, on the other hand, can reach the same result by making the practice of believer's baptism a *sine qua non* of fellowship, and by judging a man by his conformity to a rigid code. The independent position can fall into this error also, if it confuses the "new birth" of John's writings in the New Testament – that personal committal of faith of which the Pauline teaching has so much to say – with a stereotyped emotional experience. But we are trespassing into a large subject, which must be discussed more fully in later chapters.

Weaknesses occur, as always, when men fail to think through the full implications of their beliefs, or to understand what it is that they are really doing. Our next chapters will attempt to break the ground, so that conditions may be created in which such a self-assessment will be possible. They will be based upon four main and abiding insights, selected out of the welter of conflicting ideas which have characterized the Brethren movement, as those which are the most germinative and universal of their principles. We call them "the four freedoms of the Brethren":

The freedom of the Word of God in my thinking.
The freedom of the Lord Christ in my living.
The freedom of the Holy Spirit in my worship and service.
The freedom of the whole Body of Christ in my fellowship.

CHAPTER 17

THE SCRIPTURES AND THE CHURCH

THE glory of the Reformation was the rescue of the Holy Scriptures from comparative neglect. And the weakness of Protestantism has been the dream that a sect or an individual, with the Bible in hand, can from hints of expression or comparison of passages discover concealed or forgotten truths, and even construct a religious system, and set to rights the Church of all ages, notwithstanding her myriads of able, learned and pious men, her well-attested traditions, and her original contact with the Lord Himself.
Edward Miller, *The History and Doctrines of Irvingism*

"LET THE BOOK SPEAK TO THEE, JOHNNIE, THEN THOU wilt have no difficulty in speaking to the people." Such was a Quaker friend's advice to John Jewell Penstone, an early associate of John Eliot Howard in Tottenham.[1] The place of the Bible in the early Brethren movement was, as we remarked in the previous chapter, essentially the same as in the great traditions of Protestant renewal. Luther had pronounced his conscience captive to the Word of God; Calvin had built his churches and his theology on a basis of profound Biblical exposition; the Independent John Robinson had looked for "more truth yet to break forth out of His holy Word;" and John Wesley had exclaimed "Oh, give me that book! At any price, give me the book of God! I have it; here is knowledge enough for me. Let me be *homo unius libri*."[2]

The Bible, as we saw in the first chapter, was at the heart of Groves's movement of soul. Darby, too, spoke of how, in the days after his riding accident near Dublin, the Scriptures had gained "complete ascendancy" over him.[3] To the Bible, Müller and Craik also had gone at each crisis in their church and personal lives.

In going back to the Bible for their inspiration and guidance, then, the Brethren were treading in the same path as a long line of illustrious reformers. Soltau's boast quoted on page 92 was over-stated, though it became part of the legend of Brethrenism, simply because something very similar to what he claimed for the Brethren movement could be claimed with equal justice of many of its predecessors:

The organization of the Methodist Church is supposed to be a triumph of ecclesiastical statesmanship. The constructive genius of Wesley has been lauded, and he has been compared with famous constitution-builders and legislators. He would have been surprised with the eulogium. In his opinion he was not a creative statesman, but an unconscious imitator of the work of other men. His arrangements had all been anticipated. The pattern to which his Societies were unconsciously conformed was contained in the New Testament. Without any previous design, he met "occasions as they arose," and, in the end, he created a Church founded on the lines laid down in Apostolic times.[4]

The fact that each of these earlier strivings of the Spirit had developed a different form of church order is therefore a fact to be faced carefully when considering the place of Scripture in relation to church order. Virtually every form of church order has in its day claimed a complete scripturality for its own forms:

> No bishop could be more decided in maintaining the Divine origin of Episcopacy; no Presbyterian, of Commonwealth times, could be more sure of the Divine origin of ruling synods, than were these Nonconformist fathers in reference to the Divine origin of their Independency.[5]

H. Schlier has claimed that he found his way to the Roman Catholic Church *via* the New Testament, and Roman Catholic scholars have claimed that unbiased exegesis must lead to the Roman Catholic Church.[6]

There are therefore several obvious but important factors of which we must not lose sight if we are to attempt to understand the part which Scripture plays in the life and shaping of the Church. The first group of these factors relates to our own subjective approach to Scripture. It is impossible, however earnestly we may attempt it, to bring to Scripture a mind that is completely free from previous impressions. I may attempt to rid myself of all conscious prejudice, but I cannot rid myself of the influences which have made me what I am. My past experiences, my upbringing, even my heredity and my individual temperament, all leave an inevitable deposit in my mind, which colours every later addition, whether derived from Scripture or from any other source. The very words which I read, I understand in relation to that background, and therefore in a way which differs from the understanding of other men. It follows, therefore, that every conclusion which I draw from the Scripture (or from any other source) will contain a large element of myself, as well as a new element drawn from the source itself.

The second factor is closely akin to the first. When I approach Scripture, I necessarily approach it with a background, unconscious or otherwise, of traditional interpretation. I shall have absorbed a way of looking at that which I read, which will colour the conclusions which I draw from my reading. This fact often becomes apparent in a quite startling way if I hear someone from a very different tradition from my own interpret a passage of Scripture, the meaning of which I had previously taken for granted. This second factor shows that tradition has an inevitable place in relation to the authority of Scripture. Henry Soltau may genuinely have thought that he approached Scripture "freed from all tradition," and he and his fellows had indeed deliberately expunged from their minds many of the glosses which their traditional background had placed upon Scripture. The fact remained, that they all approached Scripture from within the general tradition of orthodox Protestant thought, and individually each approached Scripture from within his own more specialized traditions. It is probable, indeed, that it was a deep difference of this kind in their background traditions of Biblical interpretation that made Darby and Newton so incapable of understanding each other. Moreover, where they deliberately differed from earlier interpreters, it was often to impose upon Scripture their own system of interpretation, which rapidly hardened into as rigid a tradition as any other.

The third of this group of factors reminds us that Scripture comes to us not as an abstract set of propositions, or as a formal code of laws, but as a collection of writings which grew out of living history. Not only does this give the personal elements of which we have spoken a much greater latitude in relation to interpretation of Scripture, but it also means that Scripture itself includes matter which is directly related to the living and contemporary situation of the writers. Now the application of one and the same general principle in different sets of circumstances can lead to practical actions which appear to be inconsistent, and even directly opposed to each other. We cannot therefore simply take a custom out of Scripture, from the story of the apostolic Church, and say "we must do the same." Instead, we must first understand why that custom existed, and what principles lay behind the actions recorded.

It is this which makes the common reference to the "pattern" of the New Testament church a dangerous one. It is a slogan common to many different schools of thought (we have already seen it in the context of Methodism, and examples could have been taken from many other different denominational contexts): but we must ask what is meant by that "pattern." Is it the "pattern" of their life in the Holy Spirit, or do we look for some sort of blueprint?

This question leads us directly to the fourth factor: namely, that Scripture itself contains no specific indication as to whether the church order which is seen developing in the New Testament is in fact a "pattern" at all. This does not prove that it is not: it means that the place of Scriptural precedent in the ordering of the churches is not to be determined from the direct teaching of Scripture itself, but rather that it is to be determined by our understanding of the nature of Scriptural, and more particularly of apostolic, authority.

Now it is possible to over-emphasize the importance of each of these factors. Not one of them alters the enormous formative power of Scripture itself upon those who read it with open and impressionable minds. Nevertheless, the factors remain valid, often operating at a subconscious level, so that it is extraordinarily difficult to weigh their full effect. In ordering the churches, and particularly in relations with other

Christians, it is essential to have regard to their presence, both in our own thinking and in that of others, if we are to do common justice to our brethren in Christ.

Let us, therefore, repeat these four factors:

First, we must recognize that each mind, by its very nature, operates within a range of ideas and modes of thinking which are the product of past experience and of individual personality, and that this must to some extent colour every conclusion which is drawn by that mind.

Second, allowance must be made for the effect of the framework of Biblical interpretation which lies (often unconsciously) behind any man's approach to Scripture. Tradition is an inseparable element within Biblical interpretation.

Third, Scripture, in matters of church order, arose from the living and immediate circumstances of the early churches. This has two results. It allows a wider room for the operation of those personal idiosyncrasies of understanding which the first two factors have emphasized; and it also means that Scripture contains much that is the result of the application of general principles to particular contemporary and local circumstances. If I, in my highly different circumstances, simply copy the results of that application, I may well find that I contradict the basic principles of Scripture. This is of particular importance in relation to such subjects as the "pentecostal" practice of speaking in tongues, and the place of women's service within the church.

Fourth, the question as to whether and to what extent the ordering of New Testament churches forms a precedent for later churches, is not one to which Scripture itself gives a direct answer, but one which must be answered according to our general understanding of the scope of Scriptural and apostolic authority.

Before we apply these factors to the teachings of the early Brethren, it is well to digress to consider a further subjective feature to which weight must be given. To arrive at a correct conclusion on any subject, I must first ask the right questions (and must ask those questions in the right order). This has a corollary. Writings like the Scriptures which have arisen from living experience are related to questions which have arisen in the minds and from the circumstances of their writers, and to understand correctly what those writers say, I must therefore know what those questions were. For example, it is probable that a great deal of controversy has arisen in relation to the prophetic parts of the Bible, simply because interpreters have deduced wrongly the questions which those Scriptures were intended to answer, and therefore they have spelled out the wrong answers from Scripture. In relation to this, it is important also to notice that the forms in which ideas are expressed, or the terms in which an analysis or a controversy become crystallized, themselves have a formative influence in shaping later thinking: and often become a strait-jacket for that thinking. The legacy of the past may thus become a very real hindrance, rather than a guide. Those who have read of the contortions to which reforming elements in the Roman Catholic Church have often been reduced, in attempting to deal with the system arising from the Council of Trent, will have a ready illustration of the working of this feature.

Nevertheless, we must recognize that Scripture in part transcends this further factor in our thinking. It is an axiom of most Christian belief that there is in Scripture an element which is of deeper and wider application than to the immediate circumstances of its composition. It is by this element that the Word of God has so often spoken freshly to men and women. The principle of our last paragraph is of importance none the less, for it warns us that when we pose these wider questions to the Scriptures, we are on ground where the possibility of error is correspondingly greater. Moreover, it warns us that the immediate application of Scripture in its original context cannot be ignored: it is probable that until we have understood the immediate application, we cannot rightly understand the wider meaning. The immediate application is thus of immense regulative importance to our own deductions from Scripture.

We now turn to consider the relation of the four factors to the thinking of the early Brethren. The effect of individual backgrounds and temperaments upon their teachings has appeared plainly enough in our story. Groves's idealistic self-abandonment, Darby's self-assertive rejection of his own church, Müller's precise and businesslike mysticism, Newton's severity, and Borlase's failing health, are writ large in the deductions which they each drew from Scripture.

Further, while they rejected all conscious tradition in the matter of church order, it is equally plain (as we have already remarked) that in other matters they approached Scripture from within a very strict framework of traditional Protestant orthodoxy. The early disputes over Newton's teachings, and the outcome of the debates which arose from time to time within their churches concerning human destiny and conditionalist doctrines, make this abundantly plain. In fact, in everything except in matters of church order and eschatology, it is evident that they were inclined to take a considerably more serious view of departure from accepted Protestant doctrine than most other traditions; while in eschatology the distinctive teachings of Darbyism, as watered down by later evangelicalism, were very often given an equally prominent position with other orthodox doctrines.

It is when we consider the bearing of the last two of our four factors upon their teachings that really important features emerge. It is plain that all the early leaders regarded the Scriptures as the final court of appeal in doctrinal matters, and in practical matters of Christian living. Yet the very fact that Darby was able to teach that it was wrong to attempt to form churches on the model of the New Testament,[7] and that he could have his teaching widely accepted, shows that they gave very full regard to the local and temporary nature of parts of Scriptural practice. The fact that Darby's teachings themselves were idiosyncratic and impermanent is beside the point which we are making here: the general acceptance which his teaching had among many of the early men is a plain indication that they were not "patternists" in the sense that the early Nonconformists and the later *Needed Truth* leaders were.

Müller and Craik, like the Plymouth leaders, obviously regarded the organization and constitution of the New Testament churches as being important and authoritative guides to their own church practices. Were they therefore "patternists" in the sense in which we have just used the word? The answer to that question requires a more detailed analysis of their writings.

Their appeal to Scripture arose in the first place from their full acceptance of the basic Protestant understanding of the authority of Scripture: of that there is no doubt. They were forced the more strongly into this appeal because of their deliberate rejection of all that was consciously traditional in their church order. As William Collingwood wrote at the end of the century:

> The chief aim was to exhibit, in a Scriptural way, the common brotherhood of all believers. They recognized no special membership. That they belonged to Christ was the only term of communion; that they loved one another was the power of their fellowship. In principle, it embraced all whose faith and walk showed that they had spiritual life; in practice, all such of these as would avail themselves of it.
>
> This ideal could be attained only by a return to the absolute simplicity of the Apostolic model as found in the New Testament. To bring in anything of a contentious character would defeat it. There must be nothing that human tradition had introduced to divide God's people. None must be stumbled or grieved by the presence of what was not clearly and strictly Scriptural.[8]

Groves had written to his friend Caldecott as early as 1825, as the latter approached his ordination:

> . . . things in the Divine word, which are hard to understand, and for this reason, that we come to the consideration of them with hearts pre-occupied by a ready-made decision, more in union with the worldly systems, by which we are pressed on every side. And, against all this overwhelming influence, there is but one remedy, to read the word of God with a single view to know His will, by whom it was inspired.[9]

We are driven to further questions at this point. Did they go to Scripture in itself, or did they go to it because they regarded the apostolic authority behind the New Testament practices as the over-riding authority, Scripture being the record of that authority? We can make the question more pointed by asking another: if it could be proved that certain practices were apostolic, but were not referred to in Scripture, would they have regarded those practices as binding? The probable answer to that question would be "no:" and yet it is plain that the apostolicity which lay behind the Scriptural record was for them an essential ingredient of its authority – so that the corresponding question, whether, if it could be proved that something laid down in Scripture was contrary to apostolic authority, they would regard that point as being binding, would probably have been met by the assertion that that point would therefore be proved to be uncanonical.

> Has it then been restored, according to the Model which the Word has left upon record as the framework of that Primitive Institution, of which God Himself was the builder through the Holy Ghost? Or was the return to Apostolic doctrine, a complete redemption from the fictions, with which the power of darkness had enveloped the pure ordinances of Christ? The fundamental Protestant Rule should lead us, in common consistency, to refer to the Scriptures, not only for that which ministers to the edification of individuals, but for the form of ecclesiastical policy which God Himself has revealed in His Word, which *in its general principles*, unless unanimity be *not* a duty in the Church of Christ, must be there fully and distinctly exhibited. . . . In the Word of God, however, may be found a complete exemplar of the Divine Will, in the inspired constitution of the Apostolical Churches; and here in perfect order and symmetry exist the rules of government, edification and discipline, devised by Infinite Wisdom, for those who were to be gathered in His Name, and "builded together for an habitation of God through the Spirit."[10]

> This is a simple matter of history, for none but the Apostles were ever authorized to make enactments for the Church of Christ; and all that was ever entrusted to the Church itself, was to carry into effect those already made – the actual ministry of present order, according to the principles, and by the enactments laid down by them. Every step beyond this is necessarily evil . . .[11]

These two quotations are taken from the extremist Henry Borlase of Plymouth, and require qualification from his own writings, which will be referred to later. The more judicious Henry Craik, however, also showed that he attached considerable importance to the underlying apostolicity of that which Scripture recorded:

> This Book of the Acts constitutes not merely the most important Church History in existence, but forms, at the same time, a most interesting and instructive link between the Gospels and Epistles. It records the fulfilment of those promises which the Saviour had bequeathed to His disciples respecting the *presence* and *working* of the blessed Comforter. It answers numerous inquiries relative to the *preaching* of the Apostles – the *success* of their ministry – the *constitution* of the early churches, and the marvellous change which the diffusion of Christianity effected, both on individuals and communities. It exhibits principles and examples admirably adapted to animate and instruct the people of God in all succeeding generations; and it furnishes materials for arousing the energies of those churches which may have greatly departed from the freshness of their first love.[12]

In point of fact, any distinction between Scriptural and apostolic authority probably never arose for them: but we may deduce from their attitude to these matters that their concept of Scriptural authority was a combination of apostolic and Scriptural authority together, neither being sufficient without the other. The distinction becomes of considerable importance both in relation to the effect of later critical studies of the New Testament upon their principles, and in relation to questions of Christian unity.

The extent to which these men who looked for guidance to the apostolic practices were "patternists" in the sense in which we have used the term can now be answered. They were basically too sound in their scholarship to overlook Scripture's local and contemporary setting. Despite the apparent extreme "patternism" of the two extracts quoted from Borlase, it is important to notice that he carefully guarded against this very misunderstanding, both by his italics, and by adding a specific footnote to the second quotation:

> I believe in the actual sufficiency of scripture, not in the letter but by the Spirit. The Spirit might order by living men; *He did so*, God chose thus to order by it; by the word the Spirit now orders through living men . . . nothing but spirituality can do it, because the attempt by the letter will break down somewhere, perhaps in some great principle not coming from the same Spirit. Hence the force of the enactments, though not in literal detail unless necessary.[13]

Henry Craik, that careful and eirenical man, went even further than Borlase:

> The New Testament contains many express precepts and directions, but it is at the same time emphatically a book of principles. Neither in the records of our Lord's personal ministry, nor in the writings of His apostles, do we find every matter of minute detail expressly provided for. This must be ever kept in mind as one of the characteristic features of the new dispensation.[14]

Craik, in fact, conceded far more than most of his colleagues would have done:

> . . . it most assuredly becomes us to gather up the scattered intimations which are given us, in the writings of Evangelists and Apostles, in relation to the order and discipline of the House of God. I may be regarded as advocating very latitudinarian opinions, but I am disposed readily to admit that there are passages in the inspired writings that seem, to some extent, to favour a species of Episcopacy; others that may appear to support Presbyterianism; very many, again, that uphold Congregationalism, and others, as clearly teaching what may be described as less systematic than any of the above organizations. . . . It appears to me that the early churches were not, in all places, similarly constituted.[15]

Craik's comments are remarkable in their foreshadowing of the main theses of B. H. Streeter's *The Primitive Church*★ – a parallel which is yet more striking when we find that Craik also recognized a clear development of church order within the New Testament period itself:

> A more fully developed church organization and official position were introduced as occasion called for them. Common life in Christ was the one essential requisite for fellowship. Organization, ministry, discipline, derived all their importance from their relation to that life and its healthy manifestation. Order was secondary to spiritual vitality; legitimate and desirable, if it aided that, but worse than worthless if permitted to hinder its vigour or its growth. We hear nothing at first of Presbyters or Overseers, and the office of Deaconship appears to have been suggested by the pressure of urgent necessity. . . . the possession of spiritual gifts led to the development of rulers, teachers and evangelists, during the apostolic period.[16]

It is plain enough from these quotations that even in the Plymouth and Bristol churches the leaders were not extreme "patternists" in their approach to Scripture: that element in Brethren teaching arose later. It was Craik who described the spirit which characterized the more tolerant among the early leaders, when, in an address in 1863, he exhorted his hearers first to get rid of everything that superseded the authority of Scripture, and then, with Scripture as the one standard of judgment, to make allowance for diversity of judgment.[17]

As time passed, and as men were brought in (many of them the fruits of the revival movement) who were of rougher enthusiasms and less judicious understanding, a cruder "patternism" took hold in many places: a type of attitude well exemplified in the quotation relating to Irvingism which stands at the head of this chapter. The *Needed Truth* reaction approached Scripture in just this way. J. G. M'Vicker lived through those days, and a comment of his is worthy of quotation:

> Remember that a number of professed Christians gathering in a certain outward form, where none are received but those who are of one judgment with the leaders, where the members of Christ's body as such are not welcomed, where there is no power of God's Spirit in the worship or ministry, where Christ's voice is not heard by the believing soul, and where He is not really allowed to guide and rule, can hardly – merely because of correct form – be regarded as an *assembly of God*.[18]

The Scriptures are not to be treated in this way. They are not a constitution book for the churches. The present guidance of the Holy Spirit remains a permanent necessity in all the particular circumstances of each local church.† But in seeking that guidance, the principles and under-

★ (1929). See the Introduction pp. viii and ix. I am indebted to Mr. G. C. D. Howley for first drawing my attention to the similarity between Craik's thesis and that of Streeter.

† "The New Testament is a book of *grace* and not a book of *laws*, and the Spirit of God is not to be controlled by any human thoughts of order." From an early tract *Presbuteros – to the elders of the flock of Christ* by DSD, p. 4.

standing of the ways of God which come to us from the Scriptures remain our essential and authoritative guide.

We have been dealing with this matter of Biblical authority from the point of view of the reader's own reactions, and now we turn to consider another aspect of the question of Biblical authority, an aspect which turns on the nature of the Bible itself. The issue may be crystallized by asking the question: what effect on a movement so Bible-based have the critical studies of the last 150 years had? The answer cannot differ in any essential from the same answer in relation to any standard Protestant belief, for we have already seen that the beliefs of the early movement were firmly in the classic tradition of Protestant renewal.

To deal adequately with this question obviously requires qualifications different from those of the author, but some general comments may not be inappropriate. Developments in Biblical studies have produced a position not unlike that which arose a little earlier over the relationship of the natural sciences to Christian belief. Men have tended to overlook that while their new understanding of the natural world may have radically changed their ideas of the processes by which the world came to be, it has not really touched the basic question, which is whether or not there is a divine initiative behind the processes. So, in relation to the Bible, the bewildering succession of theories and findings which has sprung into the consciousness of the ordinary Christian from the rather over-heated world of academic Biblical scholarship, may have altered our ideas on the processes by which the Bible came to be, and it may have given a better understanding of the detailed interpretation of parts of the Bible, but it has still left open the basic question of the authority and divine nature of the Scriptures. Theories concerning the processes by which the Bible came to be can of course influence our conclusions as to the manner of Book with which we are dealing, but those influences are at best secondary to the more direct conclusions to be drawn from the effect of that Book on men and women. This evidence is historical and sociological.

Ultimately, of course, we are thrown back in our attitude to the Bible on to the same crisis as faces us in our relation to God Himself. "Whoever would draw near to God must believe that he exists and that He rewards those who seek Him."[19] Any attempt to reach God by intellectual analysis soon stultifies itself because of the very nature of the problem: it is like an attempt to define beauty by critical analysis of works of art. True knowledge of God can only begin with an act of personal response: a response which starts with basic belief or disbelief. Neither of these alternatives is in itself more logical or sensible than the other: but the positive response is that which Christianity calls "faith," and sets at the heart of its Gospel. Our attitude to the Scriptures is a counterpart to our understanding of God Himself, and is directly related to our beliefs about and our knowledge of God.

The practical effects of Biblical criticism on understanding of the Bible are important in a secondary manner. Criticism has improved understanding of grammatical and historical factors, clarified the significance of Eastern forms of thought in the Bible, provided us with a text which is closer to the original, and given us an insight into the processes by which the Bible took shape within the early church. It is doubtful whether Biblical criticism in itself does anything to weaken the radical views on church order which are distinctive of Brethren: certain it is that in matters of church order, a reader from a Brethren background finds continual echoes of his own thinking in the most surprising places in modern writings. (In passing, it may be remarked that this very fact seems to indicate that the underlying appeal in Brethren thinking on matters of church order is to the apostolic authority which underlies the Biblical record.)

Two incidental matters are worthy of comment. The first is that modern scholarship's picture of the Bible taking shape within the early church is one which should be of intense interest and importance to the developing understanding of their own church life among Brethren. The second is that the often heard distinction between the Bible *as* the Word of God, and the Bible *containing* the Word of God, seems on further analysis to be one of those peculiarly unhelpful attempts to formulate the terms of a debate which end by obscuring more than they reveal of the real beliefs of either side.

Before we close this chapter, it remains to remark on certain misuses of Scripture which can easily spring up within any movement which owes so much to the Bible. The danger of using the Bible unconsciously in a selective fashion to justify a position already held, and the danger of failing to discern how much of our understanding of the Bible arises out of a previously adopted framework of interpretation, ought to be obvious enough by now. It is necessary, nevertheless, to emphasize these two dangers again, for both continually appear in conversation and in written discussion. The most obvious sign of their appearance is seen in the tendency to transfer the adjective "scriptural" from teaching directly deduced from Scripture, to forms of action and belief which are tacitly assumed to be based on Scripture. Another symptom is a liberal use of references to unquoted texts, which are found on closer examination to bear only most indirectly on the subject in hand.

It is necessary also to re-emphasize the danger of an exaggerated "patternism" which overlooks altogether the third of our basic principles. At its worst, this tendency changes the Bible into a book of lawyer's precedents, and can end in an attitude which seems to imply that certain ways of organizing (or failing to organize) one's church life are in themselves pleasing to God. This is to revert with a vengeance to a narrow religion of form, in which the "popery of the human heart" has come full circle.

One other danger is that of an over-mystical allegorizing of the Bible. This feature has been present throughout (and before) the history of the Church, and its ludicrous medieval developments would have discredited it once for all, if the border between illustrative use of Biblical material and improper allegorization had not been so difficult to recognize. In this context, we can best call J. G. M'Vicker to our aid once more:

> The application of certain Old Testament incidents to our present circumstances is a delicate matter, and needs careful handling. Sometimes men make them mean what they themselves believe and think, and fancy that they are drawing their teaching from the Scriptures. The next speaker may see something different in them. Surely there are plain Scriptures enough to show us our path, without turning the Bible into a book of riddles, and leaving us to be dependent on the cleverest guesser.[20]

Another danger lies in an excessively mystical belief in personal inspiration from the Scripture. The Bible is not to be consulted as a sort of Delphic oracle, or as a short cut to a divine guidance that has nothing to learn from accumulated experience and spiritual wisdom. A proper understanding of its message requires open-ness of mind and the capacity for deep thought and patient learning. As we all lack a full quota of these virtues, we do well to pay attention to those who have more of them than ourselves.

My attitude to the Bible, and the things which I find in it, will not only show what sort of person I am: they will also show what sort of God I worship. The Bible can be a liberating and invigorating force, the very Word of God speaking to me: or I can use it to forge the shackles of an unbelievable bondage.

Henry Craik summed up his views on Biblical authority in words which give full scope to the whole spectrum of Biblical scholarship, and yet retain that first basic emphasis on the personal response of faith to the voice of God. With his summary we can profitably close this discussion:

> What we mean by the authority of the Bible, is the authority of the Bible when rightly read, correctly translated, and judiciously expounded and applied. Its teachings, when thus elicited, are to be received with the most entire deference.[21]

Quotation References – Chapter 17.

1. Quoted in *Chief Men Among the Brethren* (ed. Hy. Pickering) (2nd edn., undated), p. 83.
2. From the preface to *Sermons on Several Occasions*, A. C. Outler, *John Wesley* (in *A Library of Protestant Thought*) (1964), p. 89.
3. See above, p. 27.
4. *The Revival of Religion in England in the Eighteenth Century*, J. S. Simon (undated), p. 314.
5. Dr. Stoughton in *The Church of the Nineteenth Century*, quoted by Edwin Hodder, *The Life of Samuel Morley*, p. 57.

6. See G. C. Berkouwer, *The Second Vatican Council and The New Catholicism* (1965), p. 160.
7. See above, p. 125.
8. *The Brethren – A Historical Sketch*, Wm. Collingwood (1899), p. 9.
9. *Memoir*, pp. 10–11.
10. From *Reasons for Retiring from the Ministry of the Established Church* pp. 25–26, Henry Borlase. (Italics are Borlase's own.)
11. Henry Borlase, "Separation from Apostacy not Schism," *The Christian Witness*, July 1834, p. 336.
12. "A Sermon on Church Prosperity" (*c.* 1858), printed in *Biblical Expositions*, etc. (1867), p. 19. (Italics are Craik's own.)
13. *Christian Witness*, loc. cit. (Italics are Borlase's own.)
14. *New Testament Church Order*, Henry Craik (1863), p. 68.
15. Ibid., pp. 3–4.
16. Ibid., pp. 24–25.
17. *The Authority of Scripture Considered in Relation to Christian Union*, p. 17.
18. *Selected Letters*, p. 195.
19. *Hebrews* 11 : 6 (R.S.V.).
20. *Selected Letters*, p. 161.
21. *The Authority of Scripture, etc.*, p. 11.

CHAPTER 18

THE CALL OF DISCIPLESHIP

"THE lesson we all learn," her husband added, "is that in separation there is no security."

Bruce Kenrick, *Come Out The Wilderness*

OF ALL THE FEATURES THAT CHARACTERIZED THE EARLY leaders of Brethren, the most attractive was the strength of their personal devotion to Christ. It was probably the strongest of the motives which moved them, as it was certainly entirely altruistic. Men may well question many of their practices and teachings, but none can deny the force of sacrificial lives of simplicity and true saintliness.

This devotion was common to all schools among them: seen not only in Norris and Mary Groves in their giving away of their goods, or in Müller and Craik in their single-minded pursuit of the work thrust on them by the crying social needs of contemporary Bristol, or in Chapman in his tiny cottage in down-town Barnstaple. It was equally seen in Newton's sinking of his brilliant gifts in unsparing service of the Plymouth and neighbouring churches, and in Darby's delight in the simple fellowship of the mountain peasants of France and Switzerland, at a time when he might, if he had so chosen, have been looking for those glittering preferments in Law or Church to which his birth had made him heir. It was seen too in the joyful self-abandon of the later missionary pioneers and of the great revival evangelists.

Yet even this most attractive of features can be distorted, and most obviously so by extreme asceticism. Admirable as it is as a fruit of first-hand devotion, asceticism only becomes a narrow bigotry when enforced on later generations as a second- and third-hand experience. Asceticism in Christian doctrine is one of those recurring paradoxes which mark out Christianity as something both in and transcending this world. At its best it becomes a most compelling demonstration of the renunciation of worldly ambitions. Yet it has never produced a stable and enduring framework of common church life, simply because it runs counter to the basic human-ness of man's life and being.

In their ascetic tendencies, the early Brethren were children of their time, and at their strictest they did not reach the extremes which Wesley and his companions reached as early as 1744:

Q. 3. What are the Rules of an Assistant?

A. 1. Be diligent. Never be unemployed a moment, never be triflingly employed, never while away time; spend no more time at any place than is strictly necessary.

2. Be serious. Let your motto be, "holiness unto the Lord." Avoid all lightness as you would avoid hell-fire, and laughing as you would cursing and swearing. [1]

It was Wesley, after all, who, in his founding of his school for the children of his helpers, "drew up a timetable for the little boys of Kingswood which was admirably calculated to make them either lunatics or hypocrites" – including the requirement that the children should not be allowed to play! [2]

Brethrenism grew up in an evangelical environment in which the austere traditions of the eighteenth century revival had turned sour. Wesley had derived his own asceticism from à Kempis, William Law and Jeremy Taylor, and from even further back, from the ancient Eastern traditions of piety. It was a trend far older than the evangelical puritanism with which it is popularly identified.*

More subtle and therefore more serious distortions of devotedness arose from two other sources, at first sight distinct, but in fact closely related to each other. The first was their emphasis on the "heavenly calling," as a result of which they tended to overlook the Christian's part in the practical affairs of life – although this is a generalization which by no means applied to all of them. This element was nevertheless to be found in Müller as well as in Darby, although Müller's practice happily belied it, for Müller spoke of how he had been impressed as early as 1829 by "the heavenly calling of the Church of Christ, and the consequent position of the believer in this world" [3] – a form of words which was characteristic of the tendency. It is, however, associated especially with Darby's distinctive doctrine of the exclusively "heavenly" prospects of the Church. F. W. Newman detected an early version of this thinking in his "Irish clergyman" in the earliest days of their association:

What would it avail even to become a second La Place after thirty years' study, if in five and thirty years the Lord descended from heaven, snatched up all his saints to meet him, and burned to ashes all the works of the earth? [4]

But Newman was wrong in associating the tendency only with eschatology: it sprang also from a correct conviction that the Church's business was concerned with far higher things than the customary political activities of the churches around them. In essence, it was a revulsion from the Erastianism of the Established Church and from the political agitation of the Nonconformists. The strain which resulted from this, in much Brethren teaching, was neatly hit off in a *mot* of Spurgeon: "Ye men

* See Outler (ed.) *John Wesley*, Introduction.

of Plymouth, why stand ye gazing into heaven?"[4a] This tendency often prevented them from seeing the many expressions of devotion which lay to their hand in the course of the ordinary life of mankind; for this reason it distorted and restricted the outgoing flow of their love to Christ.

It is impossible, too, to dissociate the attitude of some of the early leaders from the political background of the early decades of the century. There was another side to the political agitation of the Nonconformists, for they were struggling against monstrous and unjust restrictions and handicaps, and the removal of these oppressions as a result of this agitation has immeasurably benefited every one of us. This was accomplished in the teeth of social and religious hostility of a kind which today we can barely understand. It is difficult not to feel that in their retreat into "other-worldliness" some of those leaders of early Brethren, from their upper-class Anglican backgrounds, were all too unconsciously grasping at that which would enable them to avoid facing these ugly realities of life: just as something of the same sort lay behind the retreat of the Tractarians into the ancient Catholic traditions. The immense peril of this retreat is that it confines the expression of Christian devotion to religious exercises – a limitation against which the whole example and teaching of the Lord Jesus Christ Himself cries aloud.

The second source of distortion lay in a tendency (on which we have previously remarked) to emphasize Christ's deity at the expense of His humanity. This tendency was aggravated by the Plymouth and Bethesda divisions, despite Craik's struggles against it. Its practical significance lay in a neglect of the truth of the Incarnation and thus of some of the significant consequences of Christ's identification of Himself with mankind. That identification with mankind tended to be regarded primarily in its redemptive aspects: that He was wounded for our transgressions and bruised for our iniquities was a truth in which they rightly rejoiced – but they tended to overlook the related truth that He took our infirmities and bore our diseases. Here again, they missed much of the deep impetus to their devotion which this understanding of the Incarnation would have given them. Both of these distorting influences restricted what might have been a great outflow of practical Christianity.

Nevertheless, both distortions were corrected when Christian compassion was really engaged. Müller's own work bore ample witness to this, as did that of Fegan and Barnardo and many others of the revival workers. The quotation from Dan Crawford which stands at the head of Chapter 12 of this book expresses the meaning of the Incarnation as deeply as any man has expressed it. But there is evidence enough of the unfortunate results of the distortions, to be found in that school of thought which openly decried philanthropy.

In their reaction against merely worldly ambitions in the churches, some men tended to go to the other extreme, and to write off "this world" completely as fit only for judgment. "The world" was set over against God, in forgetfulness of the fact that the Creator still worked within the world and that His disposing hand was still striving with men:

> Is not God now i' the world His power first made?
> Is not His love at issue still with sin,
> Closed with and cast and conquered, crucified
> Visibly when a wrong is done on earth?[5]

Even if they would have answered "yes" to Browning's question, yet there were those among them who were prepared to go on to declare that it was none of the Church's business. Christ's teaching that His followers were the "salt" of the earth, and His pregnant inquiry as to the salt which had lost its savour, were emasculated by this thinking as effectively as by the meaning which common speech attached to the phrase "the salt of the earth." The tendency was aggravated too by the habit of giving the concept of the Kingdom of God an exclusively eschatological meaning: of emphasising its future aspects and neglecting its present importance.

Yet Groves had given the clue to a more balanced emphasis in his exclamation of revulsion from Darby's teaching on separation:

> If ever there was a witness for God on earth, that witness was Jesus, and He never separated Himself from the synagogues; and this, if it proves nothing more, proves that *separation* is not the *only* way of witness, and yet He was emphatically "separate from sinners," not from their persons nor assemblies, but separate from their sins.[6]

Groves had been speaking in relation to separation in church fellowship, but he could have extended what he said to the whole spectrum of Christian responsibility within the world. "Separation," to many of them, often meant standing aloof, in some spiritual quarantine, from the dirt and squalor of the world; there were few who saw it as meaning engagement, if God so called a man, in that world's affairs, but with a mind and motives separated a world apart from those which characterized its victims. Yet no other interpretation can in the end, make any sort of sense out of God's actual dealings with men.

Those who did retreat into their quarantine found before long that the corruptions of the human condition, of strifes and jealousies, bigotry and foolishness, followed them even there. For, in the end, we cannot "separate" from evil in this world, for evil is within us.

Here is the paradox of the Christian ethic. The Christian ethic is not legalistic, bound by a strict code of rules and forms, but it is an ethic of freedom. But, equally, it is not an ethic of libertinism, of antinomianism, so that I may abandon law and do as I like. That is to abandon oneself to another kind of bondage, the bondage of the passions of the flesh. How does Christianity find a third way? The answer lies in the conception of the

New Birth, of an identification with Christ that is the counterpart of His identification with men in the Incarnation. With commitment to Christ, a new motivation and a new strength enters into man, the work of the Holy Spirit within him. The result is the struggle which every true Christian knows: the struggle, not between the spiritual and the material, but between the Spirit and the flesh. It is a struggle which, while this world lasts, the Christian carries into every aspect of the world in which he is placed. Devotedness to Christ is not to be seen only in my "religious" exercises: it is also to be seen in the practical application of His example in the world in which I am placed.

Quotation References – Chapter 18.

1. From the *Report of the First Annual Conference* (Friday, 29th June 1744) – reproduced in Outler, *John Wesley*, p. 145.
2. *Wesley and His Century*, W. H. Fitchett (1906), p. 494.
3. *Introduction to Passages from the Diary and Letters of Henry Craik*, p. xii.
4. *Phases of Faith*, p. 35.
4a. *Lectures to My Students (second series)* (1893), p. 36.
5. *A Death in the Desert*, Robert Browning.
6. *Memoir*, p. 374.

CHAPTER 19

THE CROWN RIGHTS OF THE REDEEMER

THE independents lit upon a new concept of human personality and responsibility, and went beyond the discoveries of the other reformers and reformations. In their meetings of believers, it was held that all who were born of the Spirit were in every way equal in the sight of God; the word might at any moment be given to any of them, and to this genuine word of God all others must pay humble and reverent attention. . . . Carried to extremes, this conviction might be thought well calculated to lead to total anarchy; yet perhaps it is not very far removed from the picture given by Paul of church meetings in Corinth; and the men who professed this view were not greatly afraid of anarchy, since they held that, where a meeting was held under the guidance of the Holy Spirit and in reliance on Him, God who is a God of order would see to it that His own will should prevail.

Stephen Neill in *The Bible in English History* (from *Churchmen Speak*, ed. P. E. Hughes, 1966).

(Concerning the seventeenth century Independents)

"THE EVANGELICAL CLERGY," WROTE R. M. BEVERLEY, one of the early Brethren teachers, "have brewed new wine, but they have not procured new bottles."[1] It was in an attempt to repair this lack that Beverley and his fellows broke from the churches of their day. Yet there was justice in a retort by Andrew Jukes, in the years after he had left the Brethren:

One special mistake both of the Quakers and of Plymouth Brethren is the notion that a form hinders the Spirit. Nothing can be a greater delusion. The Spirit, like air or water, can fill any form, if only it is received. You may, indeed, have bottles without wine; but if you wish to keep the wine the bottles are useful. It is the miserable fact that so many professed believers and ministers are "bottles without wine" which makes these Plymouth people cry out so much against bottles. But bottles have their use. All forms are bottles. Life always makes itself a form to dwell in.[2]

The absence of any separate order of ministry, full freedom of participation in Christian service, and in particular the open form of communion service, are characteristic of Brethren. The obvious danger is that a system which thus rejects restrictive "forms" in its worship should degenerate into anarchy, and that where authority is loosed, every man should do what is right in his own eyes. It was a recognition of this danger which caused Groves in the end to express himself as quite unable to join a church without properly regulated order.[3]

To understand where Brethren teaching stood in relation to these two extremes, it is necessary to understand the doctrine of the ministry which was current among them. Service within the Church was not a matter of unregulated impulse: it was rather that they tried to go back to the overriding authority of the Head of the Church Himself, and to remove those clogs which, they believed, human regulation had placed upon the exercise of His sovereignty. In principle, their basic doctrine was little different from that held by the evangelical tradition in general. Some words of Dr. J. Vernon Bartlet are apposite here:

> Accordingly the Protestant idea of the Ministry, while far from indifferent to order, is opposed to the emphasis on particular "orders," and tends to lay its stress rather on manifest God-given "gift" as essential.
> . . . ministry in the Apostolic Age had quite another origin than that suggested by the terms "devolution of authority" or "apostolic succession." It was determined by *charismatic* gifts, operative in a community conscious of special inspiration by the Spirit of God, as the link between itself and the Head of the Church. Accordingly the basis of the Church's ministry at large, whether that of the Word or other, lay in the "gift" qualifying for any form of service to the brethren in their corporate life or fellowship. Such gifts were traced ultimately to Christ, the Head of the Church, and directly to the Holy Spirit; while the corporate capacity to recognize their presence in any member was referred to the same Spirit, at work in measure in all.[4]

Certainly, Darby claimed that this was the principle behind his early thinking:

> I saw in Scripture that there were certain *gifts* which formed true ministry, in contrast to a clergy established upon another principle.[5]

According to Tregelles, Wigram had made his views quite specific:

> E. Do you admit "*a regular ministry*?"
> A. If by a regular ministry you mean a *stated* ministry (that is, that in every assembly those who are gifted of God to speak to edification will be both limited in number and known to the rest), I do admit it; but if by a regular ministry you mean an *exclusive* ministry, I dissent.[6]

Henry Craik wrote in 1863 of the New Testament churches:

> As gifts for rule or for teaching were developed, so were they recognized by apostolic appointment, or by thankful acceptance and submission on the part of those amongst whom such gifted brethren were led, in the ordering of God, to labour. The capacities for service and the corresponding spiritual qualifications were essential; the fact of recognition depended not upon mere authority but upon ascertained gifts and character; the latter constituted the foundation of the former.[7]

Yet, very soon, an "impulsive" view of ministry, fully justifying Jukes's criticism, began in many minds to be synonymous with the practice of Brethren. The reason for this development becomes apparent when we put to ourselves the further question, "How does the Head of the Church exercise His authority within the churches?" There are two possible answers. He might delegate this authority through those to whom He has given the appropriate natural and spiritual gifts (as Borlase put it – see above, p. 257), or He might exercise it by the direct impulsive movement of the Spirit on the members of the churches. Theories soon began to develop among some of them which tended to the second answer. No longer did those who developed these theories see the Holy Spirit as working through the gifts and offices with which the Church was endowed, but rather they were tending to picture His operation in terms of direct impulsive inspiration (although operating through natural functions rather than through Pentecostal manifestations.)

We may assign two causes to these developments. The former, which has already been discussed in some detail, was the evolution of Darby's thinking, aggravated by his quarrels with the Established Church (in which he found the clergy his fiercest opponents), and then by events in Vaud and in Plymouth.* The second cause is more conjectural, and is perhaps a case of arguing *post hoc, ergo propter hoc*. That cause was the considerable Quaker influx into the churches of Brethren in the late 1830s, for such impulsive views are characteristically Quaker. It is possibly significant that Müller himself should have expressed in 1843, in relation to developments in Stuttgart, opinions which certainly approached such impulsive views;[8] for Bethesda had received several additions from Quaker circles in the preceding few years, including that of James Ireland Wright, the father of Müller's future son-in-law and successor, James Wright. Müller's later practice shows, however, that such opinions were not typical of his thinking: his own temperament would have inclined him towards them, but behind him stood the perceptive Henry Craik. It is more than doubtful whether the development in Darby's views was the result of Quaker influences.† Not only would such influence from a dissenting source be contrary to what we know of him, but most of the interconnected groups of ex-Quakers were associated with the Tottenham/Bristol group of churches. or with Newton, rather than with Darby, and later they opposed Darby with some vigour. There is ample material in

* Darby wrote in his *Narrative of Facts*: "They did teach (at Plymouth) that it was by gifted members He acted *in the body*, that is, by teachers. And everyone knows that anyone's taking a part in the meeting as led of the Spirit to do so, was denounced as 'impulse'." (*Coll. Writings*, Vol. 20, p. 32n. – Stow Hill edn.)

† A tract of 1839 (not by Darby) entitled *Reply to an Article in the* Eclectic Review *for May last entitled "The Plymouth Brethren" (reprinted from* The Inquirer *for October)*, by an obviously highly informed writer quoting from a wide range of early Brethren tracts, specifically distinguishes Quaker teachings, which the writer describes as "a notion nowhere countenanced by Scripture" (pp. 19, 20). Other contemporary tracts take a similar line.

the story of Darby's own development to account for the change in his thinking.

Bartlet, in the extract which has been quoted, referred to ministry as being determined by "charismatic" gifts, and the interpretation of that word illustrates the subtle but important change which took place in the thinking of some Brethren. As Bartlet there used the word, the "charismata" were the normal abilities of teaching, government, and the like, heightened and put to use by the Holy Spirit within the churches. In theological writings, however, a habit has grown up of confining the use of the word to the more directly inspirational and impulsive "Pentecostal" phenomena of the early churches, so that "charismatic" ministry now commonly means something very different from what Bartlet meant. It was a similar transition which took place in the thinking of those early Brethren who followed Darbyite or Quaker ideas, although they confined their ideas to normal participation in worship, and did not follow the Irvingites into the Pentecostal phenomena.

Nevertheless, this development remained an aberration in the non-Darbyite congregations (within Darbyism it was much more closely woven with other elements of their thinking). Their basic doctrine of the ministry, as understood by their leading teachers, insists on complete freedom for the exercise of abilities bestowed on the individual, but does not encourage impulsive views.

The story of how the Brethren, working in this way from premises similar to those of the traditional Protestant churches, yet ended with such different practices, is instructive. The basic Protestant doctrine was that the gift given by God qualified a man for ministry within the churches. In the traditional Protestant churches expression was given to this principle in a variety of ways, but generally some form of public recognition of the existence of the gift was also regarded as necessary to safeguard decent order. In this they had plain New Testament precedent. Early Brethren were impatient with even this restriction, and relied partly upon the spiritual self-discipline of the gifted individual himself, and partly upon the judgment of the churches, to recognise the gift and to provide orderly opportunity for its use.

In practice, this clearly called for a high degree of self-control and spiritual discernment, and it soon became notorious – as many contemporary accounts from all traditions of Brethren showed – that results could be very unhappy. After a long trial, the spontaneous type of service has by now almost universally been confined (among the independent congregations) to the Lord's Supper, where it has developed a flexibility and a sense of common participation that at its best can be most memorable, and where the main activities of adoration and prayer are clearly more suitable for general exercise. Preaching at other services is normally restricted to an invited speaker, the invitations being, in theory but scarcely in practice, confined to those who are plainly gifted for the purpose. Spontaneity elsewhere is reserved for the occasional "Bible reading" or open discussion.

The extremer exclusive congregations, on the other hand, have (as might have been expected) followed Darby's line, and have imposed order in their services by a strictly enforced, unwritten, but nevertheless quasi-liturgical, form.[9]

It is because they have failed to grasp the nettle of recognition of gift that the independent Brethren have often lost an essential insight of the New Testament: the insight expressed in Ephesians 4:11, where it is the men who are equipped with the different abilities who are the gifts to the churches. Thus they have suffered from a common but fateful misunderstanding, the vague idea that every man must have his turn: an idea which ends by devaluing and devitalizing gifts which are essential to the growth of the churches.

This failure of Brethren to safeguard properly the original understanding of service within the churches has been tragic for more than themselves, because it has brought into disrepute what might have been a bold and imaginative freeing of the shackled gifts within the churches. Today the most urgent of all the problems which face them is probably that of restoring an emphasis upon the proper discovery, cultivation and deployment of the gifts given to members of the churches. They have feared that formal recognition of gift might re-create the bondage against which they originally protested, and in particular that it might be a first step towards the re-establishment of a clerical "caste." This fear is not in itself a reason for setting aside a specific insight of Scripture, and it overlooks two other principles of their position. The first is that they do not hold a professional view of the ministry, and while they recognize that some men are called to full-time service of the Word of God, they do not confine the exercise of gift to such men, but insist on full freedom for its exercise by all who possess it. "Ministry" is not thought of with those occupational overtones which are almost automatic elsewhere, but rather in terms of the exercise of talents which exist in men of varied secular callings. The second is that the basic independency of their churches is an effective barrier to the growth of a clerical autocracy.

The greatest safeguard of all will lie in a deeper understanding of all that lies within the concept of "gift" within the churches. It is especially when it is confined to narrow functions of teaching, preaching and ministry that abuses arise. When it is understood that "gift" extends to every necessary task within the church's life and witness, and that the ideal is that every member of the church should have his or her function within that life and witness made plain, then recognition becomes the open acknowledgement by the congregation of the formal place of each of its members. In this way the churches can be revolutionized by a partnership of grace in which every member has his or her own function to fulfil, without jealousy or frustration, and where the Holy Spirit will weld the individual gifts of the many into a united testimony to His power.

Again, in the present haphazard state of things, very much true gift finds no opportunity for expression, and runs to waste, simply because of natural diffidence on the part of the sensitive. It is the most forceful who tend to be heard, rather than the most gifted. An ordering of ministry provides both an incentive and an outlet for gifts which often remain unused today.

The principle has yet wider and more exciting implications. This is not the place to discuss the vogue in modern popular theology for "the rediscovery of the laity," except to say that there seems to be much in the ideas lying behind that vogue which are of importance to this discussion. Brethren thinking itself has been narrow and introspective in understanding the scope of the churches' gifts. They have tended to turn all men into "do-it-yourself" clergy, and have forgotten the immense scope of the whole field of service within the daily world into which Christians go every day. Yet, in principle, their thinking is far more radical than that of the modern discussions, which still seem to labour in the grip of old habits of thought concerning the professional ministry.

In principle, the ideal which characterises Brethren substitutes for the distinction between "clergy" and "laity," or between "the ministry" and "the people," an entirely different distinction, based upon function. It is where this distinction is not grasped, and a vague idea that all men can do the same job takes its place, that abuses arise. The new distinction does not deny that some men are called to full-time preaching, evangelism, teaching or pastoral work, or that proper provision should be made for their support. Essentially, it is a distinction of function, that seeks to allot to each man the task to which his innate abilities and the complex of personal aspirations and circumstances that make up his personal call from God, summon him. No difference of status between individuals is involved in this distinction. If there is a distinction in any form corresponding to that between "clergy" and "laity" it can lie only in the fact that some men are called to a "regular" place within the ordinary life of the human community and of God's ordinary workings within the life of mankind; while other men are called to a more dramatic place that stands in marked contrast to ordinary life – the pioneer, the mystic, the ascetic, the prophet – a place which we might call the "catastrophic," for it is directly related to that other action of God that bursts in from outside upon the world's activity, overturning and making anew: but this distinction is an entirely different one from the distinctions between the different gifts to be exercised within the churches – gifts which appear in both classes of men.

A full expression of this wider understanding involves a careful and

responsible self-assessment by each Christian of his or her own opportunities and abilities. The elders also of each church must assess responsibly
the gifts and calling of each of its members, in relation not only to the
individual church, but also in relation to the Church as a whole, in its
total witness towards the world. It is then the task of the elders to weld the
local church into a unity of witness, in fellowship with other local churches
(using that word in no denominational sense), in order that the full
potential of the gifts and calling of each member may be completely
drawn out. It should also go without saying that the sometimes violent
anti-clericalism which exists in some places among Brethren is wholly
contrary to their true understanding of the Lordship of the Head of the
Church. Where He has given gifts, those gifts are to be used for the good
of His Church, and the fact that their possessor has received an act of
public recognition by another body of Christians, or even been given a
position within that body which is felt to be inconsistent with the highest
ideals of the freedom of Christ within His Church, is irrelevant to that
obligation to recognize and to benefit from His gift.

The giving of talents within the churches, and their disposal in His own
service, are both the crown rights of the Redeemer, who is Head of the
Church. To order and utilize that gift to its best advantage, He gives other
gifts of wise oversight and of administration. Those who possess those
other gifts are in a sense stewards of the whole range of the gifts which the
Lord Jesus Christ gives to the churches, and they are responsible to the
Head of the Church to ensure that the abilities of all their fellow-members
of His Body are encouraged, nourished, and put effectively and fully to
work.

Quotation References – Chapter 19.

1. From *Examination*, p. 76.
2. *Letters of Andrew Jukes*, p. 108.
3. See above, p. 129.
4. "The Protestant Idea of Church and Ministry as Rooted in Early Christianity," in
   Evangelical Christianity, Its History and Witness (ed. W. B. Selbie), 1911, pp. 4 &
   12–13. (Italics are Bartlet's).
5. *Letters*, Vol. III, p. 300. (Letter to Tholuck, 185–.) (Italics are Darby's.)
6. Quoted S. P. Tregelles, *Three Letters*, p. 13. (Italics as Tregelles).
7. *New Testament Church Order*, p. 66.
8. See Neatby, *A History of the Plymouth Brethren*, pp. 97–100.
9. See G. F. Tripp, "Recent Liturgical Tendencies Among the Exclusive Brethren."
   Journal of the Christian Brethren Research Fellowship, April 1967, pp. 19–20.

CHAPTER 20

UNITY AND ITS EXPRESSION

I ask not, therefore, of him with whom I would unite in love, "Are you of my church, of my congregation? Do you receive the same form of church government and allow the same church officers with me? Do you join in the same form of prayer wherein I worship God?" I inquire not, "Do you receive the Supper of the Lord in the same posture and manner that I do, nor whether, in the administration of baptism, you agree with me in admitting sureties for the baptized, in the manner of administering it, or the age of those to whom it should be administered?" Nay, I ask not of you (as clear as I am in my own mind) whether you allow baptism and the Lord's Supper at all. Let all these things stand by – we will talk of them, if need be, at a more convenient season. My only question at present is this. 'Is thine heart right, as my heart is with thy heart'?"

John Wesley, *Sermon on II Kings 10:15*

"THERE WAS ONE THING MUCH INSISTED ON IN SCRIPTURE – the unity of the Church – which none of them, I thought, clearly explained or strongly inculcated."[1] So John Wesley described part of his early theological studies. The factor which Wesley missed in the writers he studied was one of the central aspirations of the early Brethren movement, as in a different way it was with Wesley.

Further definition is necessary at this point. What was this "Church" whose unity they desired? We may pass over for present purposes the subtle debates between Darby and Newton as to the standing of the faithful of pre-Christian times: for on the practical present answer to the question they were all agreed. The Church was the whole body of the faithful: of all those who were truly committed to the Lord Jesus Christ. They thus stood firmly in that long line of Protestant witness to the Church's essential nature which we saw in Wycliffe. B. W. Newton found his definition of the Church in Acts 20:28: "the Church of God which He hath purchased with His own blood." *

Their quarrel with existing forms of church life was twofold. On the one hand, they considered existing forms to be too restrictive. By requiring assent to formularies of belief, or by laying emphasis on distinctive doctrines, the churches of their time, they considered, set up barriers to the free inter-communion of true Christians. On the other hand, many of those churches were at the same time too wide, freely admitting men who

---

* Newton himself, who was in the separatist Plymouth tradition, later deprecated, in opposition to the views of Groves and his fellows, any attempt to make this definition the basis of formal unity.

had no personal faith, simply because they had received the appropriate symbol of initiation, or had made themselves amenable to the discipline of the particular body. The idea of establishment, in particular, was a cause of violent offence to them, and men such as Borlase who were prepared to dismiss the Established Church as "apostate" did so because they were deeply convinced that the requirements imposed by law upon the Church of England destroyed any possibility of reform:

> The Communion constitutes the Church; other things, properly speaking, being only accidents; and where it is corrupt, the very essence and life of the body is gone. . . . I know of nothing that a Christian has any right to demand of his fellow-man, beyond belief in free pardon and salvation by faith in Christ; and the evidence of a life conformed to that profession. . . . But these at least, in faithfulness to Christ are required. In the Communion of the Church of England, however, all distinctions are levelled; and every baptized person is considered by its rules, as qualified for admission: – "for by the law of the land, both ecclesiastical and civil, none are to be shut out from this Sacrament, but such as are notorious delinquents, and none are *notorious* but such as the sentence of the law hath, either upon their own confession, or full conviction, declared so to be."[2]

That their vision in this was not narrow, at least at this stage, is clear from Borlase's other paper *Separation from Apostacy not Schism*:

> The only way then of deciding the question, What is Schism? is to refer at once to that which is given in the Scriptures of the principles and character of the Churches. And these, by the evidence of all the Apostolic Scriptures, were each, as before said, simply a union of believers, upon the ground of the common salvation; "congregations of faithful men," ordered by the Spirit of God. Nor does it appear that any thing, beyond the mere ascertaining, as far as it was possible, that they were believers, was necessary to make them partakers of this fellowship. The whole tenor of the accounts given for our instruction prove this, and that the terms required were none other than those which make a man a member of the body of Christ, "If thou shalt confess with thy mouth the Lord Jesus Christ, and shalt believe in thine heart that God hath raised Him from the dead, thou shalt be saved." I repeat that this ground of the common Salvation is the only one which is sanctioned by Christ; that it is meeting as believers only which is Spiritual union, or which can be owned by Him. . . . Any union which has not this principle as its basis, which is brought together upon a point of secondary importance (and all else is secondary), or which enjoins anything which might prove a stumbling block to the conscience of the weak, is contrary to the mind of Christ, and is inevitably Schism.[3]

They were thus faced with a quandary. While passionately desiring unity, they knew of no existing church order which (in their view) provided an adequate form by which to express that unity. Moreover, there were other truths of freedom which could not be expressed within the forms of the existing churches, and therefore they tried new means by which they could give expression to those truths. It was at this point that an important difference of emphasis appeared. Groves and the Bristol group formed their churches in order to give positive expression to the truth as they understood it. As Müller declared in 1863:

> It is often said, for the sake of peace and union, we should not be very particular as to certain parts of truth; keep them back, and treat them as matters of no moment. I humbly state that I entirely differ from this view; for I do not see that such union is of a real, lasting, or Scriptural character.... Yet, while we hold fast the truth, *all* the truth which we consider we have been instructed in from the Holy Scriptures, we must ever remember, that it is not the degree of knowledge to which believers have attained which should unite them, but the common spiritual life they have in Jesus; that they are purchased by the blood of Jesus; members of the same family; going to the Father's house – soon to be all there: and by reason of the common life they have, brethren should dwell together in unity. It is the will of the Father, and of that blessed One who laid down His life for us, that we should love one another.[4]

Darby, on the other hand, considered himself to be withdrawing in protest against those things with which he disagreed. He had, he said:

> done no more than withdraw himself from the things he found among them, when those things appeared to him at variance with God's word, always endeavouring to "keep the unity of the spirit in the bond of peace" and remembering that word, "If thou take forth the precious from the vile, thou shalt be as my mouth," a direction of unspeakable value in the present confusion.[5]

Behind this difference of emphasis there grew up, as we have seen in Chapter 8, very different ideas of the Church's ideal structure.

If they were agreed, then, in their definition of the true Church, their definition raised, as it has always in all Protestant thinking, another need for definition. If the Church is the body of the faithful, who are those faithful, and how are they to be recognized?

The authoritative answer to that question can only be found in the New Testament itself. In explaining the Gospel which had broken upon his mind with such a shock of revelation, Paul found his key in the response which faith makes to the promise of God. So he had made Abraham the model of all who should be justified, because, at a time when Abraham had been low in despair, he had heard and believed the promise of God, and his faith had been counted to him for righteousness. When, in the Galatian letter, he had worked at the "rough block" of the Gospel which he was later to polish in the letter to the Romans, Paul had declared how for their part he and his companions had made that response: "We ourselves ... who know that a man is not justified by works of the law but through faith in Jesus Christ, even we have believed in Christ Jesus."[6] Abraham's faith had, in a sense, been blind: but now God's promises had come to a focus of atoning action in Christ, and faith was now given a final anchor-point in the open redemptive act of God in Christ. Baptism was the unifying token and symbol of faith's act of response: "in Christ

Jesus you are all sons of God, through faith. For as many of you as were baptized into Christ have put on Christ."[7]

It was a concept at once broad and simple, and, as we have seen, the earliest Brethren too accepted it as such. For proof that the necessary response of faith had been made in reality, they asked simply for active evidence of the grace of God present in a man.* As we have seen, Groves and the independents extended this also to their concept of the Church. Where Christ was, there was a valid local church.

The quarrel of these early Brethren with sacramental views of the Church is not so much, when analysed, an objection to the sacramental signs in themselves, as to the misunderstandings to which they must unavoidably give rise. A true response to God might well be sparked by the constant witness in the sacraments of the historic Church to the redemptive work of God in Christ, but the constant danger is that the sacraments themselves might assume a semi-magical† significance, as though in themselves they were the effective agents of redemption. The evangelical doctrine of justification by faith is thus not opposed to the sacraments, but rather comprehends them within itself, and safeguards them.

The constant danger in the sacramentarian's emphasis on the signs is that he comes in the end to believe that the signs in themselves accomplish that which the individual's personal response alone can accomplish, and will unlock the free grace of God. Redemption is the act of God, on the basis of the atoning work of Christ: it is available to all those who respond in truth to God. That response is an inward matter, a genuine movement of soul to God. It may be inherent in an individual's participation in one of the great Christian symbols: but to believe that the symbol by itself is effective without that inward response, or that the response cannot be made except by means of the symbol, is to reduce Christianity to superstition.

That this danger is particularly acute wherever infant baptism continues to be practised must by now be clear from history. Simply because infant baptism by definition cannot embody a conscious personal response on the part of the person baptized, it is impossible for it to avoid a basic dilemma. Either the symbol in itself is believed to effect a real change in the subject, or by itself to release the grace of God towards the subject (which must result in the error which we have just described); or it does not (in which case its justification is scanty, and the scope for misunderstanding immense). The story of exclusivism has plainly illustrated this degeneration, for the

---

* The evidence for which they asked might often have been extreme or over-scrupulous. That is another matter.

† (Apostolic succession) "transmutes the Christian minister into a sophisticated witch-doctor whose stock-in-trade is the magic of priestcraft" (P. E. Hughes in *The Credibility of the Church* [*Guidelines–Anglican Evangelicals Face the Future*, ed. J. I. Packer (1967) p. 159]).

extreme "Taylor" exclusives have today adopted what is virtually an automatic admission of the baptized child at the age of twelve: a process which cannot but result in a large admixture of unregenerate members.

Views on Christian unity must eventually go back to views on what it is that makes a Christian. Because so much modern discussion of unity avoids this essential question in the name of peace, it seems impossible to take it seriously.

In relation to this central question, the revival movement brought in another confusing factor, which has also narrowed views of unity (and particularly within a movement on which the revival had such a formative influence as it did on Brethren) to limits which are surely narrower than those of Holy Scripture. The act of personal response or committal to God, the response of faith to Him, is the Scriptural phenomenon which answers to "conversion," as that term is loosely used by evangelicalism: while the "new birth" is God's action within the one who is responding. But the revival brought with it another phenomenon: the characteristic occurrence of an emotional crisis, which, in the revival atmosphere, became identified with "conversion." This crisis undoubtedly took place with very many at the moment of their personal response of repentance and faith to God, and this was especially so in the heightened atmosphere of the revival: but it was overlooked that it could also take place in some persons, and yet leave as little trace on them as infant baptism had left on others, or, if this was noticed by the revivalists, the occurrence was explained away on the ground that the "conversion" was not genuine. Similarly, it was also overlooked that the experience took place in some who had already responded to God in the plainest possible way: or else it was explained that they were not truly "saved" before that time. This revivalist experience became a pattern experience, and thus those who had not undergone it were considered in the minds of many to be "unconverted," whatever the depth and genuineness of their faith in God.

It is essential to emphasize at this point that nothing that has been said must be allowed to detract one tittle from the vital importance of Christian conversion. The words of Christ Himself are eloquent enough in this context – as the King James Version of Matthew 18:3 renders them: "Except ye be converted, and become as little children, ye shall not enter into the kingdom of heaven." In their emphasis upon this necessity, the Brethren from the first were re-emphasizing what is perhaps the most vital element in the whole of Christianity. It was an emphasis to which they brought plain personal experience. Robert Gribble had written in 1858:

> I have on different occasions met with believers who seemed to doubt the reality of such sudden conversions as have been frequently mentioned in these *Recollections*, and it may be well to observe that I have not described any distinct case

except where it has been proved to be the work of the Holy Ghost after years of subsequent observation.

Such doubts often arise from a mistaken idea that conversion must be a *gradual*, instead of an *instantaneous* work; there can however be no period between life and death in a material body, and the analogy is strictly applicable to a sinner "dead in trespasses and sins," Ephesians ii. 1, when quickened by the Holy Spirit.[8]

J. G. M'Vicker's experience is of interest, not only for its close similarity to that of John Wesley in the previous century, but also because it illustrates both the importance of that for which he was contending, and also the dangers which a distorted understanding of what had happened could bring to the true realization of Christian unity. His diaries show a continual history of spiritual struggle until he reached peace in 1859. He complains:

I had never met any person who asked me if I was born again, or who told me that he knew God had saved him.[9]

Yet, long before, at the age of 18, he had drawn up for himself a "form of covenant":

Having been long devoted by my parents to God for the work of the ministry, and having lately had my thoughts turned to the importance of the duties, which that office involves, and the necessity of personal piety for their proper discharge, I would here, through Jesus Christ my Saviour, solemnly dedicate myself to God. To Him I devote my time, my talents, my attainments, all that I am, and all that I have, and before Him whose eye rests on me while I write, I purpose, with all the solemnity of an oath, to make His glory the great object of my life: and be it unto me according to His gracious word – "and I will be to thee a God."[10]

Six months after his crisis experience in the Revival had occurred on 26th June 1859, he wrote, in a letter of 8th December 1859:

My mind from the very first was exercised with the question, What is the Church of Christ? Is this a Church of Christ over which men have put you (M'Vicker was then a minister) to preside? I felt that it was not. The great bulk of the members there had no real faith in the Lord Jesus; they had a certain amount of knowledge, went through a certain round of duties, and that was the whole of it. Sure faith in Christ, giving them peace and joy in the Holy Ghost, they did not possess, did not even profess to have, had never been asked if they had. The whole thing was a human system – members without faith, elders without faith, a minister without faith. How could I dispense the Lord's Supper to such a gathering? What was I to do? I was in no little perplexity. Yet I felt too that here, as in everything else, my sufficiency was in God; in Him was wisdom to guide me and I sought it in faith.

The whole business of church-making and minister-making as it goes on around us, I saw to be a terrible sham. A baby is born, and after a few weeks is made, or owned – it does not matter which – as a Christian. That little Christian grows up to be a man or woman. Parents, elders, ministers, etc., tell him it is time he was "going forward," but generally without one spark of real faith. He goes forward and eats the Lord's Supper. Just such a lad is taken early, sent to school, then to college, then examined, then licensed to preach, then hands are put on his head, and he is made a minister. At no step of his progress is he ever asked if he has faith in the Lord Jesus, and in the great majority of cases he has none. Is this the Church of Jesus Christ? and are these His ministers?[11]

What M'Vicker was contending for was essentially the same as had been expressed succinctly by one of the Continental Anabaptist leaders in 1524:

Just as our forebears fell away from the true God and the knowledge of Jesus Christ and of the right faith in Him, and from the one true, common divine word, from the divine institutions, from Christian love and life, and lived without God's law and gospel in human, useless, un-Christian customs and ceremonies, and expected to obtain salvation therein, yet fell far short of it, as the evangelical preachers have declared, and to some extent are still declaring; so today, too, every man wants to be saved by superficial faith, without fruits of faith, without the baptism of test and probation, without love and hope, without right Christian practices, and wants to persist in all the old fashion of personal vices, and in the common ritualistic and anti-Christian customs of baptism and the Lord's Supper, in disrespect for the divine word . . .[12]

Conversion, in Scripture, is not presented only or even chiefly as a revivalist experience. It is a "turning about" to a new way of life – a way of life instinct with the personal apprehension of Christ. A balanced understanding of Christian conversion was expressed by Rendle Short as well as it has been by any teacher among Brethren. After summarizing the five elements in the essential Christian life, as shown by the five main groups of Biblical references to the subject (belief on a Person, and that Person Jesus Christ; repentance; a changed or purified life; open confession; and – but ambiguously – certain references which stress the importance of baptism and the Lord's Supper), he emphasized that

Faith is not just the solving of a problem. It is the motive and the driving force for living a particular kind of life.

and then he added:

This must not be interpreted to mean that all these elements have to be present and realized, in every conversion. Far from it. In the great majority of cases only one element is present to consciousness; the rest are subconscious, latent. They are unrealized at first; they come to light afterwards. That is why experiences differ so greatly. . . . In other cases there are no well-remembered and dated spiritual crises, especially with those whose experiences of eternal life began in childhood. So the door of entrance may seem to us to be painted in differing colours, but it opens on to Christ Himself, the Way, the Truth, and the Life.[13]

The importance of understanding this influence of the revival lies in the distorting effect which it has on attitudes to other Christians and to their churches. Rarely does it affect attitudes to persons within one's own fellowship, where it might be healthier, for familiarity is a common anodyne: but it is only too easy to build up invincible walls of ignorance between ourselves and those we need to meet only if we make an effort to do so. A symptom of this distortion is seen in the extreme "remnant mentality"* characteristic of some Brethren circles. It is too easy to make the grace of God seem like admission to an exclusive club, to be gained only through "right" sponsors and "right" procedure. The Church is not an exclusive club: it is the product of the free redeeming activity of a God who will have all men to be saved and come to a knowledge of the truth, but will force no man into submission against his own free will.

The only remedy for such misunderstandings is the remedy which Groves laid down: to look for Christ in another, and His Spirit in each congregation, and when they are found, to recognize the man as my true brother in Christ, and the congregation as a true church of the living God. That M'Vicker himself did that, the many other quotations we have made from his writings prove. Too few have the breadth of sympathy or vision to do so: and when today narrowness of sympathy is found in a congregation of independent Brethren it is usually because they have narrowed the grace of God to limits which are little broader than their own vision.

* I owe this phrase to Professor F. F. Bruce.

Quotation References – Chapter 20.

1. From Wesley's *Journal*, 24 January 1738 (Quoted Outler, ed., *John Wesley*, p. 46).
2. *Reasons, etc.*, reproduced in *The Present State of the Church*, pp. 12–13.
3. *The Christian Witness*, July 1834, p. 345.
4. From an address given to a Conference of Christians at Clifton in October 1863, reproduced in *Jehovah Magnified* (1876), pp. 28 ff.
5. *Reflections on the Ruined Condition of the Church* (1841), p. 2.
6. *Galatians* 2: 15, 6. (R.S.V.)
7. *Galatians* 3: 26, 7 (R.S.V.)
8. *Recollections of an Evangelist*, Robert Gribble (1858), pp. 147–8 n.
9. *Selected Letters*, p. 6.
10. Ibid., p. 2.
11. Ibid., p. 40.
12. From a letter of Conrad Grebel to Thomas Müntzer on 5 September 1524. Quoted by Harold S. Bender in *The Anabaptist Vision* (*The Recovery of The Anabaptist Vision*, ed. Guy F. Hershberger [1957]), p. 38.
13. *The Bible and Modern Research* (1944), pp. 241–46.

CHAPTER 21

THE PRESENT SITUATION

WE talk of unity in Christ but mean unity in doctrine and practice. A get-
together with a denominational church at the local level has always an
element of the unreal in it, because it is not able completely to respond to
the challenge that may be put to it, unless indeed it is willing to become
something quite different from what it is.

H. L. Ellison, *The Household Church*

WE HAVE REACHED THE POINT AT WHICH IT BECOMES
necessary to attempt a summing-up of the lessons to be drawn
from a movement like the Brethren and of its place in the
modern age.

To support a claim that the movement has a real and important thing
to say to the modern situation, it is only necessary to point to the topical
elements of today which can be traced in the thinking of the early movement. Christian unity; the "rediscovery of the laity;" the concept of a
"religionless Christianity" (if by "religion" we mean the churchly *cultus*);
the renewed emphasis on the Bible; the clash between the individual and
the organization – all these have their echoes within the early movement.
Because men of no small intellectual ability and culture faced each of these
problems well over a century ago, and in their practical and radical
approach they reached some constructive answers and also made a number
of obvious and tragic mistakes, it is worth the while of any modern thinker
to glance for a moment at what they thought and did.

For those of us who are their heirs, it is necessary to pause for a moment
to take hold of the fact that we are part of a movement which has already
in a very short history produced saints and pioneers of a calibre which is
second to none, and that the movement is still a vigorous and growing one.
It is high time that we awoke to face the real tasks of the modern world,
and we shall do so with more understanding if we have first taken a
realistic look at the experiences of our fathers.

The Brethren's claim to significance is not based upon any supposed
distinctive special virtue of the movement, for many of the things which
have been most distinctive of it are not enduring, and some are retrogres-
sive. The basis of the claim is simply that they are one of the purest
examples extant today of a strain in Christianity which has not only been
recurrent from the beginning, but will continue to recur as long as the
Church exists: for it is of the essence of the Christian Gospel. We ought to

be long past the days when men could hope for a monolithic Church, or even imagine that such an end is desirable for its own sake. The painful centuries have taught us the lesson that not one structure which involves men and women can be incorruptible or expressive of more than (at best) a part of truth. The full continuing truth is found only where every strain is present: where the conflicting weaknesses of men are balanced, and counteract their own internal evils. The Church is not spared, while it is on earth, its part in the common structure of mortality. The Spirit of God alone can bind that disparate structure into a unity: and in that transcending unity there will always be – there must always be – those churches where He will burst out at times and places of His choosing, in the liberty of His own imperious will.

Here we must repeat something which has been said at the end of Chapter 12. The independent church ideal holds within itself an essential corrective to those evils which inevitably corrupt every structure or hierarchy. History has shown that the Church is no less prone than any other structure to those evils of power. It is not that the same evils cannot arise within the single local congregation, or in the independent society or mission: they tragically can, and do. But among the truly independents (and for this purpose they must be truly independent – an organization of independent churches is a contradiction in terms) both society and the Church have a built-in corrective to the contagion of the evils of power within themselves. It is just for this reason that official power consciously or unconsciously denigrates and despises the independent, where it cannot suppress him. Instinctively, it recognizes the threat he poses to its own overweening ambition. For this same reason, no dictatorship can allow free institutions to remain genuinely free. It is precisely here that the crucial test of modern ecumenicity is found: and the signs are not always encouraging that the ecumenical movement as a whole recognizes this. The society which acknowledges, in reality and not in pretence, the free liberty of the independent, without suppression by physical or psychological pressures, alone can retain its integrity; but modern ecumenism seems bent on destroying nonconformity by Darby's plea of "one church."*

* It is not without relevance to the inability of some Brethren, also, to grasp this part of their calling by God that, when the present author made precisely this point in the course of correspondence in *The Witness* in 1965, he was met by a retort which failed even to see the point at issue. He wrote (June 1965 issue p. 229):

"For just so long as a congregation such as that which Mr. N. represents is permitted to associate with (not to say welcomed to) such a local Council, for so long will it be impossible for the totalitarianism which Mr. B. fears to take shape. The two things are, as a matter of plain constitutional fact, incompatible."

This was met by the reply (September issue, p. 348):

"His first paragraph I do not accept as fact at all. Did the faithful remnant in Israel prevent the apostate nation being cast out and judicially blinded and hardened?"

The second writer was, of course, answering a point which he thought had been made, not the point which was made.

The free appeal to Scripture must for the same reason remain an essential element in Brethren witness. We have already touched on the inter-relation between Scripture and tradition. Tradition, to bolster its own pretences, will always point to the foolishnesses and fanaticisms of private interpretation: but in doing so it overlooks the absolute necessity of paying this price, if spiritual and intellectual freedom is to be preserved. The absurd fetters which an extreme obscurantism can impose on the minds of a few men – and, be it said, on the free working of the Holy Spirit within those men's minds – are a necessary price to pay, to deliver all men from the more subtle but more absolute despotism of the officially prescribed teaching. Where the Bible remains free and accessible to all men, fanaticisms and foolishnesses will inevitably arise among a few: but only then will there be present in the Church the perpetual ferment of spiritual and intellectual liberty, for this ferment is a product of that solvent which entered history through the prophets, and finally in the person of Christ and the birth pangs of the Church; and of that divine ferment the Bible has been and will remain the carrier. This belief is not superstition: it derives from the very nature of the events which gave rise to the Bible. The Scriptures were born out of divine revolution in the affairs and lives of men, and for that reason they will always remain the source of divine revolution in the human spirit.

Ironically, the very looseness of the independent structure prevents the independents' ideals being fully developed among themselves. As has been suggested in Chapter 13, the full release of the gifts and powers of every member of the Body of Christ, and many of the most effective expressions of Christian devotion in ministration to the desperate material and spiritual needs of mankind are normally beyond the scope of an unorganized collection of independent congregations. So too are some important expressions of visible Christian unity, and (some would add, though less convincingly) so has in the past been the safeguarding of the historic faith. Yet – and this cannot be emphasized too strongly – this does not mean that independent energies can be superseded. They will always be at the grass roots, where they are a source of life to the Church. Just because every organization, including each of those structures which are the necessary carriers of much of the Church's mission, is inevitably subject to ossification or decay by its very nature as an organization, so the continually renewing energies of independents are essential feeders of life to the Church's witness. Particularly is this the case with the independent type of evangelism – and it is no accident that such a high proportion of this type of worker is found in fellowship with Brethren-type churches. The established churches are apt to look with hostility on such movements: but in the perspective of history such an attitude is tragically little-minded and foolish, for they are despising the first sources of their own renewal.

This place in the structure of the Church, means that Brethren-type congregations can never look for considerable honour or praise. They will inevitably see abilities which they have nurtured taken up by structures which seem to offer greater opportunity for development and full self-expression. Yet this very humility is their glory, and they should rejoice in this proving of their essential function within the ongoing life of the Universal Church. When those other structures have succumbed to their innate mortality, there will still be there, at the grass roots, congregations of the independent type, the fruits of the continuous activity of the Spirit of God.

Brethren-type churches have always been an irritant, even within the evangelical section of the churches. Time and again their gifts and energies are used by their fellows, only to be disclaimed with embarrassment when those fellow-sympathizers attain a degree of "respectability." No one with experience of inter-denominational evangelicalism will not have experienced this, or the unreasoning prejudice with which such churches are sometimes regarded by many who are closest to them. It is not unknown for societies of unimpeachable evangelicalism to draw freely from the gifts of independent communities, and yet to regard with extreme disfavour any of their own workers who appear to be modelling their mission practices on "Brethren lines." (This is rather difficult for the workers, for in nine cases out of ten the so-called "Brethren lines" are merely the natural means by which spontaneous forms of Christian activity express themselves.)

Some of this prejudice is probably the independents' own fault, the result of the occasional foolishnesses which seem inevitable within any association which allows wide freedom to the least gifted of its members (yet do not the most authoritarian organizations have their own foolishnesses?*). Brethren's very refusal to take a distinguishing name –though deriving from the excellent motive of not wishing to create unnecessary barriers between themselves and their brethren in Christ – assists this misunderstanding, and often gives them an un-looked-for "secret society" aura. Yet the real reasons for this prejudice may be more instinctive, and the deeper for that. These reasons lie in the consciousness that there is embedded in Brethren ideals a radicalism and a freedom that, ultimately, cannot be content with the restrictions of any organization, and that remain as a perpetual challenge and threat to any ideal which embraces less than complete freedom under God.

The short history of Brethren themselves contains within it the lessons they need for the future. They face a living contradiction within themselves; how to harness the gifts which God gives them, and at the same time to retain the freedom which is God's gift, in them, to the Church. The very statement of that dilemma shows that it is a basic dilemma of the whole Christian Church. Perhaps in this realization, then, lies the clue to

* As, for example, in Ian Henderson's *Power Without Glory* (1967), p. 173.

the part which they are called to play in the unfolding story of that Church against which the gates of Hell shall not prevail. Shall the eye say to the hand, "I have no need of you," or the head to the feet, "I have no need of you"? We need the gifts of every member of the Body of Christ. Brethren ask only that their own gifts should be understood, that they too may contribute to the growth and building up in love of that one Body of which all are members.

What has been said so far may seem to some enthusiasts to be but a feeble apology for the existence of the independent congregations. Yet, even at this level, it is plain that the place of the independent congregation expressing the Brethren's "four freedoms" is a vital one within the Church of God, and one which can be despised or ignored by the institutionalized bodies only to their own hurt.

The case for the independent does not rest there. Ecumenical publicity is directed with considerable skill at every movement or pronouncement from within the great "imperialist" churches which hints at an enlarged tolerance: and sometimes with hardly less skill at denigrating the "sectarian" independent groups. Yet the fact remains that when a question of local united action arises which calls for the sharing of the basic and deepest Christian fellowships of evangelism, prayer and the Lord's Supper, it is the independent "sectary" who is often found with his doors and heart open to his fellow Christian believer. It is such groups which can act in independence of ecclesiastical politics, and the pressures of hierarchical discipline.

The truly independent congregation is not concerned with denomination, or with ecclesiastical politics, for it is free to recognize every congregation (whatever its label or church affiliation) as a fellow "household church"* of the one great Church of Christ, when it sees in that congregation the evidences of the presence of Christ. To the independent, the long and wearisome debates over orders and their validity are pointless and irrelevant – for he knows the freedom to welcome and encourage every gift which God has been pleased to give to a fellow Christian. He asks, with John Wesley, "My only question at present is this, 'Is thine heart right, as my heart is with thy heart?'"

The duty of every congregation of independent Brethren today is written in their calling. Within their churches, there must be a revived and purified concern for the liberating Word of God, to make the Scriptures freshly alive in the context of today, as they were to their first readers. From within that new understanding their members will find awaiting them new expressions of devotedness to Christ, to be worked out within the ordinary world of which they are daily a part. Their churches are to take seriously the truth of the crown rights of the Redeemer, marking

* See H. L. Ellison *The Household Church* (1963).

the gifts and calling of each member of the congregation, trying to understand the breadth of the range of those gifts, and seeking under the guidance of wise and perceptive local leaders to release the full potential of every member, in an effective partnership of witness and service – a release, be it said, which can only be achieved if other local congregations (without distinction of denomination) are included in their perspective. Towards the whole professing Church, they bear the responsibility of the gifts of freedom and independence which God has given them. If national and world organizations are closed to them because of the independence of each of their congregations, and the absence of any organ of federation, then it is the more their duty to ensure at the local level that the vitally important understandings which God has given them should be made plain to all men. That can only be achieved by their entering into every form of fellowship and discussion which is open to them, without compromising their integrity and freedom. If this course seems dangerous, is not their Lord Himself with them, in a path to which He has called them?

The shadows of the past lie too often upon Brethren, and too often the shadows remain long after the vigour of the past has been forgotten. There are also other voices calling them, many of them of brothers in Christ with whom they have practically everything in common but their own especial calling: these voices would commit them to courses of action which would obscure that special calling which is theirs. Ultimately, they can be satisfied with nothing less than the full breadth of the fellowship of Christ. May it be given to them that their understanding of the breadth of that fellowship is not narrower than the fellowship of Christ Himself.

APPENDICES

GROVES'S LETTER TO DARBY

Milford Haven,
March 10th, 1836

My Dear D——,

As the stormy weather threatens a little delay, I am not willing to leave England without a few words in reply to your notes, and a short explanation of some other points that interest me. I have ever regretted having so few opportunities of seeing and conversing with you since my return to England, and thereby explaining many things that might have allowed us to depart on the whole more happily than now, yet I wish you to feel assured that nothing has estranged my heart from you, or lowered my confidence in your being still animated by the same enlarged and generous purposes that once so won and riveted me; and though I feel you have departed from those principles by which you once hoped to have effected them, and are in principle returning to the city from whence you departed, still my soul so reposes in the truth of your heart to God that I feel it needs but a step or two more to advance and you will see all the evils of the systems from which you profess to be separated, to spring up among yourselves. You will not discover this so much from the workings of your own soul, as by the spirit of those who have been nurtured up from the beginning, in the system they are taught to feel the only tolerable one; that not having been led like you, and some of those earliest connected with you, through deep experimental suffering and sorrow, they are little acquainted with the real truth that may exist amidst inconceivable darkness: there will be little pity and little sympathy with such, and your union daily becoming one of doctrine and opinion more than life and love, your government will become – unseen perhaps, and unexpressed, yet – one wherein, overwhelmingly, is felt the authority of *men*; you will be known more by what you witness *against* than what you witness for, and practically this will prove that you witness against all but yourselves, as certainly as the Walkerites or Glassites: your Shibboleth may be different, but it will be as *real*. It has been asserted, as I found from your dear brother W— and others, that I have changed my principles: all I can say is, that as far as I know what those principles were, in which I gloried on first discovering them in the word of God, I now glory in them ten times more since I have experienced their applicability to all the various and perplexing circumstances of the present state of the Church; allowing you to give every individual, and collection of individuals, the standing *God* gives them, without identifying yourselves with any of their evils. I ever understood our principle of union to be the possession of the common life or common blood of the family of God (for the life is in the blood); these were our early thoughts, and are my most matured ones. The transition your little bodies have undergone, in no longer standing forth the witnesses for the glorious and simple *truth*, so much as standing forth witnesses against all that they judge error, have lowered them in my apprehension from heaven to earth in their position of witnesses. What I mean is this, that then, all our thoughts were conversant about how we might *ourselves* most effectually manifest forth that life we had received by Jesus (knowing that that alone could be as the Shepherd's voice to the living children), and where we might find that life in others; and when we were persuaded we had found it, bidding them, on the Divine claim of this common life, (whether their thoughts on other matters were narrow or enlarged), to come and share with us, in the fellowship of the common Spirit, in the worship of our common head; and as Christ had received them so would we to the glory of God the Father; and further, that we were free, within the limits of the truth, to share with them in *part*, though we could not in *all*, their services. In fact, as we received them for the life, we would not *reject* them for their systems, or refuse to recognize any *part* of their systems, because we disallowed much. Trusting, that if this inter-communion could be established, to effect all we desire, by being upheld by God in walking in the light, as the Christ-like means of witnessing against any dark that might be in them, according to the rule of the Lord; John 3: 19: "This is the condemnation, that light is come into the world, and men loved darkness rather than light because their deeds were evil, neither will they come to the light lest their deeds should be reproved." A more difficult ministry of witness, than a preaching one of words, or separating one of persons, yet possessing a *much more* mighty power over the hearts of others, and a much more influential one in blessing; and which, dear brother, I know no heart more ready to acknowledge than your own. The moment the witnessing for the common life as our *bond* gives place to a witnessing *against* errors by separation of persons and preaching (errors allowably compatible with the common life), every individual, or society of individuals, first comes before the mind as those who might need witnessing against, and all their conduct and principles have first to be examined and approved before they can be received; and the position which this occupying the seat of judgment will place you in will be this: the most narrow-minded and bigoted will rule, because his conscience cannot and will not give way, and therefore the more enlarged heart must yield. It is into this position, dear D——, I feel some little flocks are fast tending, if they have not already attained it, making *light* not *life* the measure of communion. But I am told by our beloved brethren, C. and H., that if I give up this position of witnessing *against evil* in this PECULIAR WAY OF SEPARATION from the systems in which any *measure* of it is mixed up, I make our position one of simple unpardonable schism, because we might join some of the many other systems. I cannot be supposed, of course, to know fully *their* grounds of acting, but I thought I knew *yours*, at least your *original* ones. Was not the principle we laid down as to separation from all existing bodies at the outset, this: that we felt ourselves bound to separate from all individuals and systems, *so far* as they required us to do what our consciences would not allow, or restrained us from doing what our consciences required, and no further? and were we not as free to join and act with any individual, or body of individuals, as they were free *not* to require us to do what our consciences did *not* allow, or prevent our doing what they did? and in this freedom did we not feel brethren should *not* force liberty on those who were bound, nor withhold freedom from those who were free?

Did we not feel constrained to follow the apostolic rule of *not judging other men's consciences*, as to liberty, by our own; remembering it is written, "Let *not* him that eateth despise him that eateth not; and let not him which eateth not, judge him that eateth; seeing that God hath received" both the one and the other? Now it is one of these two grounds; their preventing me from, or demanding from me, other than the Lord demands, that divides me in a *measure* from every system; as my *own proper* duty to God, rather than as witnessing against THEIR evils. As any system is in its provision narrower or wider than the truth, I either stop short, or go beyond its provisions, but I would INFINITELY RATHER BEAR *with all their evils*, than SEPARATE from THEIR GOOD. These were the *then* principles of our separation and intercommunion; we had resolved never to try to *get men to act* in UNIFORMITY *further than* they FELT IN UNIFORMITY; neither by frowns, nor smiles; and this for one simple reason, that we saw no authority given us from God thus to act; nor did our experience lead us to feel it the best means at all of promoting their blessing or our common aim of a *perfect spiritual uniformity* of judgment; whilst to ourselves it afforded a *ready* OUTLET to the PROPENSITIES of the FLESH, under the appearance of spiritual authority and zeal for the truth. But in all these matters, we desired that our way might be bright as the light, and our words drop noiselessly as the dew, and if, at the last, they remained "otherwise minded," we would seek of God, that even He should reveal it unto them. There is something at present so like building what you destroyed; as if when weak you can be liberal and large, but when helpen with a little strength, the *true* spirit of sectarianism begins to bud; that being *"one of us,"* has become a stronger bond than oneness in the power of the life of God in the soul. I know it is said (dear Lady Powerscourt told me so), that so long as any terms were kept with the Church of England, by mixing up in *any* measure with their ministrations, when there was nothing to offend your conscience, they bore your testimony most patiently, but after your entire rejection of them, they pursued you with undeviating resentment, and this was brought to prove that the then position was wrong, and the present right. But all I see in this is, that whilst you occupied the place of only witnessing against those things which the divine life within themselves recognized as evil, and separating from them ONLY SO FAR as they separated from Christ, you established them as judges of themselves, and of themselves they were condemned; and at the same time you conciliated their heavenly affections, by allowing all that really was of the Lord, and sharing in it, though the system itself in which you found these golden grains, you could not away with. But the moment your position and your language implied a perfect separation, alike from the evil and the good, and a rejection of them, in consequence of their system, without discrimination, you no longer had their consciences with you, but they felt that though only a brother in a Father's house, you exercised more than a Father's power, without a Father's heart of mercy, and they, therefore, appealed from you to your common Head, both in behalf of themselves and their systems. There is no truth more established in my own mind than this: that to occupy the position of the maximum of power, in witnessing to the consciences of others, you must stand before their unbiassed judgment as evidently *wishing* to allow in them *more* than their own consciences allow, rather than less, proving that your heart of love is more alive to find a covering for faults, than your eagle eye of light to discover them. I send you this letter as we were the first to act on these principles, rather than to H— and C—, whose faith and love I do so truly desire to follow. They have written to me two very long and kind letters, which I purpose more effectually and fully to answer, by meeting the positions contained in them, in a little tract, which I hope to prepare on the voyage, and finally, to publish.

I particularly regret not meeting you at Bristol, as I had much to say to you relative to Rhenius, and other things connected with India, for my heart would naturally seek sympathy and fellowship with you and those dear brethren with whom I have no dividing thoughts relative to the great bearings of truth, or the truths themselves, in which lie the power and peace of the Gospel, – neither in the objects or principles of ministry do I differ; – my difference with you is only as to the manner in which you maintain your position of witnessing for the good against the evil. I feel no one ever expects me, when an acknowledged *visitor* in the house of another, to be answerable for the ordering of that house, or as thereby *approving* it – they would naturally come to the house in which I had control, and where the acts were looked upon as *mine*, to form such a judgment; and even in such a case, if I was but *one* among many in the government, no honest mind would make *me* responsible for faults, against which, in my place and according to my power, I protested; because I submitted to those acts in others, rather than forego a *greater* good, or incur a greater evil. If it is said man cannot discriminate, nor feel the *force* of my witness, unless I separate, not by heart and life, but by contiguity of person, altogether from all kinds of false systems, my answer is, that He, whose place it is to judge, and to whom we are called to approve our hearts, can, and to *Him*, in this matter, I am content to stand or fall.

Some will not have me hold communion with the Scotts, because their views are not satisfactory about the Lord's Supper; others with you, because of your views about baptism; others with the Church of England, because of her thoughts about ministry. On my principles, I receive them all; but on the principle of witnessing against evil, I should reject them all. I feel them all, in their several particulars, sinning against the mind and heart of Christ, and letting in, in principle, the most tremendous disorders, and it is not for me to measure the comparative sin of one kind of disobedience against another. I make use of my fellowship in the Spirit, to enjoy the common life together, and witness for that, as an opportunity to set before them those little particulars into which, notwithstanding all their grace and faithfulness, their godliness and honesty – they have fallen. Nor shall I ever feel separation from the good for the sake of the evil, to be my way of witnessing against it, till I see infinitely clearer than I do now, that it is *God's*. I naturally unite fixedly with those in whom I see and feel most of the life and power of God. But I am as free to visit other churches, where I see much of disorder, as to visit the houses of my friends, though they govern them not as I could wish; and, as I have said, I should feel it equally unreasonable and unkind, for any brother to judge me for it, though I leave him in perfect liberty to judge himself. You must not, however, dear brother, think, from anything I have said, that I shall not write freely and fully to you, relative to things in India, feeling assured in my own heart, that your enlarged and generous spirit, so richly taught of the Lord, will one day burst again those bands which narrower minds than yours have encircled you with, and come forth again, rather anxious to advance ALL the living members of the living Head into the stature of men, than to be encircled by any little bodies, however numerous, that own you for their founder. I honour, love, and respect your position in the Church of God; but the deep conviction I have that your spiritual power was incalculably greater when you walked in the midst of the various congregations of the Lord's people, manifesting forth the life and the power of the gospel, than now, is such that I cannot but write the above as a proof of my love and confidence that your mind is above considering who these remarks came from, rather than what truth there may be in them.

Yours very affectionately in the gospel,
(*Signed*) A. N. GROVES.

B. W. NEWTON'S "STATEMENT AND ACKNOWLEDGMENT RESPECTING CERTAIN DOCTRINAL ERRORS"

In the year 1835, it will be recollected by many that various false doctrines which had been introduced by Mr. Irving and others, were becoming widely disseminated amongst Christians.

Those who were concerned in the controversy with Irvingism, will remember that that doctrine attributed to Christ a sinful humanity, and set aside the union of the two natures – Divine and human – in His one Person. The following quotation from a paper of mine, published in 1835, written in confutation, will explain the nature of their doctrines. "If Christ had been (as Mr. Irving wrote) 'troubled by every evil disposition which inhereth in the fallen manhood,' and if He could have said, like the Believer, 'not I, but sin that tempteth me in my flesh,' how was not Christ personally a sinner? There are only two ways in which this question can be answered by those who maintain these doctrines. They must either deny that the evil propensity is *in itself sin*; or, consider the human nature of the Lord as something distinct from Himself *personally*. The last is, very plainly, the doctrine maintained in the 'Treatise on the Human Nature' (Mr. Irving's). I suppose a hundred quotations might be made therefrom, in which the name Christ is given not to Jesus, as being God and man in one person, but to the Word, acting in and surrounded by the flesh as by a garment. The whole purport of the book appears to be this: to represent the Incarnation as the Imprisonment, so to speak, of the Eternal Word in sinful flesh, against which He had continually to struggle, just as the Holy Spirit in us is *separate* from, and struggles against our evil nature. The flesh of our Lord, to use Mr. Irving's illustration, stood to Him in the same relation as a pit to the person who is in it, or as a garment to the person whom it covers, and thus the true doctrine of the Incarnation is denied." ("Doctrines of the Church in Newman Street, considered," in the *Christian Witness*, 1st edition, vol. II, p. 118.)

In order to meet the statements of Irvingism, it was argued, that the true doctrine of the incarnation is: that Christ is God and man in one Person; that all His actions were not those of God *simply*, nor of man *simply*; but of God and man united in one Person never to be divided; and that if holiness pertained to the Eternal Word, holiness equally pertained to that nature which He had taken into everlasting union with Himself.

To this it was objected, that we, in a sense, deified the humanity of Jesus, and virtually denied that He was really man. Many passages were quoted by the defenders of Mr. Irving's doctrine, to prove that Jesus was not only man, but man in weakness, that He had a mortal body unlike to that which Adam first had in Paradise; and they added that the cause of His body being mortal was that sin (as they said) inhered in it.

Many minds were deceived by these statements. They had been so accustomed to regard the body of the Lord Jesus, as resembling that which Adam had before he sinned in Paradise, that when they began to think of the Lord Jesus as "in the likeness of sinful flesh," they were so interested by what they felt to be a new and important branch of doctrine, and it seemed to open to their minds so much of the Scripture which they had not before considered, that many were carried away into great excesses of both thought and statement, – and were disposed to palliate, if not to receive, the evil conclusion above referred to, viz., that the cause of His body being mortal was that sin inhered in it.

In order to meet this, it was felt to be a solemn duty to endeavour to own, as far as possible, the truth that might be mingled with the error, and to seek to disentangle it from its evil connections. It was on this account that I wrote a preface, and made some additions to the paper above referred to; and in an attempt to meet, as far as possible, the minds of others, I have gone too far, and myself transgressed by overstepping the bounds of truth.

In allowing that the Lord Jesus had a body different from that of Adam in Paradise, I was right. I was right, also, in saying that inherent corruption is not the originating cause of mortality, but the one sin of Adam; "By one man sin entered into the world, and death by sin"; – I was right also in stating that the Lord Jesus partook of certain consequences of Adam's sin, of which the being possessed of a mortal body was one.

It was this that first introduced Rom. v. into the controversy, as showing that death of the body resulted from that which one man had done; and if due care had been taken to discriminate between the mode in which the consequences of Adam's transgressions reached mankind through federal headship, and the manner in which the Lord Jesus took certain of those consequences upon Himself, but not through federal headship, the error which I now have to confess would have been avoided.

If I had watched this I should have carefully avoided the referring that part of the fifth of Romans to the Lord Jesus, and I should have stated that His connection with these consequences, was in virtue of His having been made of a woman, and thus having brought Himself into association with a race on whom these penalties were resting. In other words, that when the

Eternal Word became flesh, He thereby voluntarily placed Himself in association with those on whom certain penalties, such as loss of Paradise, – hunger, – thirst, – exhaustion, – and pain had come, as consequences of the fall; – and that in virtue of such association He partook of those consequences – even all the consequences in which He could share, unconnected with personal sin.

I have invariably used the truth of His being the Son and the fact of His Divine conception, as the reason of His necessary immunity from all taint, even though born of a woman – and also as the reason of His freedom from all penalties that would, if they attached, imply personal sin, – and of His personal title (whensoever He might, according to the will of the Father, please to assert it) to immunity from all penalties of any kind whatsoever; – but I ought never to have connected Him with Adam as a federal Head; – He – being what He essentially was – was free from this, though partaking of all the common properties and infirmities of man's nature, sin only excepted.

My error in this resulted in my holding that the Lord Jesus, while perfectly free from all, even the slightest taint of sin, either original or actual, yet was under Adam, as a federal head, and thus was exposed by His position to the imputation of Adam's guilt, as it taught respecting mankind in the fifth of Romans. I saw it to be distinctly revealed that the Lord was subject to hunger, thirst, weariness, sorrow, etc., which things we know are consequences of the fall; and I erred in attributing His participation in these afflictions to a *federal* relationship to Adam.

Recent circumstances having necessitated a careful review of the whole subject, I have been led, as I above stated, to see that I was distinctly in error in holding that the Lord Jesus came by birth under any imputation of guilt or the consequences of such imputation. I see that results altogether contrary to Christian doctrine are involved in, and may fairly be deduced from this error, which I now desire explicitly to renounce, and I desire to acknowledge my error in having thus held and taught on this subject; and I hereby withdraw all statements of mine, whether in print or in any other form, in which *this error, or any of its fruits* may be found.

The doctrine in question was, I believe, first stated by me in a part of the tract above referred to against Irvingism, entitled, "Doctrines of the Church in Newman Street, considered," published in 1835, which tract was inserted in a second edition of the *Christian Witness*, in 1837 or 1838. I request that this may be considered as a withdrawal of the erroneous parts of the above-mentioned Paper, and I also desire, that any statements of mine, whether in notes or Lectures taken by others, or in any communications of my own, in which this doctrine occurs, may now be considered as withdrawn, – that they may not be regarded as now containing my sentiments, and they may no longer be circulated.

With regard to the two Tracts recently published by myself on "The Sufferings of Christ," I also request that they may be withdrawn for reconsideration.

In acknowledging the before-mentioned error, I wish explicitly to state that I do not ascribe any of Christ's living experiences to the imputation of Adam's guilt, nor ought I to have made any statements or used any words which did ascribe *any* of His sufferings to anything imputed to Him; nor yet that He had by keeping the law or by anything else to deliver Himself from such imputation or its consequences. Every such deduction must necessarily fall with the wrong doctrine on which it is based.

I do not now enter into a statement of the limitations by which this doctrine was guarded in my own mind and in my teaching: – I had supposed that the limitations which I had employed were sufficient to prevent the deductions which have been recently drawn, – and that, in many cases legitimately: – deductions, which I abhor as thoroughly as those can be by whom they have been drawn; – I trust that I can appeal to any of my writings in which the person and sacrifice of the Lord Jesus are spoken of, as well as to persons who have known me as a Christian or a teacher, for proof that deductions which go to involve the fitness of the Lord Jesus for His blessed work of atonement, could never have been contemplated by me; and that they are directly opposed to and contrasted with, the whole current of my teaching and aim and thoughts.

I wish to state distinctly, that I hold the perfectness of Christ's person and the completeness of His one sacrifice, to be truths so solemnly unquestionable, that every doctrine and opinion must be subordinated to, and guided by these leading and foundation truths; and every statement of mine on the relations of Christ, whether in my recent tracts, which I have now withdrawn, or in any other place, I wish to subject entirely to these primary truths: – I desire that every statement with regard to such subordinate truth should be strictly guarded with the limitations which the aforementioned foundation truths supply.

It is not my desire to extend the present remarks. I would merely state that I do distinctly hold, that there never was anything in the personal, relative, or dispensational positions of Christ, which could have prevented His being at any one moment of His life, the perfect and unblemished sacrifice, and that not one suffering, whencesoever originating, ever came upon Him, except because of and for the sake of *others*.

I would not wish it to be supposed that what I have now said, is intended to extenuate the error which I have confessed. – I desire to acknowledge it fully, and to acknowledge it as sin; it is my desire thus to confess it before God and His Church; and I desire that this may be considered as an expression of my deep and unfeigned grief and sorrow especially by those who may have been grieved or injured by the false statement, or by any consequences thence resulting. I trust that the Lord will not only pardon, but will graciously counteract any evil effects which may have arisen to any therefrom.

Plymouth, November 26th, 1847.   B. W. NEWTON.

THE LETTER OF THE TEN

(NOTE. The passages italicized by those who objected to this document
are reproduced here in italics also.)

DEAR BRETHREN,

Our brother, Mr. George Alexander, having printed and
circulated a statement expressive of his reasons for withdrawing from
visible fellowship with us at the table of the Lord: and these reasons being
grounded on the fact that those who labour among you have not complied
with his request relative to the judging of certain errors which have been
taught at Plymouth; it becomes needful that those of us who have incurred
any responsibility in this matter should lay before you a brief explanation
of the way in which we have acted.

And first, it may be well to mention, that we had no intimation whatever of our brother's intention to act as he has done, nor any knowledge of
his intention to circulate any letter, until it was put into our hands in print.

Some weeks ago, he expressed his determination to bring his views
before a meeting of the body, and he was told that he was quite at liberty
to do so. He afterwards declared that he would waive this, but never inti-
mated, in the slightest way, his intention to act as he has done without first
affording the church an opportunity of hearing his reasons for separation.
Under these circumstances, we feel it of the deepest importance, for relieving the disquietude of mind naturally occasioned by our brother's letter,
explicitly to state that the views relative to the person of our blessed Lord,
held by those who for sixteen years have been occupied in teaching the
word among you, *are unchanged*.

The truths relative to the divinity of His person – the sinlessness of His
nature – and the perfection of His sacrifice, which have been taught both in
public teaching and in writing for these many years past, are, through the
grace of God, those which we still maintain. We feel it most important
to make this avowal, inasmuch as the letter referred to is calculated, we
trust unintentionally, to convey a different impression to the minds of such
as cherish a godly jealousy for the faith once delivered to the saints.

We add, for the further satisfaction of any who may have had their
minds disturbed, that we utterly disclaim the assertion that the blessed Son
of God was involved in the guilt of the first Adam; or that He was born
under the curse of the broken law, because of His connection with Israel.
We hold Him to have been always the Holy One of God, in whom the

Father was ever well pleased. We know of no curse which the Saviour bore, except that which he endured as the surety for sinners – according to that Scripture, "He was made a curse for us." We utterly reject the thought of His ever having had the experiences of an unconverted person; but maintain that while He suffered *outwardly* the trials connected with His being a man and an Israelite – still in His feelings and experiences, as well as in His external character, He was entirely "separate from sinners."

We now proceed to state the grounds on which we have felt a difficulty in complying with the request of our brother, Mr. Alexander, that we should formally investigate and give judgment on certain errors which have been taught among Christians meeting at Plymouth.

1st. We considered from the beginning that it would not be for the comfort or edification of the saints here – nor for the glory of God – that we, in Bristol, should get entangled in the controversy connected with the doctrines referred to. We do not feel that, because errors may be taught at Plymouth or elsewere, therefore we, as a body, are bound to investigate them.

2nd. The practical reason alleged why we should enter upon the investigation of certain tracts issued at Plymouth was, that thus we might be able to know how to act with reference to those who might visit us from thence, or who are supposed to be adherents of the author of the said publications. In reply to this, we have to state, that the views of the writer alluded to could only be *fairly learned* from the examination of his own acknowledged writings. We did not feel that we should be warranted in taking our impression of the views actually held by him from any other source than from some treatise written by himself and professedly explanatory of the doctrines advocated. Now there has been such variableness in the views held by the writer in question, that it is difficult to ascertain what he would now acknowledge as his.

3rd. In regard to these writings, Christian brethren, hitherto of unblemished reputation for soundness in the faith, have come to different conclusions as to the actual amount of error contained in them. The tracts some of us knew to be written in such an ambiguous style, that we greatly shrunk from the responsibility of giving any formal judgment on the matter.

4th. As approved brethren, in different places, have come to such different conclusions in reference to the amount of error contained in these tracts, we could neither desire nor expect that the saints here would be satisfied with the decision of one or two leading brethren. Those who felt desirous to satisfy their own minds, would naturally be led to wish to peruse the writings for themselves. For this, many among us have no leisure time; many would not be able to understand what the tracts contained, because of the mode of expression employed; and the result, there is much reason to fear, would be such perverse disputations and strifes of words, as minister questions rather than godly edifying.

5th. Even some of those who now condemn the tracts as containing doctrine essentially unsound, did not so understand them on the first perusal. Those of us who were specially requested to investigate and judge the errors contained in them, felt that, under such circumstances, there was but little probability of our coming to unity of judgment touching the nature of the doctrines therein embodied.

6th. *Even supposing that those who inquired into the matter had come to the same conclusion, touching the amount of positive error therein contained, this would not have guided us in our decision respecting individuals coming from Plymouth. For supposing the author of the tracts were fundamentally heretical, this would not warrant us in rejecting those who came from under his teaching, until we were satisfied that they had understood and imbibed views essentially subversive of foundation truth*; especially as those meeting at Ebrington-street, Plymouth, last January, put forth a statement, disclaiming the errors charged against the tracts.

7th. The requirements that we should investigate and judge Mr. Newton's tracts, appeared to some of us like the introduction of a fresh test of communion. It was demanded of us that, in addition to a sound confession and a corresponding walk, we should, as a body, come to a formal decision about what many of us might be quite unable to understand.

8th. We remembered the word of the Lord, that "the beginning of strife is as the letting out of water." We were well aware that the great body of believers amongst us were in happy ignorance of the Plymouth controversy, and we did not feel it well to be considered as identifying ourselves with either party. We judge that this controversy had been so carried on as to cause the truth to be evil spoken of; and we do not desire to be considered as identifying ourselves with that which has caused the opposer to reproach the way of the Lord. At the same time we wish distinctly to be understood that we would seek to maintain fellowship with all believers, and consider ourselves as particularly associated with those who meet as we do, simply in the name of the Lord Jesus.

9th. We felt that the compliance with Mr. Alexander's request would be the introduction of an evil precedent. *If a brother has a right to demand our examining a work of fifty pages, he may require our investigating error said to be contained in one of much larger dimensions; so that all our time might be wasted in the examination of other people's errors, instead of more important service.*

It only remains to notice the three reasons specially assigned by Mr. Alexander in justification of his course of action. To the first, viz., "that by our not judging this matter, many of the Lord's people will be excluded from communion with us" – we reply, that unless our brethren can prove, either that error is held and taught amongst us, or *that individuals are received into communion who ought not to be admitted, they can have no scriptural warrant for withdrawing from our fellowship.* We would affectionately entreat such brethren as may be disposed to withdraw from communion for the reason assigned, to consider that, except they can prove allowed evil in life or doctrine, they cannot, without violating the principles on which we meet, treat us as if we had renounced the faith of the Gospel.

In reply to the second reason, viz., "that persons may be received from Plymouth holding evil doctrines" – we are happy in being able to state, that ever since the matter was agitated, we have maintained that persons coming from thence – if suspected of any error – *would be liable to be examined on the point*; that in the case of one individual who had fallen under the suspicion of certain brethren amongst us, not only was there private intercourse with him relative to his views, as soon as it was known that he was objected to, but the individual referred to – known to some of us for several years as a consistent Christian – actually came to a meeting of labouring brethren for the very purpose that any question might be asked him by any brother who should have any difficulty on his mind. Mr. Alexander himself was the principal party in declining the presence of the brother referred to, on that occasion, such inquiry being no longer demanded, inasmuch as the difficulties relative to the views of the individual in question, had been removed by private intercourse. We leave Alexander to reconcile this fact, which he cannot have forgotten, with the assertion contained under his second special reason for withdrawing.

In regard to the third ground alleged by Mr. Alexander, viz., that by not judging the matter, we lie under the suspicion of supporting false doctrine, we have only to refer to the statement already made at the commencement of this paper.

In conclusion, we would seek to impress upon all present the evil of treating the subject of our Lord's humanity as a matter of speculative or angry controversy. One of those who have been ministering among you from the beginning, feels it a matter of deep thankfulness to God, that so long ago as in the year 1835,* he committed to writing, and subsequently printed, what he had learned from the Scriptures of truth relative to the meaning of that inspired declaration, "The Word was made flesh.' He would affectionately refer any whose minds may be now disquieted, to what he then wrote, and was afterwards led to publish. If there be heresy in the simple statements contained in the letters alluded to, let it be pointed out; if not, let all who are interested in the matter know that we continue unto the present day, "speaking the same things."   (Signed)

Henry Craik	Edmund Feltham
George Müller	John Withy
Jacob Henry Hale	Samuel Butler
Charles Brown	John Meredith
Elijah Stanley	Robert Aitchison

The above paper was read at meetings of brethren at Bethesda Chapel, on Thursday, June 29th, and on Monday, July 3rd, 1848.

* *Pastoral Letters* by H. Craik.

THE TOTTENHAM STATEMENT

SPECIAL circumstances having occurred in connexion with Christians, who, from time to time, are or may be, making application to be received as in communion at the Lord's Table, we desire to make known our individual convictions and collective judgment as to the path which we believe to be well-pleasing to the Lord in this matter; and in which we desire to walk.

1. We find our centre of union with each other, and with all saints, in Christ, as *one in Him*, and our power of fellowship by the Holy Ghost.

2. We therefore desire to receive to the Lord's Table those whom he has received; time being allowed for confidence to be established in our minds that those whom we receive are indeed the Lord's, and opportunity afforded for inquiring into and clearing away any imputation or occasion of scandal in any so applying.

3. We welcome to the table, on individual grounds, each saint, not because he or she is a member of this or that gathering or denomination of Christians nor because they are followers of any particular leader, but on such testimony as commends itself to us as being sufficient.

4. We distinctly refuse to be parties to any exclusion of those who, we are satisfied, are believers – except on grounds personally applying to their individual faith and conduct.

Adopted by Brethren at Tottenham the 4th of March 1849.

CHRONOLOGICAL TABLE
OF THE FORMATIVE YEARS OF THE MOVEMENT

1793	Birth of J. L. Harris (13 Feb.).
1795	Birth of A. N. Groves (1 Feb.).
1800	Birth of J. N. Darby (18 Nov.).
1803	Birth of R. C. Chapman (4 Jan.).
1805	Birth of Henry Craik (8 Aug.).
	Birth of George Müller (27 Sept.).
1807	Birth of B. W. Newton (12 Dec.).
1815	Robert Gribble starts evangelization in N. Devon.
c.1816	The "Western Schism" of evangelical clergymen.
c.1822	Beginning of Groves's Bible studies.
1825	Groves's *Christian Devotedness*.
	Mr. and Mrs. Groves accepted for Bagdad by C.M.S.
	J. N. Darby ordained deacon.
	Müller's conversion in Halle.
1826	Craik joins Groves in Exeter.
	Groves's visits to Dublin begin.
1827	Groves's suggestion to Bellett on free celebration of Lord's Supper.
	F. W. Newman visits Dublin.
	Archbishop Magee's charge to the Irish clergy.
	Groves gives up his plans for ordination.
	Cronin's and Stokes's groups meeting in Dublin.
1828	Groves breaks with C.M.S.
	Darby's *On the Nature and Unity of the Church of Christ* (1st edn.).
	Groves's suggestion to Bellett on freedom of ministry.
	Craik moves to Teignmouth.
1829	Groves sails for Bagdad (12 June).
	Müller visits Teignmouth.
	Darby's group meets in Dublin (Nov.) with Cronin.
1830	Stokes's group joins Darby's group in Dublin. Church meets in Aungier Street, Dublin.
	Darby visits Oxford University (early summer) and meets Newton and others.
	Party leave Dublin for Bagdad.
	Müller settles in Teignmouth. Marries Mary Groves (1 Oct.).

Church under Leonard Strong meeting in Georgetown, British Guiana.

1831   Bulteel's Oxford sermon (6 Feb.).
(About this time) Foundation of Plymouth church.
Beginning of Irvingite manifestations in London (30 Apr.).
First Powerscourt Conference (Oct.).
J. L. Harris joins Plymouth church after resigning curacy.

1832   B. W. Newton vacates Exeter College fellowship on marriage (15 Mar.).
Müller and Craik visit Bristol (Mar.) and settle there (25 May).
Darby's clash with Archbishop Whateley.
Foundation of church at Bethesda, Bristol (13 Aug.).
(About this time) Henry Borlase resigns curacy and joins Plymouth church.
R. C. Chapman moves to Barnstaple.

1833   The Powerscourt controversy (Sept.).
(About this time) Wigram founds church in London.
Groves moves to India.

1834   First issue of *The Christian Witness* in Plymouth (Jan.).
Groves arrives in U.K. from India (Jan.).
Müller founds Scriptural Knowledge Institution (Feb.).
Torquay church founded under John Vivian.

1835   (About this time) Churches founded in Bath and Salcombe.
Beginning of "Beaconite" controversy among Quakers.
S. P. Tregelles joins Plymouth church.
Death of Henry Borlase (Nov.).
Müller announces plans for Orphan House (9 Dec.).

1836   Groves leaves for India with Bowden and Beer (1 Mar.).
Müller opens first Orphan House (11 Apr.).
Foundation of church in Westport (Ireland): Darby's clash with Archbishop le-Poer Trench.

1837   Foundation of church in Hereford.
(About this time) foundation of churches in Kendal and Stafford.
Darby's first visit to Geneva.

1838   (About this time) Bible and Tract Depot started in Plymouth.
W. H. Dorman leaves Independents at Islington (26 June).
Foundation of church in Tottenham.
Accessions from Methodist controversy in Yorkshire (Wm. Trotter).
Growth of controversy over prophetic teachings of Darby and Newton.

1839   Darby in Geneva.
1840   Gideon Chapel (Bristol) given up.
Ebrington Street Chapel built in Plymouth.

Darbyite dispute begins in Vaud and Geneva.

John Meyer leaves Switzerland for British Guiana.

1842   Jukes founds church in Hull.

Dissension in Vaud and Geneva.

1843   Müller leaves for Germany (9 Aug.–6 Mar. 1844). Church founded in Stuttgart.

1845   Darby leaves Switzerland for Plymouth (Mar.).

Dispute at Plymouth over Newton's control of the church.

Müller announces plans for building his own orphan homes. (Nov.).

1846   Plymouth dispute spreads to London.

Rawstorne Street, London, exclude Newton (Dec.).

1847   Disclosure of Newton's erroneous teachings (July).

Newton's *Statement and Acknowledgment Respecting Certain Doctrinal Errors* (26 Nov.).

1848   Ebrington Street disclaim the errors (10 Jan.).

The Bath meeting concerning the dispute. (May).

Darby announces his breach with Bethesda (May).

The Letter of the Ten (June).

Darby's circular excommunicating Bethesda (26 Aug.).

The "exclusive" churches separate from the independents.

1849   First of Müller's own-built orphan homes opened (Mar.).

Evangelical movement starts in Florence in association with Count Guicciardini.

1850   Imprisonment of Count Guicciardini in Florence (7 May).

1853   Death of A. N. Groves (20 May).

J. G. Deck moves to New Zealand.

1855   John Morley devotes himself to full-time Christian work.

(About this time) Beginnings in South Africa.

1858   Darby's articles in *The Bible Treasury* lead to controversy within "exclusives."

Guicciardini and Rossetti in Italy.

1859   Mid-century revival starts in Ireland (14 March).

J. G. M'Vicker joins with Brethren.

1860   Beginnings in Malaya.

1862   Wm. Lincoln accedes to movement.

T. J. Barnardo converted among Brethren.

1863   Opening of Merrion Hall, Dublin.

Spread of the independent Brethren in the wake of the revival.

George Brealey settles in Blackdown Hills.

1866   Death of Henry Craik (22 Jan.).

Beginning of Barnardo's social work.

1867   Foundation of church in Clapton, North London.

1868   Henry Moorhouse in Chicago, meets D. L. Moody.

1869   Settled work in Spain begins.

1870   (About this time) Donald Ross joins with Brethren.

1871   Richard W. Owens in New York.

1872   Opening of Fegan's first orphan home.
Start of *The Missionary Echo* (later *Echoes of Service*).

1875   Baedeker in Berlin.

1876   Gordon Forlong to New Zealand. Harrison Ord to Australia.

1877   Baedeker in Russia.

1879   Donald Ross in N. America. Alexander Marshall in Canada.
John Hambleton to Australia. C. H. Hinman to New Zealand.
Beginning of the first major division within the "exclusive" churches ("Kelly" division).

1881   F. S. Arnot sails for Africa.

1882   Death of J. N. Darby (29 Apr.).
Beginnings in Argentina.

1884   Many American and other "exclusives" break with the extremer British "exclusives" under J. B. Stoney ("Grant" division).

1886   Arnot reaches Katanga.

1888   W. G. Smith in Tokyo.

1889   Dan Crawford and Walter Fisher sail for Africa.

1890   Many Continental "exclusives" break with the extremer British "exclusives" under F. E. Raven and J. B. Stoney ("Lowe" division).

1892   "Needed Truth" secession from independents.

1898   Death of Müller (10 Mar.).

1902   Death of Chapman (12 June).

1905   Foundation of the Allianz Bibelschule in Berlin (from 1919 in Wiedenest, Rhineland).

1906   Death of William Kelly (27 Mar.).

1908   Remaining moderates leave extremer British "exclusives" in "Glanton" division.

BIBLIOGRAPHY

I. GENERAL SURVEYS OF THE MOVEMENT

ANON, "The Brethren Since 1870." cyclostyled 1966. From the moderate "exclusive" standpoint.

ANON ("An Irish Clergyman"), "The History and Doctrines of the Plymouth Brethren." Undated. An unpublished B.D. thesis of Trinity College, Dublin.

BAIRD, T., *Back to the Beginning*. 1919. An American sketch of Brethren missionary work.

BASS, CLARENCE B., *Backgrounds to Dispensationalism* (1960). A study of J. N. Darby's theology. Fails to understand the position of non-Darbyite Brethren.

BEATTIE, DAVID J., *Brethren, The Story of a Great Recovery* (1940). Traces the foundation of many independent congregations in Britain.

BROADBENT, E. H., *The Pilgrim Church* (1931). (Chaps 16 and 17). Brief summary, from the independent standpoint.

BRUCE, F. F., *Who are the Brethren?* A brief pamphlet introduction.

D.J.C. "The Lord's Testimony" (*c.* 1955). Pamphlet from an "exclusive" splinter group.

CARSON, J. C. L., *The Heresies of the Plymouth Brethren* (1877). Bitterly hostile. Unreliable.

COLLINGWOOD, WILLIAM, "The 'Brethren'; A Historical Sketch" (1899). Pamphlet. From the independent standpoint.

CROSKERY, T., *Plymouth Brethrenism: A Refutation of its Principles* (1879). Hostile, and largely irrelevant to the main movement.

DABNEY, R. L., "The Theology of the Plymouth Brethren." In *Discussions Evangelical and Theological* (1891, reprinted 1967). Largely irrelevant to the main movement.

ELLISON, H. L., *The Household Church; Apostolic Practice in a Modern Setting* (1963). Largely concerned with the practical running of a church but contains a brief survey of the movement from the independent standpoint.

GARDINER, A. J. (*Ed.*), *The Recovery and Maintenance of the Truth* (1951). A collection of documents on the various "exclusive" divisions, from the extreme "exclusive" standpoint.

IRONSIDE, H. A., *An Historical Sketch of the Brethren Movement* (1942). An objective account from an American pastor formerly with Brethren.

LANG, G. H., *The Churches of God* (1959, revision of 1928 edition). A practical and doctrinal dissertation, but containing much matter relating to the history of the movement.

LANG, G. H., *The Local Assembly*. 5th edn. 1955. A survey of the differences between independent and "exclusive" Brethren, from the independent standpoint.

MASELLI, DOMENICO, *Tra Risveglio e Millennio* (Turin, 1974). History of the early days of the Brethren movement in Italy.

MEARNS, *Christian Truth and Plymouthism* (1875). Hostile.

MILLER, ANDREW, *The Brethren: A Brief Sketch of their Origin, Progress and Testimony* (c. 1880). From the moderate "exclusive" standpoint.

MOEDE, GERALD F., "Assemblies of Brethren" in World Council of Churches *Faith and Order Paper No. 61* (1972) (reprinted from *The Ecumenical Review* Vol. 24, No. 2, April 1972). An excellent summary of Continental Darbyism. Only incidental references to main movement.

MUDDITT, B. H., *The New Fellowship* (1975).

NEATBY, W. B., *A History of the Plymouth Brethren* (2nd edn. 1902). For long the standard work, but now badly out-dated.

NOEL, N., *The History of the Brethren*. 2 Vols. 1936. Grossly misnamed. Largely an almost incoherent account of "exclusive" quarrels.

PERRET, PAUL, "Coup d'oeil sur l'Histoire et les Principes des Frères Appelés 'Frères Larges'" (cyclostyled c. 1946). A valuable summary from the Swiss independent churches.

PIEPKORN, A. C., *Plymouth Brethren (Christian Brethren), A Brief Study* (1970). An excellent brief objective study from a North American viewpoint, printed in *Concordia Theological Monthly* for March 1970, and reprinted in the *Journal* of the Christian Brethren Research Fellowship No. 25 of Sept. 1973.

REID, WILLIAM, *Plymouth Brethrenism Unveiled and Refuted* (3rd edn. 1880). Bitterly hostile. Unreliable.

ROBERTS, THEODORE. "A short Account of the Brethren Movement" (1926). Pamphlet. From the independent standpoint.

ROWDON, H. H., *The Origins of the Brethren* (1967). University doctoral thesis of 1965.*

SHORT, A. RENDLE, *The Principles of "Open Brethren"* (1913). Contains a useful historical summary.

SMART, JOHN, *Historical Sketch of Assembly Missions* (undated). A brief survey from the U.S.A.

SOLTAU, H. W., "They Found it Written, or Those Called by Some the Brethren, Who Are They, What Are Their Doctrines?" (containing a reprint of the 1851 Census report on "The Brethren and Their Doctrines"). Undated pamphlet. An address by an early leader.

* Now enlarged and published as *The Origins of the Brethren* (1967).

STUNT, W. T. AND OTHERS, *Turning the World Upside Down* (1972). The "Echoes of Service" centenary history. A massive and indispensable source book on that major part of Brethren missionary work connected with "Echoes of Service."

TAYLOR, J. R., "Who Are the Plymouth Brethren?" In *The World Christian Digest* for July 1959. A useful summary from an independent Brethren missionary in Argentina.

TEULON, J. S., *The History and Teaching of the Plymouth Brethren* (1883). A moderate criticism from an Anglican standpoint.

TROTTER, MRS. EDWARD, *Undertones of the Nineteenth Century* (1905). An interesting comparison of Brethren and Tractarianism. More poetical than objective.

VEITCH, T. S., *The Story of the Brethren Movement* (c. 1940). From an independent standpoint, but brief and disappointing.

WILSON, BRYAN R. (Ed.), *Patterns of Sectarianism* (1967). Contains balanced and scholarly articles on "The Early Development of the Plymouth Brethren" (P. L. Embley), "The Churches of God: Pattern and Practice" – the *Needed Truth* movement – (G. Willis and B. R. Wilson) and "The Exclusive Brethren: A Case Study in the Evolution of a Sectarian Ideology" (B. R. Wilson).

2. MATERIAL ON INDIVIDUAL ASPECTS OF THE HISTORY

(i) Primary Material
(in approximate chronological order of subject matter).

The Religious Belief of James Buchanan (1834, reprinted 1955). (With MS letter of James Quinn to F. R. Coad, 11 December 1956.)

Letters Concerning Their Principles and Order from Assemblies of Believers in 1818–1820 (reprinted 1889).

GRIBBLE, ROBERT, *Recollections of an Evangelist* (1858).

GROVES, MRS. (ed.), *Memoir of the Late Anthony Norris Groves, containing extracts from his Letters and Journals* (2nd edn. 1857).

GROVES, A. N., *Christian Devotedness* (1825).

Interesting Reminiscences of the Early History of "Brethren," containing extracts from a letter from J. G. Bellett to James McAllister, with notes by J. N. Darby, G. V. Wigram, E. Cronin, and J. B. Stoney; and a letter from J. G. Bellett to J. N. Darby of 1 Sept. 1864.

DARBY, J. N., *Letters* (3 vols.) (The Stow Hill edition is quoted in the body of this book.)
Other writings of J. N. Darby are collected in his *Collected Writings* (ed. Wm. Kelly), and in the volumes of *The Christian Witness* (Plymouth 1834–41). References in this book are appropriately designated to one of these sources or to individual pamphlets.

NEWMAN, F. W., *Phases of Faith* (1850).

BRENTON, L. C. L., "A Sermon preached in the Parish Church of Stadhampton, Oxford, on Sunday 11 Dec. 1831."

WELCH, EDWIN, Articles "Dissenters' Meeting Houses in Plymouth to 1852," in *Transactions of the Devonshire Association*, Vol. 94, 1962, and a similar article covering 1852–1939 in Vol. 99, 1967.

HALL, P. F., *Discipleship: or, Reasons for Resigning his Naval Rank and Pay.* (London reprint: undated.)

ANON, *Reply to an Article in the* Eclectic Review *for May last entitled "The Plymouth Brethren" (reprinted from* The Inquirer *for October)* (1839). An important apologetic, quoting from writings of important early Brethren.

MÜLLER, GEORGE, *Autobiography of George Müller* (compiled from *The Narrative of the Lord's Dealings with George Müller*, by G. Fred Bergin, 1905).

TAYLER, W. E. (Ed.), *Passages from the Diary and Letters of Henry Craik of Bristol* (1866).

STONEY, MISS. MS notes relating to the early Brethren in Dublin (in possession of Mr. O. W. Ware of Capetown).

DORMAN, W. H., *Reasons for Retiring from the Independent or Congregational Body and from Islington Chapel.* Revised edn. 1862.

NEWTON, B. W., MS letters, reminiscences and other material in the possession of Mr. C. E. Fry of Newport, Isle of Wight. (Much of this material is copied into a separate MS book, to which references in this book are designated.)

CROSSLEY, E. and ANDREWS, A. *(Eds.), Extracts from the Writings of the late Henry Borlase on subjects connected with the Present State of the Church.* 1892 (reprinting material of 1836).

The Christian Witness. Bound in volumes for the period of its issue in Plymouth, 1834–1841.

COLE, W. H., Reminiscences of the Plymouth Meeting of "Brethren," 1902. (Reprinted in G. H. Lang, *Anthony Norris Groves*, 2nd edn. 1949.)

BEVERLEY, R. M., *An Inquiry into the Scriptural Doctrine of Christian Ministry (c.* 1841).

TREGELLES, S. P., Three Letters to the Author of *A Retrospect of Events that have taken place amongst the Brethren* (1849, 2nd edn. 1894).

NEWTON, B. W., "A Statement and Acknowledgment Respecting Certain Doctrinal Eerrors" (26 Nov. 1847).

REYNOLDS, G., *Mr. B. W. Newton and His Traducers*, with extracts from statements by Dr. Tregelles and Edward Dennett in support of Newton (1906).

TROTTER, W., *The Whole Case of Plymouth and Bethesda.* 1849.

TREGELLES, S. P., *Prisoners of Hope*, being letters from Florence relative to the Persecution of Francesco and Rosa Madiai. 1852.

CHAPMAN, ROBT. C., *Letters of the late Robert Cleaver Chapman* (1903).

TREGELLES, S. P., *Pastoral Relations* (1862).

CRAIK, HENRY, *New Testament Church Order* (1863).

CRAIK, HENRY, *The Authority of Scripture Considered in Relation to Christian Union* (1863).

CRAIK, HENRY, *Biblical Expositions, Lectures, etc.* (1867).

MÜLLER, GEORGE, *Jehovah Magnified, a collection of addresses* (1876).

NEWTON, B. W., *Propositions for the Solemn Consideration of Christians* (1864).

M'VICKER, J. G., *Selected Letters with Brief Memoir of J. G. M'Vicker* (1902).

HORNER, W. B., Printed open letter of November 1883 explaining the withdrawal from exclusive Brethren of the writer, a well known publisher of their works.

Letter from A. Stunt, C. Morgan and F. Stunt to William Lincoln. (MS), 14 Oct. 1864.

Report of Three Days Meetings for Prayer and Addresses on the Sure Word of Prophecy, held in Freemasons' Hall, May 9th, 10th and 12th 1864.

Notes of a Conference held at Leominster, October 6th to 10th, 1884.

ARNOT, F. S., *Garenganze, or Seven Years' Pioneer Mission Work in Central Africa* (1889).

CRAWFORD, DAN, *Thinking Black, Twenty-four years without a break in the Long Grass of Central Africa* (1912).

CRAWFORD, DAN, *Back to the Long Grass, My Link with Livingstone* (1923).

"A Statement of the Position of Bethesda." 1906. Printed privately in hope of a reconciliation with some "exclusives."

REDWOOD, A. McD., "Clarence High School, Bangalore, India" (Cyclo-styled. 1958).

"A New Testament Church in 1955." Report of the High Leigh Conference of Brethren, 16–19 September 1955.

"Christian Unity." Report of the Swanwick Conference of Brethren. June 1964.

"Assemblies in Britain and Other Parts." 1959. Unofficial address book of British churches of independent Brethren.

"Der Kleine Wegweiser." 1966. The like for Germany.

A Prayer Guide. The list of missionaries supported through "Echoes of Service," Bath.

(ii) Secondary Material

(in approximate chronological order of subject matter).

ROWDON, H. H., "Secession from the Established Church in the Early Nineteenth Century." In *Vox Evangelica* No. 3 (1964).

NOTT, L. P., *Gideon 1810–1910; The Vicissitudes of a City Chapel* (1909).

DAVIES, E. T. and others, *Bethesda Church, Great George Street, Bristol* (1917).

STUNT, T. C. F., "Irvingite Pentecostalism and the Early Brethren." In the *Journal* of the Christian Brethren Research Fellowship. Dec. 1965.

Early Brethren and the Society of Friends (1970). C.B.R.F. Occasional Paper No. 3.

LANGFORD, DR., "An account of the Brethren in Hereford" 1958.

HITCHCOCK, H. C., "A Little of our History." In *The Brook Street Chapel, Tottenham Magazine* for Nov./Dec. 1962.

ROWDON, H. H., "A Nineteenth-Century Nestorius." In *Vox Evangelica* No. 1 (1962).

BRUCE, F. F., "The Humanity of Jesus Christ." In the *Journal* of the Christian Brethren Research Fellowship, Sept. 1973, No. 24.

COAD, F. R., *Prophetic Developments, with particular reference to the early Brethren Movement* (1966).

MACKINTOSH, C. H., "Fifteenth Letter to a Friend." In *Things New and Old*, Vol. XVIII (1875), pp. 317–328.

FORREST, J. W., "The Missionary Reporter." In the *Journal* of the Christian Brethren Research Fellowship, May 1971.

GROVES, E. K., *Conversations on Bethesda Family Matters*, 2nd edn. 1885.

GROVES, E. K., *George Müller and His Successors* (1906).

"Clapton Hall, Alkham Road, Stoke Newington, N.16" (1867–1967). The centenary booklet.

LEONARD, A., *Betchworth "After Many Days" (1857–1960)*. An account of a village church in Surrey springing largely from the preaching of Richard Weaver and Henry Moorhouse (1960).

CORDINER, JAMES, *Fragments from the Past*; an Account of people and events in the Assemblies of Northern Scotland (1961).

WALKLEY, VICTOR G., *A Church Set on a Hill* (1972). The Centenary History of Edgmond Hall, Eastbourne.

SURRIDGE, F. W., *The Finest of the Wheat* (1950). An account of the church at Bridford Mills, Devon.

JONES, MALCOLM V., "Some Notes on Dostoyevsky, Tolstoy and the 'Redstokisty'" in *Slavonica*, publication of the Dept. of Slavonic Studies, University of Nottingham, No. 1, May 1968.

DOODSON, A. T., *The Search for the Truth of God* (1947). The "Needed Truth" apologia.

OXLEY, C. A., "The 'Needed Truth' Assemblies." In the *Journal* of the Christian Brethren Research Fellowship (April 1964).

PORTEOUS, *Brethren in the Keelhowes* (1876).

MURDOCH, A., *Life Among the Close Brethren* (1890).

PAYNE, W. and WILSON, C. T. W., *Missionary Pioneering in Bolivia, with some Account of work in Argentina* (c. 1904).

Echoes Quarterly Review. A periodical devoted to missionary work of independent Brethren. Several issues (the journal dates from 1949) have carried useful reviews of the history of various mission fields in which Brethren had worked.

Echoes Missionary Surveys. A range of booklets issued over many years, containing surveys of individual mission fields.

BROUGHTON D. G., *Mongolian Plains and Japanese Prisons* (1947).

NEWTON, K. J., *Brethren Missionary Work in Mysore State* (1975).

HARLOW, R. E., *The Cross in the Southern Sky* (1967).

ROTBERG R. I., *Christian Missionaries and the Creation of Northern Rhodesia 1880–1924* (1965).

SLADE, RUTH, M. *English-Speaking Missions in the Congo Independent State* (1959).

WEST, J. F., *Faroe: the Emergence of a Nation* (1972).

SAUER, E., *50 Jahre Missionshaus Bibelschule Wiedenest: Ein Zeugnis von der Gnade Gottes* (1955).

ANDREWS, J. S., "The Wiedenest Bible College." In the *Journal* of the Christian Brethren Research Fellowship, May 1971.

TRIPP, G. F., "Recent Liturgical Tendencies Among the Exclusive Brethren." In the *Journal* of the Christian Brethren Research Fellowship, April 1967.

ROWDON, H. H., "The Early Brethren and the Ministry of the Word." In the *Journal* of the Christian Brethren Research Fellowship, January 1967.

TINDER, D. (Ed.), "The Brethren Movement in the World Today." A collection of contemporary comment. *Journal* 25 of the Christian Brethren Research Fellowship, Sept. 1973.

(iii) Biographical Material

(in alphabetical order of the biographical subject)

General	PICKERING, Henry, *Chief Men Among the Brethren* (2nd edn. 1931). A collection of biographical sketches.
	HUTCHINSON, J. G., *Irish Evangelists now with the Lord* (1969).
Anderson, Sir R.	MOORE-ANDERSON, A. P., *Sir Robert Anderson, K.C.B., Ll.D. A Tribute and a Memoir* (1919).
Arnot, F. S.	BAKER, ERNEST, *The Life and Explorations of Frederick Stanley Arnot* (1921).
Arnott, Anne	ARNOTT, ANNE, The Brethren (1969).
	Journey into Understanding (1971).
Aroolapen, J. C.	LANG, G. H., *The History and Diaries of an Indian Christian* (1939).
Baedeker, F. W.	LATIMER, R. S., *Dr. Baedeker and His Apostolic Work in Russia* (1907).

Barnardo, T. J.   WYMER, NORMAN, *Father of Nobody's Children* (1955).

Beer, Patricia   BEER, PATRICIA, Mrs. Beer's House (1968).

Bellett, J. G.   BELLETT, L. M., Recollections of the late J. G. Bellett (1895).

Bevan, Mrs. F.   ANDREWS, J. S., "Frances Bevan, Translator of German Hymns." In *The Evangelical Quarterly* for Oct. 1962 and Jan. 1963. *And* "The Recent History of the Bevan Family," ibid., April 1961.

Broadbent, E. H.   LANG, G. H., *Edmund Hamer Broadbent* (1946).

Brealey, George   BREALEY, W. H. J., *Always Abounding* (1897).

WHITE, R. H., *Strength of the Hills, the Story of the Blackdown Hills Mission* (1964).

Bruce, F. F.   GASQUE, W. W. and MARTIN R. P., *Apostolic History and the Gospel* (Essays presented on his 60th birthday) (1970).

COAD, F. R., editor. *The Contribution of Frederick Fyvie Bruce* (C.B.R.F. Journal 22, November 1971).

Burton, A. M.   PITT, F. W., *Windows on the World* (approx. 1937).

Capper, W. M.   CAPPER, W. M., *Questions Colleagues Have Asked Me* (1972).

Butcher, F.   COOPER, RANSOME W., *A Brief Memoir of the Life and Labours of Frederick Butcher* (1955).

Cavan, Earl of   *Frederick John William, eighth Earl of Cavan, a Life Sketch* (c. 1888).

Chapman, R. C.   BENNET, W. H., *Robert Cleaver Chapman of Barnstaple* (1902).

HOLMES, F., *Brother Indeed* (1956).

Collingwood, Wm.   COLLINGWOOD, W. G., Unpublished memoir in MS.

ANON, Obituary in "The Christian" for 9 July 1903.

Crawford, Dan   TILSLEY, G. E., *Dan Crawford, Missionary and Pioneer in Central Africa* (1929).

Darby, J. N.   TURNER, W. G., *John Nelson Darby* (expanded edn. 1944).

Fisher, Walter   FISHER, W. SINGLETON and HOYTE, JULIAN, *Africa Looks Ahead, the Life Stories of Walter and Anna Fisher of Central Africa* (1948).

Fisk, E. G.   FISK, E. G., *The Cross versus the Crescent* (1972).

Gosse, P. H.   GOSSE, EDMUND, *The Life of Philip Henry Gosse, F.R.S.* (1890).

GOSSE, EDMUND, *Father and Son* (1907).

ANDREWS, J. S., "Philip Henry Gosse, F.R.S." In *The Library Association Record* for June 1961.

Groves, A. N.   LANG, G. H., *Anthony Norris Groves* (2nd edn. 1949).

Hake, William   CHAPMAN, R. C. (Ed.), *Seventy Years of Pilgrimage being a memorial of William Hake* (1890).

Hooke, S. H.   GRAHAM, E. C., *Nothing Is Here for Tears* (1969).

Hurditch, C. Russell   "SEPTIMA" (Mrs. H. Grattan Guinness). *Peculiar People* (1935).

Jukes, Andrew   JEAFFRESON, H. H. (Ed.), *Letters of Andrew Jukes, with Short Biography* (1903).

Kelly, William   WREFORD, HEYMANN, *Memories of the Life and Last Days of William Kelly* (1906).

Köhler, Christof   In SAUER, ERICH, *50 Jahr Missionshaus Bibelschule Wiedenest* (1955).

Laing, Sir John W.   HARRISON, GODFREY, *Life and Belief in the experience of John W. Laing, C.B.E.* (1954).

Lang, G. H.   LANG, G. H., *An Ordered Life* (1959).

Lees, James   COOPER, RANSOME W., *James Lees, Shepherd of Lonely Sheep in Europe* (1959).

Marsh, C. R.   MARSH, C. R., *Too Hard for God?* (1970). *Streams in the Sahara* (1972).

Moorhouse, Henry   MACPHERSON, JOHN, *Henry Moorhouse, the English Evangelist* (undated).

Müller, George   PIERSON, A. T., *George Müller of Bristol* (6th edn. 1901).

HARDING, W. H., *The Life of George Müller.* 1914.

MÜLLER, MRS. (Ed.), *The Preaching Tours and Missionary Labours of George Müller* (2nd edn. 1889).

M'Kendrick, James   M'KENDRICK, JAMES, *What We Have Seen & Heard* (1914).

Newton, B. W.   FROMOW, G. H. (Ed.), *B. W. Newton and Dr. S. P. Tregelles, Teachers of the Faith and Future* (1959).

North, Brownlow   MOODY-STUART, K., *Brownlow North: the Story of his Life and Work* (1904).

Olley, John   CLAPHAM, J. W. and TAYLOR, N. J., *John Olley, Pioneer Missionary to the Chad* (1966).

Ross, Donald   ROSS, C. W. (Ed.), *Donald Ross, Pioneer Evangelist of the North of Scotland and U.S.A.* (approx. 1904).

Schofield, A. T.   SCHOFIELD, A. T., *Behind the Brass Plate, Life's Little Stories* (undated).

Short, A. Rendle   CAPPER, W. M. and JOHNSON, D. *Arthur Rendle Short, Surgeon and Christian* (1954).

van Sommer, James	Stunt, T. C. F., "James Van Sommer, an Undenominational Christian and Man of Prayer." In the *Journal* of the Christian Brethren Research Fellowship, Aug. 1967.
St. John, Harold	St. John, Patricia, *Harold St. John, A Portrait* (1961).
Swan, Charles A.	Ingleby, A. G., *Pioneer Days in Darkest Africa* (undated).
Tatford, F. A.	McNicol, J., *Twentieth Century Prophet* (1971).
Thomson, A. A.	Thomson, A. A., *The Exquisite Burden* (1935). A fictional work containing half-disguised autobiography.
Tregelles, S. P.	See op. cit. under "Newton, B. W." above.
Vine, W. E.	Ruoff, P. O., *W. E. Vine, His Life and Ministry* (1951).
Warns, J.	In Sauer, Erich, *50 Jahre Missionshaus Bibelschule Wiedenest* (1955).

3. Hymnology

Allen, C. J., *Hymns and the Christian Faith* (1966).

Andrews, J. S., "Brethren Hymnology." In *The Evangelical Quarterly* for Oct.–Dec. 1956 (and *The Life of Faith*, 5 & 12 Dec. 1957).

Andrews, J. S., "Frances Bevan: Translator of German Hymns." In *The Evangelical Quarterly*, Oct.-Dec. 1962 and Jan.-Mar. 1963.

Beattie, D. J., *Stories and Sketches of Our Hymns and Their Writers* (1934).

Julian, J., *A Dictionary of Hymnology*.

Hine, Stuart K., The Story of "How Great Thou Art" (Nov. 1958), published privately in *Russian Melodies and Hymns of Other Lands*.

According to Allen (op. cit. p. 114), there have been "at least" twenty-four Brethren compiled hymnbooks. This figure probably excludes some of the more personal compilations, among which are *The Mitchley Supplements* (c. 1955–65), to the inter-denominational hymnbooks of the Scripture Union (compiled originally for the use of the church at Mitchley Hill, Sanderstead, Surrey), the *Remembrance Hymns* of I. Y. Ewan and his companions (1935), and *Additional Hymns of Worship* compiled by A. J. Atkins, Alan Fairhead and O. C. Hartridge (c. 1955). Books in common use at the communion service (an inter-denominational collection is normally used at more general services) are:

Hymns of Light and Love (1900).
The Believers Hymn Book (1884) (supplement 1959).
Hymns of Truth and Praise (U.S.A., 1971).
"Echoes of Service" Missionary Hymnal (undated).
Christian Worship (1976).

These hymnals are used by independents. The exclusive groups use their different editions of *Hymns for the Little Flock* (appearing under other titles in some editions).

Collections of individual compositions include those by:

CHAPMAN, R. C., *Hymns and Meditations* (1871).

DARBY, J. N., *Spiritual Songs* (1883).

DENNY, SIR E., *Hymns and Poems* (Last and definitive edn. 1889).

Verse collections include:

BEVAN, MRS. F., *Hymns of Ter Steegen, Suso and Others* (First Series, 1894).

BEVAN, MRS. F., *Hymns of Ter Steegen and Others* (Second Series, undated).

TAIT, J. M. S., *Bells and Pomegranates* (1946).

BEVIR, E. L., *Poems* undated (*c.* 1923).

SHAW, LUCI, *Listen to the Green* (1971).

4. BACKGROUND WORKS

(i) Works Quoted Containing Incidental References

COLLINGWOOD, W. G., *The Life and Work of John Ruskin* (2 Vols. 1893).

ELLIOTT-BINNS, L. E., *English Thought 1860–1900. The Theological Aspect* (*1956*).

EVANS, J. J. (Ed.), *Memoir and Remains of the Rev. James Harington Evans, late minister of John Street Chapel.* 1852.

JAMES, WILLIAM, *The Varieties of Religious Experience* (1902).

LITCHFIELD, MRS. HENRIETTA (*Ed.*), *Emma Darwin: A Century of Family Letters 1792–1896* (1915).

MADDEN, MRS. HAMILTON, *Memoir of the late Right Rev. Robert Daly, D.D., Lord Bishop of Cashel* (1875).

MOODY, W. R., *The Life of Dwight L. Moody* (undated).

HODDER, EDWIN, *The Life of Samuel Morley* (3rd edn. 1887).

POWLES, L. V., *The Faith and Practice of Heretical Sects* (2nd edn. 1962).

SIRR, J. D. A., *A Memoir of the Honorable and Most Reverend Power le-Poer Trench, last Archbishop of Tuam* (1845).

SOMMER, DUDLEY, *Haldane of Cloan* (1960).

STEVENSON, R. L., *Travels with a Donkey in the Cevennes* (1879).

WEYMOUTH, R. F. (*Tr.*), *The New Testament in Modern Speech* (edn. of 1905).

WILLEY, BASIL, *More Nineteenth Century Studies – A Group of Honest Doubters* (1956).

(ii) General Works

The Oxford Dictionary of the Christian Church (1957, 1974).

BAINTON, R. L., *Here I stand; a Life of Martin Luther* (1950).

BALLEINE, G. R., *A History of the Evangelical Party in the Church of England* (1908).

BERKOUWER, G. C., *The Second Vatican Council and the New Catholicism* (1965).

BRUNNER, EMIL, *The Misunderstanding of the Church* (Eng. trans. 1952).

CARRON, T. W., *The Christian Testimony through the Ages* (1956).

COOMER, DUNCAN, *English Dissent Under the Early Hanoverians* (1946).

FITCHETT, W. H., *Wesley and His Century, A Study in Spiritual Forces* (1906).

BROWN, FORD, K., *Fathers of the Victorians* (1961).

FROOM, LeR. E., *The Prophetic Faith of Our Fathers* (1950).

FROOM, LeR. E., *The Conditionalist Faith of Our Fathers*. 1966.

GROVES, C. P., *The Planting of Christianity in Africa* (1948).

HERSHBERGER, GUY F. (*Ed.*), *The Recovery of the Anabaptist Vision* (1957).

HOHLENBERG, J., *Søren Kierkegaard*. Eng. trans. 1954.

KINNEAR, ANGUS, *Against the Tide: the Story of Watchman Nee* (1973).

LATOURETTE, K. S., *A History of Christianity* (1954).

MILLER, EDWARD, *The History and Doctrines of Irvingism* (1878).

ORR, J. EDWIN, *The Second Evangelical Awakening in Britain* (1949).

ORR, J. EDWIN, *The Light of the Nations* (1965).

OUTLER, ALBERT C. (*Ed.*), *John Wesley* (1964).

PARKER, G. H. W., *The Morning Star; Wycliffe and the Dawn of the Reformation* (1965).

SELBIE, W. B. (*Ed.*), *Evangelical Christianity, Its History and Witness* (1911).

SIMON, JOHN S., *The Revival of Religion in England in the Eighteenth Century* (37th Fearnley Lecture, undated).

TAYLOR, DR. and MRS. HOWARD, *Biography of James Hudson Taylor* (abridged edn. 1965).

TREVELYAN, G. M., *History of England* (3rd edn. 1945).

TRUEBLOOD, D. E., "The Paradox of the Quaker Ministry." In *The Friends' Quarterly* for April 1961.

VERDUIN, L., *The Reformers and Their Stepchildren* (1964).

VIDLER, A. R., *The Church in an Age of Revolution, 1789 to the present day* (1961).

WALTON, ROBERT C., *The Gathered Community* (1946).

WILSON, DANIEL, *The Pilgrim Fathers* (1849).

5. ADDENDA

SCARFE, ALAN, "The Evangelical Wing of the Orthodox Church in Romania." In *Religion in Communist Lands*, Vol. 3, No. 6 (Nov.–Dec. 1975).

BROMLEY, E. B., *They Were Men Sent From God*. A Centenary Record of Gospel Work in the Godaveri Delta, India (1937).

HOGG, C. F., *What We Saw in Africa* (1940).

STEER, ROGER, *George Müller: Delighted in God* (1975).

INDEX

INDEX